C++ Without Fear

C++ Without Fear

A Beginner's Guide That Makes You Feel Smart

Brian Overland

PRENTICE
HALL
PTR

Prentice Hall Professional Technical Reference
Upper Saddle River, New Jersey 07458
www.phptr.com

Library of Congress Cataloging-in-Publication Data is on file at the Library of Congress

© 2005 Pearson Education, Inc.
Publishing as Prentice Hall Professional Technical Reference
Upper Saddle River, New Jersey 07458

Prentice Hall PTR offers excellent discounts on this book when ordered in quantity for bulk purchases or special sales. For more information, please contact: U.S. Corporate and Government Sales, 1-800-382-3419, corpsales@pearsontechgroup.com. For sales outside of the U.S., please contact: International Sales, international@pearsoned.com.

Printed in the United States of America

First Printing

ISBN 0-321-24695-0

Pearson Education Ltd.
Pearson Education Australia Pty., Limited
Pearson Education South Asia Pte. Ltd.
Pearson Education Asia Ltd.
Pearson Education Canada, Ltd.
Pearson Educación de Mexico, S.A. de C.V.
Pearson Education—Japan
Pearson Malaysia S.D.N. B.H.D.

To all the great teachers I have known,
and to Fara and Skyler, who will not be forgotten

Contents

Chapter 9 — Some Advanced Programming Techniques — 219

Chapter 10 — Getting Yourself Object Oriented — 245

Preface

In my ten years at Microsoft, I found the top-level programmers ("software development engineers," we called them) to be an interesting breed. Once you got them to open up and talk about their projects, they could be an articulate and passionate group.

The trick was to get beyond the initial barrier, to convince them that you spoke their language. Experienced programmers sometimes divide the world into two groups: those who are "technical" and those who are not. At times a yawning gap seems to exist between them, like that between people with perfect pitch and those without.

For programmers, the dividing line these days is most often the ability to program in C++. This attitude stems from the perception of C++ as difficult to learn.

This book is dedicated to the idea that C++ need not be difficult. It's often a more challenging language than Basic, to be sure, but with the right kind of help, you can master the tricks of C++.

Why a New C++ Book?

Introductory programming books for C++ exist aplenty. But many—probably the great majority—are "introductory" only in the sense that they don't assume knowledge of C++ specifically. They usually assume that you've programmed in another language before, preferably in several.

This book does not make that assumption. All that's required is that you're comfortable with a computer and that you've run applications such as a word processor or e-mail reader.

Once you narrow the available C++ texts down to those that require no programming experience at all, there's a much smaller group of books from which to choose.

What Else Is New about This Book?

The book you hold in your hand stresses the fundamentals of programming. Yet even if you have programmed before (maybe you've taken a basic course in high school or college), you may find this a useful review. This book delves into the topic of how to think like a programmer . . . and why specific language features matter. The why is as important as the how.

People learn best when they get the benefit of several learning methods reinforcing one another. Therefore, every topic in this book is introduced by a general discussion with short program-code examples, accompanied by the following:

▶ *A complete program example.* Usually I provide a complete example that can be run and tested. The emphasis in this book is on short examples that do something interesting and useful and, when possible, something fun.

▶ *Programming exercises.* Each example has a series of accompanying exercises, in which I encourage you to modify the example or write similar programs, so that from the beginning you're writing C++ code. Answers to these exercises provided on the accompanying CD in the folder "Example Code and Answers to Exercises."

▶ *Generous use of illustrations.* Many so-called beginning texts don't use this approach at all. But I often find that the right figures can clarify an abstract concept. One picture is worth a thousand lectures, sometimes.

▶ *A special "How It Works" section for every major example in the book.* How-to-program texts are notorious for giving you a long example followed by a couple of paragraphs of text. That's not the approach of this book. Complete examples are listed so that you can see everything in context. But after each example, I go back and dissect the program a couple of lines at a time, explaining how and why each bit of the program does what it does.

Multiple Learning Paths: What Fits You Best

In addition to the multiple learning techniques just described, this book contains frequent *Interludes,* where the more curious reader will find additional background and explanations why C++ features work the way they do. If you're eager to just get C++ programs working, you may want to skip the *Interludes* and return to them later. One of the advantages of this book is that it accommodates multiple learning paths.

Unlike some texts, this book does not start with an exhaustive description of all language features such as data types, control structures, and operators. That would be like learning French by spending months memorizing nouns rather than learning to speak a complete sentence. This book focuses on getting real programs to work, right away.

At the same time, it's helpful to have access to a thorough-but-concise summary of language features. This book provides that summary in a series of convenient appendixes.

What If You Already Have a Programming Background?

If you already know another programming language but are new to C++, that's not a problem. Certain ideas in programming never get old: what it means to think like a programmer, what's going on just beneath the surface, why the language is constructed the way it is. This review of programming fundamentals may be of interest anyway. But if not, you can speed through the first chapter or two. C++ gets challenging quickly enough.

What Is Not Covered?

The goal of this book is to make you comfortable and conversant in C++, including objected-oriented programming features (classes and objects) that, although a relatively advanced topic, are at the heart of C++. The goal is not to teach every last bit of language syntax or to describe how every statement is translated into machine behavior (that is, how it is implemented), although in some places I do discuss that.

In my view, the good majority of beginning texts make the mistake of trying to cover every obscure corner of the language, even though there is ample room in intermediate to advanced books to handle those topics.

In case you are a C++ expert or otherwise a guru perusing this book, or you have some familiarity with the scope of the language, here is a summary of what's in C++ but is not covered in this book. (Consider this a "truth in advertising" disclaimer.)

▶ **Bit fields and bit operations**. Bit operations can occasionally be useful for programs that must make extreme use of compact space, but in general, bit operations are rarely necessary. This is a good advanced topic. Likewise, I don't cover the **union** keyword (another feature used for compaction).

▶ **Windows and GUI programming**. These are difficult subjects, deserving of their own book (or three). Visual C++ requires understanding of a complex architecture and thorough knowledge of object-oriented programming systems (OOPS). Reading this book first will give you a background in OOPS.

▶ **Templates and STL (Standard Template Library)**. This is another good topic for an advanced book. A template is a way of creating a generalized data structure in which an abstract mechanism can be combined with any number of specific data types. The template-defining capability was not originally in the C++ specification, although it is now standard.

Although this book does cover exception handling—a way to respond to runtime errors—I don't stress it, because it is most appropriate in complex programs and not likely to be as useful to a beginner.

Why Should Anyone Start with C++?

Some people will tell you that C++ is unsuitable for beginners; therefore, unless you're in the elite of talented and experienced programmers, you shouldn't bother. I don't agree with that.

There are some good reasons for learning C++ early in your programming career. People used to spend a lot of time mastering the C language first. Yet C is rarely used for real work anymore. Now students learn it primarily as a stepping-stone to C++. But this makes little sense. You can pick up some bad habits learning C. It's better to go directly to C++. C++ is now the language of choice for systems programmers as well as for writing commercial software—including games, graphics, and business-oriented programs.

Some other languages (notably Microsoft's Visual Basic) are more forgiving. But as with C, Basic can encourage bad habits. C++ offers any learner some unique rewards.

▶ Like the C language, C++ is a systems-programming language. In learning about C++ (at least in this book) you'll learn a lot about how things work in the computer and why they do.

▶ Unlike C, C++ is a good implementation of object-oriented programming. This is an approach to programming in which you create intelligent data structures, especially well suited to things such as graphics programming. Object-oriented programming also lets you define new types that in effect expand the capabilities of the language itself. In learning object-oriented programming, you'll learn more about the current state of software design and where it's going.

The first half of this book focuses on the fundamentals of C++: how to get a program to work and accomplish basic tasks. From the beginning, however, it does get you to start using and understanding objects.

The second half focuses more completely on object-oriented programming, with special emphasis on how you can use it to write useful—and reusable—program code.

To Get Started . . .

This book provides an added bonus: an accompanying CD with a free compiler, which is the language translator needed to write and execute programs in C++. All the programming examples in this book have been tested and retested with this compiler. The examples also work with compilers such as C++ in Microsoft Visual Studio.NET, although you'll need to follow the special instructions in Chapter 1 for use with that environment.

To install the free C++ compiler, just insert the CD into a PC and follow the instructions in the README.TXT file in the root directory.

This compiler is a free shareware version of GNU C++. You are free to use it to build and distribute your own programs. It also comes with a free development environment, so (as described in Chapter 1), you can write programs and then build them (translate them into executable form) at the touch of a single keystroke.

Tips and Tricks: What Do I Watch Out For?

Perhaps what gives C-based languages their reputation for being more difficult than some others is that they have some "gotchas"—things that will catch you off guard if you don't have a friendly mentor standing next to you to steer you around the pitfalls.

As much as anything, this book is about keeping you safe from the gotchas. For too many people, the ability to program is gained only after making the same unnecessary mistakes over and over.

Above all, I hope to communicate some of what makes the subject, at least at times, so interesting. Software development can test your patience as you track down elusive bugs. But the concepts can be fascinating. In our new century, programming computers has become the new kind of craftsmanship, the new mode of fashioning fine tools, for a world that runs on information.

Acknowledgments

This book exists because of the efforts of Laura Lewin (my agent) and Peter Gordon, who believed strongly in the need for the book and convinced me to write it. Peter shaped its direction from the beginning, particularly with regard to the role of C/C++ issues and object-oriented programming. He was assisted by Bernard Gaffney, who shepherded the draft through its early stages of submission, review, and rewrites. Peter was also assisted by Chanda Leary-Coutu, who put together a great marketing plan, and Lara Wysong, the production coordinator.

During copy editing and production, I was lucky enough to work with Kathy Glidden of Stratford Publishing Services and Brian Wright. They accommodated last-minute changes and a good deal of discussion on styles, even while under pressure to get a book out quickly.

Many people contributed to the book through technical review and close examination of every line of code—saving the author from having to learn of certain errors after going to press. (Nothing is ever perfect, but the standard for this book was a "zero defect" goal in which we didn't leave in obvious errors.) For some of these people I have only a last name, but among the most helpful reviewers were Mary Dageford, Bill Locke, Shauna Kelly, and Matthew Johnson.

Matthew was especially helpful with his suggestion for an improved greatest-common-factor algorithm. I think I once learned that algorithm in an advanced-placement math class, but that was more years ago than I'd like to admit.

Dick Bower contributed the index, as well as finding some small errors that somehow got past everybody else. He showed that he obviously followed the text extremely well.

I'd also like to thank Microsoft engineer John Bennett, who contributed useful insights on array indexing and random-number generation.

Finally, I would especially like to thank my cousins Darren and Kevin Oke, who provided some of the earliest feedback and encouragement.

The accompanying CD-ROM contains a free C++ compiler—the software needed for programs to work. All the sample programs in this book are designed to run on any fairly recent C++ compiler. However, if you have a compiler released before 2000, it is possible that some examples might not run. If that happens, just move on to the next example—or install the compiler provided on the CD.

Your First C++ Programs

There's nothing to fear about C++ programming—really! Like all programming languages, it's just a way to give logically precise directions to a computer. C++ can get as complicated as you want, but the easy way to start learning is to use it to solve fundamental programming tasks. That's the approach here.

In the first couple of sections, I review the basic concepts of programming. If you've programmed in any language, you might want to skip these, or review them briefly. But if you stick around, I promise to not be too long-winded.

Thinking like a Programmer

Programming may not be exactly like any activity you've ever done. Basically, you're just giving instructions—but doing so in a logical, systematic manner.

Computers Do Only What You Tell Them

Computers do only what you tell them: This is the most important rule in this book, especially if you are new to programming. By using a computer language such as C++, Visual Basic, Pascal, or FORTRAN you give the computer a list of things to do; this is the *program*.

I once ran a computer lab in Tacoma, Washington (famous for being America's most stressful city). One of the students was a little man who wore a straw hat and old clothes. Every day he'd come to me with a stack of copies of *The Daily Racing Form* and say that if we could just enter that information into the computer we could make millions of dollars getting it to pick winning horses for us.

That's not how it works. A computer needs information, of course—that's program *data*. But it also needs to know what to do with that data. The instructions that tell it what to do (for reasons I'll go into later) are called program *code*.

Determine What the Program Will Do

So, to get a computer to do anything it has to be told exactly what to do.

Up until now, you've probably used a computer by running programs other people (such as Bill Gates and his friends) have written for you. To this extent you've been an *end user*—commonly referred to as a *user* for short.

Now, by writing programs yourself, you'll promote yourself into the next higher echelon of computer people. Now you'll decide what a program does. You'll make things happen.

But a computer—more so than Dustin Hoffman in *Rain Man*—is the ultimate idiot savant. It can never guess what you want. It can never make independent judgments. It is extremely literal and will carry out precisely what you tell it to do, no matter how stupid. Therefore, you have to be careful to say what you mean.

You can't even give the computer a command that might seem relatively clear to a human such as, "Convert a number from Celsius to Fahrenheit for me." Even that's too general. Instead, you have to be more specific, writing down steps such as these:

1 Print the message "Enter Celsius temperature: "

2 Get a number from the keyboard and store it in the variable ctemp.

3 Convert to Fahrenheit by using the formula ftemp = (ctemp * 1.8) + 32.

4 Print the message "The Fahrenheit temperature is: "

5 Print the value of the variable ftemp.

If you have to go through this much trouble just to do something simple, why even bother? The answer is that once a program is written you can run it over and over. And though programs take time to write, they usually execute at lightning speed.

Write the Equivalent C++ Statements

After you've determined precisely what you want your program to do, step by step, you need to write down the equivalent C++ statements. A statement is roughly the C++ equivalent of a sentence in English; it can perform one or more actions or it can create a piece of data—as you'll see later in the chapter.

For example, say you want your program to do the following:

1 Print the message "The Fahrenheit temperature is: "

2 Print the value of the variable ftemp.

You'd translate these steps into the following C++ statements:

```
cout << "The Fahrenheit temperature is: ";
cout << ftemp;
```

Remember, the goal of programming is to get the computer to do a series of specific tasks. But the computer understands only its own native language—*machine code*—which consists of 1s and 0s. Back in the 1950s, programmers did write out instructions in machine code, but this was exceedingly difficult and time-consuming.

To make things easier, computer engineers developed programming languages such as FORTRAN, Basic, and C, which enabled humans to write programs bearing at least some resemblance to English.

To write a program, you may want to start by writing *pseudocode*—an approach I often use in this book. Pseudocode is similar to English, but it describes the action of the program in a systematic way that reflects the logical flow of the program. For example, here's a simple program written in pseudocode.

If a is greater than b

    Print "a is greater than b."

Else

    Print "a is not greater than b."

Once you've written pseudocode, you're not far from having a C++ program. All you need to do is look up the corresponding C++ statement for each action.

```
if (a > b)
    cout << "a is greater than b.";
else
    cout << "a is not greater than b.";
```

The advantage of a programming language is that it follows rules that allow no ambiguity. C++ statements are so precise that they can be translated into the 1s and 0s of machine code without guesswork.

It should come as no surprise that programming languages have strict rules of syntax. These rules are more consistent (and usually simpler) than rules in a human language. From time to time I summarize these rules. For example, here's **if-else** syntax:

```
if (condition)
    statement
else
    statement
```

The words in bold are *keywords;* they must be entered into the program exactly as shown. Words in italics (also called *placeholders*) represent items you supply.

The application that translates C++ statements into machine code is called a *compiler*. I'll have a lot more to say about compilers in the upcoming section, "Building a C++ Program." First, however, let's review some key definitions.

Some Nerdy Definitions—A Review

I like to avoid jargon. I really do. But let's be candid. When you start learning programming, you enter into a world that requires some new terminology. The following provides some definitions you need to survive in this world.

application

Essentially the same thing as a program, but seen from a user's point of view. An application is a program that a user runs to accomplish some task. A word processor is an application; so is an Internet browser or a database manager. Even a *compiler* (see below) is an application, but of a very special kind, because it's used by programmers. To put the matter simply, when your program is written, built, and tested, it's an application.

code

Another synonym for "the program," but seen from the programmer's point of view. "The code" is the series of statements and supporting syntax that make up a program; this can refer to *machine code* (1s and 0s) or to *source code* (C++ statements). The use of the term "code" stems from the days when all programmers wrote in machine code. Each machine instruction is encoded into a unique combination of 1s and 0s and is therefore the computer's code for doing some action. Programmers have continued to talk about "code" even when using languages such as C++, Java, FORTRAN, or Visual Basic. (For more information, see the definition of *source code*.)

Also, the term "code" is sometimes used to differentiate between the passive information in a program (its data) and the part of the program that performs actions (its code).

compiler

The language translator that takes C++ statements (C++ source code) as input and outputs the program in machine-code form. This is necessary because the computer itself—its central processing unit (CPU)—only understands machine code.

data

The information stored by a program, to be manipulated or displayed. At its most basic level, this information consists of words and/or numbers (although it can be organized into much more interesting types of data called "classes" and "objects").

machine code

The CPU's native language, in which each computer instruction consists of a unique combination (or *code*) of 1s and 0s. It is still possible to program in machine code, but this requires looking up each instruction, as well as having knowledge of the CPU's architecture—all of which is outside the scope of this book.

Languages such as C++ provide a way to write programs that are closer to English, but still logically precise enough to be translated into machine code. C++ provides other helpful features as well.

program

A series of instructions to be carried out by a computer along with initial data. As I mentioned earlier, a program can take time to write but once completed usually executes at lightning-fast speed, and it can be run over and over.

source code

A program written out in a high-level language such as C++. The source code consists of the C++ statements that make up your program. Source code needs to be translated into machine code before it can actually run on a computer.

Machine code, as I've mentioned, consists of 1s and 0s, but is usually represented in hexadecimal code (base 16), so that machine code looks something like:

```
08 A7 C3 9E 58 6C 77 90
```

It's not obvious what this does, is it? Unless you look up all the instruction codes, such a program is incomprehensible—which is why very few people use machine code to write programs anymore. In contrast, source code at least bears some semblance to English. For example, C++ source code looks like this:

```
if (salary < 0)
    print_error_message();
```

statement

Usually one line of a C++ program. A statement in C++ corresponds roughly to a sentence in a natural language such as English. C++ also supports complex structures made up of one or more smaller statements; these correspond roughly to compound statements in English. Most C++ statements perform an action, although some perform many actions.

user

The person who runs a program—that is, the person who uses the computer to do something useful such as edit a text file, read e-mail, explore the Internet, or balance a checkbook. The more official name for user is *end user*.

While I was at Microsoft, the user was the person who caused most of the trouble in the world, but he or she was also the person who paid all the bills and generated all the profits. When you start designing serious programs, you must consider the needs of the user carefully and try to anticipate everything that may go wrong.

Although it's easy for a programmer to look down on users, the first user of a program is almost always . . . the programmer himself! After you write a program, you're probably going to be the first person (and sometimes the only person) to run and test it. So, remember you are always a user as well as a programmer.

What's Different about C++?

Most of the things I've just said about C++ apply to other programming languages such as Pascal, Java, FORTRAN, and Basic. These are all *high-level languages,* meaning they do not correspond closely to machine code but use keywords (such as "if" and "while") that resemble English, however remotely.

But if all these languages do essentially the same thing (provide an easier way to write programs than is possible with machine code), why are there so many?

Each language was developed for a different purpose. Basic, for example, was designed to be easy to learn and to use. As a result, it permitted loose syntax that unfortunately can lead to bad programming habits. Still, Microsoft developed Visual Basic into a powerful, convenient, quick application-building tool for Windows.

Pascal was developed for use in academic environments to teach sophisticated programming concepts. Where Basic is fast and loose in its syntax rules, Pascal is elaborate and full of complex syntax. It's a good language, but most programmers prefer something that imposes fewer restrictions.

C was originally designed for writing operating systems. While its syntax enforces more structure (and better habits) than Basic, it's a clean language that supports shortcuts and makes it possible to write more concise programs. The straightforward but comprehensive syntax of C has proven extremely popular with programmers through the years. Another advantage of C is that it imposes few restrictions, so anything possible in machine code can almost always be accomplished in C.

So what about C++?

The major difference between C and C++ is that C++ adds the ability to do *object-oriented programming.* This is an approach especially well suited to working with complex systems such as graphical user interfaces and network environments. As an object-oriented programmer you would ask:

1 What are the major kinds of data (that is, information) in the problem to be solved?

2 What operations should be defined for each kind of data?

3 How do the data objects interact with each other?

Interlude

What about Java and C#?

When object-oriented programming caught on in the late 1980s, several attempts were made to create an object oriented version of C. Bjarne Stroustrup created the first such language to achieve wide acceptance. That language, C++, is still in wide use today (a fact to which the existence of this book attests).

But C++ is not quite the final word on the development of an object-oriented version of C. Two new languages—Java and C#—are close enough to C and C++ to be called "C-based," but each language is a little different.

There are a number of differences among the three languages. C++ was designed to be backward-compatible with C for the most part, and a number of C coding tricks (some strongly discouraged by today's gurus) continue to work in C++ but are not even thinkable in Java and C#.

Java and C# are application-building tools not suited to writing operating systems. Although they adopt a great deal of C/C++ syntax, they do not, for example, enable access of arbitrary memory addresses. Also, some people consider them purer implementations of object-oriented programming.

With regard to each other, the differences between Java and C# syntax are not that great. Java was developed by Sun Microsystems as a platform-independent language; C# was developed by Microsoft for its .NET platform. They differ in platform and support libraries.

Although I've referred to C++ as a tool for writing operating systems, you can just as easily use it to create business programs, game programs, and programs for personal use. It provides greater freedom than some other languages, including the freedom to make low-level errors. That's why I try to steer you past potential "gotchas."

The good news is that if you learn C++ you should find Java or C# easy to pick up. C++ is also an easier language for people to learn if they've had experience with C.

In learning object-oriented programming, I've found that it's much easier if you've mastered basic statement syntax first. Therefore, I don't focus too much on object orientation until Chapter 10.

But I do introduce some objects—pieces of data that can respond to operations—early in the book. For example, in this chapter, I use **cout**, a data object not part of the C language. In C you'd print information by calling a function, which is a predefined series of statements. But when you use **cout** you're sending data to an object that—in a real sense—*knows how* to display information.

So instead of thinking "I'll call a function that prints this text on the screen," you think "I'll send this text to **cout**, which represents console output, and let it worry about how to do the printing."

This turns out to a superior way of doing things for a number of reasons—some more obvious and some less so. In particular, **cout** (the console output object) knows how to print many kinds of data, and—more important—that knowledge can be extended to any new data type whatsoever. The object-oriented approach is not restricted to a limited series of data formats as in the old-fashioned C-language approach.

What it means to send commands to an object and how that differs from old-fashioned programming is one of the major themes of this book—and the focus of the last half.

Building a C++ Program

Writing a program is actually only the first step of creating an application. In the next few sections I will outline all the steps you go through.

Enter the Program Statements

To write a C++ program (or most any other kind of program, for that matter), you need some way to enter the program statements. There are a couple of ways to do this:

▶ You can use a text editor, such as Microsoft Word or Notepad, an application that comes with Windows. Actually, most *any* text editor will do. If you use this approach, you must save the document (or rather source file) in plain-text format.

▶ You can enter text in an integrated development environment (IDE). A development environment is a text editor combined with other helpful programming tools. Microsoft Visual Studio is a development environment.

Once you've entered the program statements (and checked for errors), you can proceed to build the program.

Build the Program (Compile and Link)

Building the program is the process of converting your source code (C++ statements) into an application that can be run. If the program is correctly written this is usually as easy as pressing a function key. The process actually breaks down into two steps.

The first step *compiles* the program by translating C++ into machine code (also called "object code"). If that step is successful, the next step runs the *linker,* which combines this machine code with code from the C++ library.

The C++ library (also called the "runtime library" in techie circles) contains functions you call to do common tasks. (*Function* is another word for sub routine.) For example, the library contains the standard **sqrt** (square root) function so that you don't have to calculate square roots yourself. It also contains subroutines that send data to the monitor and know how to read and write to data files on the hard disk.

The accompanying figure summarizes how the build process works. Remember, if you use an integrated development environment these steps are automated for you; you simply press a function key.

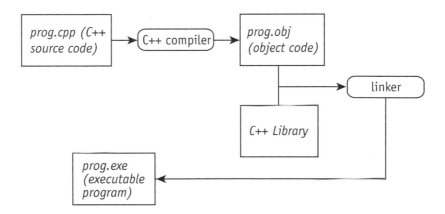

If the build was successful, you can pat yourself on the back; neither the compiler nor the linker found errors. But does that mean you're finished? Not quite. The compiler catches grammatical (syntax) errors. But there are many errors it cannot find.

Consider this analogy. Suppose you have the following sentence:

The moon is made green cheese.

This is not a grammatically correct sentence in English. To fix the grammar you'd insert the word "of":

The moon is made *of* green cheese.

Now the sentence has no syntax errors. But if something is grammatically correct does that necessarily mean it's a correct statement in the larger sense—that is, a true statement of fact? Of course not. To make the previous statement true you'd need to insert the word "not" in this case.

The moon is *not* made of green cheese.

Programming languages are similar. The C++ compiler determines if you have a syntactically correct program; if not, the compiler reports the exact line at which the error occurred. But the larger question, the question of *whether the program behaves correctly in all cases,* is not so obvious. Which brings us to the next step.

Test the Program

After you've succeeded in building a program, you need to run it a few times to verify it does exactly what you want it to do. In the case of a serious program—a program to be given or sold to other people—you may need to test it many times. (And in fact large software companies have entire departments that do nothing else.)

The errors you look for at this stage are called *program-logic errors.* With these errors you've used the syntax of the language correctly (there are no misplaced commas, for example) but for some reason the program doesn't behave the way you want it to.

Program-logic errors can be far more elusive than syntax errors. Suppose the program prints the wrong number or abruptly stops executing for no apparent reason. Which statement caused the problem? The answer is not always obvious. There may be many causes; for example, you may have made assumptions that are valid in some cases but not others. The process of testing a program and determining the source of a problem is called *debugging.*

Revise As Needed

If the program runs correctly, you're done. But if it has program-logic errors as just described, you need to determine the source of errors, go back and make changes to the C++ source code, and then rebuild the program.

With complex pieces of software, you may need to go through this cycle many times. Such a program may take a good deal of testing to verify that the program behaves correctly in all cases. Until you've completed such testing and revision, the program isn't really done. But with simple programs, you can usually get away with a moderate amount of testing.

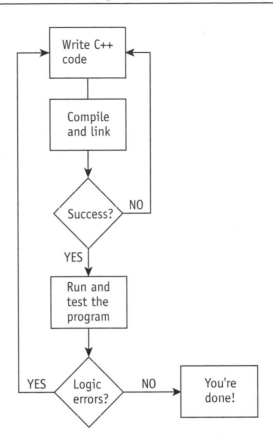

Installing Your Own C++ Compiler

If you have your own C++ compiler, you can use it to compile and run the examples in this book. For best results you should use a recent version of C++, but the examples are written so that they work with a variety of C++ compilers.

You can also install the GNU C++ compiler provided on the CD that accompanies this book. This is a free shareware compiler for MS-DOS environments; from Windows, you can run the compiler by first opening an MS-DOS command window. You are free to distribute any programs you create with the GNU compiler. The CD also provides the RHIDE development environment, which you can use to write and test programs.

To install the compiler, locate the README.TXT file on the root of the CD and follow directions. The CD also contains "Sample Code and Answers" directory. Its subdirectories contain answers to all the exercises in the book.

Note ▶ The CD also contains source files for the compiler. You don't need to install these unless you choose to.

Example 1.1. *Print a Message*

To start programming, open a new source file and enter the code listed below. If you're using the RHIDE development environment, choose the New command from the File menu. Then type in the source code exactly as shown. If you're using Microsoft Visual Studio, follow the instructions I give in the section "If You're Using Microsoft Visual Studio," on the next page.

Note ▶ You have to do a couple of things differently with Visual Studio, so don't expect the code to compile correctly until you consult that section.

print1.cpp

```cpp
#include <iostream>
using namespace std;

int main() {
    cout << "Never fear, C++ is here!";
    return 0;
}
```

The fifth line, beginning with **cout,** doesn't have to be indented a fixed number of spaces. Also, the space between words and punctuation (such as "<<") can contain any number of white spaces.

But you have to watch out for a couple of things: first, case-sensitivity matters. C++ is fussy about uppercase versus lowercase letters. Don't capitalize anything except for the text inside quotation marks. Also, make sure you remember the semicolon (;) at the end of the second, fifth, and sixth lines.

After entering the program, save it as print1, compile, and run it. Here's what the program prints when correctly entered and run:

```
Never fear, C++ is here!
```

If You're Using the RHIDE Environment

If you installed the shareware version of C++ described in the previous section, here's how to compile and run the program:

1 Save the program as print1.cpp if you haven't already. (You can pick a different name for the program if you want, but always use the extension .cpp.) Within RHIDE choose Save from the File menu.

2 Press F9 to build the program.

3 If you don't receive any error messages, the program compiled and linked successfully. Congratulations! If you received error messages, then either you didn't install the compiler successfully or you mistyped part of the example. Go back and check to make sure you typed every character—including the punctuation—exactly as shown.

4 Once the program successfully compiles, test it by first leaving RHIDE. From the File menu choose DOS Shell.

5 Once in the DOS Shell, type the name of the program:

```
print1
```

6 When done testing the program, type:

```
exit
```

Note ▶ You can also run programs from within RHIDE, but control is instantly passed back to RHIDE after the program is run, so unless the program pauses you don't get a good look at the output. That's why I recommend using the DOS Shell command.

If You're Using Microsoft Visual Studio

If you're using Microsoft Visual Studio to write C++ programs, there are a couple of extra things you need to do. Visual Studio is an excellent tool for writing programs, but it's designed primarily for the creation of serious Windows applications, not simple programs (which are the first things you should really be doing if new to C++).

To write a program in Visual Studio you first have to set up the right kind of project. (*Project* is Visual Studio lingo for all the files that go together to form a program.)

1 From the File Menu choose the File submenu, and from there choose the New command. Or you can click the New Project button if it is currently displayed near the middle of the screen.

2 Fill out the dialog box by clicking "Console Application" as the project type. Also, enter the program name—in this case, print1—and click OK.

3 If the file print1.cpp is not displayed, look for it in the list of filenames on the left side of the screen and double-click it.

Before you enter any C++ code, first delete all the code you see in the print1.cpp file except the following:

```
#include <stdafx.h>
```

This statement *always* needs to be included in console applications (that is, non-Windows applications) created with Visual Studio. If you're using Visual Studio to follow this book, remember to always insert this line at the beginning of every program.

The print1.cpp code should therefore look like this (with the added line shown in bold):

```
#include <stdafx.h>
#include <iostream>
using namespace std;

int main() {
    cout << "Never fear, C++ is here!";
    return 0;
}
```

To build the program just press F7. This launches both the compiler and linker.

If you succeed, congratulations! You're on your way. If the program does not build successfully, go back and make sure you entered every line verbatim.

To then run the program, press CTRL+F5. Although there are other ways to run the program from within Visual Studio, this is the only way that avoids the problem of the MS-DOS window flashing input on the screen and then disappearing immediately. CTRL+F5 (Start without debugging) runs the program and then prints a helpful "Press any key to continue" message, so you have a chance to look at the output.

How It Works

Believe it or not, this simple program has only one real statement. You can think of the rest as a template for now—stuff you have to include but can safely ignore. (If you're interested in the details, the upcoming "Interlude" discusses the **#include** directive.)

The syntax below shows standard, required items in bold. For now, don't worry about why it's necessary, just use it. In between the braces ({}) you insert the actual lines of the program—which in this case consist of just one statement.

```
#include <iostream>
using namespace std;
```

```
int main() {
    Enter_your_statements_here!
    return 0;
}
```

This program has only one real statement (which you insert into the fifth line above).

```
cout << "Never fear, C++ is here!";
```

What is **cout**? This is an *object*—a concept I'll discuss a lot more in the second half of the book. In the meantime, all you have to know is that **cout** stands for "console output." In other words, it represents the computer screen. When you send something to the screen, it gets printed just as you'd expect!

In C++ you print output by using **cout** and a leftward "stream" operator (<<) that shows the flow of data from a value (in this case, the text string Never fear, C++ is here!) to the console. You'll never get the use of **cout** wrong if you visualize it this way.

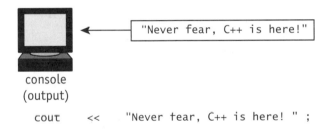

console
(output)

cout   <<   "Never fear, C++ is here! " ;

Don't forget the semicolon (;). Every C++ statement must end with a semicolon, with only a few exceptions.

For technical reasons, **cout** must always appear on the left side whenever you use it. Data in this case flows to the left. Use the leftward "arrows," which are actually two less-than signs (<<) combined together.

The following table shows other simple uses of **cout**.

STATEMENT	ACTION
cout << "Do you C++?";	Prints the words "Do you C++?"
cout << "Hello!";	Prints the word "Hello!"
cout << "Hi there, sailor!";	Prints the words "Hi there, sailor!"

EXERCISES

Exercise 1.1.1.   Write a program that prints the message "Get with the program!" If you want, you can work on the same source file used for the featured example and alter it as needed. (Hint: alter only the text inside the quotation marks; otherwise, reuse all the same programming code.)

Exercise 1.1.2.   Write a program that prints your own name.

Interlude

What about #include and "using"?

I said that the fifth line of the program is the first "real" statement of the program. I glossed over the first line:

```
#include <iostream>
```

This is an example of a C++ *preprocessor directive,* a general instruction to the C++ compiler. A directive of the form

```
#include <filename>
```

loads declarations and definitions that support a part of the C++ standard library. Without this directive, you could not use **cout**.

If you've used older versions of C++ and C you may wonder why no specific file (such as a ".h" file) is named. The filename "iostream" is a *virtual* include file, which has information in a precompiled form.

If you're new to C++, just remember you have to use **#include** to turn on support for specific parts of the C++ standard library. Later, when we start using math functions such as **sqrt** (square root), you'll need to switch on support for the math library:

```
#include <math.h>
```

Is this extra work? Yes. Could C++ have been designed without it? Maybe. "Include" files originally came about because of a distinction between the core C language and the standard runtime library. (Advanced C/C++ programmers sometimes avoid the library or modify it.) Library functions and objects—though indispensable to beginners—are treated just like user-defined functions, which means (as you'll learn in Chapter 4), they have to be declared. That's what included files do: they save you from having to declare things yourself.

Interlude

▼ *continued*

You also need to put in a **using** statement. This enables you to refer directly to objects such as **std::cout**. Without this statement you'd have to print messages this way:

```
std::cout << "Never fear, C++ is here!";
```

We're going to be using **cout** (and its cousin **cin**) quite a lot—as well as another **std** symbol named **endl**—so for now it's easier just to put a **using** statement at the beginning of every program.

Advancing to the Next Print Line

With C++, text sent to the screen does not automatically advance to the next physical line. You have to print a *newline* character to do that. If you don't print a newline, all the text gets printed on the same physical line. (Exception: If you never print a newline, the text may automatically wrap when the current physical line fills up, but this usually produces an ugly result.)

One way to print a newline is to use the predefined constant **endl**. Like **cout**, the **endl** constant is part of the **std** namespace:

```
std::cout << "Never fear, C++ is here!" << std::endl;
```

But as long as you place this statement at the beginning of the program:

```
using namespace std;
```

you don't need to qualify each use of **cout** and **endl**; so you can write the print statement as:

```
cout << "Never fear, C++ is here!" << endl;
```

Note ▶ The "endl" name is short for "end line"; it is therefore spelled "end ELL," not "end ONE."

Another way to print a newline is to insert the characters \n. This is an escape sequence, which C++ interprets as having a special meaning rather than interpreting it literally. The following statement has the same effect as the example above.

```
cout << "Never fear, C++ is here!\n";
```

Example 1.2.   *Print Multiple Lines*

The program in this section prints messages across several lines. If you're follow-ing along and entering the programs, remember once again to use uppercase and lowercase letters exactly as shown—although you can change the capitaliza-tion of the text inside quotation marks and the program will still run.

```cpp
print2.cpp

    #include <iostream>
    using namespace std;

    int main() {
        cout << "I am Blaxxon," << endl;
        cout << "the godlike computer." << endl;
        cout << "Fear me!" << endl;

        return 0;
    }
```

Save the program as print2.cpp and then compile and run it as explained ear-lier for Example 1.1.

How It Works

This example is similar to the first one I introduced. The main difference is this example uses newline characters. If these characters were omitted, the program would print

```
I am Blaxxon,the godlike computer.Fear me!
```

which is not what you want.

Conceptually, the accompanying figure shows how the statements in the pro-gram work:

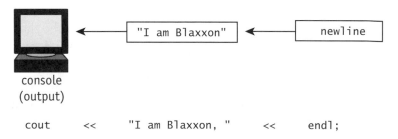

You can print any number of separate items this way—though again they won't advance to the next physical line without a newline character (**endl**). You could send several items to the console with one statement.

```
cout << "This is a " << "nice " << "C++ program.";
```

which prints the following when run:

```
This is a nice C++ program.
```

Or you can embed a newline like this:

```
cout << "This is a" << endl << "C++ program.";
```

which prints:

```
This is a
C++ program.
```

This example, like the previous one, returns a value. "Returning a value" is the process of sending back a signal—in this case to the operating system or development environment. You return a value by using the **return** statement:

```
return 0;
```

The return value of **main** is a code sent to the operating system in which 0 indicates success. All the examples in this book return 0.

Note ▶ Return values are more useful for other kinds of functions, which you'll learn about in Chapter 4. Returning a value from **main** is one of those annoying things that may not seem useful at first, but that you just need to *do*. (Note: some programs do choose to return values other than 0, to indicate specific problems.) For now, returning 0 from **main** is just one of those things you need to put in the program to make sure it is correct. "Why do I have to do that?" asks the child. "Because I said so," says the father.

EXERCISES

Exercise 1.2.1. Remove the newlines from the example in this section, but put in extra spaces so none of the words are crammed together. (Hint: remember that C++ doesn't automatically insert a space between output strings.) The resulting output should look like this:

```
I am Blaxxon, the godlike computer. Fear me!
```

Exercise 1.2.2. Alter the example so it prints a blank line between each two lines of output—in other words, make the results double-spaced rather than single-spaced. (Hint: print *two* newline characters after each text string.)

Interlude

What Is a String?

From the beginning, I've made use of text inside of quotes, as in the statement

```
cout << "Never fear, C++ is here!";
```

Everything outside the quotes is part of C++ syntax. What's inside the quotes is data.

Actually, all the data stored on computer is ultimately numeric. But depending on how data is used it can be interpreted as a string of printable characters. That's the case here.

You may have heard somewhere of ASCII code. "Never fear, C++ is here!" in this example is ASCII data. The characters 'N', 'e', 'v', 'e', 'r', etc., are stored in individual bytes in which each is a numeric code corresponding to a printable character.

I'll talk a lot more about this kind of data in Chapter 7. The important thing to keep in mind is that text enclosed in quotes is considered data, as opposed to a command. This kind of data is considered a string of text, or more commonly just a *string*.

Storing Data: C++ Variables

If all you could do was print silly messages, C++ wouldn't be too useful. The point is usually to get new data from somewhere—such as end-user input—and then do something interesting with it.

Such operations require *variables:* these are locations into which you can place data. You can think of variables as magic boxes that hold values. As the program proceeds, it can read, write, or alter these values as needed. The upcoming example uses variables named ctemp and ftemp to hold Celsius and Fahrenheit values, respectively.

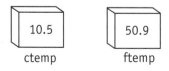

How do values get put into variables? One way is through console input. In C++ you can input values by using the **cin** object, representing (appropriately enough) console input. With **cin** you use a stream operator showing data flowing to the right ($>>$).

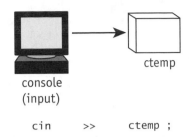

console
(input)

```
cin    >>    ctemp ;
```

Here's what happens in response to this statement. (The actual process is a little more complicated, involving the checking of an "input buffer," but what follows is essentially how it works in a simple program.)

1 The program suspends running and waits for the user to enter a number.

2 The user types a number and presses ENTER.

3 The number is accepted and placed in the variable ctemp (in this case).

4 The program resumes running.

So if you think about it a lot happens in response to the statement

```
cin >> ctemp;
```

But before you can use a variable in C++ you must declare it. This is an absolute rule, and it makes C++ different from Basic, which is sloppy in this regard and doesn't require declaration. (Generations of Basic programmers have banged their heads against their terminals as they've discovered errors cropping up from Basic's laxness about variables.)

This is important enough to justify restating, so I'll make it a cardinal rule:

✳ In C++ you must declare a variable before using it.

To declare a variable you have to first know what *data type* to use. This is a critical concept in C++ as in most other languages.

Introduction to Data Types

A variable is something you can think of as a magic box into which you can place information—or rather *data*. But what kind of data?

All data on a computer is ultimately numeric, but it is organized into one of three basic formats: integer, floating-point, and text string.

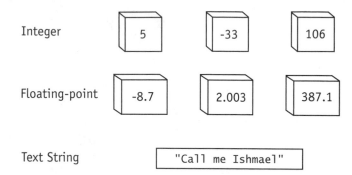

There are several differences between floating-point and integer format. But for beginning programs the rule is simple:

* **If you need to store numbers with fractional portions, use a floating-point variable; otherwise, use integer.**

The main floating-point data type in C++ is **double**. This may seem like a strange name: it stands for "double-precision floating point." There is also a single-precision type (**float**) but its use is rare. When you need the ability to retain fractional portions, you'll get better results—and fewer error messages—if you stick to **double**.

A **double** declaration has the following syntax. Note this statement is terminated with a semicolon (;), just as most kinds of statements are.

```
double   variable_name;
```

You can also use a **double** declaration to create a series of variables.

```
double   variable_name1, variable_name2, ...;
```

For example, this statement creates a **double** variable named aDouble:

```
double   aDouble;
```

This statement creates a variable of type **double**.

aDouble

The next statement, which uses the more complex syntax, declares four **double** variables named b, c, d, and amount:

```
double   b, c, d, amount;
```

The effect of this statement is equivalent to the following:

```
double  b;
double  c;
double  d;
double  amount;
```

The result of these declarations is to create four variables of type **double**.

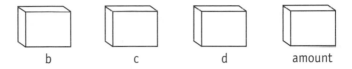

b   c   d   amount

Interlude | ## Why Double Precision, Not Single?

Double precision is like single precision, except it's better. Double precision supports a greater range of values and does so with better accuracy. (Yes, loss of accuracy is possible with floating-point variables; this is a topic I'll return to in later chapters.)

Because double precision is more accurate, it is the preferred floating-point type in C++; before C++ performs floating-point calculations it converts all values to double precision if they're not already in that format. C++ also stores floating-point constants in double precision unless you specify otherwise (for example, by using the notation 12.5F instead of 12.5).

Double precision has one drawback: it requires more space—specifically, eight bytes rather than four bytes (in PC environments). That's not even a factor for simple programs, because math coprocessors support eight-byte operations directly. It's only a factor when you have large amounts of floating-point values to be stored on disk. Then, and only then, should you consider using the single-precision type, **float**.

Example 1.3. *Convert Temperatures*

I don't know about you, but every time I go to Canada I have to convert Celsius temperatures to Fahrenheit in my head. If I had a handheld computer, it would be nice to tell it to do this conversion for me; computers are good at that sort of thing.

Here's the conversion formula. The asterisk (*), when used to combine two values, means "multiply by."

Fahrenheit = (Celsius * 1.8) + 32

Now, a useful program wouldn't just calculate a single temperature value and then be done for all time. If that were the case, it would be easier to just use the Windows Calculator program! No, a really useful program will take *any* value input for Celsius and then convert it. This requires the use of some new features:

▶ Getting user input, and

▶ Storing the value input in a variable.

Here is the complete program. Open a new source file, enter the code, save it as convert.cpp. Then compile and run.

convert1.cpp

```cpp
#include <iostream>
using namespace std;

int main() {
    double  ctemp, ftemp;

    cout << "Input a Celsius temp and press ENTER: ";
    cin >> ctemp;
    ftemp = (ctemp * 1.8) + 32;
    cout << "Fahrenheit temp is: " << ftemp;

    return 0;
}
```

Programs are easier to follow when you add comments, which in C++ are notated by double slashes (//). Comments are ignored by the C++ compiler itself (that is, they have no effect on program behavior) but are useful for humans. Here is the commented version.

convert2.cpp

```cpp
#include <iostream>
using namespace std;

int main() {

// Declare floating-pt variables.
```

convert3.c, cont.

```
    double  ctemp, ftemp;

// Prompt and input value of ctemp (Celsius Temp).

    cout << "Input a Celsius temp and press ENTER: ";
    cin >> ctemp;

// Calculate ftemp (Fahrenheit Temp) and output it.

    ftemp = (ctemp * 1.8) + 32;
    cout << "Fahrenheit temp is: " << ftemp;

    return 0;
}
```

This commented version, though it's easier for humans to read, takes more work to enter. In following the examples in this book, you can always omit the comments or choose to add them in later. Remember this cardinal rule for comments:

 C++ code beginning with double slashes (//) is a comment and is ignored by the C++ compiler to the end of the line.

Adding comments is always optional, but it is a good idea—especially if any humans (including you) are going to have to ever look at the C++ code.

How It Works

The first statement inside of **main** declares variables (of type **double**) ctemp and ftemp, which store Celsius temperature and Fahrenheit temperature, respectively.

```
    double  ctemp, ftemp;
```

This gives us two locations at which we can store numbers. Because they have type **double**, they can contain fractional portions. Remember that **double** stands for "double-precision floating point."

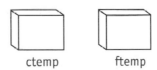

ctemp   ftemp

The next two statements prompt the user and then store input in the variable ctemp. Assume that the user types "10". Then the numeric value 10.0 gets put into ctemp.

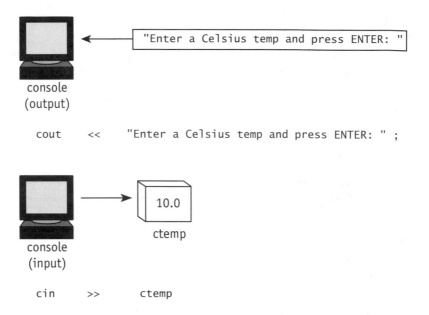

cout   <<   "Enter a Celsius temp and press ENTER: " ;

cin   >>   ctemp

In general, you can use similar statements in your own programs to print a prompting message and then store the input. The prompt is very helpful—because otherwise the user may not know when he's supposed to do something.

Note ▶ Although the number entered in this case was "10" it is stored as 10.0. In purely mathematical terms 10 and 10.0 are equivalent, but in C++ terms the notation "10.0" indicates the value is stored in floating-point format rather than integer format. This turns out to have important consequences, as I'll explain in the next chapter.

The next statement performs the actual conversion using the value stored in ctemp to calculate the value of ftemp:

```
ftemp = (ctemp * 1.8) + 32;
```

This statement contains an *assignment;* the value on the right side of the equal sign (=) is evaluated and then copied to the variable on the left side. This is one of the most common kinds of statements in C++.

Again, assuming "10" was input by the user, the accompanying diagram shows how data would flow in the program:

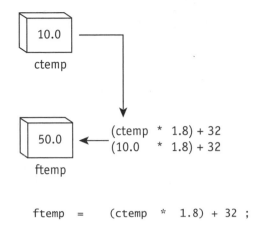

```
ftemp   =    (ctemp  *  1.8) + 32 ;
```

Finally, the program prints the result—in this case, 50.

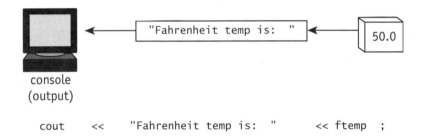

```
cout    <<    "Fahrenheit temp is:  "     << ftemp  ;
```

Variations on the Example

If you look at the last example carefully, you might ask yourself if it is really necessary to declare two variables instead of one.

Actually, it isn't. Welcome to the world of optimization. The following version improves on the first version of the program by getting rid of ftemp and combining the conversion and output step together. This doesn't always work—in a more complex program we might need to hold on to the Fahrenheit value—but here it works just fine.

convert3.cpp
```cpp
#include <iostream>
using namespace std;

int main() {
```

convert3.cpp, cont.

```
// Declare ctemp as a floating-pt variable.

    double  ctemp;

// Prompt and input value of ctemp (Celsius Temp).

    cout << "Input a Celsius temp and press ENTER: ";
    cin >> ctemp;

// Convert ctemp and output results.
    cout << "Fahrenheit temp is: " << (ctemp * 1.8) +
        32;

    return 0;
}
```

Do you detect a pattern by now? With the simplest programs the pattern is usually

1 Declare variables.

2 Get input from the user (after printing a prompt).

3 Perform calculations and output results.

For example, the next program does something different, but it should look familiar. This program prompts for a number and then prints the square (the number times itself). The statements are similar to those in the last example; the only things that are different are the name of the variable (n) and the particular calculation involved (n * n).

square.cpp

```
#include <iostream>
using namespace std;

int main() {

// Declare n as a floating-pt variable.

    double  n;
```

square.cpp, cont.

```cpp
// Prompt and input value of n.

    cout << "Input a number and press ENTER: ";
    cin >> n;

// Calculate and output the square.

    cout << "The square is: " << n * n;

    return 0;
}
```

EXERCISES

Exercise 1.3.1.   Rewrite the example so it performs the reverse conversion: input a value into ftemp (Fahrenheit) and convert to ctemp (Celsius). Then print the results. (Hint: the reverse conversion formula is ctemp = (ftemp – 32) / 1.8.)

Exercise 1.3.2.   Write the Fahrenheit-to-Celsius program using only one variable, ftemp. This is an optimization of Exercise 1.3.1.

Exercise 1.3.3.   Write a program that inputs a value into a variable n and outputs the cube (n * n * n). Make sure the output statement uses the word "cube" rather than "square."

Exercise 1.3.4.   Rewrite the example square.cpp using the variable name "num" rather than "n." Make sure you change the name everywhere "n" appears.

A Word about Variable Names and Keywords

This chapter has featured the variables ctemp, ftemp, and n. Exercise 1.3.5 suggested you could replace "n" with "num" as long as you did the substitution consistently throughout the program. So "num" is a valid name for a variable as well.

I could have chosen from an endless variety of variable names instead of "n" or "num". For example, I could give some variables the names "terminator2003", "killerRobot", and "GovernorOfCalifornia".

So, which variables names are permitted and which are not? Answer: you can use any name you want as long as you follow these rules:

▶ The first character should be a letter. It cannot be a number. Technically, the first character can be an underscore (_), but the C++ library uses that naming convention internally, so it's best to avoid starting a name that way.

▶ The rest of the name can be a letter, number, or an underscore (_).

▶ You must avoid words that already have a special predefined meaning in C++.

Words with special meaning in C++ are called "keywords." One such word is **main**. Other keywords include the standard C++ data types such as **int**, **float**, and **double**. Still other keywords include **if**, **else**, **while**, **do**, **switch**, and **class**.

It isn't necessary to sit down and memorize all the C++ keywords—although many programming books suggest you do that! You only need to know that if you try using a name that conflicts with one of the C++ keywords, the compiler will respond with a message referring to a keyword conflict or syntax error. In that case, try a different name.

EXERCISE

Exercise 1.3.5.   In the following list, which of the following words are legal variable names in C++ and which are not? Review the rules just mentioned as needed.

```
x
x1
EvilDarkness
PennslyvaniaAve1600
1600PennsylvaniaAve
Bobby_the_Robot
Bobby+the+Robot
whatThe???
amount
count2
count2five
5count
main
main2
```

Chapter 1   *Summary*

Here are the main points of Chapter 1:

▶ Creating a program begins with writing C++ source code. This consists of C++ statements, which bear at least some resemblance to English. (Machine code, by contrast, is completely incomprehensible unless you laboriously look up the meaning of each combination of 1s and 0s.) But before the program can be run it has to be translated into machine code, which is all that the computer ultimately understands.

▶ The process of translating the C++ statements into machine code is called *compiling*.

▶ After compiling, the program also has to be linked to standard functions stored in the C++ library. This process is called *linking*. After this step is successfully completed you have an executable program.

▶ Fortunately, if you have a development environment, the process of compiling and linking a program (called *building* the program) is automated so you need only press a single function key.

▶ Simple C++ programs have the following general form:

```cpp
#include <iostream>
using namespace std;

int main() {
    Enter_your_statements_here!
    return 0;
}
```

▶ To print output, use the **cout** object. For example:

```cpp
cout << "Never fear, C++ is here!";
```

▶ To print output and advance to the next line, use the **cout** object and send a newline character (**endl**). For example:

```cpp
cout << "Never fear, C++ is here!" << endl;
```

▶ Almost every C++ statement is terminated by a semicolon (;). One exception is that you don't put a semicolon after a preprocessor directive.

▶ Double slashes (//) indicate a comment; all text to the end of the line is ignored by the compiler itself but is helpful for humans who have to maintain the program.

▶ Before using a variable, you must declare it. For example:

```cpp
double x;      // Declare x as a floating-pt variable.
```

▶ Variables that may store a fractional portion should have type **double**. This stands for "double-precision floating point." The single-precision type (**float**) should only be used when storing large amounts of floating-point data on disk, in cases where storage space is precious.

▶ To get keyboard input into a variable you can use the **cin** object. For example:

```
cin >> x;
```

▶ You can also put data into a variable by using assignment (=). This operation evaluates the expression on the right side of the equal sign (=) and places the value in the variable on the left side. For example:

```
x = y * 2;    // Multiply y times 2, place result in x.
```

2 Decisions, Decisions

Once you know how to do input, output, and data calculations, you're on your way to writing real C++ programs. But there's more to programming than that. The most useful programs have behavior: *the ability to respond to conditions.*

In effect, computers make decisions. That's what this chapter is all about.

We'll start by looking at some simple programs. By the end of the chapter, you'll have the tools to do something interesting: perform a prime-number test. For large numbers especially, that job is a difficult one for humans, but it's perfect for a computer.

But First, a Few Words about Data Types

But before you look at computer decision-making, it's important to understand data. Ultimately, all information on a computer is a series of 1s and 0s. What gives the information meaning is how it's organized into meaningful units, called *data types*.

When learning mathematics, you didn't have to worry about types. A number is a number is a number. All these expression are mathematically equivalent:

   3   3.0   three   2+1

But computer languages and systems are different from pure math. It's not enough to have a value: you have to have a way to store it. In Chapter 1, I referred to a variable as a "magic box," but it might be more accurate to say that a variable is a bucket that can hold data—and like all buckets, it's not infinite. It can only hold so much information.

Unlike the world of pure math, the world of computers is one in which data is often a precious resource.

Chapter 1 developed examples using floating-point data. The current chapter uses integer data. The most important difference, as I mentioned, is that floating-point values can contain a fractional portion whereas integer cannot.

But there's more to it than that. Underneath the covers, integer and floating-point formats look nothing alike. Most of the time the differences are invisible to you: you just use the type you need and leave it to C++ to take care of the details. But sometimes the compiler warns you about "conversions" or "loss of data," and in those cases it's useful to know what the compiler is talking about.

Here's how a single value, 150, is stored in integer and in floating-point formats. (I've made a few simplifying assumptions. Actually, floating-point format uses binary rather than decimal representation.)

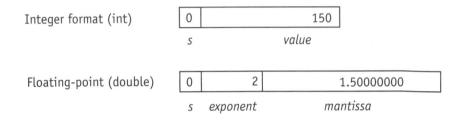

The sign bit, s, indicates whether the amount is positive or negative, with 0 indicating a non-negative number.

The exponent field is what makes floating-point format different from integer format—and also more flexible. Consider the problem of storing 10 to the 18th power. Here's the number written out:

1,000,000,000,000,000,000

You can't store this value in an integer variable. There isn't enough room. But a floating-point variable can store this value easily—it's simply a matter of using a sufficiently high exponent field. (The exponent would be 18 if the computer used decimal format. In binary, which is what the computer really uses, the exponent value is several times that.) Here's a concise way of representing this number in C++ code:

```
1e18
```

The point here is that you need to use the right data type for the right job. To store a whole number, such as 2 or 3, you can use floating-point storage if you choose (as with the number 150 in the earlier example). But the floating-point format takes up more space and is more complex than integer format. You're making the computer work harder than necessary. It's better to use integer format when you're working with whole numbers only, as long as those numbers are in the standard integer range (about plus or minus two billion, or two thousand million).

In some rare cases a floating-point field cannot store an integer precisely. This happens only with the largest integer values. Yet this is another reason to avoid using floating-point format when you're only working with whole numbers.

You declare an integer variable by using syntax similar to that for declaring a **double**. The **int** type is a standard integer value (four bytes wide on most any PC these days).

```
int variable_name;
```

Constant values are also stored in integer or floating-point format. The presence of a decimal point automatically causes the value to be stored as floating point. A number such as 3.141592 obviously requires floating-point format and so is stored as a **double**. But because it contains a decimal point, the numeral 3.0 is also stored as a **double**. If it's notated as 3, it's stored as an **int**.

And this is significant because C++ will oblige you and supply data conversions without complaint, but only if it can do so without potential loss of data. For example, an **int** constant has to be converted to floating-point before it can be assigned to a **double**.

```
double x;
x = 3;          // OK: convert from int
```

The C++ compiler does not complain in this case, because **double** format can hold any value that can be stored as an **int**.

But in this next example, a floating-point value (3.7) has to be converted to an integer. The compiler goes ahead and does the required conversion, but it issues a warning message saying that you may be losing data.

```
int n;
n = 3.7;        // Warning: convert from double to int
```

The result here is that the fractional portion 0.7 is dropped so that the value 3 is stored in the variable n.

What's less obvious is that this next statement—which looks so innocent—results in the same warning, because the ".0" says "I'm in floating-point format." To the C++ compiler, any conversion from floating-point to integer format is automatically suspect.

```
n = 3.0;        // Warning: convert from double to int
```

Despite the warning, the program still works correctly in this case since 3.0 is mathematically equivalent to 3. But most programmers like to get rid of warnings from the compiler—they're annoying and they give the lingering impression that something is wrong. The way to get rid of warnings here is to supply a cast, which says to the compiler, "Convert to **int** type." Because the conversion is done deliberately in this case, the compiler assumes you know what you're doing and does not issue the warning.

```
n = static_cast<int>(3.0);
```

Or better yet, you could make the constant an integer rather than a floating-point numeral; then there's no problem, because you're just assigning a constant in **int** format to an **int** variable.

```
n = 3;
```

The general form of the **static_cast** operator, by the way, is:

static_cast<*type*>(*expression*)

This **static_cast** operator takes the specified *expression* and returns a new expression with the same mathematical value but with the indicated *type*.

There are several cast operators supported by standard versions of C++ (all but the oldest, out-of-date versions). The **static_cast** operator is the most common of these; its use is straightforward. The others have more specialized uses.

Interlude

For C Programmers

If you have come from a C programming background, you may look at the C++ cast operators and wonder, why do the extra work of typing in all those extra characters? After all, the statement

```
n = static_cast<int>(3.0);
```

could be written more concisely in C as:

```
n = (int) 3.0;
```

In truth this shorter usage will work, although there are some C++ gurus who would be mad at me for letting you know that. C++ was designed from the beginning to be backward-compatible with C, and for this reason the shorter C-style data cast still works.

But there are some reasons for adopting the longer C++ style. Each of the C++ casts has a narrower purpose. For example, the **static_cast** operator can cast from **int** to **double** type, but it cannot cast from one type of pointer to another. (If you're a non-C programmer reading this, don't worry, I'll explain what pointers are in Chapter 6.) The latter is a special kind of cast

▼ continued

Interlude

that can have bizarre results if you're not exactly sure why you're doing it. Casting between pointer types has its own operator, **reinterpret_cast.**

Each of the four C++ casts (**static, dynamic, const,** and **reinterpret**) has a specialized usage, unlike the C cast, which is general. Use of the C++ casts therefore makes it easier to understand what the cast is for as you're perusing someone's C++ code.

The C-style casts, though more concise, are being strongly discouraged now. There is no guarantee that the ANSI C++ specification will continue to support C-style casts forever.

Decision Making in Programs

Decision making in a program is limited. A computer can only carry out instructions that are absolutely clear and precise.

In some ways this is a good thing; in other ways it's a challenge. The good news is the computer will always do exactly what you say. The bad news is the computer will always do exactly what you say—no matter how goofy. Once again, this is one of the cardinal rules of programming—maybe *the* cardinal rule:

✳ **A computer can only carry out instructions that are absolutely clear.**

In the case of decision making, this means the computer has no such thing as discretion or judgment. It can only follow mathematically precise rules: for example, comparing two values to see if they are equal.

Only in the realm of artificial intelligence (AI) do computer scientists suggest that a computer can have anything you might call judgment. But AI is the exception that proves the rule. A sophisticated decision-making program consists of thousands or even millions of individual instructions, each of which is simple, precise, and clear. (And that's how IBM's Deep Thought program can beat an international grandmaster at chess!)

If and if-else

The simplest way to program behavior is to say, "If A is true, then do B." That's what the C++ **if** statement does. Here is the simple form of the **if** statement syntax:

```
if (condition)
    statement
```

There are more complex forms of this statement, which we'll get to in a moment. But first consider an **if** statement that compares two variables, x and y. (Assume that these have already been declared as required.)

```
if (x == y)
    cout << "x and y are equal.";
```

This is strange. There are two equal signs (==) here instead of one (=). This is not a typo. C++ has two separate operators in this regard: one equal sign means assignment, which copies values into a variable; two equal signs test for equality.

Note ▶   As you progress in your C++ career, you'll find that using assignment (=) where you meant to use test-for-equality (==) is one of the most common errors. The problem is that assignment (=) inside a condition is legal; it just doesn't do the right thing. (The upcoming Interlude discusses the issue further.)

What if instead of executing just one statement in response to a condition you want to do a whole series of things? The answer is to use a *compound statement* (also called a "statement block"):

```
if (x == y) {
    cout << "x and y are equal." << endl;
    cout << "Isn't that nice?";
    they_are_equal = true;
}
```

The significance of this syntax is either all these statements are executed or none of them is. If the condition (x equal to y in this case) is not true, program control jumps past the end of the compound statement—in other words, it jumps to the first statement after the closing brace (}).

The opening and closing braces ({}) determine where the compound statement begins and ends. This can be plugged into **if** statement syntax because of another cardinal rule:

✱   **Anywhere you can use a statement in C++ syntax you can use a compound statement.**

Technically, a compound statement is just another kind of statement. Note that the compound statement itself is not terminated by a semicolon (;)—only the statements inside are. This is one of those exceptions to the semicolon rule I referred to in the last chapter.

Here's the **if** statement syntax again:

```
if (condition)
    statement
```

Applying the cardinal rule I just stated, we can insert a compound statement for the *statement:*

```
if (condition) {
    statements
}
```

where *statements* are zero or more statements.

You can also specify actions to take if the condition is *not* true. This is completely optional. As you might guess, this variation uses the **else** keyword.

```
if (condition)
    statement1
else
    statement2
```

As usual, either *statement1* or *statement2,* or both, can be a compound statement. Now you have the complete **if** syntax.

Here's a brief example.

```
if (x == y)
    cout << "x and y are equal";
else
    cout << "x and y are NOT equal";
```

This code can be rewritten to use compound-statement style, even though it's not strictly necessary.

```
if (x == y) {
    cout << "x and y are equal";
} else {
    cout << "x and y are NOT equal";
}
```

All **if** and **if-else** code can be written this way, so curly braces always appear even though the resulting statement blocks include only one statement each. Personally, I don't always use this approach because it's extra work, even though some programmers strongly recommend it.

The advantage of this approach (in which you always use compound statements with **if** syntax) is you can later go back and add a statement or two within the braces without making the code incorrect. My approach is usually to add the braces as needed, but you may prefer this more cautious approach.

Interlude

Why Two Operators (= and ==)?

If you've used another programming language such as Pascal or Basic, you may wonder why = and == are two separate operators. After all, Basic uses a single equal sign (=) for both assignment and test-for-equality, using context to tell them apart.

In C and C++, the following code is freely permitted. Yet it almost always produces the wrong behavior.

```
if (x = y)              // WRONG! Assignment!
    cout << "x and y are equal";
```

What this example does is (1) assign the value of y to x and (2) use that value as the test condition. If this value is nonzero, it is considered "true." Consequently, if y is any value other than zero, the condition above is always considered true and the statement is always executed!

Here is the correct version, which will do what you want:

```
if (x == y)             // CORRECT: test for equality
    cout << "x and y are equal";
```

Here, x == y is an operation that tests for equality and returns "true" or "false" as appropriate. The important thing to remember is not to confuse test-for-equality with assignment (x = y), which copies data to x and returns "true" on any nonzero value.

Why allow this potential source of problems? Well, the designers of C decided to give it more flexibility than other languages, and C++ inherits these features. In particular, nearly every expression in C or C++ returns a value, and this extends to assignment (=), which is considered "an expression with a side effect." So, you can initialize three variables at once by doing this:

```
x = y = z = 0;   // Set all vars to 0.
```

which is equivalent to:

```
x = (y = (z = 0));   // Set all vars to 0.
```

Each assignment beginning with the rightmost one (z = 0) returns the value that was assigned (0), which is then used in the next assignment (y = 0). In other words 0 is passed along three times, each time to a new variable.

C++ therefore treats "x = y" as an ordinary expression that returns a value, just like any other.

Interlude

▼ *continued*

And there'd be nothing wrong with that except for another C rule inherited by C++: *any value can be used as a condition*. Therefore, the compiler does not stop you if you write statements like this:

```
if (x = y)
    //...
```

So be extra careful about where you use a single equal sign (=) and where you use double equal signs (==).

Example 2.1.   *Odd or Even?*

Okay, enough preliminaries. It's time to look at a complete program that uses decision making. This is a simple, almost trivial, example, but it introduces a new operator (%) and shows the **if-else** syntax in action.

This program takes a number from the keyboard and reports whether it is odd or even. This is a trivial operation but illustrates simple use of the **if** statement.

---

even1.cpp

```
#include <iostream>
using namespace std;

int main() {
    int  n, remainder;

// Get a number from the keyboard.

    cout << "Enter a number and press ENTER: ";
    cin >> n;

// Get remainder after dividing by 2.

    remainder = n % 2;

// If remainder is 0, the number input is even.

    if (remainder == 0)
        cout << "The number is even.";
```

▼ *continued on next page*

---

even1.cpp, cont.

```
    else
        cout << "The number is odd.";

    return 0;
}
```

Once again, if you are following along and want to enter this example by hand, the comments—lines beginning with double slashes (//)—are optional.

How It Works

The first statement of the program declares two integer variables, n and remainder.

```
int  n, remainder;
```

The next thing the program does is get a number and store it in the variable n. This should look familiar by now:

```
cout << "Enter a number and press ENTER: ";
cin >> n;
```

Now it's just a matter of performing a test on n to see if it is odd or even. How do you do that? Answer: you divide the number by 2 and look at the remainder. If the remainder is 0 the number is even (in other words divisible by 2). Otherwise, it's odd.

That's exactly what's done here. The next statement divides by 2 and gets the remainder. This is called *modulus* or *remainder* division. The result is stored in a variable named (appropriately enough) "remainder."

```
remainder = n % 2;
```

The percent sign (%) loses its ordinary meaning in C++ and instead signifies remainder division. Here are some sample results:

EXAMPLE	THE REMAINDER FROM DIVISION IS	REMARKS
3 % 2	1	Odd.
4 % 2	0	Even.
25 % 2	1	Odd.
60 % 2	0	Even.
25 % 5	0	Divisible by 5.
13 % 5	3	Not divisible by 5.

After dividing n by 2 and getting the remainder, we get a result of either 0 (even) or 1 (odd). The **if** statement compares the remainder to 0 and prints the appropriate message.

```
if (remainder == 0)
    cout << "The number is even.";
else
    cout << "The number is odd.";
```

Notice the double equal signs (==) used in this code. As I mentioned before, a test-for-equality requires double equal signs—a single equal sign (=) means assignment. If I'm getting repetitive on this subject, it's because when I was first learning C, I made this mistake too many times myself!

Incidentally, here is the same code written in compound-statement style, which some programmers prefer on general principle:

```
if (remainder == 0) {
    cout << "The number is even.";
} else {
    cout << "The number is odd.";
}
```

Optimizing the Code

The version of the odd-or-even program I just introduced is not as efficient as it could be. The remainder variable is not really necessary. This version is a little better:

```
even2.cpp

    #include <iostream>
    using namespace std;

    int main() {
        int  n;

    // Get a number from the keyboard.

        cout << "Enter a number and press ENTER: ";
        cin >> n;
```
▼ continued on next page

even2.cpp, cont.

```
// Get remainder after dividing by 2.
// If remainder is 0, the number input is even.

    if (n % 2 == 0)
        cout << "The number is even.";
    else
        cout << "The number is odd.";

    return 0;
}
```

This version performs modulus division inside the condition, comparing the result to 0.

EXERCISE

Exercise 2.1.1.   Write a program that reports whether a number input is divisible by 7. (Hint: if a number is divisible by 7, that means you can divide it by 7 and get a remainder of 0.)

Introducing Loops

One of the most powerful concepts in any programming language is that of loops. In this section you'll see how a few lines of C++ can set up an operation to be performed (potentially) thousands of times.

When a program is in a loop, it performs an operation over and over just as long as a condition is true. The simplest form is the classic **while** statement:

```
while (condition)
    statement
```

As with **if**, you can make replace *statement* with a compound statement, which in turn lets you put as many statements inside the loop as you want.

```
while (condition) {
    statements
}
```

As with the **if** statement, **while** evaluates the *condition* and then executes the *statement* if the condition is true. The difference is **while** repeats the operation over and over until the condition is false.

More specifically, the program reevaluates the *condition* after each and every execution of the *statement*. If the *condition* is still true, the *statement* is executed

```
label1:  ◄
    if (condition) {
        statement
        goto label1;
    }
```

again. Here is how a **while** statement can be represented in terms of **if** and **goto** statements. (A **goto** statement is a direct jump to a program location.)

Or, to express the idea in terms closer to English:

1 Test the *condition*. If true, execute steps 2 and 3. (Otherwise, we're done; skip to the first statement after the end of the loop.)

2 Execute the *statement*.

3 Go back to Step 1.

About the simplest example of **while** is a loop that prints the numbers 1 to N, where N is a number input at the keyboard. We'll look first at this program in *pseudocode* form, meaning the steps are written out in English.

By convention, C and C++ programmers use variable names with lowercase letters: using "n," for example, rather than "N." The language itself doesn't enforce this convention; you can use uppercase letters as much as you want. This book follows the lowercase convention, using uppercase letters only occasionally. For the next page or so, I use the variable names "I" and "N," because it makes the pseudocode easier to follow.

At the beginning of a program, you need to declare variables. Assume that I and N (which we'll later replace with "i" and "n") are declared as integers. This makes sense because these variables will never need to hold a fractional portion.

Here's how to print the numbers from 1 to N:

1 Get a number from the keyboard and store in N.

2 Set I to 1.

3 While I is less than or equal to N,

    3A Output I to the console.

    3B Add 1 to I.

The first two steps initialize the integer variables I and N. I is set directly to 1. N is set by keyboard input. Assume that the user inputs "2".

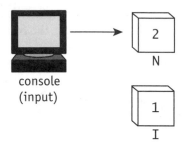

console
(input)

Step 3 is the interesting one. The program first considers whether I (which is 1) is less than or equal to N (which is 2). Since I *is* less than N, the program carries out steps 3A and 3B. First it prints the value of I.

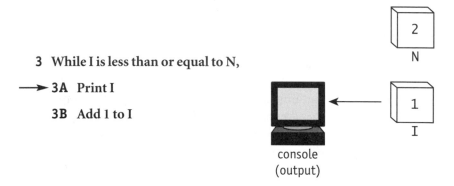

3 While I is less than or equal to N,

──▶ **3A Print I**

    3B Add 1 to I

console
(output)

Then it increases the value of I by 1 (called *incrementing*).

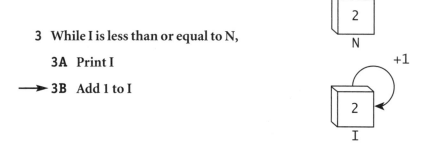

3 While I is less than or equal to N,

    3A Print I

──▶ **3B Add 1 to I**

Having carried out these steps, the program performs the comparison again. Because this is a **while** statement, not an **if** statement, the program continues to perform the steps 3A and 3B until the condition is no longer true.

The condition is still true (because the values are equal) so the program continues.

3 While I is less than or equal to N,

⟶ **3A Print I**

  3B Add 1 to I

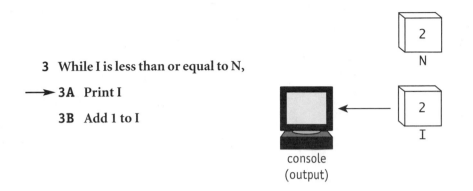

console
(output)

After printing the new value of I, the program increments I again.

3 While I is less than or equal to N,

  3A Print I

⟶ **3B Add 1 to I**

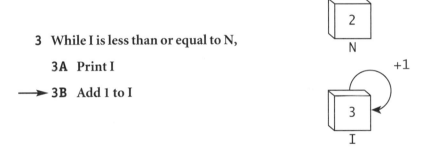

The program performs the test once more. Because I is now greater than N, the condition (Is I less than N?) is no longer true. The program ends. 3 is never printed. The output of the program, in this case, is:

    1 2

Because the user input 2, the loop executed twice. But with a large input for N (say, 1024) the loop would continue many more times.

If you're new to programming, this may come as a revelation: here's a program a few steps long that could (depending on the value input for N) print millions of numbers! The theoretical value of N has no limit except for the maximum integer size; the largest number that can be stored in an **int** variable is approximately two billion (that is, two thousand million).

In extreme cases, the limitations of data storage can affect what you can do with **while** statements, which is why I started the chapter by talking about data types.

Interlude | **Infinite Loopiness**

Can you set the loop condition in such a way that it will *always* be true? And if so, what happens? The answer is (1) yes, it's a common programming error; and (2) the loop will run until the computer loses power, the hardware gives out, there's a software interrupt, or—if none of those things happens first—it will run until one day billions of years from now the sun goes supernova and destroys the Earth. This is called an "infinite loop," and it's not pretty.

To avoid infinite loops, you need to exercise care with **while** and other kinds of loops (which we'll get to later in this chapter). Make sure you set the condition, the loop statement, and the initial settings so the loop eventually terminates.

Example 2.2.   *Print 1 to N*

Now let's use C++ code to implement the loop described in the last section. All this takes is a simple **while** loop using compound-statement syntax so that two statements are executed each time through the loop.

Here and in the remainder of the book I stick to the standard C++ convention of using lowercase letters for variable names.

count1.cpp

```cpp
#include <iostream>
using namespace std;

int main() {
    int  i, n;

// Get a number from the keyboard and initialize i.

    cout << "Enter a number and press ENTER: ";
    cin >> n;
    i = 1;
    while (i <= n) {           // While i less than or equal to n,
        cout << i << " ";      //    Print i,
        i = i + 1;             //    Add 1 to i.
    }

    return 0;
}
```

Note that some of the comments are on the same line as the C++ statements. This works because a comment begins with the double slashes (//) and continues to the end of line. Comments can be on their own lines or to the right of the statements.

The program, when run, counts to the specified number. For example, if the user inputs "6", the program prints

1 2 3 4 5 6

How It Works

This example introduces a new operator, although I'm sure you've surmised what it does. This is the less-than-or-equal-to test.

i <= n

The less-than-or-equal-to operator (<=) is one of several relational operators, all of which return true or false.

OPERATOR	MEANING
==	Test for equality
!=	Test for inequality (greater than or less than)
>	Greater than
<	Less than
>=	Greater than or equal to
<=	Less than or equal to

If you followed the logic in the section "Introducing Loops," the loop itself is straightforward. The braces ({}) create a compound-statement, so the **while** loop executes two statements each time through rather than one.

```
while (i <= n) {        // While i less than or equal
                        // to n,
    cout << i << " ";   //   Print i,
    i = i + 1;          //   Add 1 to i.
}
```

If you think about it, you'll see that the last number to be printed is n—which is what we want. As soon as i becomes greater than n, the loop ends and the output statement never executes for that case. The first statement inside the loop is:

```
cout << i << " ";   //   Print i,
```

This statement adds a space after i is printed. This is so the output is spaced like this:

```
1 2 3 4 5
```

rather than this:

```
12345
```

The loop then adds 1 to i before continuing to the next cycle. This ensures that the loop eventually ends, because i will sooner or later become greater than n (at which point the loop condition will fail).

```
i = i + 1;          //   Add 1 to i.
```

EXERCISES

Exercise 2.2.1. Write a program to print all the numbers from n1 to n2, where n1 and n2 are two numbers specified by the user. (Hint: you'll need to prompt for two values, n1 and n2, then initialize i to n1 and use n2 in the loop condition.)

Exercise 2.2.2. Alter the example so it prints all the numbers from n to 1 in reverse order. For example: 5 4 3 2 1. (Hint: to decrement a value inside the loop use the statement i = i – 1;).

True and False in C++

What exactly are "true" and "false"? Are these values stored in the computer in numeric form just like any other?

Indeed they are. Every Boolean (i.e., relational) operator returns 1 or 0:

IF THE CONDITION EVALUATED IS	THE EXPRESSION RETURNS
true	1
false	0

Also, any nonzero value fed to a condition is interpreted as true. So in this example, the statements are always executed:

```
// ALWAYS EXECUTED!

if (1) {
    // Do some stuff.
}
```

This next case creates one of those notorious infinite loops I referred to earlier:

```
// INFINITE LOOP!

while (1) {
    // Do some stuff.
}
```

Because all the relational operators return 1 or 0 you can declare an integer variable and use it as a Boolean "flag"—a variable that stores a true-or-false value. For example:

```
int is_less_than;

is_less_than = (i < n); // Store the value true (1) if
                        //  i is less than n.
```

The variable is_less_than stores the result of testing a condition. We'll make practical use of a similar variable (is_prime) later in this chapter.

Interlude

The bool Data Type

The most recent versions of C++ support a special **bool** ("Boolean") data type, which is similar to an integer type but is capable of only holding two values: true (1) or false (0). Any nonzero integer assigned to a **bool** variable causes it to hold the value true (1). If your compiler supports the **bool** type, it is preferable to **int** in this situation because the purpose of a **bool** variable is more readily apparent: it holds a true/false value.

```
bool is_less_than;

is_less_than = (i < n);   // Store the value true
                          // (1) if
                          //  i is less than n.
```

The Increment Operator (++)

The designers of C, the language on which much of C++ is based, had an obsession for creating shortcuts. One of the favorite shortcuts among programmers has always been the increment operator (++). This operator adds 1 to a variable. For example:

```
n++;              // n = n + 1
```

Consider the loop of the last section:

```
while (i <= n) {          // While i less than or equal to n,
    cout << i << " ";     //    Print i,
    i = i + 1;            //    Add 1 to i.
}
```

The second statement inside the loop can be replaced with a statement using the increment operator, producing:

```
while (i <= n) {          // While i less than or equal to n,
    cout << i << " ";     //    Print i,
    i++;                  //    Add 1 to i.
}
```

So far this substitution has saved only a few keystrokes. But it gets better. The item i++ is "an expression with a side effect"—meaning it produces a value *and* performs an action. Specifically, i++ is an expression with the same value as i, but after i++ is evaluated it adds 1 to i. So the loop can be shortened to:

```
while (i <= n) {            // While i less than or equal to n,
    cout << i++ << " ";   // Print i and then add 1 to i.
}
```

Do you see what this does? The statement prints out the current value of i and then increments it. Now we don't need the compound-statement syntax, so the loop can be shortened even further to:

```
while (i <= n)              // While i less than or equal to n,
    cout << i++ << " ";   // Print i and then add 1 to i.
```

But this kind of programming, while a nice shortcut, can be risky. In a complex statement that features multiple uses of i, side effects produce impossible-to-predict results. The only safe policy is to use i++ in its own statement or in a statement in which the variable appears just once.

You might wonder if there is a corresponding operator for subtraction. In fact, C++ has four increment/decrement operators. Here *var* means any variable.

OPERATOR	ACTION
var++	Return the current value of *var*, then add 1 to var.
++*var*	Add 1 to *var*: then return the result.
var−−	Return the current value of *var*, then subtract 1 from it.
−−*var*	Subtract 1 from *var*, then return the result.

Statements vs. Expressions

Until now, I've gone blithely along using the
These are fundamental terms in C++ so it's i.

These are difficult to define except by us:
thing you can say for sure about statements is t
one or more functions, and (2) a function, in t.
statements.

In general you recognize a statement by its use o
Here's an example:

```
cout << i++ << " ";
```

A simple statement is usually one line of a C++ program. But remember that
a semicolon terminates a statement, so it's legal (though not recommended) to
put two statements on a line:

```
cout << i << " ";  i++;
```

Fine, you say. So what's an expression? That's a closely related concept, but
the difference is important. An expression in C++ is anything that produces a
value with the exception of **void** expressions. That includes constants, variables,
and everything created with the help of operators.

Here's a sample list of expressions, along with descriptions of what value each
produces.

```
x                    // Returns value of x
12                   // Returns 12
x + 12               // Returns x + 12
x == 33              // Test for equality: returns 1 or 0
x = 33               // Assignment: returns value assigned
                     //    (33)
num++                // Returns value of num before
                     //    incrementing
i = num++ + 2        // Complex expression; returns new
                     //    value of i
```

Because these are expressions, any of these can be used as part of a larger
expression including assignment (=). The last three have *side effects*. x = 33 alters
the value of x, and num++ alters the value of num. The last example changes the
value of both num and i.

Any expression can be turned into a statement by following it with a semicolon.

```
num++;
```

The fact that any expression can be turned into a statement this way makes some strange statements possible. You can, for example, turn a constant into a statement:

    35;

But this statement does exactly nothing. Usually, you'll only see an expression turned into a statement if it has the potential to change a value, print output, or perform some other useful activity.

Introducing Boolean (Short-Circuit) Logic

Sometimes you need words like "and," "or," and "not" to express a complex condition. This is just common sense. For example, here (in pseudocode) is a condition that uses "and":

    If age > 12 and age < 20
        The subject is a teenager

To express conditions using "and," computer programmers use *Boolean algebra,* named for nineteenth-century mathematician George Boole. Boolean algebra does just what you'd expect.

Specifically, the subexpressions "age > 12" and "age < 20" are each evaluated, and if both are true, the overall expression

    age > 12 and age < 20

evaluates to true.

The following table summarizes the three Boolean (logical) operators in C++.

Table 2.1: Boolean Operators

SYMBOL	OPERATION	C++ SYNTAX	ACTION
&&	AND	*expr1* && *expr2*	Evaluate *expr1* and *expr2*. If both are true, return the value true; otherwise return false.
||	OR	*expr1* || *expr2*	Evaluate *expr1* and *expr2*. If at least one of these is true, return the value true; otherwise return 0.
!	NOT	! *expr1*	Evaluate *expr1*. If it's zero, return the value true; otherwise return false.

So the earlier example using "and" is expressed this way in C++:

```
if (age > 12 && age < 20)    // if age > 12 AND age < 20
    cout << "The subject is a teenager.";
```

The Boolean operators && and || have lower precedence than the relational operators (<, >, >=, <=, !=, and ==), which in turn have lower precedence than arithmetic operators such as addition (+) and multiplication (*). (But note that logical negation (!) has high precedence. See Appendix A for a complete summary of precedence order.)

Precedence is the rule that determines what operations are resolved in what order. Higher-precedence operators are applied before lower-precedence operators. Consequently, the following statement does what you'd probably expect:

```
if (x + 2 > y && a == b)
    cout << "The data passes the test";
```

This means "If x+ 2 is greater than y, and a is equal to b, then print the message." On the other hand, you can always achieve greater clarity by using parentheses.

```
if (((x + 2) > y) && (a == b))
    cout << "The data passes the test";
```

In C++ the "and" and "or" operators (&& and ||) employ short-circuit logic: This means the second operand is evaluated only if it needs to be. For example, with an "and" operation (&&), if the first operand is false, the second operand is never evaluated. Similarly, with an "or" operation (||) if the first operand is true, the second operand is never evaluated.

Note ▶ Don't confuse the Boolean operators with the bitwise operators (&, |, ^, and ~). C++ supports both but each group works a little differently; they are not combined as in Basic. The bitwise operators compare each bit in one operand to the corresponding bit in the other. Although in many cases bitwise operators produce the same results as Boolean operators, in many cases they do not. One important difference is bitwise operators do not use short-circuit logic; that fact can have significant consequences if the second operand has any kind of side effects.

Interlude

What Is "true"?

In some areas, C++ is more lax than other programming languages. The Boolean operators—&&, ||, and !—can take any numeric or Boolean expressions as input. Any nonzero expression is considered "true." Some programmers take advantage of this behavior to write shortcuts:

▼ *continued on next page*

Interlude

▼ *continued*

```
if (n && b > 2)
    cout << "n is nonzero and b is greater than 2.";
```

But this aspect of C++ also means that it's possible to write some really strange bits of code like the following:

```
if (1.05 && 33)
    cout << "Both 1.05 and 33 are nonzero.";
```

Expressions such as 1.05 && 33 are nearly meaningless and should be avoided. Many programmers, in fact, dislike the use of any conditions other than ones that have obvious true/false values (such as x > 0).

Example 2.3.   *Testing a Person's Age*

This section demonstrates a simple use of the AND operator (&&). The program here determines whether a number is in a particular range—in this case the range of teen numbers 13 through 19.

range.cpp

```cpp
#include <iostream>
using namespace std;

int main() {
    int  n;

    cout << "Enter an age and press ENTER: ";
    cin >> n;

    if (n > 12 && n < 20)
        cout << "Subject is a teenager.";
    else
        cout << "Subject is not a teenager.";

    return 0;
}
```

How It Works

This brief program uses a condition made up of two relational tests:

```
n > 12 && n < 20
```

Because Boolean "and" (&&) has lower precedence than relational operations (> and <), the "and" operation is performed last. The test performs as if written this way:

```
(n > 12) && (n < 20)
```

Consequently, if the number input is greater than 12 and less than 20, the condition evaluates to true and the program prints the message, "Subject is a teenager."

EXERCISE

Exercise 2.3.1.   Write a program to test a number for being in the range 0 to 100, inclusive.

Introducing the Math Library

Up until now, I've used C++ standard library for the support of input-output streams. That enabled the code to use **cout** and **cin**, and it's why the programs had to include the following line:

```
#include <iostream>
```

Now I'm going to introduce one of the math functions. You can use any of the C++ operators (such as +, *, -, /, and %) without library support, because operators are intrinsic to the language itself. But to use any of the special mathematics functions, you need to include the line:

```
#include <math.h>
```

Math functions include trigonometric functions (**sin**, **cos**, **tan**, **asin**, **acos**, **atan**, etc.), logarithmic functions (**log**, **log10**), exponential functions (**pow**, **exp**), and other goodies. This chapter uses just one math function: **sqrt**, which returns a square root.

```
#include <math.h>
//...

double x;
x = sqrt(2.0);        // Assign the square root of 2 to x
```

Programmers affectionately refer to **sqrt** as the "squirt" function. As with all math functions, this function accepts and returns a value of type **double**. If you assign the result to an integer, C++ drops the fractional portion (and also issues a warning message).

```
int  n;
n = sqrt(2.0);   // This places the value 1 into n,
                 //   after truncating 1.41421 to 1.
```

You may have noticed what appears to be an inconsistency here. The subjects of the **#include** directives are `iostream` and `math.h`... one includes a .h extension and the other doesn't. The explanation lies in the fact that math.h is an actual file; iostream is a "virtual" include file that exists in a precompiled form. The C++ language is in a state of transition, and right now you need to use both "iostream" and "math.h" to ensure the best chances of working with all compilers. Eventually, all library support will be handled with virtual include files so C++ code will become more consistent.

```
#include <iostream>
#include <math.h>
```

Example 2.4.   *Prime–Number Test*

Now we have enough C++ tools to do something interesting and useful: determine whether a number input is a prime number. A prime number is a number divisible only by itself and 1. It's obvious that 12,000 is not prime (since it's a multiple of 10), but it's not at all obvious whether 12,001 is.

Determining whether a number is prime is a classic case of something that's difficult for humans but—with the right program—is easy for computers. Here's the code.

```
prime1.cpp

    #include <iostream>
    #include <math.h>
    using namespace std;

    int main() {
        int  n;   // Number to test for prime-ness
        int  i;   // Loop counter
        int  is_prime;   // Boolean flag
```

prime1.cpp, cont.

```cpp
        // Assume that a number is prime until proven
        // otherwise

        is_prime = true;

        // Get a number from the keyboard.

        cout << "Enter a number and press ENTER: ";
        cin >> n;

        // Test for prime-ness by checking for divisibility
        //   by all whole numbers from 2 to sqrt(n).

        i = 2;
        while (i <= sqrt(static_cast<double>(n))) {
                                    // While i is <= sqrt(n),
            if (n % i == 0)         // If i divides evenly
                                    //   into n,
                is_prime = false;   // n is not prime.
            i++;                    // Add 1 to i.
        }

        // Print results

        if (is_prime)
            cout << "Number is prime.";
        else
            cout << "Number is not prime.";

        return 0;
    }
```

When the program is run, if the user enters "12000" the program will print:

```
Number is not prime.
```

To discover what happens with 12001, I'll leave you to run the program for yourself.

Note ▶ When running the program, enter "12000" not "12,000". A C++ program doesn't normally expect or permit commas inside of numerals. (The only exception would be if you wrote a program so that it expected a comma in the thousand's place, which is not a trivial thing to do.)

How It Works

The core of the program is the following loop. Note that to avoid data-conversion problems, the integer n needs to be cast to type **double** before being passed to the **sqrt** function; this is because the function takes and returns values of type **double**.

```
while (i <= sqrt(static_cast<double>(n))) {
                            // While i is <= sqrt(n),
    if (n % i == 0)         // If i divides evenly into n,
        is_prime = false;   //   n is not prime.
    i++;                    // Add 1 to i.
}
```

Let's look at this a little more closely. Here's a pseudocode (English language) version of this loop:

Set i to 2.
While i is less than or equal to the square root of n,
   If n is divisible by the loop counter (i),
      n is not prime.
   Add 1 to i.

The loop tests n for divisibility by each whole number, starting with 2. The loop stops at the square root of n, because if it were going to find divisors (numbers that divide into n evenly) it would have found them before that point. A little reasoning shows why this is true: if n had a divisor greater than its square root, it would have to have a divisor less than its square root as well. (If $a * b = n$ and $a > sqrt(n)$, then $b < sqrt(n)$.)

If you don't fully understand the mathematical reasoning involved, don't worry. What's important here is how you can use C++ to implement the procedure.

The divisibility test itself uses the modulus operator (%) introduced near the beginning of the chapter. You may recall that this operator performs division and returns the remainder. If the second number perfectly divides the first, the remainder is 0; therefore, this second number (i, in this case) is not prime.

```
if (n % i == 0)
    is_prime = false;
```

The beginning of the program assumes that the number is prime (is_prime = true), so if no divisors are found, the result is true. The values **true** (1) and **false** (0) are predefined in C++.

Optimizing the Program

There are several ways this program can be improved, but the most important change is: once the first divisor of n is found, the loop should immediately stop. There is no reason to continue since that would only waste CPU time.

The C++ **break** keyword lets you exit the nearest enclosing loop. Here is the revised code:

```
i = 2;
while (i <= sqrt((static_cast<double>(n)))) {
    if (n % i == 0) {
        is_prime = false;
        break;
    }
    i++;
}
```

Note how braces ({}) are used here to create a compound statement (that is, a statement block) for the **if** statement, because two actions must be taken. In this case, the braces are not optional if you want the program to work correctly.

Another way to improve the code is through initialization. In C++, variables may be initialized when declared—using any expression to the right of the equal sign. For example:

```
int  is_prime = true;
```

EXERCISE

Exercise 2.4.1. Optimize the program further by calculating the square root of n just once rather than over and over as was done in the example. To perform this optimization, you'll need to declare another variable and set it to the square root of n. The type should be **double**. You can then use this variable in the **for** loop condition. Write a complete program that includes this optimization, as well as the ones mentioned under "Optimizing the Program."

Chapter 2 *Summary*

In this chapter we covered the following concepts.

▶ Use the right data type for the right job. A variable that can never have a fractional portion should be given type **int** (the standard integer format in C++) unless it exceeds the range limitation of the **int** type—over two billion (two thousand million). Because floating-point format uses an internal exponent field it can store much larger values if needed.

▶ You can declare integer variables by using the **int** keyword followed by a variable name and semicolon. (You can also declare multiple variables, separating adjacent variable names with a comma.)

```
int  variable_name;
```

▶ Constants have **int** or **double** type as appropriate. Any value with a decimal point is automatically considered a floating-point value: 3 is stored as an **int**, but 3.0 is stored as a **double** because it is notated with a decimal point.

▶ The simplest decision-making structure in C++ is the **if** statement:

```
if (condition)
    statement
```

▶ The **if** statement has an optional **else** clause, so you can use this form:

```
if (condition)
    statement
else
    statement
```

▶ Anywhere you can use a statement, you can use a *compound* statement (also called a "statement block"), which consists of one or more statements enclosed in braces ({}).

```
if (condition) {
    statements
}
```

▶ Don't confuse assignment (=) with test-for-equality (==). The latter compares two values and returns true (1) or false (0). Assignment returns the value that was assigned. Here's a correct use of the two operators:

```
if (x == y)
    is_equal = true;
```

▶ The **while** statement executes a statement (or compound statement) repeatedly, as long as the specified condition is true. More specifically, after each execution of *statement*, the *condition* is reevaluated. If true, then *statement* is executed again.

```
while (condition)
    statement
```

▶ The modulus operator performs division and then returns the remainder. For example, the result of the following expression is 3:

```
13 % 5
```

▶ A statement is (most commonly) one line of a C++ program, terminated by a semicolon (;). Also, some statements are made up of a series of smaller statements. These may span multiple lines.

▶ An expression is a value formed by a variable, constant, or any number of subexpressions combined with C++ operators (including assignment). Expressions can be used inside of larger expressions.

▶ An expression can be turned into a statement by adding a semicolon. For example:

```
num++;
```

▶ The increment operator is convenient shorthand for adding 1 to a number. This creates an expression with a side effect.

```
cout << n++;    // Print n and then add 1 to n.
```

▶ You can use the C++ Boolean operators AND (&&), OR (||), and NOT (!) to create complex conditions.

The Handy, All-Purpose "for" Statement

3

Some tasks are so common that C++ provides special syntax just to represent them with fewer keystrokes. An example is the increment operator (++) introduced in Chapter 2. Because adding 1 to a variable is so common, C++ provides this operator to add 1 even though you could get away without it.

```
n++;    // Add 1 to n.
```

*Another case is the **for** statement. Its only purpose in life is to make certain kinds of **while** loops more concise. But this turns out to be so useful that programmers come to rely on it heavily. I use it throughout the rest of this book.*

*You'll find that once you use it a few times the **for** statement becomes second nature. Unfortunately, it looks strange the first time you see it. And to be frank, most instruction books don't do a great job of explaining it. To address this problem, I am giving the **for** statement its own chapter.*

Loops Used for Counting

As you worked with **while** loops in Chapter 2, you may have noticed that a common purpose of a loop is to count to a number—in the process, performing some action a specific number of times. For example:

```
i = 1;
while(i <= 10) {
    cout << i << " ";
    i++;
}
```

After all is said and done, what's really going on here is the computer counting from 1 to 10. That's something computers are good at. A loop variable gets an initial value of 1 and then is incremented each time through the loop. You can summarize what happens this way:

1 Set i to 1.

2 Perform the loop action.

3 Set i to 2.

4 Perform the loop action.

5 Set i to 3.

6 Perform the loop action.

7 Continue in this manner up to, and including, i being set to 10.

In other words, perform the loop 10 times, each time giving a different value to i. In loops of this kind (which are extremely common in programming), certain actions are always performed. We can identify three such actions:

initializer: evaluated just once, before the loop begins

                        ── *condition*

```
i = 1;
while (i <= 10) {
    cout << i << " ";
    i++;
}                      ── increment: evaluated after each
                          execution of the loop statement
```

It would be nice to have a way to express these actions in one succinct statement. Then it would be easy to write a loop that counts to 10.

Introducing the "for" Loop

The **for** statement provides just such a mechanism, letting you specify the *initializer, condition,* and *increment.*

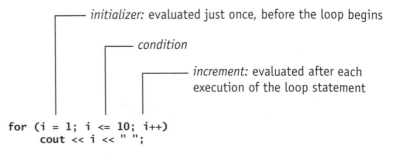

initializer: evaluated just once, before the loop begins

── *condition*

increment: evaluated after each execution of the loop statement

```
for (i = 1; i <= 10; i++)
    cout << i << " ";
```

This is not only more concise but a lot tidier. All the settings that control operation of the loop are placed between parentheses. More formally, here is the syntax of the **for** statement along with the equivalent **while** loop.

Look at that example of the **for** statement again:

```
for (i = 1; i <= 10; i++)
    cout << i << " ";
```

In mentally deciphering the **for** statement, remember to identify the three expressions between the parentheses as the *initializer, condition,* and *increment*—in that order. Here's how they're used in this case.

1 The *initializer* is the expression $i = 1$. This is evaluated just once, before the loop executes. In this case, i gets the initial value of 1.

2 The *condition* is $i <= 10$. This is the same loop condition you'd use if you were writing the code as a **while** loop. The effect here is to keep cycling the loop as long as i is less than or equal to 10.

3 The *increment* is the expression i++. This is evaluated at the bottom of the loop. That is to say, i is increased by 1 after each execution of the statement inside the loop (the "body of the loop," as it were).

Again, this **for** loop is equivalent to the **while** loop identified earlier:

```
i = 1;                    // Set i to 1.
while(i <= 10) {          // While i is less than or
                          // equal to 10,
    cout << i << " ";     //    Print i, along with a
                          //    space.
    i++;                  //    Add 1 to i.
}
```

I've found that, even with all this discussion of syntax and equivalent loops, a structure such as **for** can still be fuzzy until you look at a lot of examples. That's the purpose of the next section.

A Wealth of Examples

I'll start with a slight variation of the example you've already seen. The loop variable, i, is initialized to 1 (i = 1) and the loop continues while the condition (i <= 5) is true. This is the same as the earlier example except that the loop only counts to 5.

```
for(i = 1; i <= 5; i++)
    cout << i << " ";
```

This produces the output:

```
1 2 3 4 5
```

The next example runs from 10 to 20 rather than 1 to 5.

```
for(i = 10; i <= 20; i++)
    cout << i << " ";
```

This produces the output:

```
10 11 12 13 14 15 16 17 18 19 20
```

Here the *initializer* is i = 10 and the *condition* is i <=20. These expressions determine the initial and terminal settings of the loop. (The condition terminates the loop when it is no longer true; therefore, the highest value of i will be 20 in this case.)

These settings do not have to be constants. In this next example they are determined by variables. The loop counts from n1 to n2.

```
n1 = 32;
n2 = 38;
for (i = n1; i <= n2; i++)
    cout << i << " ";
```

This produces the output:

```
32 33 34 35 36 37 38
```

The *increment* expression can be any expression at all; it does not have to be i++. You can just as easily use i– –, which causes the **for** loop to count downward. Note the use of greater-than-or-equal-to (>=) in the condition in this example.

```
for(i = 10; i >= 1; i--)
    cout << i << " ";
```

This produces the output:

```
10 9 8 7 6 5 4 3 2 1
```

The **for** statement is highly flexible. By changing the *increment* expression, you can count by 2 rather than by 1.

```
for(i = 1; i <= 11; i = i + 2)
    cout << i << " ";
```

This produces the output:

```
1 3 5 7 9 11
```

As a final example you don't have to use i as the loop variable. Here's an example that uses a loop variable named j:

```
for(j = 1; j <= 5; j++)
    cout << j * 2 << " ";
```

This produces the output:

```
2 4 6 8 10
```

Note that in this case the loop statement prints j * 2, which is why this loop prints even numbers.

Interlude

Does "for" Always Behave like "while"?

I said that a **for** loop is a special case of **while** and performs exactly as the corresponding **while** loop would. That's *almost* true. There is one minor exception—which for the purposes of this entire book and 99.9 percent of all the code you will ever write—you don't need to worry about. The exception involves the **continue** keyword. You can use this keyword in a loop, placing it in its own statement to say, "Advance immediately to the next cycle of the loop."

```
continue;
```

This is a kind of "Advance directly to Go" statement. It doesn't break out of the loop (which the **break** keyword does), it simply speeds things up.

The difference in behavior is this: in a **while** loop, the **continue** statement neglects to execute the *increment* (i++) before advancing to the next cycle of the loop. In a **for** loop, the **continue** statement does execute the *increment* before advancing. This second behavior would usually be the behavior you'd want, and that provides one more reason why **for** is useful.

Example 3.1.   *Printing 1 to N with "for"*

Now we'll apply the **for** statement in a complete program. This example does the exact same thing as Example 2.2 on page 48: it prints all the number from 1 to n. But this version is more compact.

```
count2.cpp

    #include <iostream>
    using namespace std;

    int main() {
        int  i, n;

    // Get a number from the keyboard and initialize i.

        cout << "Enter a number and press ENTER: ";
        cin >> n;

        for (i = 1; i <= n; i++)    //   For i = 1 to n,
            cout << i << " ";       //        Print i.

        return 0;
    }
```

The program when run counts to the specified number. For example, if the user inputs "9" the program prints

1 2 3 4 5 6 7 8 9

How It Works

This example features a simple **for** loop, similar to the first example of a **for** statement shown earlier. The only difference is that the loop condition in this example uses n, a number the program gets from the user.

```
        cout << "Enter a number and press ENTER: ";
        cin >> n;
```

The loop prints numbers from 1 to n, where n is the number entered.

```
        for (i = 1; i <= n; i++)    //   For i = 1 to n,
            cout << i << " ";       //        Print i.
```

To review:

▶ The expression i = 1 is the *initializer* expression; this is evaluated just once, before the loop is executed. This initial value of i is therefore 1.

▶ The expression i <= n is the *condition*. This is checked before each loop cycle to see if the loop should continue. If for example n is 9, the loop terminates when i reaches 10, so the loop is not executed for the case of i equal to 10.

▶ The expression i++ is the *increment* expression, which is evaluated after each execution of the loop statement. This drives the loop by adding 1 to i each time.

The program logic is therefore:

```
Set i to 1.
While i is less than or equal to n,
    Print i,
    Add 1 to i.
```

EXERCISES

Exercise 3.3.1. Use the **for** statement in a program that prints all the numbers from n1 to n2, where n1 and n2 are two numbers specified by the user. (Hint: you'll need to prompt for the two values and then, inside the **for** statement, initialize i to n1 and use n2 in the loop condition.)

Exercise 3.3.2. Rewrite the example so that it prints all the numbers from n to 1 in reverse order. For example, the user enters 5 and the program prints 5 4 3 2 1. (Hint: in the **for** loop, initialize i to n, use the condition i >= 1, and subtract 1 from i in the increment step.)

Statement Blocks with "for"

Up until now, I've used the following statement in the body of every loop.

```
cout << i << " ";
```

Of course you don't have to use this statement. You don't have to print the value of i; in fact, you don't have to print out anything at all. I chose this statement for its value in demonstrating what a loop does. You can do a lot of other things in a loop.

As with **if** and **while** you can use a statement block with **for**:

```
for (initializer; condition; increment) {
    statements
}
```

As before, this syntax follows from the rule that wherever you can use a statement in C++ you can also use a compound statement.

Here is an example that executes two statements inside a **for** loop:

```
for (i = 1; i <= 10; i++) {
    cout << "The square root of " << i << " is ";
    cout << sqrt(i) << endl;
}
```

This is equivalent to:

```
i = 1;
while (i <= 10) {
    cout << "The square root of " << i << " is ";
    cout << sqrt(i) << endl;
    i++;
}
```

Declaring Loop Variables on the Fly

One of the added benefits of the **for** statement is that you can use it to declare a variable that has scope local to the **for** loop itself. The variable is declared "on the fly" for the express use of the **for** loop itself. For example:

```
for (int i = 1; i <= n; i++)   //   For i = 1 to n,
    cout << i << " ";          //        Print i.
```

Here, i is declared inside the *initializer* expression of the **for** statement.

If you use this technique you don't need to declare i separately from the loop. You could rewrite Example 3.1 this way:

---

count3.cpp

```
#include <iostream>
using namespace std;

int main() {
    int  n;

// Get a number from the keyboard.

    cout << "Enter a number and press ENTER: ";
    cin >> n;
```

count3.cpp, cont.

```
    for (int i = 1; i <= n; i++)    //  For i = 1 to n,
        cout << i << " ";           //  Print i.

    return 0;
}
```

Example 3.2.

Prime-Number Test with "for"

For this section I return to the prime-number example of Example 2.4 (page 58), showing how to write that program using a **for** loop rather than **while**. This example does something more interesting than just print the value of i; it determines whether a number input is a prime number. (Remember, a number is prime if it is evenly divisible only by itself and 1.)

The same basic logic is involved as in Example 2.4. Forgive me if this seems a little redundant.

The logic of a prime-number test is:

Set i to 2.
While i is less than or equal to the square root of n,
   If i divides evenly into n,
     n is not prime.
   Add 1 to i.

The **for**-loop version uses exactly the same approach: when compiled it carries out the same instructions as the **while** loop. However, because the essential nature of a **for** loop is to perform counting—in this case counting from 2 to the square root of n—we can think of it a little differently. Conceptually this approach is simpler:

For all whole numbers from 2 to the square root of n,
   If i divides evenly into n,
     n is not prime.

Here is the complete program for testing whether a number is a prime number. Again, this is a version of the program described in Example 2.4, so most of it should look familiar.

prime2.cpp

```
#include <iostream>
#include <math.h>
using namespace std;
```

▼ *continued on next page*

prime2.cpp, cont.

```cpp
int main() {
    int  n;    // Number to test for prime-ness
    int  i;    // Loop counter
    int  is_prime;   // Boolean flag

    // Assume that a number is prime until proven
    // otherwise

    is_prime = true;

    // Get a number from the keyboard.
    cout << "Enter a number and press ENTER: ";
    cin >> n;

    // Test for prime-ness by checking for divisibility
    //   by all whole numbers from 2 to sqrt(n).

    for (i = 2; i <= sqrt((double) n); i++) {
        if (n % i == 0)
            is_prime = false;
    }

    // Print results

    if (is_prime)
        cout << "Number is prime.";
    else
        cout << "Number is not prime.";

    return 0;
}
```

When the program is run, if the user enters "23", the program prints:

```
Number is prime.
```

How It Works

The beginning of the program uses **#include** directives to provide needed C++ library support. The C++ library is used here because the program will be calling the **sqrt** function to get the square root of a number.

```
#include <iostream>
#include <math.h>
```

The rest of the program defines **main**—the main (and so far, only) function. The first thing **main** does is define the three variables the program will use.

```
int  n;    // Number to test for prime-ness
int  i;    // Loop counter
int  is_prime;   // Boolean flag
```

Though is_prime is an integer variable, its function is to store a value of true (1) or false (0). Note that if your version of C++ supports the **bool** type, this would be a logical place to use it:

```
bool  is_prime;   // Boolean flag
```

If the program cannot find a divisor for n it should conclude that the number is prime. Therefore, is_prime gets a default setting of true. In other words, if is_prime isn't specifically set to false then it will (correctly) reflect the fact that the number is prime.

```
// Assume that a number is prime until proven
// otherwise

is_prime = true;
```

The heart of the program is the **for** loop that performs the prime-number test. As I described in Chapter 2, it's only necessary to test for divisors up to the square root of n. If a divisor is not found by then, the number being tested has no divisors, other than itself and 1.

The expression n % i uses the modulus operator (%) to perform a division and get the remainder. This remainder is 0 if i divides evenly into n—in which case n is not prime.

```
for (i = 2; i <= sqrt((double) n); i++) {
    if (n % i == 0)
        is_prime = false;
}
```

Remember how a **for** loop works: The first expression in parentheses is the *initializer,* the second expression is the *condition,* and the last is the *increment.* This **for** loop is therefore equivalent to:

```
i = 2;
while (i <= sqrt((double) n)) {
    if (n % i == 0)
        is_prime = false;
    i++;
}
```

Notice that the **for**-loop version includes only one statement inside the loop—this embedded statement is an **if** statement. The braces ({}) are legal since you can always have a compound statement with only statement between the braces. Yet their only purpose here is clarity. The **for** loop works just as well if you write it this way, without the braces:

```
for (i = 2; i <= sqrt((double) n); i++)
    if (n % i == 0)
        is_prime = false;
```

As I mentioned in Chapter 2, some programmers advise against *ever* writing a **for** or **if** statement without adopting statement-block syntax (that is, use of the braces) even when they are not strictly necessary. In this case, leaving in the braces—at least for the **for** statement—is probably a good idea because they make the program easier to follow.

EXERCISE

Exercise 3.2.1.   Revise the example so that it uses more optimal code. When you consider the lightning-fast speed of today's microprocessors, it's unlikely you'll see a difference in execution speed, although if you attempt to test an extremely large number, say, over a billion, you might see a slight difference in response time. (By the way, good luck in finding a prime number in that range, if you're just looking for one by chance. Prime numbers become rarer as you get into larger values.)

In any case, the following changes to code make the program more efficient for large numbers:

▶ Calculate the square root of n only once, by declaring a variable square_root_of_n and determining its value before entering the **for** loop. This variable should be a **double** variable to avoid compiler warnings.

▶ Once a divisor of n is found you don't need to look for any more. Therefore, in the **if** statement inside the loop, add a **break** statement (breaking out of the loop) after setting is_prime to false.

I described both of these optimizations in Chapter 2. The point of this exercise is to work them in with the **for** statement.

Comparative Languages 101: The Basic "for" Statement

If you've programmed in Basic or FORTRAN you've seen statements something like the C++ **for** statement, whose purpose is to count from one number to another. For example, this Basic loop prints all the whole numbers from 1 to 10:

```
For i = 1 To 10
    Print i
Next i
```

The Basic "For" statement has the advantage of clarity and ease of use. It admittedly takes fewer keystrokes to use than C++ **for**.

But against that, the advantage of the C++ **for** statement is that it's infinitely more flexible. "Infinitely" is an awfully strong word, so it requires some justification.

One way in which the C++ **for** statement is so much more flexible is that you can use it with any three valid C++ expressions. The condition (the middle expression) does not even have to be a Boolean expression such as "i < n", although using other kinds of expressions can be a risky practice. For the purposes of evaluating a condition in an **if, while,** or **for** statement, remember that any nonzero value is considered "true."

The **for** statement does not even require you to use all three expressions (*initializer, condition,* and *increment*). If any of these are missing, they are ignored. If the *condition* is omitted it's considered "true" by default, setting up an infinite loop.

```
for(;;) {
    // Infinite loop!
}
```

An infinite loop is usually a bad thing, as I suggested in Chapter 2. But if you have some way to break out of it (for example, by using the **break** statement), it may be perfectly fine. In the following example the user can break out of the loop by entering the value 0.

```
for (;;) {
    // Do some stuff...

    cout << "Enter a number and press ENTER: ";
    cin >> n;
    if (n == 0)
        break;

    // Do some more stuff...
}
```

Chapter 3   *Summary*

Let's refresh our understanding of the basic points of Chapter 3.

▶ The purpose of a **for** statement is usually to repeat an action while counting to a particular value. The statement has this following syntax:

```
for (initializer; condition; increment)
    statement
```

This is equivalent to the following **while** loop:

```
initializer;
while (condition) {
    statement
    increment;
}
```

▶ A **for** loop behaves exactly like its **while**-loop counterpart (just described), with one exception: the **continue** statement increments the loop variable before advancing to the top of the next loop cycle.

▶ As with other kinds of control structures, you can always use a compound statement with **for** by using opening and closing braces ({}):

```
for (initializer; condition; increment) {
    statement
}
```

▶ A variable such as i in the following example is called a *loop variable:*

```
for (i = 1; i <= 10; i++)
    cout << i << " ";
```

▶ In the *initializer* expression you can declare a variable "on the fly." This declaration gives the variable scope locale to the **for** loop itself, meaning that changes to the variable don't affect variables of the same name declared outside the loop.

```
for (int i = 1; i <= 10; i++)
    cout << i << " ";
```

▶ As with **if** and **while**, the loop condition of a **for** statement can be any valid C++ expression; any nonzero value is considered "true." But it is good to stick to genuine Boolean expressions, such as x > 0 and a = = b.

▶ You can omit any and all of the three expressions inside the parentheses of the **for** statement (*initializer, condition, increment*). If the condition is omitted the loop is executed unconditionally. (In other words, the loop is infinite.) Remember to use a **break** statement to get out of it.

```
for (;;) {

    // Infinite loop!
}
```

Functions: Many Are Called

From the earliest days of computers, one of the major goals of programmers has been to avoid having to write the same group of statements over and over. This is the search for reusability, and it is a major reason why object-oriented programming (OOP) was developed. But the most basic technique for writing reusable code is the use of functions—often known as procedures or subroutines in other languages.

A function is a group of related statements that accomplish a specific task. Once you define a function you can execute it whenever you need to. Beyond that functions provide a way to divide a complex program into smaller, more doable tasks. Without this division of labor, serious programming would be just about impossible.

The Concept of Function

If you've followed the book up until this point, you've already seen use of a function—specifically the **sqrt** function, which takes single a number as input and returns a result.

```
double sqrt_of_n = sqrt(n);
```

Executing a function and using its result (that is, its return value) is referred to as a *function call*.

The C++ concept of function is not far removed from the mathematical concept of function, if you recall your high-school or college algebra. A function takes zero or more inputs and returns an output, called a *return value*.

Here's another example—this one is a hypothetical example and is not part of the C++ standard library. This function takes two inputs and returns their average.

```
cout << avg(1.0, 4.0);
```

81

Assuming the **avg** function was properly written, this line of code would print the number 2.5.

Fundamentally, the idea here is similar to that of the **sqrt** function: take some inputs and return an output. You can think of the function call this way:

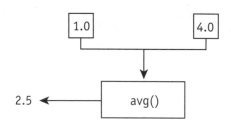

A function can also have zero inputs, as is the case with the **rand** function, which returns a random integer:

```
n = rand();
```

Parentheses are used in the call to **rand**; parentheses are *always* present during a C++ function call even when there are no inputs. This turns out to be helpful because it makes it absolutely clear when you're making a function call and when you're not.

Broadly speaking, functions fall into two categories. These aren't really different—they all follow the same rules—but there's a difference in the amount of work you have to do:

▶ Some functions are supplied by the C++ standard library. These have already been written and compiled, so you don't have to define what they do.

▶ Functions not supplied by the C++ library have to be supplied by the program itself. You define what these do.

Both of these kinds of functions follow one of the all-important, unbreakable rules of C++:

✻ **You must completely declare type information for a function before calling it. You can only be excused from this requirement if an "include" file does the job of declaring it for you (as the math.h file does for the sqrt function).**

This is why the **#include** directive is useful when you work with library functions. For example, including "math.h" frees you from having to declare any math function—including **sqrt**—before using that function.

```
#include <math.h>
//...
cout << "square root of 2 is " << sqrt(2.0);
```

If a function is not declared in an "include" file, you have to declare it yourself—ideally at the beginning of the source code. Why, you may ask, is this necessary?

One answer relates to the problem of multiple modules—when you have source code placed in more than one file. The definition of a function may be in a different source file from a statement that calls it, so without an explicit declaration the compiler has no way to get type information for the function. And without that information, there's no way to check and see if the function is being used correctly.

Beyond that, getting in the habit of declaring a function before using it is good programming practice. Because it is strict about type information, C++ occasionally requires a little extra work. But this work proves to be time well spent.

Function Calls and the Flow of the Program

For the rest of the chapter, I'm going to be concerned with user-defined functions. Along the way I'll make use of the **sqrt** and **rand** library functions, but otherwise everything said in this chapter applies to the task of creating and calling functions you define yourself.

Conceptually, the best way to think of a C++ function is as *a specific task.* A program may accomplish many tasks. If it's a commercial program, like Microsoft Word, it may accomplish hundreds or even thousands of tasks. What makes complex software possible is that you can write individual functions, each with a limited job to do. Each function can then be individually developed and tested.

Imagine a programmer had to write a serious, full-featured word processor and had to do so by writing a single block of code. The job would be impossible. Even Bill Gates and Paul Allen couldn't do it. But a programmer can write a series of functions that accomplish specific tasks—such as "load a file" or "paste text from the Clipboard"—and then call upon these as needed. This approach makes writing complex software doable.

Once a function is written you can call it any number of times. Every time the function is called, program execution is temporarily transferred away from the current function (such as **main**) and over to the definition of the function being called. The next figure shows how this might happen in a simple program.

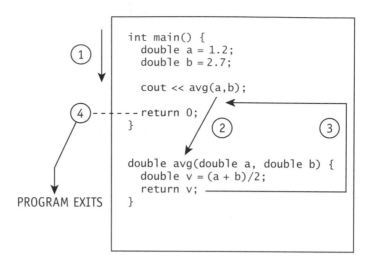

Here's how program execution flows in this example:

1 The program begins as always by automatically executing **main** (which runs until there is a function call or the program ends).

2 A function call to avg transfers control from **main** to the avg function.

3 The avg function runs until it reaches a **return** statement or the function ends. At that point, control is returned back to **main**, at the statement just after the function call.

4 **main** resumes execution. The statement return 0; returns control back to the operating system. The program is done.

From this logic, you may conclude that it's possible to define functions that are never executed. That's true. Only **main** is guaranteed to be executed. Other functions run only when they are called.

The Basics of Using Functions

I strongly recommend the following approach for creating and calling user-defined functions:

▶ At the beginning of your program, *declare* the function in prototype form. This is a declaration that contains type information only.

▶ Somewhere in your program, *define* the function. This tells what the function does.

▶ You can then execute the function from anywhere else in the program. This is known as *calling* the function. You can do this any number of times.

You may be asking, "Do I have to both declare and define the function? And what's the difference?"

You must provide complete type information for a function before you call it—C++ requires you tell it exactly what kind of data is going in and out. One way to do that is to define a function before it's called in **main**. But such an approach becomes unwieldy in a large program where you can't remember which function calls which first.

So, to avoid this problem, the best approach is to declare all your functions at the beginning of the program. Then you can place the function definitions in any order.

Step One: Declare (Prototype) the Function

A function declaration (or "prototype") provides type information only. It has this syntax:

```
type  function_name (argument_list);
```

The *type* is a recognized data type such as **int**, **float**, or **double**, which tells what kind of value the function returns (what it passes back). If the function does not return a value, use the special type **void** here (**void** means "an empty type").

The *argument_list* is a list of zero or more argument names—separated by commas if there is more than one—each preceded by the corresponding type name.

For example, the following statement declares a function named avg, which takes two arguments of type **double** and returns a **double** value.

```
double avg(double x, double y);
```

The *argument_list* may be empty, which indicates that it takes no arguments. For example, this statement declares a function get_todays_date, which returns an **int** value:

```
int get_todays_date();
```

Note ▶ C++ differs from C in this regard. A declaration with an empty argument list does not mean, as it does in C, that the argument list is undetermined. It means that the function cannot have any arguments. This is one of the fixes that has to be made to C code before porting it to C++. Another difference is that C++ requires the prototype style of declaration described in this section.

Here are some other function-declaration examples:

```
void print_spaces(int n);    // Declare print_spaces function;
                             // Takes one integer argument,
                             //   returns no value (void).
```

```
double get_odds(int a, int b);   // Declare get_odds; takes
                                 //    two integer arguments and
                                 //    returns a double.
int is_prime(int n);             // Declare is_prime function;
                                 // Takes one integer argument
                                 // and returns an integer value.
```

Step Two: Define the Function

The function definition tells what the function does. It uses this syntax:

```
type  function_name (argument_list) {
      statements
}
```

Most of this looks like a declaration. The only thing that's different is that the semicolon is replaced by a series of statements between two braces ({}).

The *statements* portion of the syntax can contain as few as zero statements. But the braces are required even in that case. Here's an example that uses one statement in the definition:

```
double avg(double x, double y) {
    return (x + y) / 2;
}
```

This same function can be written as a longer version—although this takes up more space to do exactly the same thing. Notice that this version declares its own variable, named v. (The variable is *local*; it's not recognized outside the function.)

```
double avg(double x, double y) {
    double v = (x + y) / 2;
    return v;
}
```

The **return** statement specifies that the function returns the amount $(x + y) / 2$.

Functions with **void** return type do not return a value (although the **return** statement with no argument can still be used to exit early from the function). Here is a simple example of a definition of a function with **void** return type and—in this particular case—no arguments.

```
void print_messages() {
    cout << "You just attempted an illegal action." <<
        endl;
    cout << "This will not be allowed." << endl;
    cout << "Try not to do that ever again." << endl;
}
```

Step Three: Call the Function

Once a function is declared and defined it can be used—or rather "called"—any number of times from any function. For example:

```
n = avg(9.5, 11.5);
n = avg(5, 25);
n = avg(27, 154.3);
```

A function call is an expression: as long as it returns a value other than **void**, it can be used inside of a larger expression. For example:

```
z = x + y + avg(a, b) + 25.3;
```

When the function is called, the values specified in the function call are passed as function arguments. Here's how a call to the avg function works with sample values 9.5 and 11.5 as input.

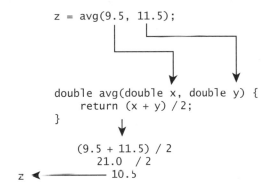

Another call to the function might pass different values—in this case 6 and 26:

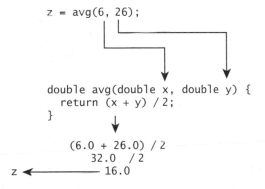

The values 6 and 26 are integer values. C++ converts these values to type **double** without complaint. But when you go in the reverse direction—assigning a **double** return value to an **int** variable—the compiler issues a warning advising you that some values in the larger range may not fit in the smaller range.

By using a cast, you inform the compiler that you're aware of the issue but want to proceed with the assignment anyway. Remember the data-cast syntax from Chapter 2:

```
static_cast<type> (expression)
```

When you use this expression, you avoid the warning message. For example:

```
int i = static_cast<int>(avg(3.5, 10));
```

Example 4.1.   *Triangle-Number Function*

This section shows a function call in the context of a complete program. The triangle totals all the whole numbers from 1 to the number specified. For example, the triangle number for 5 is:

```
triangle(5) = 1 + 2 + 3 + 4 + 5 = 15
```

The triangle number for 7 is:

```
triangle(7) = 1 + 2 + 3 + 4 + 5 + 6 + 7 = 28
```

It's a fairly easy task to write a program that includes and tests this function. Here is the code:

triangle.cpp

```cpp
#include <iostream>
using namespace std;

// Function must be declared before being used.
int triangle(int num);

int main() {
    int n;
    cout << "Enter a number and press ENTER: ";
    cin >> n;
    cout << "Function returned " << triangle(n);
    return 0;
}

// Triangle-number function.
```

triangle.cpp, cont.

```cpp
// Return 1 + 2 + ... + n
int triangle(int n) {
    int i;
    int sum = 0;
    for (i = 1; i <= n; i++)        // For i = 1 to n,
        sum = sum + i;              //    Add i to sum
    return sum;
}
```

How It Works

This code is straightforward. First, a function declaration (or "prototype") is placed at the beginning of the program.

```cpp
int triangle(int num);
```

Given this declaration, any statement may now call the triangle function. All that's required is that the function is defined somewhere in the program.

A statement in **main** calls the function:

```cpp
cout << "Function returned " << triangle(n);
```

The value of n is obtained from the keyboard. Assume that the user types in "4". In that case the function call passes the value 4 to argument n:

```cpp
cout << "Function returned" << triangle(4);


        int triangle (int n){
            int i:
            int sum = 0

            for(i = 1; i<= n;i++)
                sum = sum + i;
            return sum;
        }

                10
```

The program then prints the value returned, 10 (because $1 + 2 + 3 + 4 = 10$). The result is as if this value replaced the function call:

```cpp
cout << "Function returned " << 10,
```

Here's the definition of the triangle function. The function declares its own variables and uses a **for** loop that cycles n times.

```
int triangle(int n) {
    int i;
    int sum = 0;
    for (i = 1; i <= n; i++)      // For i = 1 to n,
        sum = sum + i;            //   Add i to sum
    return sum;
}
```

The loop totals all the whole numbers from 1 to n, accumulating this total in the variable sum. Again, if the value 4 is input by the user, the **for** loop cycles four times, each time incrementing i by 1.

VALUE OF I DURING ONE CYCLE OF THE LOOP	ACTION OF THE LOOP STATEMENT	VALUE OF SUM AFTER THIS ACTION
1	Add 1 to sum	1
2	Add 2 to sum	3
3	Add 3 to sum	6
4	Add 4 to sum	10

The function then returns the final value of sum, in this case "10".

```
return sum;
```

Variables i and sum are *local* to the triangle function because they are declared inside the function definition. When a variable is local, other functions can have a variable with the same name and what happens in one function won't affect what happens in another. For example, **main** and triangle can both have a variable named i, and when triangle changes the value of i it doesn't affect the value of i in **main**.

When the function declares the local variable sum, it initializes it to 0. C++ is liberal about initialization, enabling you to initialize a variable to any valid expression (not just to a constant expression as is required in C.)

```
int sum = 0;
```

Optimizing the Program

The designers of the C language realized that incrementing a variable (whether in a loop or another context) is one of the most common things you can do in a program. With their obsession for creating shortcuts, they saw that adding a value to a variable is common and should therefore have a shorthand version. (It also translates into an efficient CPU instruction.) We've already seen how to add 1 to a variable:

```
i++;
```

This is our old friend the increment operator. It adds 1 to the variable. But what if you want to add a number other than 1? That's what the addition-assignment operator (+=) is for.

For example, the following statement adds 5 to the variable n:

```
n += 5;        // n = n + 5
```

Like every other kind of expression in C++ (other than a call to a **void** function), the expression n += 4 returns a value: specifically, it returns the new value assigned to n. Consequently, the following two expressions are equivalent since both return the value of i after incrementing:

```
++i
i += 1
```

The expression sum = sum + i in the triangle function can be replaced with sum += i, producing:

```
int triangle(int num) {
    int i;
    int sum = 0;
    for (i = 1; i <= num; i++)    // For i = 1 to n,
        sum += i;                 //   Add i to sum.
    return sum;
}
```

All the arithmetic operators (as well as some others you haven't seen yet) have a corresponding assignment operator. Here *var* is any variable and *expr* is any valid expression.

OPERATOR	MEANING
var += expr	*var = var + expr*
var -= expr	*var = var - expr*
var *= expr	*var = var * expr*
var /= expr	*var = var / expr*

EXERCISES

Exercise 4.1.1.   Write a program that defines and tests a factorial function. The factorial of a number is the product of all whole numbers from 1 to N. For example, the factorial of 5 is 1 * 2 * 3 * 4 * 5 = 120. (Hint: you can use code similar to that for Example 4.1, changing just a few lines.)

Exercise 4.1.2.   Alter the program for Exercise 4.1.1 so it uses the multiplication-assignment operator *=. (For example, the expression n *= 4 multiplies n by 4.)

Exercise 4.1.3.   Write a function named print_out that prints all the whole numbers from 1 to N. Test the function by placing it in a program that passes a number n to it, where this number is entered from the keyboard. The print_out function should have type **void**; it does not return a value. The function can be called with a simple statement:

```
print_out(n);
```

Example 4.2.   *Prime-Number Function*

Chapter 2 ended with an example that was actually useful: determining whether a specified number was a prime number or not.

Wouldn't it be even better to be able to test a number for prime-ness whenever you wanted? If the test is written as a function it can be executed any number of times simply by using function calls. Then you don't have to keep running and rerunning the program to test multiple numbers.

The following program uses the prime-number example from Chapters 2 and 3 but places the relevant C++ statements into their own function is_prime.

```
prime3.cpp
    #include <iostream>
    #include <math.h>
    using namespace std;

    // Function must be declared before being used.
    int prime(int n);

    int main() {
        int i;
```

prime3.cpp, cont.

```cpp
    // Set up an infinite loop; break if user enters 0.
    // Otherwise, evaluate n from prime-ness.
        while (1) {
            cout << "Enter a number (0 to exit)";
            cout << "and press ENTER:";
            cin >> i;
            if (i == 0)                 // If user entered 0,
                break;                  // EXIT
            if (prime(i))               // Call prime(i)
                cout << i << " is prime" << endl;
            else
                cout << i << " is not prime" << endl;
        }
        return 0;
}


    // Prime number function. Test divisors from
    //  2 to sqrt of n. Return false if a divisor
    //   found; otherwise, return true.
    int prime(int n) {
        int i;
        for (i = 2; i <= sqrt((double) n); i++) {
            if (n % i == 0)             // If i divides n
                                        // evenly,
                return false;           //  n is not prime.
        }
        return true;    // If no divisor found, n is prime.
}
```

How It Works

Again, this program adheres to the pattern of (1) declaring function type information at the beginning of the program ("prototyping" the function), (2) defining the function somewhere in the program, and (3) calling the function from **main**.

The prototype says that the prime function takes an integer argument and returns an integer value. (This is actually a Boolean—that is, true/false—value, but C++ allows you to store such values in an **int** type since true and false are represented as 1 and 0, respectively.)

```
int prime(int n);
```

The function definition is a variation on the prime-number code from Chapter 3, which used a **for** loop. If you compare the code here to Example 3.2 on page 73 you'll see only a few differences. This version uses function-code syntax, of course:

```
int prime(int n) {
    int i;
    for (i = 2; i <= sqrt((double) n); i++) {
        if (n % i == 0)          // If i divides n evenly,
            return false;        //  n is not prime.
    }
    return true;    // If no divisor found, return true.
}
```

Another difference is that instead of setting a Boolean variable is_prime, this version returns a Boolean result. The logic here is:

For all whole numbers from 2 to the square root of n,
> If n is evenly divisible by the loop variable (i),
>> Return the value false immediately.

Remember that the modulus operator (%) carries out a division of two integers and returns the remainder. If this remainder is 0, then the second number is a divisor of the first.

The action of the **return** statement here is key. This statement returns immediately—causing exit from the function and passing control back to **main**. There's no need to use **break** to get out of the loop:

```
for (i = 2; i <= sqrt((double) n); i++)
    if (n % i == 0) {
        return false;
        break;              // not necessary
    }
```

The loop in the main function calls the prime function. The use of a **break** statement here provides an exit mechanism so the loop isn't really infinite. As soon as the user enters "0" the loop terminates and the program ends.

Here I've added a comment showing where the loop exits:

```
while (1) {
    cout << "Enter a number (0 to exit)";
    cout << "and press ENTER";
    cin >> i;
    if (i == 0)              // If user entered 0, EXIT
```

```
        break;
      if (prime(i))         // Call prime(i)
        cout << i << " is prime" << endl;
      else
        cout << i << " is not prime" << endl;
  }
```

The rest of the loop calls the prime function and prints the result of the prime-number test. Note that the prime function returns a true/false value, and so the call to prime(i) can be used as an if/else condition.

EXERCISES

Exercise 4.2.1. Optimize the prime-number function by calculating the square root of n only once during each function call. Declare a local variable sqrt_of_n of type **double**. (Hint: a variable is local if it is declared inside the function.) Then use this variable in the loop condition.

Exercise 4.2.2. Rewrite **main** so that it tests all the numbers from 2 to 20 and prints out the results, each on a separate line. (Hint: use a **for** loop, with i running from 2 to 20.)

Exercise 4.2.3. Write a program that finds the first prime number greater than one billion (1000000000).

Local and Global Variables

Nearly every programming language in existence (machine code being the major exception) has a concept of local variable. This means that as long as two functions mind their own data, as it were, they won't interfere with each other.

That's definitely a factor in the last example (Example 4.2). Both **main** and prime have a local variable named i. If i is not local—that is, it is shared between functions—then consider what can happen.

First, the main function executes prime as part of evaluating the **if** condition. Let's say that i has the value 24.

```
  if (prime(i))
      cout << i << " is prime" << endl;
  else
      cout << i << " is not prime" << endl;
```

The value 24 is passed to the prime function.

```
// Assume i is not declared here, but is global.
int prime(int n) {
    for (i = 2; i <= sqrt((double) n); i++)
        if (n % i == 0)
            return false;
    return true;    // If no divisor found, n is prime.
}
```

Look what this function does. It sets i to 2 and then tests it for divisibility against the number passed, 24. This test passes—because 2 does divide into 24 evenly—and the function returns. But i is now equal to 2 instead of 24.

Upon returning, the program executes

```
cout << i << " is not prime" << endl;
```

which prints:

```
2 is not prime
```

This is not what was wanted, since we are testing the number 24!

So, to avoid this problem, declare variables local unless there is a good reason not to. If you look back over Example 2.3 you'll see that i is local; **main** and prime each declare their own version of i.

Is there ever a good reason to not make a variable local? Yes, although if you have a choice, it's better to go local because you want functions interfering with each other as little as possible.

You can declare global—that is, nonlocal—variables by declaring them outside of any function definition. It's usually best to put all global declarations near the beginning of the program, before the first function. A global variable is recognized from the point it is declared to the end of the file.

For example, you could declare a global variation named status by declaring it before **main**:

```
#include <iostream>
#include <math.h>
using namespace std;

int status = 0;

void main () {
    // ...
}
```

Now the variable named status may be accessed by any function. Because this variable is global, there is only one copy of it; if one function changes the value of status, this reflects the value of status that other functions see.

Recursive Functions

So far, I've only shown the use of **main** calling other functions defined in the program, but in fact any function can call any function.

But can a function call itself?

Yes. And as you'll see in a moment, it's not as crazy as it sounds. You can also have two functions call each other, and for a certain class of programs (such as the program that produced the C++ compiler itself) this can be useful. That's another reason I recommended putting all function declarations at the beginning of the program: because if two functions call each other, it would be logically impossible to define every function before using it.

The technique of a function calling itself is called *recursion*. The obvious problem is the same one for infinite loops: if a function calls itself, when does it ever stop? The problem is easily solved, however, by putting in some mechanism for stopping.

Remember the triangle function from Example 4.1 (page 88)? We can rewrite this as a recursive function:

```
int triangle(int n) {
    if (n <= 1)
        return 1;
    else
        return n + triangle(n - 1);  // RECURSION!
}
```

For any number greater than 1 the triangle function issues another call to itself but with a lower number. Eventually, the function triangle(1) is called. In that case the **if** statement causes the cycle to stop: triangle(1) just returns the value 1. There is a literal "stack" of calls made to the function, each with a different argument for n, and now they start returning. (The stack is a last-in-first-out mechanism maintained internally that keeps track of the argument values for all pending function calls.)

You can picture how a call to triangle(4) would be executed this way:

```
triangle(4)
    ↓
    4 + triangle(3)
            ↓
            3 + triangle(2)
                    ↓
                    2 + triangle(1)
                            ↓
                            1
```

Many functions that use a **for** statement can be rewritten so they use recursion instead. But does it always make sense to use that approach?

The example here is not an ideal one. It causes the program to store all the values 1 through n on the stack, rather than simply totaling them up directly in a loop. This approach is not nearly as efficient as a standard looping approach—although with the speed and storage capacities of modern computers it would be difficult to tell the difference. The next section makes a much better and more efficient use of recursion.

Example 4.3.   *Greatest Common Factor (GCF)*

Some problems make better use of recursive solutions than others. One of the best examples of a recursive solution is a classic method for computing greatest common factors (GCFs). Later in the book (starting in Chapter 11), we'll return and make use of this solution as an important foundation for the Fraction class.

This method is a beautiful algorithm—beautiful because of its simplicity, elegance, and the fact that it ends up saving a great many CPU cycles compared to a more brute-force approach.

To understand the method, recall the use of the modulus operator (%), which was introduced in Chapter 2. This operator divides the first number by the second and returns the remainder. Consider this expression:

```
215 % 100
```

This expression divides 215 by 100 and returns the remainder, in this case 15.

Armed with this operator, we can now state an elegant solution for finding the greatest common factor between two integers—that is, the largest number that divides evenly into both inputs.

To find the greatest common factor (GCF) for A and B:

If A % B equals 0,
    Return B
Else
    Return GCF(B, A % B)

As with other recursive algorithms, this method has both a general case and a terminal case (A % B equals 0). Every recursive algorithm must have at least one terminal case, to avoid infinite regress. (One such case is sufficient.)

The reason why the terminal case works should be clear: if A % B equals 0, then B divides evenly into A; therefore, B is the greatest common factor since it divides both itself and A. For example, if A is 4 and B is 2, then 4 % 2 equals 0 (2 divides 4 evenly), so 2 is the greatest common factor of 4 and 2.

The reason why the general case works is less obvious, assuming you haven't spent your life studying number theory. But running a few cases should convince you that the method works. Keep in mind the form of the general procedure:

GCF(A, B) =>   GCF(B, A % B)

Take the example of 300 and 500. The greatest common factor is 100. Let's see if our method produces this result.

In the first step, we compute 300 % 500. When you attempt to divide 500 into 300, the result is 0, with a remainder of 300. 300 % 500 is therefore 300.

GCF(300, 500) => GCF(500, 300 % 500)
                 GCF(500, 300)

So far, this has accomplished nothing but rearrangement of the two numbers such that the higher number is first. But we're just getting started. In the next step 300 divides into 500 with a remainder of 200—a useful result.

GCF(500, 300) => GCF(300, 500 % 300)
                 GCF(300, 200)

Do you see that now we're getting somewhere? We are actually very close to the answer. The next step involves dividing 200 into 300 and getting the remainder . . . which is—surprise!—100.

GCF(300, 200) => GCF(200, 300 % 200)
                 GCF(200, 100)

In the next (and final) step we calculate 200 % 100. The result is 0; we have reached our terminal condition (the second number divides the first evenly) and the answer is therefore 100.

You can run this method an endless number of times and, as long as you run it correctly on any two positive integers, it will always work. Here is another example, using 45 and 35.

GCF(A, B)	A % B
GCF(45, 35)	10
=> GCF(35, 10)	5
=> GCF(10, 5)	0

Again we reach the terminal condition (A % B equals 0), so the answer is the final value of B, in this case 5.

Probably the hardest thing about this method is convincing yourself it works. But once you agree it works, it's an easy matter to write the function. Here is a program that includes this function and performs repeated tests.

```
gcf1.cpp

    #include <iostream>
    using namespace std;

    int gcf(int a, int b);

    int main() {
        int a = 0, b = 0;
        while(1) {
            cout << "Enter a number (0 to quit): ";
            cin >> a;
            if (a == 0)
                break;
            cout << "Enter 2nd number: ";
            cin >> b;
            cout << "GCF = " << gcf(a, b) << endl;
        }
        return 0;
    }

    int gcf(int a, int b) {
        if (a % b == 0)
            return b;
        else
            return gcf(b, a % b);
    }
```

How It Works

After providing the usual program header (the **#include** directive and the **using** statement), the program first prototypes the greatest-common-factor function (gcf). This prototype declares gcf as a function that takes two integer arguments (a, b) and returns an integer result.

```
int gcf(int a, int b);
```

The main function begins by declaring two variables, a and b. These happen to use the same names as the arguments to the gcf function. The reuse of names is not required here (n and m could have been used, for example) but it does not cause a conflict either. Each call to gcf will get its own copy of a and b, which (as arguments) work like local variables.

```
int a = 0, b = 0;
```

Within **main**, the **while** loop does several things: (1) it gets a number from the user, (2) it exits the loop by using a **break** statement if the user enters 0 for this first number, (3) it gets another number, and (4) it prints the greatest common factor by calling gcf.

```
while(1) {
    cout << "Enter a number (0 to quit): ";
    cin >> a;
    if (a == 0)
        break;
    cout << "Enter 2nd number: ";
    cin >> b;
    cout << "GCF = " << gcf(a, b) << endl;
}
```

This is a classic case of a loop that looks like an infinite loop but really isn't, because it does have an exit condition—it's just that the exit condition is in the middle of the loop rather than the top.

The loop prints out the greatest common factor and starts over again. The process repeats until the user enters 0 for the first number.

The gcf function itself is easy to write. All you have to do is look at the GCF algorithm shown earlier and translate the statements into C++.

```
int gcf(int a, int b) {
    if (a % b == 0)
        return b;
    else
        return gcf(b, a % b);
}
```

EXERCISES

Exercise 4.3.1. Revise the program so it shows all the steps involved in the algorithm. Here is sample output:

```
GCF(300, 500) =>
GCF(500, 300) =>
CGF(300, 200) =>
GCF(200, 100) =>
GCF = 100
```

(Hint: to make this happen, what is the first thing the gcf function should do?)

Exercise 4.3.2. Is it possible to revise the gcf function so it calculates the expression a % b only once per call? If so, write this more optimal solution.

Exercise 4.3.3. What is the trade-off involved in this "better" solution alluded to in Exercise 4.3.2? How much work is saved? Is there a cost, however small, in program space? (Note that time vs. space is a classic trade-off in designing and optimizing programs.)

Example 4.4. *Prime Factorization*

The prime-number examples we've looked at so far are fine, but they have a limitation. For example, they tell you that a number such as 12,001 is not prime, but they don't tell anything more. It would be nice to know *why* 12,001 isn't prime—that is, what numbers actually divide into this monster?

What you'd like to do is to generate the *prime factorization* for any requested number. This would show us exactly what prime numbers divide into that number. For example, if the number 36 was input, we'd get:

```
2, 2, 3, 3
```

If 99 was input, we'd get

```
3, 3, 11
```

And if a prime number was input, the result would be the number itself. For example, if 17 was input, the output would be 17.

This may sound like a tall order, but actually we have almost all the programming code to do this already. Only a few changes need to be made to the prime-number code.

The key to getting a prime factorization is the ability to get the lowest divisor and then continue factoring the remaining quotient. To get all the divisors for a number n:

For all whole numbers from 2 to the square root of n,
    If n is evenly divisible by the loop variable (i),
        Print i followed by a comma, and
        Rerun the function on n / i, and
        Exit the current function
If no divisors found, print n itself

This logic is a recursive solution, which we can implement in C++ by having the function get_divisors call itself.

prime4.cpp

```cpp
#include <iostream>
#include <math.h>
using namespace std;

void get_divisors(int n);

int main() {
    int i, n;
    cout << "Enter a number and press ENTER: ";
    cin >> n;
    get_divisors(n);
    return 0;
}

// Get divisors function
//  This function prints all the divisors of n,
//  by finding the lowest divisor, i, and then
//  rerunning itself on n/i, the remaining quotient.
void get_divisors(int n) {
    int i;
    double sqrt_of_n = sqrt((double) n);
    for (i = 2; i <= sqrt_of_n; i++)
        if (n % i == 0) {                // If i divides n
                                         // evenly,
            cout << i << ", ";           //    Print i,
            get_divisors(n / i);         //    Factor n/i,
            return;                      //    and exit.
        }
    // If no divisor is found, then n is prime;
    //  Print n and make no further calls.
    cout << n;
}
```

How It Works

As always, the program begins by declaring the functions it will use—in this case, there is one function other than **main** (which never needs to be declared). The new function is get_divisors.

Also, the beginning of the program includes the two files iostream.h and math.h because the program uses **cout**, **cin**, and **sqrt**. You don't need to declare **sqrt** directly, by the way, because this is done for you in math.h.

```
#include <iostream>
#include <math.h>
using namespace std;

void get_divisors(int n);
```

The **main** function itself does little. All it does is get a number from the keyboard and then call get_divisors, which does nearly all the work.

```
void main() {
    int i, n;
    cout << "Enter a number and press ENTER: ";
    cin >> n;
    get_divisors(n);
}
```

The get_divisors function is the interesting part of this program. This is something we haven't seen before: a function with **void** return value. This means that it doesn't pass back a value, but it still uses the **return** statement to exit early.

```
void get_divisors(int n) {
    int i;
    double sqrt_of_n = sqrt((double) n);
    for (i = 2; i <= sqrt_of_n; i++)
        if (n % i == 0) {           // If i divides n evenly,
            cout << i << ", ";      //    Print i,
            get_divisors(n / i);    //    Factor n/i,
            return;                 //    and exit.
        }
    // If no divisor is found, then n is prime;
    //  Print n and make no further calls.
    cout << n;
}
```

The heart of this function is a loop that tests numbers from 2 to the square root of n (which has been calculated and placed in the variable sqrt_of_n).

```
for (i = 2; i <= sqrt_of_n; i++)
    if (n % i == 0) {           // If i divides n evenly,
        cout << i << ", ";      //    Print i,
        get_divisors(n / i);    //    Factor n/i,
        return;                 //    and exit.
    }
```

If the expression n % i == 0 is true, that means that the loop variable i divides evenly into n. In that case, the function does several things: (1) it prints out the loop variable, which is a divisor, (2) it calls itself recursively, and (3) it exits.

The function calls itself with the value n/i. Because the factor i is already accounted for, the function needs to get the prime-number divisors for *the remaining factors* of n; these are contained in n/i.

If no divisors are found that means that the number being tested is prime. The correct response is to print this number and stop.

```
cout << n;
```

For example, suppose that 30 is input. The function tests to see what the lowest divisor of 30 is. The function prints the number 2 and then reruns itself on the remaining quotient, 15 (because 30 divided by 2 is 15).

During the next call, the function finds the lowest divisor of 15. This is 3, so it prints 3 and then reruns itself on the remaining quotient, 5 (because 15 divided by 3 is 5).

By the time the function is finished, it has printed out the numbers 2, 3, and 5, which is indeed the factorization of 30.

Visually, here's how a call to the get_divisors function works in this case. Each call to get_divisors gets the lowest divisor and then (unless the number being tested is prime) makes another call.

```
get_divisors(30)
       |
       v
   print "2," -----> get_divisors(15)
                            |
                            v
                        print "3," -----> get_divisors(5)
                                                 |
                                                 v
                                             print "5"
```

Interlude

For Math Junkies

A little reflection shows why the lowest divisor is always a prime number. Suppose a number, A, is the lowest divisor but is not a prime. A number that's not prime must have at least two divisors of its own, B and C.

But if A divides evenly into a number, then B and C divide the number evenly as well. This should be intuitively obvious, but the mathematical demonstration for it (if you need it) is easy.

▼ *continued on next page*

▼ *continued*

n = Am   (where m is some whole number)

n = (BC)m   (because A = BC)

n = B(Cm)   therefore B divides evenly into n

So if A divides evenly into n, then so do A's divisors (B and C). These divisors are of course lower than A itself. Therefore, A cannot be the lowest divisor.

The hypothesis that the lowest divisor is not prime results in a contradiction. The lowest divisor, therefore, must be prime.

Look at it another way. Any number divisible by 4 (a non-prime) is also divisible by 2 (a prime). Any number divisible by 9 (a non-prime) is also divisible by 3 (a prime). The prime factors will always be found first as long as you keep looking for the lowest divisor.

EXERCISES

Exercise 4.4.1.   Rewrite the **main** function for Example 4.4 so that it prints the prompt message "Enter a number (0 = exit) and press ENTER". The program should call get_divisors to show the prime factorization and then prompt the user again until he or she enters 0. (Hint: if you need to, look at the code for Example 4.2 on page 93.)

Exercise 4.4.2.   Write a program that calculates factorials by use of a recursive function. Remember that a factorial is the product of all whole numbers from 1 to N in which N is the number specified. For example, factorial(5) = 5 * 4 * 3 * 2 * 1.

Exercise 4.4.3.   Modify Example 4.4 so that it uses a *nonrecursive* solution. You will end up having to write more code. (Hint: to make the job easier, write two functions: get_all_divisors and get_lowest_divisor. The **main** function should call get_all_divisors, which in turn has a loop: get_all_divisors calls get_lowest_divisor repeatedly, each time replacing n with n/i, where i is the divisor that was found. If n itself is returned then the number is prime and the loop should stop. Further hint: to write this loop, you may want to make it an infinite loop that terminates from inside with a **break** statement.)

Example 4.5.   *Random–Number Generator*

Aren't you fascinated by prime numbers? Aren't they your favorite thing in the world?

Well, maybe not. So let's turn to something a little more fun: a random-number generator. A random-number generator is at the heart of many game programs.

The test program simulates any number of dice rolls. It does this by calling a function rand_0toN1, which takes an argument n and randomly returns a number from 0 to n − 1. For example, if the number 10 is passed as an argument the function returns a number from 0 to 9. The main function uses rand_0toN1 by specifying 6 as an argument and adding 1 to the result, thus getting a number from 1 to 6.

When run, the program prints output like this:

    3 4 6 2 5 3 1 1 6

Here is the program code:

dice.cpp

```cpp
#include <iostream>
#include <math.h>
#include <stdlib.h>
#include <time.h>
using namespace std;

int rand_0toN1(int n);

int main() {
    int n, i;
    int r;

    srand(time(NULL)); // Set a seed for random-num.
                       // generation.
    cout << "Enter number of dice to roll: ";
    cin >> n;
    for (i = 1; i <= n; i++) {
        r = rand_0toN1(6) + 1;      // Get a number from
                                    // 1 to 6

        cout << r << " ";           // Print it out
    }
    return 0;
}

// Random 0-to-N1 Function.
// Generate a random integer from 0 to N-1, giving each
//  integer an equal probability.
//
int rand_0toN1(int n) {
    return rand() % n;
}
```

How It Works

The beginning of the program has to include a number of files to support the functions needed for random-number generation:

```
#include <iostream>
#include <math.h>
#include <stdlib.h>
#include <time.h>
using namespace std;
```

Make sure you include the last three here—math.h, stdlib.h, and time.h—whenever you use random-number generation.

Random-number generation is actually a difficult problem in computing because computers by their nature follow deterministic rules—which by definition are nonrandom. The solution of the C++ library is to generate what's called a "pseudo-random" sequence by taking a number and performing a series of complex transformations on it.

But to do this, it needs a number as random as possible to start off the sequence. That's what the following statement does, by getting the system time and using it as a seed. The word *seed* in this context is just a fancy term for "the first number in the sequence." Each pseudo-random number is produced through deterministic—but highly complex—mathematical transformations on the previous number in the sequence.

```
srand(time(NULL));
```

NULL is a predefined value that means a data address that points nowhere. Essentially, NULL is equivalent to 0 but needs to be used here because an address expression is expected. (I'll explain more about address expressions in Chapter 6.) In any case, you don't need to worry about it. The effect of "time(NULL)" is simply to get the current time.

Every program that uses random numbers should execute this statement first. The system time changes too quickly for a human to guess what it will be precisely, and even a tiny difference in the value of the seed causes radical changes in the resulting sequence. This is a practical application of what Chaos theorists call the Butterfly Effect.

Note ▶ You can, if you choose, use 0 rather than NULL. Some C++ programmers prefer 0, in fact, as it is less reflective of old-fashioned "C-style." In any case, both `time(NULL)` and `time(0)` will work. Remember that the meaning of NULL is essentially (or nearly) the same as 0.

The rest of **main** prompts for a number and then prints the quantity of random numbers requested. A **for** loop makes repeated calls to rand_0toN1, a function that returns a random number from 0 to n – 1:

```
for (i = 1; i <= n; i++) {
    r = rand_0toN1(6) + 1;      // Get a number from
                                // 1 to 6
    cout << r << " ";           // Print it out
}
```

Here is the function definition for the rand_0toN1 function. Simple, isn't it?

```
int rand_0toN1(int n) {
    return rand() % n;
}
```

The rand() function returns a number that may be anywhere in the range for the **int** type. This may be a relatively small number, but it's just as likely to be a rather large number, such as 1,336,588.

The problem, of course, is we don't want such a large number as a result. What we want is a number from 0 to 9 (if 9 is input for n) or 0 to 5 (if 6 is input).

This is where our old friend—the modulus operator (%) that we've already made so much use of—comes to the rescue. Remember that this operator performs division between two integers and returns the remainder. Now if you divide by 6 (for example) you must get a remainder of 0, 1, 2, 3, 4, or 5. You cannot possibly get a higher or lower result no matter how large the first operand is.

Furthermore, when performed on a random large number, the modulus 6 operation should produce one of these six numbers (0, 1, 2, 3, 4, 5) with equal frequency. There is no reason for one or another of these results to be favored.

The result, therefore, is a random integer in the range 0 to n–1, just as we wanted.

EXERCISE

Exercise 4.5.1. Write a random-number generator that returns a number from 1 to N (rather than 0 to N-1), where N is the integer argument passed to it.

Chapter 4 *Summary*

In this chapter we discussed the following important concepts:

▶ In C++ you can use functions to define a specific task just as you might use a "subroutine" or "procedure" in another language. C++ uses the name *function* for all such routines, whether they return a value or not.

▶ You need to declare all your functions (other than **main**) at the beginning of the program so that C++ has the type information required. Function declarations, also called "prototypes," use this syntax:

```
type  function_name (argument_list);
```

▶ You also need to define the function somewhere in the program to tell what the function does. Function definitions use this syntax:

```
type  function_name (argument_list) {
  statements
}
```

▶ A function executes (runs) until it ends or until the **return** statement is executed. A return statement that passes a value back to the caller has this form:

```
return expression;
```

▶ A return statement can also be used in a **void** function (function with no return value) just to exit early, in which case it has a simpler form:

```
return;
```

▶ Local variables are declared inside a function definition; global variables are declared outside all function definitions, preferably before main. If a variable is local, it is not shared with other functions; two functions can each have a variable named i (for example) without interfering with each other.

▶ Global variables enable functions to share common data but such sharing provides the possibility of one function interfering with another. It's a good policy not to make a variable global unless there's a clear need to.

▶ The addition-assignment operator (+=) provides a concise way to add a value to a variable. For example:

```
n += 50;                    // n = n + 50
```

▶ C++ functions can use recursion—meaning that they call themselves. (A variation on this is when two or more functions call each other.) This technique is valid as long as there is a case that terminates the calls. For example:

```
int triangle(int n) {
    if (n <= 1)
        return 1;
    else
        return n + triangle(n - 1);  // RECURSION!
}
```

Arrays: We've Got Their Number

*The last couple of chapters have had a theme: once you define a task (no matter how simple or how complex) you can ask the computer to perform it any number of times. We've seen this principle at work in **while** loops and **for** loops, as well as functions. It's this fact—more than any other—that demonstrates the power of computer software.*

But the magic of computers lies not just in the fact they can perform an arbitrarily large number of repetitions. They can also work on arbitrarily large amounts of data.

An "array" is an arbitrarily large collection of data indexed by number. With a few keystrokes—as you'll see in this chapter—you can create array data structures of any size. Then, by using loops, you can process the data structure with just a few lines of code. Loops and arrays go hand in hand. Together they help make programs not just powerful but—more important—useful.

A First Look at C++ Arrays

Suppose you're writing a program to analyze the scores given by five judges in a new event, the Olympic kite-flying contest. All five scores need to be stored for a while so you can measure a number of statistical properties: range, average, median, standard deviation, and so on.

Assume for the moment that the five judges are anonymous; we haven't been given their identities—only their scores. One way to store the information is to just declare five variables. Since the scores have a fractional portion (0.1 being the lowest score and 9.9 being almost the highest) you'd declare **double** as the type.

```
double  scores1, scores2, scores3, scores4, scores5;
```

That's a fair amount to enter. Wouldn't it be nice to just enter the word "scores" once and tell C++ to declare five variables for you?

That's exactly what happens when you declare an array. Here's what it would look like for this example:

```
double  scores[5];
```

This declaration creates five data items of type **double** and places them next to each other in memory. In C++ executable statements (statements that actually do the work) these items are referred to as scores[0], scores[1], scores[2], scores[3], and scores[4]. The numbers between brackets are called *indexes*.

| scores[0] | scores[1] | scores[2] | scores[3] | scores[4] |

In the remainder of the code you can perform operations on each of these items just as if it were an individual variable.

```
scores[0] = 2.7;        // Judge #0 assigns a low score.
scores[2] = 9.5;        // Judge #2 assigns a high score.
scores[1] = scores[2];  // Judge #1 copies Judge #2.
```

After these operations are performed, the array looks like this:

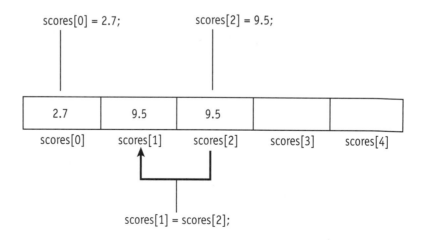

With five elements, the use of an array can make for more concise program code. But that's nothing compared to what can be saved with large arrays. A five-element array is quite short. Consider how much labor you save if you have an array with a *thousand* elements. This is just as easy to declare as a smaller array:

```
int  votes[1000];      // Declare an array with 1,000
                       // elements
```

This declaration creates an array with one thousand elements, running from votes[0] to votes[999].

Initializing Arrays

If you look at the figures in the last section, you see that I left some locations blank. That's because the data items were never assigned a value. But in that case what values *do* they hold? This is the issue of initialization.

Referring to a variable you've forgotten to initialize can end up producing garbage ("garbage" being a highly technical term for a variable with a meaningless value). If a variable is going to be used as a loop counter and is explicitly assigned a value later on (for example in a **for** statement), you can get away with not initializing it. Otherwise, initialization is always a good idea. You can initialize a variable when it's declared.

```
int  sum = 0;
```

You can even initialize variables declared on the same line.

```
int  sum = 0, fingers = 10;
```

And finally, you can initialize an array with the use of something called an *aggregate*. This approach uses a simple notation involving curly braces and commas:

```
double  scores[5] = {0, 0, 0, 0, 0};
int  ordinals[10] = {0, 1, 2, 3, 4, 5, 6, 7, 8, 9};
```

Each of these lines is terminated with a closing curly brace followed by a semicolon (};). This is an exception to the rule that you don't follow a brace with a semicolon. A class or data declaration *always* ends with a semicolon whether braces are involved or not.

Note ▶ If a variable or an array is global, then by default C++ initializes it to zero. (In the case of arrays, C++ initializes every item to zero.) But local variables do not get initialized at all if you don't do it. Global variables not initialized contain zero; local variables not initialized contain garbage.

Zero-Based Indexing

You may have noticed by now that in C++, arrays work a little differently from the way you might expect. If you have N items they are not numbered 1 to N, but 0 to N-1. Again, for an array declared this way:

```
double  scores[5];
```

the elements are:

```
scores[0]
scores[1]
scores[2]
scores[3]
scores[4]
```

No matter how you declare an array, the highest index number (in this case 4) will always be *one less than* the size of the array (in this case 5). This may seem counterintuitive.

But seen from another angle, it makes perfect sense. The index number in a C or C++ array is not an ordinal number (that is, a position) so much as it is an *offset*. That is, the index number of an element is a measure of the distance from the beginning of the array.

How far is the first element from the beginning of an array? That's right: it is no distance away at all . . . it is zero positions away! The index number of the first element is therefore 0. This is worth stating as another cardinal rule:

✱   **In a C++ array of size N elements, the index numbers run from 0 to N-1.**

Interlude | ## Why Use Zero-Based Indexes?

Most other languages, such as FORTRAN and COBOL, use 1-based indexing. The declaration ARRAY(5) in FORTRAN creates an array with indexes running from 1 to 5. This is admittedly a little more natural for beginners.

But regardless of what language they are written in, all programs must be translated into machine code. This code is what the CPU actually executes.

At the machine level, array indexing is handled through offsets: a register (a special memory location inside the CPU itself) contains the address of an array—actually, the address of the first element. Another register contains an offset, such as the distance to the desired element.

Interlude

▼ *continued*

What is the offset of the first element? That's right: zero, just as in C++. With a language such as FORTRAN, the 1-based index must first be translated into a 0-based index by subtracting by 1. Then it is multiplied by the size of each element. To get the element with index I:

address of element I = base address + ((I − 1) * size of each element)

In a 0-based language such as C++ the subtraction no longer has to be done. This results in a slightly more efficient calculation at run time.

address of element I = base address + (I * size of each element)

Even though it results in only a slight saving of CPU cycles, it's very much in the spirit of C-based languages to use this approach, because it better reflects what the CPU does.

Example 5.1. *Print Out Elements*

Let's start by looking at one of the simplest programs possible that uses an array. The rest of the chapter gets into more interesting programming challenges.

```cpp
print_arr.cpp

#include <iostream>
using namespace std;

int main() {
    int i;
    double scores[5] = {0.5, 1.5, 2.5, 3.5, 4.5};

    for(i = 0; i < 5; i++) {
        cout << scores[i] << " ";
    }

    return 0;
}
```

The program, when run, prints

```
0.5  1.5  2.5  3.5  4.5
```

How It Works

The program uses a **for** loop that sets the loop variable i to a series of values: 0, 1, 2, 3, 4, corresponding to the range of indexes in the array named scores.

```
for(i = 0; i < 5; i++) {
    cout << scores[i] << "   ";
}
```

This kind of loop is extremely common in C++ code, so you often see these expressions used with **for**: i = 0, i < SIZE_OF_ARRAY, and i++.

The loop cycles five times, each time with a different value for i.

VALUE OF I	ACTION OF THE LOOP	VALUE PRINTED
0	Print scores[0]	0.5
1	Print scores[1]	1.5
2	Print scores[2]	2.5
3	Print scores[3]	3.5
4	Print scores[4]	4.5

You can also understand the action of this loop visually. The following figure demonstrates the action of the first two cycles of the loop.

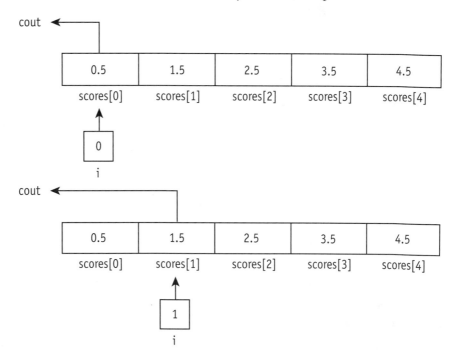

EXERCISES

Exercise 5.1.1. Write a program that initializes an array of eight integers with the values 5, 15, 25, 35, 45, 55, 65, and 75, and then prints each of these out. (Hint: instead of using the loop condition i < 5, use i < 8 because in this case there are eight elements.)

Exercise 5.1.2. Write a program that initializes an array of six integers with the values 10, 22, 13, 99, 4, and 5. Print each of these out and then print their sum.

Exercise 5.1.3. Write a program that prompts the user for each of seven values, stores these in an array, and then prints each of them out followed by the total. You will need to write two **for** loops for this program: one for collecting data and another for calculating the sum and printing out values.

Example 5.2. ## How Random Is Random?

The last example in Chapter 4 introduced a random-number function, rand_0toN1. As I mentioned in that chapter, programmed randomness—the calculated lack of order and predictability—is problematic, because it's a self-contradictory idea. The best you can do is use the system time and then perform a series of complex math transformations. True randomness may not be a theoretical possibility.

But is it a *practical* possibility? That is, can a C++ program simulate the results of randomness so well that it becomes a practical impossibility for a user to predict random numbers in advance? And if we ask a program to output a series of these numbers, do they behave in a way that has all the qualities we'd expect of a true random sequence?

The rand_0toN1 function outputs an integer from 0 to N − 1, where N is the argument to the function. We can use this function to get a series of numbers from 0 to 9 and count how many we get of each digit. What you'd expect to happen is:

▶ Each of the ten digits should be produced about one-tenth of the time.

▶ But the digits shouldn't be produced with absolutely equal frequency. Especially with a small number of trials, you should see variation. However, as the number of trials increases, the ratio of actual hits to expected hits for each digit (one-tenth of the total number) ought to get closer and closer to 1.0.

A program can test this theory by using an array of ten integers to register the results. The program could be written with ten independent variables, each collecting data for one of the numbers 0 to 9, but it would involve a great deal more code, as you'll see. Arrays make this program much easier to write.

When the program is run, it will prompt for a number of trials. It will then report the total number of hits for each of the numbers 0 to 9. Here's what sample output for 20,000 trials should look like.

```
Enter number of cases to do: 20000
0: 1950      Accuracy: 0.975
1: 2026      Accuracy: 1.013
2: 1897      Accuracy: 0.9485
3: 2102      Accuracy: 1.051
4: 2019      Accuracy: 1.0095
5: 1997      Accuracy: 0.9985
6: 1999      Accuracy: 0.9995
7: 1969      Accuracy: 0.9845
8: 2033      Accuracy: 1.0165
9: 2008      Accuracy: 1.004
```

With 20,000 trials you should get instant response. Depending on your computer, it may take millions of trials before you get a noticeable delay; then it's only a few seconds. I have run this program with as many as two billion trials (input: 2000000000). My desktop computer, which is a few years old, takes 28 minutes to respond in that case. But your computer may respond faster.

It's interesting to run this program repeatedly with different values for N. You should find that as the number of trials increases, the accuracy (the ratio of actual hits to expected hits) does, in fact, get closer to 1.0.

Here's the code for this program.

stats.cpp

```cpp
#include <iostream>
#include <stdlib.h>
#include <time.h>
#include <math.h>
using namespace std;

int rand_0toN1(int n);

int hits[10];

int main() {
    int n;
```

stats.cpp, cont.

```
    int i;
    int r;

    srand(time(NULL));      // Set seed for random
                            // numbers.
    cout << "Enter number of trials to run"
    cout << "and press ENTER: ";
    cin >> n;

    // Run n trials. For each trial, get a number from
    //   0 to 9 and then increment the corresponding
    //   element in the hits array.

    for (i = 1; i <= n; i++) {
        r = rand_0toN1(10);
        hits[r]++;
    }

    // Print all the elements in the hits array,
    //   along  with the ratio of hits to the EXPECTED
    //   hits (n / 10).

    for (i = 0; i < 10; i++) {
      cout << i << ": " << hits[i] << " Accuracy: ";
      cout << static_cast<double>(hits[i]) / (n / 10)
        << endl;
    }

    return 0;
}

// Random 0-to-N1 Function.
// Generate a random integer from 0 to N-1.
//
int rand_0toN1(int n) {
    return rand() % n;
}
```

How It Works

The program begins with a couple of declarations:

```
int rand_0toN1(int n);
int hits[10];
```

The rand_0toN1 function is declared here because it is going to be called by **main**. The declaration of hits creates an array of ten integers, ranging in index from 0 to 9. Because this array is global (declared outside of any function), all its elements are initialized to 0.

The main function begins by defining three integer variables—i, n, and r—and by setting the seed for the sequence of random numbers. Remember, this needs to be done in every program that uses random-number generation.

```
srand(time(NULL));    // Set seed for random numbers.
```

The program then prompts for the value of n. This should look familiar by now.

```
cout << "Enter number of trials to run"
cout << "and press ENTER: ";
cin >> n;
```

The next part of the program sets up a **for** loop that operates on an array as part of its operation.

```
// Run n trials. For each trial, get a number from
//  0 to 9 and then increment the corresponding
//  element in the hits array.

for (i = 1; i <= n; i++) {
    r = rand_0toN1(10);
    hits[r]++;
}
```

This loop performs n trials, where n may be a large number such as 20,000. During each cycle, the loop gets a random number r between 0 and 9 and then scores this as a "hit" for the number chosen, by adding 1 to the appropriate array element. At the end of the process, the element hits[0] contains the number of 0s generated, hits[1] contains the number of 1s generated, and so on.

The expression hits[r]++ saves a lot of programming effort. If you weren't using an array, you'd have to write a series of if/else statements like this:

```
if (r == 0)
    hits0++;
```

```
   else if (r == 1)
       hits1++;
   else if (r == 2)
       hits2++;
   else if (r == 3)
       hits3++;
   // etc.
```

Because we're working with arrays, what would otherwise take twenty lines of code takes only one! This single statement adds 1 to whatever element is selected by r. For example, if r equals 1, hits[1] is incremented. If r equals 2, hits[2] is incremented. And so on.

```
       hits[r]++;
```

The rest of **main** consists of a loop that prints all the elements of the array. This action reports the results and is run after all the trials have been performed. As before, this code is much more concise than would be the case if we weren't using an array.

```
// Print all the elements in the hits array, along
//  with the ratio of hits to the EXPECTED hits
//  (n / 10).

for (i = 0; i < 10; i++) {
    cout << i << ": " << hits[i] << "    Accuracy: ";
    cout << static_cast<double>(hits[i]) / (n / 10)
         << endl;
}
```

Note that the cast to **double** type is necessary here to force a floating-point result for the ratio of actual hits to expected hits. Otherwise, the program performs integer division, which simply throws away any remainder.

The rand_0toN1 function is the same function I introduced at the end of Chapter 4.

```
// Random 0-to-N1 Function.
// Generate a random integer from 0 to N-1.
//
int rand_0toN1(int n) {
    return rand() % n;
}
```

EXERCISES

Exercise 5.2.1. Alter Example 5.2 so that it generates not 10 different values, but five: in other words, use the rand_0toN1 function to get a 0, 1, 2, 3, or 4. Then perform the requested number of trials in which you'd expect each value of the five values to be produced one-fifth of the time.

Exercise 5.2.2. Alter the example so that it can work with any number of values, simply by changing one setting in the program. You can do this with a **#define** directive near the beginning of the code. This directive instructs the compiler to replace all occurrences of a symbolic name (in this case, "VALUES") with the specified text.

For example, to generate five different values, first put the following directive at the beginning of the code:

```
#define VALUES 5
```

Then use the symbolic name VALUES wherever the program refers to the number of possible values. For example, you'd declare the hits array as:

```
int hits[VALUES];
```

From then on, you can control the number of different values by going back and changing one line—the **#define** directive—with a different number and then recompiling. The beauty of this approach is that the behavior of the program can be so easily modified by that one line of code.

Exercise 5.2.3. Rewrite the code in **main** so that it uses a loop similar to the one in Example 4.3 (page 98), allowing the user to keep rerunning sessions of any number of times until he or she enters 0 to terminate the program. Before each session, you need to reinitialize all the elements of the hits array to 0. You can do that either by including a **for** loop that sets each element to 0, or by calling a function that contains this loop.

Strings and Arrays of Strings

To do the examples in the remainder of this chapter, I'm going to have to get a little ahead of the story and show how to declare arrays of strings. In Chapter 7, we'll return to the subject of strings.

Up until now, I've shown the use of string literals—or rather, string constants. For example, to print a message you'd use a line of code like this:

```
cout << "What a good C++ am I.";
```

You can have string variables, just as you can have integer and floating-point variables. These require a strange-looking **char*** notation. For example, the following code first stores the string in the variable message and then prints it:

```
char *message = "What a good C++ am I";
cout << message;
```

The rest of this chapter uses arrays of strings. The declarations look just like those for arrays of numbers, except that the **char*** notation must be used for the array's data type. For example:

```
char *members[4] = {"Sally", "Alex", "George",
    "Martha" };
```

To refer to an individual string in executable code, use array notation (but you don't use the * operator when printing the string). For example:

```
cout << "The leader of the club is " << members[0];
```

This prints out:

```
The leader of the club is Sally.
```

Because the names of the members are all stored in the array, we can use a loop to efficiently print all of them out. For example, this code

```
for (i = 0; i < 4; i++)
    cout << members[i] << endl;
```

prints out this list of names:

```
Sally
Alex
George
Martha
```

Example 5.3. *Card Dealer #1*

Now we're ready to have some fun. The example in this section uses two arrays of strings—ranks and suits—to simulate the dealing of a card from a standard deck of 52 playing cards.

This example has one major limitation: the same card may be dealt again before the rest of the deck has been exhausted. The behavior simulated is the act of dealing a card, noting it, and then putting it back and reshuffling before dealing another card. In later sections, I'll develop a technique for preventing a card from being redealt.

This example, at least, shows some of the basic code you need for a card-dealing program, even though in some ways it's not yet complete.

```
dealer1.cpp

#include <iostream>
#include <stdlib.h>
#include <time.h>
#include <math.h>
using namespace std;

int rand_0toN1(int n);
void draw_a_card();

char *suits[4] =  {"hearts", "diamonds", "spades",
                      "clubs"};
char *ranks[13] = {"ace", "two", "three", "four", "five",
                   "six", "seven", "eight", "nine",
                   "ten", "jack", "queen", "king" };

int main() {
    int n, i;

    srand(time(NULL));       // Set seed for random
                             // numbers.

    while (1) {
        cout << "Enter no. of cards to draw (0 to"
        cout << "exit): ";
        cin >> n;
        if (n == 0)
            break;
        for (i = 1; i <= n; i++)
            draw_a_card();
    }
    return 0;
}

// Draw-a-card function
// Performs one card-draw by getting a random 0-4 and
//   a random 0-12. These are then used to index the
```

dealer1.cpp, cont.

```
//   string arrays, ranks and suits.
//
void draw_a_card() {

    int r;          // Random index (0 thru 12) into
                    // ranks array
    int s;          // Random index (0 thru 3) into
                    // suits array
    r = rand_0toN1(13);
    s = rand_0toN1(4);
    cout << ranks[r] << " of " << suits[s] << endl;
}


// Random 0-to-N1 Function.
// Generate a random integer from 0 to N-1.
//
int rand_0toN1(int n) {
    return rand() % n;
}
```

How It Works

The key to this example is the use of the two global arrays declared: suits and ranks.

```
char *suits[4] =  {"hearts", "diamonds", "spades",
                       "clubs"};
char *ranks[13] = {"ace", "two", "three", "four", "five",
                       "six", "seven", "eight", "nine",
                       "ten", "jack", "queen", "king" };
```

Each of these is an array of strings that can be indexed just like any other array. The suits array has four elements indexed by the numbers 0 to 3. The ranks array has 13 elements indexed by the numbers 0 to 12.

By happy coincidence, the rand_0toN1 function produces numbers the same way that C++ arrays are indexed: with a number running from 0 to N-1 (where N is the number of elements). This makes the program easier to write.

The draw_a_card function manages all the work associated with drawing one card.

```
void draw_a_card() {
    int r;          // Random index (0 thru 12) into
                    // ranks array
    int s;          // Random index (0 thru 3) into
                    // suits array

    r = rand_0toN1(13);
    s = rand_0toN1(4);
    cout << ranks[r] << " of " << suits[s] << endl;
}
```

The program calls the rand_0toN1 function, specifying the argument 13. We get back a random integer from 0 to 12: these correspond to all the elements in the ranks array. Therefore, each of the 13 rank values will be selected with equal probability.

```
    r = rand_0toN1(13);
```

The program then calls rand_0toN1, specifying the argument 4. We get back a random integer from 0 to 3, corresponding to all the elements in the suits array.

```
    s = rand_0toN1(4);
```

Now all the function has to do is select two strings and print them, and we're done.

```
    cout << ranks[r] << " of " << suits[s] << endl;
```

EXERCISE

Example 5.3.1. Write a program that randomly selects from a bag of eight objects. Each object can be red, blue, orange, or green, and it can be a ball or a cube. Assume the bag contains one object for each combination (one red ball, one red cube, one orange ball, one orange cube, and so on). Write code similar to Example 5.3, using two string arrays—one to identify colors and the other to identify shapes.

Example 5.4.   *Card Dealer #2*

The next step in writing a complete card-dealing program is to select a single number at random, and then use this number to get both suit and rank. Such an approach makes it possible later on to create an array that tracks the status of each card. The program generates a random number from 0 to 51 and then maps this number to a unique combination of suit and rank.

Each card-draw here is still treated as an independent event. The next section adds the logic to simulate a real deck of cards, in which a card can't be drawn a second time.

In the following code, the new lines (or lines to be changed) are in bold. The rest of the code is identical to that in Example 5.3.

dealer2.cpp

```cpp
#include <iostream>
#include <stdlib.h>
#include <time.h>
#include <math.h>
using namespace std;

int rand_0toN1(int n);
void draw_a_card();

char *suits[4] =  {"hearts", "diamonds", "spades",
                   "clubs"};
char *ranks[13] = {"ace", "two", "three", "four", "five",
                   "six", "seven", "eight", "nine",
                   "ten", "jack", "queen", "king" };

int main() {
    int n, i;

    srand(time(NULL));       // Set seed for random
                             // numbers.

    while (1) {
        cout << "Enter no. of cards to draw (0 to"
        cout << "exit): ";
        cin >> n;
        if (n == 0)
            break;
        for (i = 1; i <= n; i++)
            draw_a_card();
    }
    return 0;
}
```

▼ *continued on next page*

dealer2.cpp, cont.

```cpp
// Draw-a-card function
// Performs one card-draw by getting a random 0-4 and
//  a random 0-12. These are then used to index the
//  string arrays, ranks and suits.
//
void draw_a_card() {
    int r;          // Random index (0 thru 12) into
                    // ranks array
    int s;          // Random index (0 thru 3) into
                    // suits array

    int card;

    card = rand_0toN1(52);     // Get random number
                               // from 0 to 51

    r = card % 13;             // r = random 0 to 12
    s = card / 13;             // s = random 0 to 3
    cout << ranks[r] << " of " << suits[s] << endl;
}

// Random 0-to-N1 Function.
// Generate a random integer from 0 to N-1.
//
int rand_0toN1(int n) {
    return rand() % n;
}
```

How It Works

There are just four new lines in the program . . . but I felt these important enough to base an entire example on. These statements are all part of the draw_a_card function.

```cpp
int card;
card = rand_0toN1(52);     // Get random number 0 - 51
r = card % 13;             // r = random 0 to 12
s = card / 13;             // s = random 0 to 3
```

For each card drawn, this version of the program only makes one call to rand_0toN1. This approach is consistent with the general goal here: to select a single number that corresponds to a unique card.

The card drawn must have a combination of suit and rank that no other card has. Given a number between 0 and 51, the program determines a unique suit and rank combination.

One way to do that would be to create two more arrays:

```
int rank_chooser[52] = {0, 1, 2, 3, 4, 5, 6, 7, 8, 9, 10, 11, 12,
                        0, 1, 2, 3, 4, 5, 6, 7, 8, 9, 10, 11, 12,
                        0, 1, 2, 3, 4, 5, 6, 7, 8, 9, 10, 11, 12,
                        0, 1, 2, 3, 4, 5, 6, 7, 8, 9, 10, 11, 12,
};

int suit_chooser[52] = {0, 0, 0, 0, 0, 0, 0, 0, 0, 0, 0, 0, 0, 0,
                        1, 1, 1, 1, 1, 1, 1, 1, 1, 1, 1, 1, 1, 1,
                        2, 2, 2, 2, 2, 2, 2, 2, 2, 2, 2, 2, 2, 2,
                        3, 3, 3, 3, 3, 3, 3, 3, 3, 3, 3, 3, 3, 3,
};
```

You could then get r and s values by indexing into these arrays:

```
r = rank_chooser[card];
s = suit_chooser[card];
```

The values generated this way would be unique, as you can see by examining the arrays. For example, a card value of 12 would result in r and s values of 12 and 0, respectively, while a card value of 25 would result in r and s values of 12 and 1.

This solution—indexing into these arrays—is equivalent to the following mathematical operations:

```
r = card % 13;          // r = random 0 to 12
s = card / 13;          // s = random 0 to 3
```

As you may recall from earlier chapters, the modulus operator (%) performs division between two integers and returns the remainder. The action here is to divide by 13 and produce a number from 0 to 12—the same values as in the rank_chooser array.

Division between two integers returns the quotient, rounded down, and discards the remainder. This produces a number from 0 to 3—the same values as in the suit_chooser array.

So, by using these mathematical operations you save yourself the trouble of creating the arrays rank_chooser and suit_chooser. The results are the same.

EXERCISE

Exercise 5.4.1.   Write a program for the scenario described in Exercise 5.3.1. This exercise features eight objects, each of which has a unique combination of color (red, blue, orange, green) and shape (ball, cube). Use an approach similar to that in Example 5.3, in which you generate one random number for each object picked and then use this number to generate a unique combination of two numbers—one that selects the color and another that selects the shape.

Example 5.5.   *Card Dealer #3*

Now that we know how to use a number from 0 to 51 to represent a deck of cards, we can add the final piece of the puzzle. An accurate card-dealing program must remember which card was drawn and then avoid drawing that card again.

There are two ways to do this. One is to initialize a 52-element array so that each element represents a position in a deck, assign each a card value, and then "shuffle" the deck by doing a series of random swaps.

The approach I adopt here is one that I find a little simpler and definitely easier to write: I use a 52-element array, in which each element corresponds to a card. The content of an element is a true/false value indicating whether or not the corresponding card has been selected yet. Once a card is picked, this array is updated to show that the card should be skipped in the future.

Here is the program. As before, only the new lines of code are in bold. All other lines of code are identical to those in the previous example.

```
dealer3.cpp

    #include <iostream>
    #include <stdlib.h>
    #include <time.h>
    #include <math.h>
    using namespace std;

    int rand_0toN1(int n);
    void draw_a_card();
    int select_next_available(int n);

    char *suits[4] = {"hearts", "diamonds", "spades",
                      "clubs"};
```

```
char *ranks[13] = {"ace", "two", "three", "four",
                   "five",
               "six", "seven", "eight", "nine",
               "ten", "jack", "queen", "king" };

int card_drawn[52];
int cards_remaining = 52;

int main() {
    int n, i;

    srand(time(NULL));        // Set seed for random
                              // numbers.

    while (1) {
        cout << "Enter no. of cards to draw (0 to"
        cout << "exit): ";
        cin >> n;
        if (n == 0)
            break;
        for (i = 1; i <= n; i++)
            draw_a_card();
    }
    return 0;
}

// Draw-a-card function
// Performs one card-draw by getting a random 0-4 and
//  a random 0-12. These are then used to index the
//  string arrays, ranks and suits.
//
void draw_a_card() {
    int r;          // Random index (0 thru 12) into
                    // ranks array
    int s;          // Random index (0 thru 3) into
                    // suits array
    int n, card;

    n = rand_0toN1(cards_remaining--);
    card = select_next_available(n);
```

▼ *continued on next page*

```
        r = card % 13;              // r = random 0 to 12
        s = card / 13;              // s = random 0 to 3
        cout << ranks[r] << " of " << suits[s] << endl;
    }


    // Select-next-available-card function.
    // Find the Nth element of card_drawn, skipping over
    //   all those elements already set to true.
    //
    int select_next_available(int n) {
        int i = 0;

        // At beginning of deck, skip past cards already
        // drawn.

        while (card_drawn[i])
            i++;

        while (n-- > 0) {        // Do the following n times:
            i++;                       // Advance to next card
            while (card_drawn[i])  // Skip past cards
                i++;                   //   already drawn.
        }
        card_drawn[i] = true;      // Note card to be drawn
        return i;                  // Return this number.
    }

    // Random 0-to-N1 Function.
    // Generate a random integer from 0 to N-1.
    //
    int rand_0toN1(int n) {
        return rand() % n;
    }
```

How It Works

The version of the program uses an additional function select_next_available to determine what card to draw. The program uses a global integer variable cards_remaining to remember how many cards are remaining in the deck.

```
int cards_remaining = 52;
```

Every time a card is drawn, this variable is decreased by 1.

The draw_a_card function first gets a random integer based on the value of cards_remaining. That integer is then passed to the select_next_available function.

```
n = rand_0toN1(cards_remaining--);
card = select_next_available(n);
```

The job of select_next_available is to count through the array n + 1 times, each time skipping over cards that have already been drawn. These cards are marked by a value of true (1) in the card_drawn array. For example, here's how you'd count ahead three:

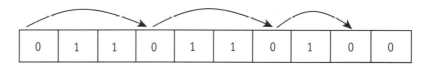

| 0 | 1 | 1 | 0 | 1 | 1 | 0 | 1 | 0 | 0 |

card_drawn array

The code for select_next_available finds the first available card by skipping past all the drawn cards at the beginning of the array.

```
while (card drawn[i])
    i++;
```

It then counts n more available cards, each time skipping over items already drawn.

```
while (n-- > 0) {        // Do the following n times:
    i++;                 // Advance to next card
    while (card_drawn[i])  // Skip past cards
        i++;             //  already drawn.
}
```

This loop uses n-- > 0 as the **if** condition. If n has a value greater than zero, the condition is considered true; n is then decremented. The effect of the condition is to cycle through the loop n times.

When select_next_available has finally arrived at the card to be drawn, it does two things: it sets the index number to true (1) in the card_drawn array and then returns the index to the caller.

```
card_drawn[i] = true;    // Note which card to draw.
return i;                // Return this number.
```

Optimizing the Program

If you're a careful programmer, you may note that this program has one gaping flaw: if the user attempts to deal more than 52 cards, no procedure exists for resetting the deck (in effect, reshuffling) and starting over. Instead, the program ends up going outside the bounds of the card_drawn array. The result can be disaster, as the code that writes array values ends up overwriting other areas of memory. Therefore, it's important to handle this situation in some way.

Probably the most user-friendly is to detect this condition at the beginning of the draw_a_card function, then respond by resetting the global array card_drawn and the global variable cards_remaining to their original values at the start of the program.

```
if (cards_remaining == 0) {
    cout << "Reshuffling." << endl;
    cards_remaining = 52;           // Reset cards_remaining.
    for (int i = 0; i < 52; i++)    // Reset all the values
        card_drawn[i] = false;      //  in card_drawn array.
}
```

The **for** loop here makes use of a trick introduced in Chapter 3. We need a variable i for the use of this particular loop, but i was not yet declared in the draw_a_card function. The effect of the expression int i = 0 is to declare i "on the fly" and initialize it to 0. The variable i is given scope local to the **for** loop: changes to i inside this loop can't affect the value of i in other contexts.

There's a second feature of the program that is less than optimal. If you review the code for the select_next_available function, you'll see that it performs the same **while** loop (the code that performs the "skip ahead" activity) in more than one place. You can fold these together by realizing that the function advances through the array not n times, but n + 1 times. (For example, an input of 0 counts to the first available item, an input of 1 counts to the second available item, and so on.)

The improved, shorter version is:

```
int select_next_available(int n) {
    int i = -1;

    n++;  // Set up for n + 1 counting operations

    while (n-- > 0) {       // Do the following n times:
        i++;                        // Advance to next card
        while (card_drawn[i])   // Skip past cards
            i++;                    //  already drawn.
```

```
    }
    card_drawn[i] = true;    // Note which card to draw.
    return i;                // Return this number.
}
```

Note that i is initialized to -1 rather than 0 in this version. That's because picking the first element should increment i to 0, not to 1.

EXERCISE

Exercise 5.5.1. Write a similar program for a bag that contains the eight objects described earlier: each item has a unique combination of color (red, blue, orange, green) and shape (ball, cube). Every time an object is picked from the bag it can't be picked again, so the number of possible choices decreases by one. The logic should be identical to that in Example 5.5, but the arrays and initial settings will differ. You may also want to give your variables different names such as items_remaining and (for the integer array) items_picked.

A Word to the Wise

While looking at the examples in this chapter you may have a question: what happens if you attempt to access an array element that does not exist? That is, what if you use an index number that's not supported?

The answer is that C++ is untrustworthy in this regard. For example, you declare an array of size 5 but for some reason attempt to write to an element with index 5. This should not be legal, because the last element has index number 4.

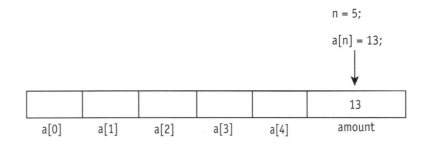

C++ doesn't stop you. Instead, the operation proceeds at the memory location where array[5] would be *if it existed*. The result is that a piece of data outside of the array is overwritten. This can create bugs that are very difficult to track down.

Why does C++ permit this? Why doesn't it check the array index and then disallow operations that overwrite other areas of memory?

Some programming languages do, in fact, make such a check. But an illegal array-access can't necessarily be determined when the program is compiled. In the example here, the value of n may not be known until the program is run. Languages such as Basic and FORTRAN therefore have to put in a runtime check before each and every array-element access. This causes programs to run less efficiently.

C++ and its predecessor C were designed with the philosophy that the programmer knows what he or she is doing. C/C++ programs are faster and more compact than those created by other languages. But in return for this greater efficiency, you need to take care that the array indexes in your programs do not go out of bounds.

2-D Arrays: Into the Matrix

Most computer languages provide the ability not only to create ordinary, one-dimensional arrays but to create multidimensional arrays as well. C++ is no exception.

Two-dimensional arrays in C++ have this form:

```
type  array_name[size1][size2];
```

The number of elements is `size1 * size2`, and the indexes in each dimension are 0-based, just as in one-dimensional arrays. For example, consider this declaration.

```
int  matrix[10][10];
```

This creates a 10-by-10 array having 100 elements. Each dimension has index numbers running from 0 to 9. The first element is therefore matrix[0][0] and the last element is matrix[9][9].

To process such an array programmatically, you need to use a nested loop with two loop variables. For example, this code initializes all the members of the array to 0:

```
int i, j;

for (i = 0; i < 10; i++)
    for (j = 0; j < 10; j++)
        matrix[i][j] = 0;
```

The way this works is:

▶ i is set to 0, and a complete set of cycles of the inner loop—with j ranging from 0 to 9—is done first.

▶ One cycle of the outer loop is then complete; i is incremented to the next higher value, which is 1. Then all the cycles of the inner loop run again, with j (as always) ranging from 0 to 9.

▶ The process is repeated until i is incremented past its terminal value 9.

Consequently, the values of i and j will be (0, 0), (0, 1), (0, 2), . . . (0, 9), at which point the inner loop is complete, i is incremented, and the inner loop begins again: (1, 0), (1, 1), (1, 2) . . . In all, 100 operations will be performed, because each cycle of the outer loop—which runs 10 times—performs 10 cycles of the inner loop.

In C++ arrays, the index on the right changes the fastest. This means that the elements matrix[5][0] and matrix[5][1] are next to each other in memory.

Incidentally, compound statement syntax (which uses braces to explicitly define where a loop begins and ends) can be used here as with all control structures. Here's what this one would look like. It's a little more work, but its meaning is clearer.

```
int i, j;

for (i = 0; i < 10; i++) {
    for (j = 0; j < 10; j++) {
        matrix[i][j] = 0;
    }
}
```

Chapter 5   *Summary*

Chapter 5 has been about the use of arrays in C++. Some important points:

▶ Use bracket notation to declare an array in C++. Declarations have this form:

```
type  array_name[number_of_elements];
```

▶ For an array of size n, the elements have indexes ranging from 0 to n -1. For example, the following statement assigns the number 3 to the first element.

```
scores[0] = 3;
```

▶ You can use loops to efficiently process arrays of any size. For example, assume an array was declared with SIZE_OF_ARRAY elements. The following loop sets every element to 0:

```
for(i = 0; i < SIZE_OF_ARRAY; i++)
    my_array[i] = 0;
```

▶ You can use aggregates—a list of values between set braces—to initialize arrays.

```
double  scores[5] = {6.8, 9.0, 9.0, 8.3, 7.1 };
```

▶ Use the **char*** notation to declare a string variable. For example:

```
char *name = "Joe Bloe";
```

▶ You can declare arrays of strings just as you can declare other kinds of arrays. For example:

```
char *names[4] = {"John", "Paul", "George", "Ringo" };
```

▶ When you print a string or a member of a string array, don't use the * operator.

```
cout << "The organization of the group was " << names[0];
```

▶ C++ does not check array bounds for you at runtime. Therefore, you need to show care that you don't write array-access code that overwrites other areas of memory.

▶ Two-dimensional arrays are declared this way:

```
type  array_name[size1][size2];
```

Pointers: Getting a Handle on Data

Perhaps more than anything else, the C-based languages (of which C++ is a proud member) are characterized by the use of pointers—variables that store memory addresses. The subject sometimes gets a reputation for being difficult for beginners. It seems to some people that pointers are part of a plot by experienced programmers to wreak vengeance on the rest of us (because they didn't get chosen for basketball, invited to the prom, or whatever).

But a pointer is just another way of referring to data. There's nothing mysterious about pointers; you will always succeed in using them if you follow simple, specific steps. Of course, you may find yourself baffled (as I once did) that you need to go through these steps at all—why not just use simple variable names in all cases? True enough, the use of simple variables to refer to data is often sufficient.

But sometimes, programs have special needs. What I hope to show in this chapter is why the extra steps involved in pointer use are often justified.

The Concept of Pointer

The simplest programs consist of one function (**main**) that doesn't interact with the network or operating system. With such programs, you can probably go the rest of your life without pointers.

But when you write programs with multiple functions, you may need one function to hand off a data address to another. In C and C++ this is the only way a function can change the value of arguments passed to it. This is called *pass by reference*.

Note ▶ C++ features an alternative technique for enabling pass by reference, which I'll introduce in Chapter 12, but the underlying mechanics are similar. It's best to understand pointers first.

A pointer is a variable that contains an address. For example, suppose you have three **int** variables, a, b, c, and one pointer variable, p. Assume that a, b, and c are initialized to 3, 5, and 8, and the pointer is initialized to point to a. In that case, the layout of the computer's memory might look like this:

	Value	Address
a	5	1000
b	3	1004
c	8	1008
p	1000	1012

This figure assumes that variables a, b, c, and p have numeric addresses 1000, 1004, 1008, and 1012. Data addresses vary from one system to another, but the distances between the addresses are uniform. The **int** type and all pointer types on a 32-bit system take up four bytes each; a variable of type **double** takes up eight bytes.

All memory locations on a computer have a numeric address—even though you almost never know or care what it is. Yet at the level of machine code, addresses are about the only thing the CPU understands! A reference to a variable Num in your program, for example, is translated into a reference to a numeric address. (The compiler, linker, and loader assign this address to Num, so you don't have to think about it.)

Pointer usage is about *indirect* memory reference. CPUs are optimized to do these references efficiently, which is one reason why C-based languages encourage their use. At runtime an address is loaded into an on-board CPU register, which is then used to access items in memory.

Interlude What Do Addresses Really Look Like?

In the last section, I assumed that the variables a, b, and c had the physical addresses 1000, 1004, and 1008. While this is possible, it's unlikely—just a shot in the dark.

Actually, when hard-core programmers represent bit patterns or addresses, they use the hexadecimal numbering system. This means base 16 rather than base 10.

There's a good reason for using hexadecimal notation. Because 16 is an exact power of 2 (2 * 2 * 2 * 2 = 16), each hexadecimal digit corresponds to a unique pattern of exactly four binary digits—no more, no less. Table 6.1 shows how hexadecimal digits work.

Interlude

▼ *continued*

Table 6.1: Hexadecimal Equivalents

HEXADECIMAL DIGIT	EQUIVALENT DECIMAL	EQUIVALENT BINARY
0	0	0000
1	1	0001
2	2	0010
3	3	0011
4	4	0100
5	5	0101
6	6	0110
7	7	0111
8	8	1000
9	9	1001
A	10	1010
B	11	1011
C	12	1100
D	13	1101
E	14	1110
F	15	1111

The advantage of using hexadecimal notation for addresses is you can tell how wide an address is just by looking at it. One hexadecimal digit always corresponds precisely to four binary digits. The address 0x8000 has four hexadecimal digits. (The "0x" prefix is the C++ notation that means the number is hexadecimal.) Four hexadecimal digits correspond precisely to 16 binary digits. The math is very simple: $4 * 4 = 16$.

In contrast, it's hard to tell how many binary digits (or bits) the decimal number 1000 corresponds to. The answer is 10 bits. (Did you know that?) But decimal 5000 requires 13 bits to represent in binary. Decimal-to-binary is vastly more difficult than hexadecimal-to-binary; therefore, systems programmers favor hexadecimal.

On nearly all personal computers still in use today addresses are not 16 bits wide, but 32. An address such as 0x8FFF1000 is a 32-bit address, because it has eight hexadecimal digits ($8 * 4 = 32$). 0x00002222 is also a 32-bit address, because the assumption is that the leading zeros are preserved.

▼ *continued on next page*

Interlude

▼ *continued*

When personal computers were introduced in the 1970s, 16-bit addresses were the norm. The number of possible addresses were 2 to the 16th power, or 64k. That meant that no matter how many memory cards you purchased, the processor simply couldn't recognize more than 64k of memory.

The 8086 processor, utilized in the IBM PC and the early clones that followed, used a 20-bit address system, which supported up to 16 "segments" each of which could be 64k. (Again, this made 64k a magic number.) Addressable memory increased to a little more than one megabyte—better than 64k, but still woefully inadequate by today's standards.

By the mid 1990s, 32-bit addresses became the standard and Microsoft Windows fully supported it. Software was rewritten and recompiled so that it stopped using the awkward segmented addressing mode and went to clean 32-bit addresses. The number of possible memory addresses is now 2 to the 32nd power, or somewhat more than four *billion*—an upper limit of four gigabytes! But at the rate which memory is improving, it's only a matter of time until hardware capabilities exceed this limit. Stay tuned to see what workarounds computer architects devise when that day comes.

Declaring and Using Pointers

A pointer declaration uses the following syntax:

```
type  *name;
```

For example, you can declare a pointer p, which can point to variables of type **int**:

```
int  *p;
```

At the moment, the pointer is not initialized. All we know is that it can point to data objects of type **int**. Does this type matter? Yes. The base type of a pointer determines how the data it points to is interpreted. Assign it to point to some other type, and the wrong data format will be used. The pointer p has type **int***; so it should only be able to point to **int** variables.

The next statements declare an integer n, initialize it to 0, and assign its address to pointer p.

```
int n = 0;
p = &n;              // p now points to n!
```

The ampersand (&) is another new operator. Its purpose in life is to get an address. Again, you don't really care what the numeric address is; all that matters is that p contains the address of n—that is, p *points to* n.

After these statements are executed, a possible memory layout for the program is:

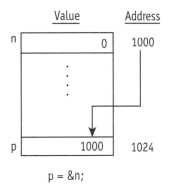

p = &n;

Here comes the interesting part. There are a couple of ways to use a pointer variable. One is to change the value of p itself.

```
p++;      // Point to next item in memory.
```

This adds 1 to p, which makes it point to the variable in memory after n. The effects are unpredictable except in the case of array elements, which I describe later in the section "Pointers and Array Processing." Otherwise, this kind of operation should be avoided.

The other way to use a pointer is more useful—at least in this case. Applying the indirection operator (*) says "the thing pointed to by this pointer." Therefore, assigning a value to *p has the same effect as assigning to n, because n is what p points to.

```
*p = 5;     // Assign 5 to the int pointed to by p.
```

So, this operation changes the thing that p points to, not the value of p itself. Now the memory layout looks like this:

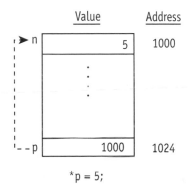

*p = 5;

The effect of the statement, in this case, is the same as "n = 5". The computer finds the memory location pointed to by p and puts the value 5 at that location.

You can use a value pointed to by a pointer both to get and to assign data. Here's another example of pointer use:

```
*p = *p + 3;    // Add 3 to the int pointed to by p.
```

The value of n changes yet again—this time from 5 to 8. The effect of this statement is the same as n = n + 3. The computer finds the memory location pointed to by p and adds 3 to the value at that location.

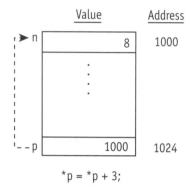

$$*p = *p + 3;$$

To summarize, when p points to n, referring to *p has the same effect as referring to n. Here are more examples:

WHEN P POINTS TO N, THIS STATEMENT	HAS THE SAME EFFECT AS THIS STATEMENT
*p = 33;	n = 33;
*p = *p + 2;	n = n + 2;
cout << *p;	cout << n;
cin >> *p;	cin >> n;

But if using *p is the same as using n, why bother with *p in the first place? The answer is that (among other things) it achieves pass by reference—in which a function can change the value of an argument. Here's how it works:

▶ The caller of a function passes the address of a variable to be changed. For example, the caller passes &n (the address of n).

▶ The function has a pointer argument such as p that receives this address value. The function can then use *p to manipulate the value of n.

The next section shows a simple example that does just that.

Example 6.1. *The Double-It Function*

Here's a program that uses a function named double_it, which doubles the value of a variable passed to it—or, more specifically, it doubles the value of a variable whose address is passed to it. That may sound a little convoluted, but the example should help make it clear.

```
double_it.cpp
    #include <iostream>
    using namespace std;

    void double_it(int *p);

    int main() {
        int a = 5, b = 6;
        cout<< "Value of a before doubling is " << a << endl;
        cout<< "Value of b before doubling is " << b << endl;
        double_it(&a);      // Pass address of a.
        double_it(&b);      // Pass address of b.
        cout<< "Value of a after doubling is " << a << endl;
        cout<< "Value of b after doubling is " << b << endl;
        return 0;
    }
    void double_it(int *p) {
        *p = *p * 2;
    }
```

How It Works

This is a straightforward program. All the main function does is:

▶ Print the values of a and b.

▶ Call the double_it function to double the value of a, by passing the address of a (&a).

▶ Call the double_it function to double the value of b, by passing the address of b (&b).

▶ Print the values of a and b again.

This example needs pointers to work. You could write a version of double_it that took a simple **int** argument, but such a function would do nothing.

```
void double_it(int n) {    // THIS DOESN'T WORK!
    n = n * 2;
}
```

The problem here is that when an argument is passed to a function, the function gets a copy of the argument. But upon return, that copy is thrown away. But if the function gets the address of a variable, then it can use that address to make changes *to the original copy of the variable itself.*

Here's an analogy. Getting a variable passed to you is like getting photocopies of a secret document. You can view the information, but you have no access to the originals. But getting a pointer is like getting the location and access codes for the original documents; you not only get to look at them, you can make changes!

So to enable a function to change the value of a variable, use pointers. This function does that by declaring an argument p, a pointer to an integer:

```
void double_it(int *p);
```

This declaration says that "the thing pointed to by p" has **int** type. Therefore, p itself is a pointer to an **int**.

The caller must therefore pass an address, which it does by using the address operator (&).

```
double_it(&a);



void double_it(int *p) {
    *p = *p * 2
}
```

Visually, here's the effect of these statements in terms of the memory layout. The address of a is passed to the function, which then uses it to change the value of a.

	Value	Address			Value	Address
a	5	1000		a	10	1000
b	6	1004		b	6	1004
p	1000	1160		p	1000	1060

p ◄— &a   *p = *p * 2;

The program then calls the function again, this time passing the address of b. The function uses this address to change the value of b.

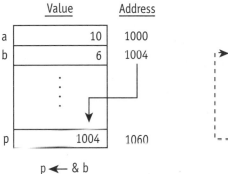

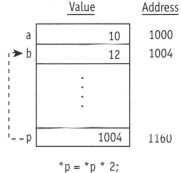

$$p \leftarrow \& b \qquad\qquad *p = *p * 2;$$

EXERCISES

Exercise 6.1.1.   Write a program that calls a function triple_it that takes the address of an **int** and triples the value pointed to. Test it by passing an argument n, which is initialized to 15. Print out the value of n before and after the function is called. (Hint: the function should look similar to double_it in Example 6.1, so you can use that code and make the necessary alterations. When calling the function, remember to pass &n.)

Exercise 6.1.2.   Write a program with a function named convert_temp: the function takes the address of a variable of type **double** and applies Centigrade-to-Fahrenheit conversion. A variable that contains a Centigrade temperature should, after the function is called, contain the equivalent Fahrenheit temperature. Initialize a variable named temperature to 10.0 and print out the value before and after the function is called. Hint: the relevant formula is F = (C * 1.8) + 32.

Swap: Another Function Using Pointers

The double_it function showcased in the last section is fine for illustrating some basic mechanics, but it's probably not something that would appear in a real program. Now I'll move onto a function called swap, which you should find much more useful.

Suppose you have two **int** variables and you want to swap their values. It's easy to do this with a third variable temp, whose function is to hold a temporary value.

```
temp = a;
a = b;
b = temp;
```

Now wouldn't this be useful to put into a function that you could call whenever you needed to? Yes, but as I explained earlier, unless the arguments are passed by reference, changes to the variables are ignored.

Here's another solution. This one uses pointers to pass by reference.

```
// Swap function.
// Swap the values pointed to by p1 and p2.
//
void swap(int *p1, int *p2) {
    int temp = *p1;
    *p1 = *p2;
    *p2 = temp;
}
```

The expressions *p1 and *p2 are integers, and you can use them as you would any integer variables. The effect here is to swap the values pointed to by p1 and p2. Therefore, if you pass the addresses of two integer variables a and b, the values of those variables get swapped.

Literally, here's what the three statements inside the function do:

1 Declare a local variable named temp and initialize it to the value pointed to by p1.

2 Assign the value pointed to by p2 to the value pointed to by p1.

3 Assign the value temp to the value pointed by p2.

p1 and p2 are addresses, and they do not change. The data that's altered is the data *pointed to* by p1 and p2. This is easy to see with an example.

Assume that big and little are initialized to 100 and 1, respectively.

```
int big = 100;
int little = 1;
```

The following statement calls the swap function, passing the addresses of these two variables. Note the use of the address operator (&) here.

```
swap(&big, &little);
```

Now if you print the values of these variables, you'll see the values have been exchanged, so that now big contains 1 and little contains 100.

```
cout << "The value of big is now " << big << endl;
cout << "The value of little is now " << little;
```

Note that the memory addresses of big and little do not change. But the values *at* those addresses change. This is why the indirection operator (*) is often called the "at" operator. The statement *p = 0 alters the value stored *at* address p.

Example 6.2.   *Array Sorter*

Now it's time to show the power of this swap function. First I need to clarify that pointers are not limited to pointing only to simple variables—although I used that terminology at first to keep things simple. An **int** pointer (for example) can point to any memory location that stores an **int** value. This means that it can point to elements of an array, as well as pointing to a variable.

For example, here the swap function is used to swap the values of two elements of an array named arr:

```
int arr[5] = {0, 10, 30, 25, 50};
swap(&arr[2], &arr[3]);
```

Why am I so proud of this fact? Because given the right procedure, you can use the swap function to sort all the values of an array.

Consider a typical array. Take a look at arr again—this time with the data jumbled around.

30	25	0	50	10
arr[0]	arr[1]	arr[2]	arr[3]	arr[4]

Here's an obvious solution to the sorting problem. You can easily verify that it works.

1 Find the lowest value and put that value in arr[0].

2 Find the *next* lowest value and put that value in arr[1].

3 Continue in this manner until you get to the end.

Don't laugh. This simple, brute-strength approach is not as dumb as it seems. A slight refinement gives us the essence of the classic selection-sort algorithm, which is what I use here. Here's the more refined version, where a[] is the array and n is the number of elements.

```
For i = 0 to n – 2,
    Find the lowest value in the range a[i] to a[n – 1]
    If i is not equal to the index of the lowest value found,
        Swap a[i] and a[index_of_lowest]
```

That's the basic plan. The effect will be to put the lowest value in a[0], the next lowest value in a[1], and so on. Note that by

```
For i = 0 to n – 2
```

I mean a **for** loop in which i is set to 0 during the first cycle of the loop, 1 during the next cycle of the loop, and so on, until i is set to n - 2, at which point it completes the last cycle. Each cycle of the loop places the correct element in a[i] and then increments i.

Inside the loop, a[i] is compared to a range that includes itself and all *the remaining elements* (the range a[i] to a[n - 1], which includes all elements on the *right*). By the time every value of i has been processed through the loop, the entire array will have been sorted.

Here's an example illustrating the first three cycles of the loop. The essence of the procedure is to compare each element in turn to all the elements on its right, swapping as needed.

Swap a[0] with the lowest element in this range

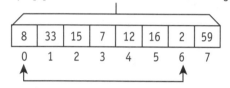

Swap a[1] with the lowest element in this range

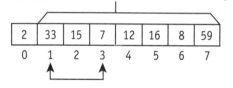

Swap a[2] with the lowest element in this range

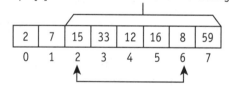

But how do we find the lowest value in the range a[i] to a[n - 1]? Remember we must be careful never to throw away an element, because we'll need it later. We need another algorithm.

What the following algorithm does is (1) start by assuming that i is the lowest element and so initialize "low" to i; and (2) whenever a lower element is found, this becomes the new "low" element.

To find the lowest value in the range a[i] to a[n – 1]:

Set low to i

For j = i + 1 to n − 1,
    If a[j] is less than a[low]
        Set low to j

This algorithm uses two additional **int** variables, j and low: j is another loop variable, and low is an integer that gets set to the index of the lowest element found so far. Whenever a lower element is found, the value of low gets updated.

We then combine the two algorithms together. After this, it's an easy matter to write the C++ code.

For i = 0 to n − 2,
    Set low to i
    For j = i + 1 to n − 1,
        If a[j] is less than a[low]
            Set low to j
    If i is not equal to low,
        Swap a[i] and a[low]

Here's the complete program that uses this algorithm to sort an array:

sort.cpp

```cpp
#include <iostream>
using namespace std;

void sort(int n);
void swap(int *p1, int *p2);
int a[10];

int main () {
    int i;
    for (i = 0; i < 10; i++) {
        cout << "Enter array element #" << i << ": ";
        cin >> a[i];
    }
    sort(10);
    cout << "Here are all the array elements, sorted:"
      << endl;
    for (i = 0; i < 10; i++)
        cout << a[i] << " "?;
    return 0;
}
```

▼ continued on next page

```
// Sort array function: sort array named a, having n
// elements.
//
void sort (int n) {
    int i, j, low;
    for(i = 0; i < n - 1; i++) {
        // This part of the loop finds the lowest
        //  element in the range i to n-1; the index
        //  is set to the variable named low.
        low = i;
        for (j = i + 1; j < n; j++)
            if (a[j] < a[low])
                low = j;
        // This part of the loop performs a swap if
        //  needed.
        if (i != low)
            swap(&a[i], &a[low]);
    }
}

// Swap function.
// Swap the values pointed to by p1 and p2.
//
void swap(int *p1, int *p2) {
    int temp = *p1;
    *p1 = *p2;
    *p2 = temp;
}
```

How It Works

Only two parts of this example are directly relevant to understanding pointers. The first is the call to the swap function, which passes the addresses of a[i] and a[low]:

```
swap(&a[i], &a[low]);
```

An important point here is that you can use the address operator (&) to take the address of array elements, just as you can with variables.

The other part of the example that's relevant to pointer use is the function definition for swap, which I described in the previous section.

```
// Swap function.
// Swap the values pointed to by p1 and p2.
//
void swap(int *p1, int *p2) {
    int temp = *p1;
    *p1 = *p2;
    *p2 = temp;
}
```

As for the sort function, the key to understanding it is to note what each part of the main loop does. The main **for** loop successively sets i to 0, 1, 2 . . . up to and including n – 2. Why n – 2? Because by the time it gets to the last element (n – 1), all the sorting will have been done. (There is no need to compare the last element to itself.)

```
for(i = 0; i < n - 1; i++) {
    //...
}
```

The first part of the loop finds the lowest element in the range that includes a[i] and all the elements *to its right*. (Items on the left of a[i] are ignored, since they've already been sorted.) An inner loop conducts this search using a variable j, initialized to start at i + 1 (one position to the right of i).

```
low = i;
for (j = i + 1; j < n; j++)
    if (a[j] < a[low])
        low = j;
```

This, by the way, is an example of a *nested loop*, and it's completely legal. A **for** statement is just another kind of statement; therefore, it can be put inside another **if, while,** or **for** statement, to any degree of complexity.

The other part of the loop has an easy job. All it has to do is ask whether i differs from the index of the lowest element (stored in the variable "low"). Remember that the != operator means "not equal." There's no reason to do the swap if a[i] is already the lowest element in the range; that's the reason for the **if** condition here.

```
if (i != low)
    swap(&a[i], &a[low]);
```

EXERCISES

Exercise 6.2.1.   Rewrite the example so that instead of ordering the array from low to high, it sorts the array in reverse order: high to low. This is actually much easier than it may look. The new program must look for the highest value in each range. You should therefore rename the variable low as "high". Otherwise, you need change only one statement; this statement involves a comparison. (Hint: that comparison is not part of a loop condition.)

Exercise 6.2.2.   Rewrite the example so that it sorts an array with elements of type **double**. (This supports more flexibility for the user to enter values into the array.) It's essential that you rewrite the swap function to work on data of the right type. But note that you should not change the type of any variables that serve as loop counters or array indexes—such variables should always have type **int**, regardless of the rest of the data.

Pointer Arithmetic

Although pass-by-reference is the most obvious example, especially when you are first learning C++, pointers have a number of important uses. One of these is efficiently processing arrays. This is not an essential feature of the language, but it is often favored by programmers trying to write the tightest possible code.

Suppose you declare an array:

```
int arr[5] = {5, 15, 25, 35, 45};
```

The elements arr[0] through arr[4], of course, can all be used like individual integer variables. You can, for example, write statements such as `arr[1] = 10;`.

But what is the expression `arr` itself? Can `arr` ever appear by itself?

Yes: `arr` is a constant that translates into an address—specifically, the address of the first element. Because it's a constant, you cannot change the value of `arr` itself. You can, however, use it to assign a value to a pointer variable:

```
int *p;
p = arr;
```

The statement `p = arr` is equivalent to this:

```
p = &arr[0];
```

So we've found a more concise, cleaner way to initialize a pointer to the address of the first element arr[0]. Is there a similar technique for the other elements? You betcha. For example, to assign p the address of arr[2]:

```
p = arr + 2;                    // p = &arr[2];
```

In fact, under the covers, C++ interprets all array references as pointer references. A reference to arr[2] translates into:

```
*(arr + 2)
```

If you've been paying close attention all along, you may at first think this looks wrong. We add 2 to the address of the start of the array, arr. But arr is an **int** array, not an array of bytes. The element arr[2] is therefore not two but rather eight bytes away (four for each integer—assuming you are using a 32-bit system)! Yet this still works. Why?

It's because of *pointer arithmetic*. Only certain arithmetic operations are allowed on pointers and other address expressions (such as arr). These are:

▶ *address_expression + integer*

▶ *integer + address_expression*

▶ *address_expression - integer*

▶ *address_expression – address_expression*

When an integer and an address expression are added together, the result is another address expression. Before the calculation is completed, however, the integer is automatically *scaled* by the size of the base type. The C++ compiler performs this scaling for you.

$$new\_address = old\_address + (integer * size\_of\_base\_type)$$

So, for example, if p has base type **int**, adding 2 to p has the effect of increasing it by 8—because 2 times the size of the base type (4 bytes) yields 8.

Scaling is an extremely convenient feature of C++ because it means that when a pointer p points to an element of an array and it is incremented by 1, this always has the effect of making p point to the next element:

```
p++;      // Point to next element in the array.
```

This in turn makes the code in the next section easier to write. It's also worth stating another cardinal rule. This is one of the most important things to remember when using pointers.

✱   **When an integer value is added or subtracted from an address expression, the compiler automatically multiplies that integer by the size of the base type.**

Address expressions can also be compared to each other. Again, you should not make assumptions about a memory layout except where array elements are involved. The following expression is always true:

```
&arr[2] < &arr[3]
```

which is another way of saying that the following is always true, just as you'd expect:

```
arr + 2 < arr + 3
```

Pointers and Array Processing

Because pointer arithmetic works the way it does, functions can access elements through pointer references rather than array indexing. The result is the same, but the pointer version (as I'll show) executes slightly faster.

In these days of incredibly fast CPUs, such minor speed increases make little difference for most programs. CPU efficiency was far more important in the 1970s, with its comparatively slow processors. CPU time was often at a premium.

But for a certain class of programs, the superior efficiency gained from C and C++ can still be useful. C and C++ are the languages of choice for people who write operating systems, and subroutines in an operating system or device driver may be called upon to execute thousands or even millions of times a second. In such cases, the small efficiencies due to pointer usage can actually matter.

Here's a function that uses direct pointer reference to zero out an integer array of size n elements.

```
void zero_out_array(int *p, int n) {
    while (n-- > 0) {        // Do n times:
        *p = 0;             //    Assign 0 to element
                            //      pointed to by p.
        p++;                //    Point to next element.
    }
}
```

This is a remarkably compact function, which would appear more compact still without the comments. (But remember that comments have no effect whatsoever on a program at runtime.)

Here's another version of the function using code that may look more familiar.

```
void zero_out_array2(int *arr, int n) {
    int i;
    for (i = 0; i < n; i++) {
        arr[i] = 0;
    }
}
```

But this version, while nearly as compact, runs a bit slower. Here's why: in the loop statement, the value of i must be scaled and added to arr each and every time through the loop, to get the location of the array element arr[i].

```
arr[i] = 0;
```

This in turn is equivalent to:

```
*(arr + i) = 0;
```

It's actually worse than that, because the scaling effect has to be done at run-time; so at the level of machine code the calculation is:

```
*(arr + (i * 4)) = 0;
```

The problem here is that the address has to be recalculated over and over again. In the direct-pointer version the address arr is only figured in once. The loop statement does less work:

```
*p = 0;
```

Of course, p has to be incremented each time through the loop; but both versions have a loop variable to update. Incrementing p is no more work than incrementing i.

Conceptually, here's how the direct-pointer version works. Each time through the loop, *p is set to 0 and then p itself is incremented to the next element. (Because of scaling, p is actually increased by 4 each time through the loop, but that's an easy operation.)

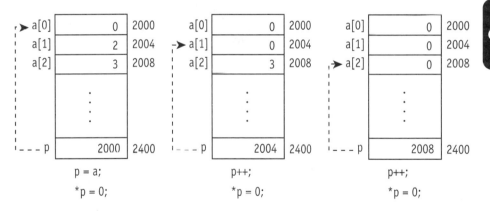

Example 6.3. *Zero Out an Array*

Here's the zero_out_array function in the context of a complete example. All this program does is initialize an array, call the function, and then print the elements so that you can see that it worked. It's not very exciting in and of itself, but it does show how this kind of pointer usage works.

zero_out.cpp

```cpp
#include <iostream>
using namespace std;

void zero_out_array(int *arr, int n);
int a[10] = {1, 2, 3, 4, 5, 6, 7, 8, 9, 10};

int main() {
    int i;
    zero_out_array(a, 10);
    // Print out all the elements of the array.
    for (i = 0; i < 10; i++)
        cout << a[i] << "  ";
    return 0;
}


// Zero-out-array function.
// Assign 0 to all elements of an int array of size n.
//
void zero_out_array(int *p, int n) {
    while (n-- > 0) {       // Do n times:
        *p = 0;             //     Assign 0 to element
                            //       pointed to by p.
        p++;                //     Point to next element.
    }
}
```

How It Works

I explained how the function zero_out_array works in the previous section, "Pointers and Array Processing." Again, the key to understanding that function is to remember that adding 1 to a pointer makes it point to the next element of an array:

```cpp
p++;
```

The other thing that's notable about this program example is that it demonstrates how to pass an array in C++. The first argument to the function is the array name. Remember that usage of an array name translates into the address of the beginning of the array (i.e., the address of its first element).

```cpp
zero_out_array(a, 10);
```

To pass an array, therefore, just use the array name. The function must expect an address expression (i.e., a pointer) as the argument type. Here the function expects an argument of type **int***, so using the array name as the argument is correct behavior: as I mentioned, this statement passes the address of the first element.

This behavior may seem a little inconsistent if you're not used to it. Remember that passing a simple variable causes a copy of the value to be passed; passing an array name passes an address. For a simple array with base type **int**, the array name has type **int***. (A two-dimensional array name has type **int****.)

Optimizing the Program

Strictly speaking, the technique described here does not optimize anything, in the sense of generating different instructions to be executed at runtime. You can, however, write even more compact code if you have a mind to.

As I've mentioned, the designers of C (the forerunner to C++) had an obsession for being able to write the most compact statements possible. This is why it's often possible to do multiple things in a single statement. This kind of programming can be dangerous unless you know what you're doing. Nevertheless. . . .

The **while** loop in the zero_out_array function does two things: zero-out an element and then increment the pointer so it points to the next element:

```
while (n-- > 0) {
    *p = 0;
    p++;
}
```

If you recall from past chapters, p++ is just an expression, and expressions can be used within larger expressions. That means we can combine the pointer-access and increment operations to produce:

```
while (n-- > 0)
    *p++ = 0;
```

What in the world does this do? To properly interpret *p++, I have to talk about two aspects of expression-evaluation that I've glossed over until now: precedence and associativity. Operators such as assignment (=) and test-for-equality (==) have relatively low precedence, meaning that they are applied only after other operations are resolved.

The pointer-indirection (*) and increment (++) operators have the same level of precedence as each other, but (unlike most operators) they associate right-to-left. Therefore, the statement *p++ = 0; is evaluated as if it were written this way:

```
*(p++) = 0;
```

This means: Increment pointer p but only after using its value in the operation

```
*p = 0;
```

Incidentally, using parentheses differently would produce an expression that is legal but not, in this case, useful.

```
(*p)++ = 0;   // Assign 0 to *p and then increment *p.
```

The effect of this statement would be to set the first array element to 0 and then to 1; p itself would never get incremented.

Whew! That's a lot of analysis required to understand a tiny piece of code. You're to be forgiven if you swear never to write such cryptic statements yourself. But now you're forearmed if you come across such code written by other C++ programmers.

Note ▶   Appendix A summarizes precedence and associativity for all C++ operators.

EXERCISES

Exercise 6.3.1.   Rewrite Example 6.3 to use direct-pointer reference for the loop that prints out the values of the array. Declare a pointer p and initialize it to start of the array. The loop condition should be p < a + 10.

Exercise 6.3.2.   Write and test a copy_array function that copies the contents of one **int** array to another array of same size and base type. The function should take two pointer arguments. The operation inside the loop should be:

```
*p1 = *p2;
p1++;
p2++;
```

If you want to write more compact but cryptic code, you can use this statement:

```
*(p1++) = *(p2++);
```

or even the following, which means the same thing:

```
*p1++ = *p2++;
```

Chapter 6   *Summary*

Several useful points were brought up in the discussion of pointers. These are summarized as follows:

▶ A pointer is a variable that can contain a numeric memory address. You can declare a pointer by using the following syntax:

```
type *p;
```

▶ You can initialize a pointer by using the address operator (&):

```
p = &n;              // Assign address of n to p.
```

▶ Once a pointer is initialized, you can use the indirection operator (*) to manipulate data pointed to by the pointer.

```
p = &n;
*p = 5;              // Assign 5 to n.
```

▶ To enable a function to manipulate data (pass by reference), pass an address.

```
double_it(&n);
```

▶ To receive an address, declare an argument having pointer type.

```
void double_it(int *p);
```

▶ An array name is a constant that translates into the address of its first element.

▶ A reference to an array element a[n] is translated into the pointer reference:

```
*(a + n)
```

▶ When an integer value is added to an address expression, C++ performs scaling, multiplying the integer by the size of the address expression's base type.

```
new_address = address_expression + (integer *
size_of_base_type)
```

▶ The unary operators * and ++ operators associate right-to-left. Consequently, this statement:

```
*p++ = 0;
```

does the same thing as the following statement, which sets *p to 0 and then increments the pointer p to point to the next element:

```
*(p++) = 0;
```

Strings: Analyzing the Text

7

Most computer programs, at some point in their life, have to communicate with a human being. Especially as you begin to write programs to be used by other people, it's important to give the user a clue to what's going.

For the console-based applications in this book, you have to use words and text in English or some other natural language (as opposed to a computer language— though sometimes I suspect that for some programmers, computer language may actually come more naturally). Working with language involves the use of text strings.

Using strings to print simple messages is easy enough. Strings get more interesting when you pick apart, combine, or analyze them. That's what this chapter is all about.

Note ▶ The last two sections in this chapter present an easier-to-use string type that is supported on more recent C++ compilers.

Text Storage on the Computer

Back in Chapter 1, I said the computer stores text numerically, just like any other kind of data. The difference is that with text data, each byte is an ASCII code that corresponds to a particular character. Suppose I created a string by using the following declaration:

```
char *str = "Hello!";
```

C++ allocates exactly seven bytes—one byte for each character and one for the terminating null byte (more about that in a moment). Here's what the string data looks like in memory:

163

Actual data:	72	101	108	108	111	33	0
ASCII code for:	'H'	'e'	'l'	'l'	'o'	'!'	(null)

You can turn to Appendix D and see the ASCII code for every character. In reality, the computer doesn't actually store alphanumeric characters; it only stores numbers. When and how, then, do the numeric values get translated into text characters?

The answer is this translation happens at least two times: when data is typed at the keyboard and when it's displayed on the monitor. For example, when you type an "H" at the keyboard, a series of actions happen at a low level that result in the ASCII for "H" (72) getting read into your program, which then stores that code in a data area.

The rest of the time, a text string is just a series of numbers—or more specifically, a series of bytes ranging in value from 0 to 255. But as programmers, we can think of C++ storing text characters in memory, one byte at a time.

Interlude

How Does the Computer Translate Programs?

Programming books sometimes point out that the CPU doesn't understand the C++ language. All the C++ statements must be translated into machine code before they can be executed. But who does the translation?

Oh, that's no mystery, say the programming books; the translation is done by the compiler—which itself is a computer program. But in that case, the computer is doing the translation.

When I was first learning how to program, this seemed to me an insolvable paradox. The CPU (the "brain" at the heart of the computer) doesn't understand a word of C++, yet it performs the translation between C++ and its own internal language. How in the world is that possible? Isn't that a contradiction?

A large part of the answer is this: C++ source code is stored in a text file, just as you might store an essay or a memo. But text characters, as I've pointed out, are stored in numeric form. When the compiler works on this data, therefore, it's doing another form of number crunching, evaluating data and making decisions according to logically precise rules.

Interlude

▼ *continued*

In case that doesn't clear things up, imagine this: you have the task of reading letters from a person who knows Japanese but no English. You, meanwhile, know English but not one word of Japanese.

But suppose you have an instruction book that tells you how to translate Japanese characters into their English-language equivalent. The instruction book itself is written in English, so you have no problem using it.

So, even though you don't understand Japanese, you're able to translate all the Japanese you want, by carefully following instructions.

That's what a computer program is, really: an instruction book read by the CPU. A computer program is an inert thing—a sequence of instructions and data—yet the "knowledge" inside a computer arises from its programs. Programs enable a computer to do all kinds of clever things—including translating a text file containing C++.

A compiler, of course, is a very special program, but what it does is not at all strange or impossible. As a computer program, it's an "instruction book," as described. What it tells how to do is to read a text file containing C++ source code, and output another instruction book: this output is your C++ program in executable form.

Did some programmers have to write machine code at some point in time? Yes. For example, the very first compilers had to be written in machine code. Later on, old compilers could be used to write new compilers . . . so that through a bootstrap process, even the most skilled programmers could rely on the writing of machine code less and less.

7

It Don't Mean a Thing If It Ain't Got That String

If you read Chapter 5, "Arrays: We've Got Their Number," you may have guessed what a string is: an array. More specifically, a string is an array of base type **char**.

Technically, **char** is an integer type, one byte wide, large enough to store 256 different values (ranging from 0 to 255). This is more than enough to contain all the different ASCII codes for the standard set of characters, including uppercase and lowercase letters, as well as numbers and a large set of punctuation marks.

There are several variations on string-declaration technique. You can create a **char** array of a definite size, but no initial values:

```
char str[10];
```

This creates a string that can hold up to 10 bytes but has yet to be initialized. (Remember that if it is global, all the values in the array are initialized to 0 by default, but if it is local, the values can be anything.) More often than not, programmers give a string an initial value when they declare it, like this:

```
char str[10] = "Hello!";
```

This declaration creates the array shown, and associates the starting address with str. (Remember that the name of an array always translates into its starting address.) In this figure, I've dispensed with showing the numeric codes and show only the character represented.

Space reserved for the string

| H | e | l | l | o | ! | \0 | | | |

The character "\0" is C++ notation for a null character: it means the actual value 0 is stored in this byte (as opposed to 48, the ASCII code for the digit "0").

String data terminates with a null byte. This is necessary because the computer needs a way of determining where the string ends. Some programming languages, such as Basic, use a hidden data structure to contain length information, but C and C++ don't use that approach.

If you don't specify a definite size, but initialize the string anyway, C++ allocates just enough space needed for the string (including its null-terminator byte).

```
char s[] = "Hello!";
char *p  = "Hello!";
```

The effect of these two statements is roughly the same. (The difference is that "s" is an array name and is therefore a constant, unlike p, which can point to different values.) C++ allocates just enough space in the data segment, and assigns the starting address to s or p:

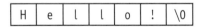

| H | e | l | l | o | ! | \0 |

String-Manipulation Functions

Just as you can call functions to crunch numbers (the **sqrt** and **rand** functions are but two examples), you can call functions to manipulate strings. The important thing to remember about these functions is that they take pointer arguments—that is, they get the addresses of the strings—but they work on the string data pointed to.

Here are some of the most commonly used string functions:

Table 7.1: C++ Common String Functions

FUNCTION	DESCRIPTION
strcpy(*s1*, *s2*)	Copy contents of s2 to destination string s1.
strcat(*s1*, *s2*)	Concatenate (join) contents of s2 onto the end of s1.
strlen(*s*)	Return length of string s (not counting terminating null).
strncpy(*s1*, *s2*, *n*)	Copy s2 to s1, but copy no more than n characters (not counting the null).
strncat(*s1*, *s2*, *n*)	Concatenate contents of s2 onto the end of s1, copying no more than n characters (not counting the null).

Possibly the most common of all are **strcpy** ("string copy") and **strcat**, which stands for "string concatenation." Here's an example of their use:

```
char s[80];
strcpy(s, "One");
strcat(s, "Two");
strcat(s, "Three ");
cout << s;
```

This produces the output:

```
OneTwoThree
```

This example, while relatively simple, illustrates some important points to keep in mind:

▶ The string variable, s, must be declared with enough space to hold all the characters in the resulting string. This is critical. C++ does nothing to ensure that there is space enough to hold all the string data necessary; this is your responsibility.

▶ Although the string is not initialized, a total of 80 bytes are reserved for it. This example assumes that storing 80 characters (including the null) will be sufficient.

▶ The string literals "One", "Two", and "Three" are all used as arguments. When a string literal appears in code, C++ allocates space for the string in the data segment, and returns the address of the data; that is, in the C++ code, a string name evaluates to an address. Therefore, "Two" and "Three" are interpreted as address arguments, just as required.

The action of the statement:

```
strcat(s, "Two");
```

looks like this:

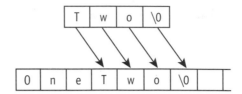

Alternatively, you can concatenate one string onto another by using string variables:

```
strcat(s1, s2);
```

There's a risk with these string functions, as you can already see: How do you guarantee, really, that the first string is large enough to include space for the existing string data along with the new?

One approach is to make the target string so large you don't think it will ever be exceeded. That can work for simple programs.

A more secure technique is to use the **strncat** and **strncpy** functions. Each of these functions avoids copying more than N characters (not including the null byte). For example, the following operation is guaranteed not to exceed the memory allocated for s1.

```
char s1[20];
// . . .
strncpy(s1, s2, 19);
strncat(s1, s3, 19 – strlen(s1));
```

You may notice that the limit of characters to copy here is 19, not 20. It's necessary to leave one extra byte for the terminating null.

Example 7.1.   *Building Strings*

Let's start with a simple string operation: building a string out of smaller strings. The following program gets a couple of strings from the user (by calling the **getline** function, described later), builds a larger string out of these smaller strings, and then prints the results.

```
buildstr1.cpp
```
```
#include <iostream>
#include <string.h>
using namespace std;
```

buildstr1.cpp, cont.

```cpp
int main() {
    char str[600];
    char name[100];
    char addr[200];
    char work[200];

    // Get three strings from the user.

    cout << "Enter name and press ENTER: ";
    cin.getline(name, 99);
    cout << "Enter address and press ENTER: ";
    cin.getline(addr, 199);
    cout << "Enter workplace and press ENTER: ",
    cin.getline(work, 199);

    // Build the output string, and then print it.

    strcpy(str, "\nMy name is ");
    strcat(str, name);
    strcat(str, ", I live at ");
    strcat(str, addr);
    strcat(str, ",\nand I work at ");
    strcat(str, work);
    strcat(str, ".");

    cout << str;

    return 0;
}
```

Here's a sample session using this program.

```
Enter name and press ENTER: Niles Cavendish
Enter address and press ENTER: 123 Mayfair Street
Enter work and press ENTER: Bozo's Carnival of Fun

My name is Niles Cavendish, I live at 123 Mayfair Street,
and I work at Bozo's Carnival of Fun.
```

How It Works

This example starts with a new include-file directive:

```
#include <string.h>
```

This is needed, because it brings in declarations for the **strcpy** and **strcat** functions. As a general rule, using any standard-library function that begins with the three letters "str" requires you to include the string.h file.

The first thing that the main function does is to declare a series of strings to hold data. The program assumes that these strings are sufficiently large that they won't be exceeded:

```
char str[600];
char name[100];
char addr[200];
char work[200];
```

It seems absurd that you'd ever want to enter a name longer than 100 characters, so these limits are probably sufficient, especially if you're writing the program for your own use.

But of course any such limits *can* be exceeded, and if you write programs for large numbers of other people, it's wise to assume that users are going to test every limit they can at some point. (This problem is addressed in Exercise 7.1.1.)

The other part of the example that's new is the use of the **getline** function:

```
cin.getline(name, 99);
```

This function call, by the way, uses an internal dot (.). This is not a typo. I explain more about this syntax in the next section. For now, just remember to include the dot.

The **getline** function gets an entire line of input: all the characters input before the user pressed ENTER. The first argument (in this case, name) specifies the destination to copy the characters to. The second argument specifies the maximum number of characters to copy; this should never be more than N-1, where N is the number of bytes allocated for the string.

After getting input into the three strings—name, addr, and work—the program builds the string. The first call is to **strcpy**, which copies string data to the beginning of str. (Calling **strcat** wouldn't produce correct results in this case, unless you knew that the first byte of str was a null—not a safe assumption here.)

```
strcpy(str, "\nMy name is ");
```

The characters "\n" are a C++ *escape sequence:* This means that they are not intended literally, but instead represent a special character. In this case, the characters "\n" denote a newline character.

The program builds the rest of the string by calling **strcat** repeatedly.

```
strcat(str, name);
strcat(str, ", I live at");
strcat(str, addr);
strcat(str, ",\nand I work at ");
strcat(str, work);
strcat(str, ".");
```

EXERCISES

Exercise 7.1.1. Rewrite the example so that it cannot exceed the limits of str. For example, you'd replace the statement

```
strcat(str, addr);
```

with the statement

```
strncat(str, addr, 599 - strlen(str));
```

Exercise 7.1.2. After completing Exercise 7.1.1, test it by experimenting with different limitations for the str string. It helps if you replace the number 600 with the symbolic constant STRMAX, putting the following **#define** directive at the beginning of the program. During preprocessing, this directive causes the compiler to replace occurrences of STRMAX in the source code with the indicated text (599).

```
#define STRMAX 599
```

You can then use STRMAX+1 to declare the length of str:

```
char str[STRMAX+1];
```

and then use STRMAX to determine how many bytes to copy:

```
strncpy(str, "\nMy name is ", STRMAX);
strncat(str, name, STRMAX - strlen(str));
```

The beauty of this approach is that if you need to change the maximum string size, you need only change one line of code (the line containing the **#define** directive) and then recompile.

Interlude

What about Escape Sequences?

Escape sequences can create some odd-looking code, if you're not used to them. Consider this statement:

```
cout << "\nand I live at";
```

This has the same effect as:

```
cout << endl << "and I live at";
```

The key to understanding a strange-looking string such as "\nand" is to remember this rule:

✳ **In C++ source code, when the compiler reads a backslash (\), the very next character is interpreted as having a special meaning.**

Aside from "\n", which represents a newline, other escape sequences include "\t" (tab) and "\b" (backspace).

Now, if you have an inquiring mind, you may be asking: How do I print an actual backslash?

The answer is simple. Two backslashes in a row (\\) represent a single backslash. For example, consider this statement:

```
cout << "\\nand I live at";
```

This prints the following text:

```
\nand I live at
```

Reading String Input

So far, I've been treating data input in a simplistic way. In previous examples, I assumed that the user types a number—for example, "15"—and that this value gets directly entered into the program. Actually, there's more to it than that.

All the data entered at a keyboard is initially text data: this means ASCII codes. So, when you're a user and you type the digits "1" and "5" at the keyboard, the first thing that happens is that these characters get put into the input stream.

Input stream:

	32	49	53	32	
Actual data: · · · | | | | | · · ·
ASCII code for: | (sp) | '1' | '5' | (sp) | |

The **cin** object, which has been told to get a number, analyzes this text input and produces a single integer value: in this case the value 15. That number gets assigned to an integer variable in a statement such as this one:

```
cin >> n;
```

If the type of n were different (say, if it had type **double**), a different conversion would be called for. Floating-point format requires a different kind of value to be produced. Normally, the **cin** object handles all this for you.

The next couple of sections look at ways to bypass the process that **cin** uses, so you can gain more control over interpreting input. Doing so requires a little more work on your part, but provides more flexibility in how you interact with the user.

The last section introduced the **getline** function, which has some strange-looking syntax:

```
cin.getline(name, 99);
```

This is our first look at member functions. The dot (.) is necessary to show that **getline** is a member of the object **cin**. Admittedly, there's some new terminology here.

I'll explain a lot more about objects starting in Chapter 10. For now, think of an object as a data structure that comes with built-in knowledge of how to do certain things. The way you call upon an object's abilities is to call a member function:

```
object.function(arguments)
```

Here's how to think about this syntax: The *object* is what the function applies to—in this case, **cin**. The *function* in this case is **getline**. There are other objects that support the **getline** function, but I won't introduce those until later. (For the record, file-input objects, introduced in Chapter 8, also support this function.)

Calling **cin.getline** is an alternative to getting input by using the stream operator (>>):

```
cin >> var;
```

We've seen this kind of statement used to get **int** and **double** data. Can you use it with strings? Yes.

```
cin >> name;
```

The problem with this statement is that it doesn't do what you might expect. Instead of getting an entire line of input—that is, all the data that the user types before pressing ENTER—it gets data up to the first white space ("white space" being programmerese for a blank space, tab, or newline). So, given this line of input:

```
Niles Cavendish
```

the effect of "cin >> name" would be to copy the letters "Niles" into the string variable, name, while "Cavendish" would remain in the input stream. (It would be left there to be picked up by the next input operation.)

The general operation of **cin** is:

▶ C++ holds all input in a hidden string buffer until the user presses ENTER. No input is forwarded until that happens. If the program needs input, it sits and waits.

▶ Once input is available, the stream operator (>>) reads no more than one field at a time—ending at a white space. Any unused input is left for the next use of >>.

So, assume the user types in the following and then presses ENTER.

```
50 3.141592 Joe Bloe
```

This works fine if you're expecting two numbers and two strings separated by a blank space. Here's the statement that would successfully read the input:

```
cin >> n >> pi >> first_name >> last_name;
```

But in general, the use of the stream input operator gives you a lack of control. I avoid it myself, except for simple test programs. One of the limitations of this operator is that it doesn't allow you to set a default value. Suppose you prompt for a number:

```
cout << "Enter number: ";
cin >> n;
```

If the user presses ENTER without typing anything, nothing happens. The computer just sits there, waiting for the user to type a number and press ENTER again. If the user keeps pressing ENTER, the program will wait forever, like a stubborn child.

Personally, I think it's much better to have the program support the behavior implied by the following prompt:

```
Enter a number (or press ENTER to specify 0):
```

Wouldn't you find it convenient to have 0 (or whatever number you choose) as a default value? But how do you implement this behavior? This next example demonstrates how.

Note ▶   If you use the **getline** function at all, you may find that further operations using the stream input operator (>>) do not work correctly. This is because the **getline** function and the stream-input operator make different assumptions about when a newline character is "consumed." It's a good idea to stick to one approach or the other.

Example 7.2. *Get a Number*

The following program gets numbers and prints their square roots, until the user either types "0" or presses ENTER directly after the prompt.

```cpp
get_num.cpp

    #include <iostream>
    #include <string.h>
    #include <math.h>
    #include <stdlib.h>
    using namespace std;

    double get_number();

    int main() {
        double x;

        for (;;) {
            cout << "Enter a number (press ENTER to exit): ";
            x = get_number();
            if (x == 0.0)
                break;
            cout << "The square root of x is: " << sqrt(x);
            cout << endl;
        }
        return 0;
    }

    // Get-number function.
    // Get number input by the user, taking only the first
    //   numeric input entered. If user presses ENTER with
    //   no input, then return a default value of 0.0.
    //
    double get_number() {
        char s[100];

        cin.getline(s, 99);
        if (strlen(s) == 0)
            return 0.0;
        return atof(s);
    }
```

You can use this same function code (get_number) in all your programs, as a better way of getting numeric input.

How It Works

The program begins by including the string.h and math.h files, which bring in type information for string functions and math functions, respectively. (The latter is needed to do square roots.) It also declares the get_number function up front:

```cpp
#include <iostream>
#include <string.h>
#include <math.h>
#include <stdlib.h>
using namespace std;

double get_number();
```

What the main function does should be familiar by now. It performs an infinite loop, which is terminated when 0 is returned by the get_number function. When any value other than zero is entered, the program calculates a square root and prints the results.

```cpp
for (;;) {
    cout << "Enter a number (press ENTER to exit): ";
    x = get_number();
    if (x == 0.0)
        break;
    cout << "The square root of x is: " << sqrt(x);
    cout << endl;
}
```

What's new here is mainly the get_number function itself. When this function calls **getline**, it gets no more and no less than an entire line of input (although all characters after the first 99 are thrown away, because the second argument to the function is 99 in this case). If the user presses ENTER directly after the prompt, **getline** returns an empty string—that's a string of length 0.

```cpp
double get_number() {
    char s[100];

    cin.getline(s, 99);
    if (strlen(s) == 0)
```

```
            return 0.0;
        return atof(s);
    }
```

Once the input line is stored in the local string, s, it's a trivial matter to return 0 if the string is empty.

```
    if (strlen(s) == 0)
        return 0.0;
```

The constant, 0.0, is equal to 0 but is stored in **double** format rather than integer format. (Remember that every constant containing a decimal point is considered a floating-point number by C++.) The function itself also has return type **double**, so using 0.0 saves the program from having to do an unnecessary conversion.

If the length of string s is not 0, then there's data in the string that needs to be converted. Because we're not relying on the stream operator (>>), the get_number function must take responsibility for interpreting data itself. It therefore needs to examine the characters read—the ASCII codes sent from the keyboard—and produce a **double** value.

Fortunately, the C++ standard library supplies a handy function—**atof**—for doing just that, and we can make use of it here. The **atof** function takes string input and produces a floating-point (**double**) value, just as its cousin **atoi** produces an **int** value.

```
    return atof(s);
```

This is a function defined in stdlib.h (which is why that file had to be included at the beginning of the program). This function has a sibling function, **atoi**, that does the same thing for integers:

```
    return atoi(s);        // Return an int value.
```

EXERCISE

Exercise 7.2.1. Rewrite Example 7.2 so that it only accepts integer input. (Hint: you'll want to change all types directly affected, from **double** to **int** format—including constants.)

Example 7.3. *Convert to Uppercase*

Later in the chapter, in Exercise 7.4 (page 181), I'm going to do some fancy string manipulation by referring to individual characters. First, however, I'll show a simple example that accesses individual characters.

upper.cpp

```cpp
#include <iostream>
#include <string.h>
#include <ctype.h>
using namespace std;

void convert_to_upper(char *s);

int main() {
    char s[100];

    cout << "Enter string to convert and press ENTER: ";
    cin.getline(s, 99);

    convert_to_upper(s);
    cout << "The converted string is:" << endl;
    cout << s;

    return 0;
}

void convert_to_upper(char *s) {
    int i;
    int length = strlen(s);

    for (i = 0; i < length; i++)
        s[i] = toupper(s[i]);
}
```

How It Works

The main purpose of this example is to show that you can manipulate individual characters of a string. To pass a string to a function, you pass its address. To do that, of course, you just give the name of the string. (This is the standard procedure to pass any kind of array.)

```cpp
convert_to_upper(s);
```

The function uses the argument passed—which, after all, is an address—to index into the string data.

```
void convert_to_upper(char *s) {
    int i;
    int length = strlen(s);

    for (i = 0; i < length; i++)
        s[i] = toupper(s[i]);
}
```

This example introduces a new function, **toupper**. This function, along with a number of others, is declared in the ctype.h include file. The two functions, **toupper** and **tolower**, operate on individual characters:

Table 7.2: toupper **and** tolower **Functions**

FUNCTION	DESCRIPTION
toupper(*c*)	If c is a lowercase letter, return the uppercase equivalent; otherwise return c as is.
tolower(*c*)	If c is an uppercase letter, return the lowercase equivalent, otherwise return c as is.

The following statement therefore converts a character to uppercase (if it is a lowercase letter), and replaces the original character with the result.

```
s[i] = toupper(s[i]);
```

EXERCISES

Exercise 7.3.1. Write a program that is similar to Example 7.3, but converts the string input to all lowercase. (Hint: use the **tolower** function from the C++ library.) Use the function name "convert_to_lower" rather than "convert_to_upper".

Exercise 7.3.2. Rewrite Example 7.3 so that it uses direct pointer reference—described at the end of Chapter 6—rather than array indexing. If you have reached the end of the string, the value of the current character is a null-terminator, so you can test for the end-of-string condition by using *p == '\0'. You can also use *p itself as the condition, because it is nonzero if it's not pointing to a zero (or null) value.

```
while (*p++)
    // Do some stuff...
```

Individual Characters vs. Strings

C++ makes a big distinction between individual characters and strings. A lot depends on whether you use single or double quotation marks.

The expression `'A'` represents a single character. During compilation C++ replaces this expression with the ASCII value for a letter 'A', which happens to be 65 (decimal).

On the other hand, the expression `"A"` represents a string of length 1. When C++ sees this expression, it places two bytes in the data area:

▶ The ASCII code for the letter `'A'`, as above.

▶ A null terminating byte.

This is a string that takes up two bytes—one for the 'A' value and one for the terminating null.

The C++ compiler then replaces the expression `"A"` *with the address* of this two-byte array. `'A'` and `"A"` are fundamentally different, because one is converted to an integer value, whereas the other represents a string and so is converted to an address.

This may seem like a lot to digest, but just remember to pay close attention to the quotation marks. The following code gives a good example of how they can be intermixed correctly:

```
char s[] = "A";
if (s[0] == 'A')
    cout << "The first letter of the string is 'A'. ";
```

This produces a correct result. But a comparison such as the following produces completely wrong results, or may not be allowed by the compiler:

```
if (s[0] == "A")                    // WRONG!
    //...
```

This fragment attempts to compare an element of the string array s with an address expression, `"A"`. The cardinal rules are:

✱ Expressions in single quotation marks (such as `'A'`) are treated as integer values after translation into ASCII codes. They are not arrays.

✱ Expressions in double quotation marks (such as `"A"`) are arrays of char, and as such are translated into addresses.

This distinction matters in the next example.

Example 7.4. *Analyze Input*

The ultimate ability in getting input is to take an entire input line and analyze its contents. This section demonstrates how. The following program gets a line of input from the user and recognizes a new "field" wherever it sees a comma. For example, given the following line of input,

    Me, Myself, Joe Bloakes

the program extracts the strings "Me", "Myself", and "Joe Bloakes". Then it stores these strings in an array and prints out the contents, so that you can verify that the program worked.

Once you know how to use commas as field delimiters, you can use any kind of delimiter you want.

Note ▶ You can achieve similar results simply by using the **strtok** ("string tokenizer") function, which I briefly describe in Appendix E. However, even though **strtok** would work fine in this example—and therefore save a fair amount of coding—it is very useful to know how to analyze input in a customized way. Then, if you ever need to analyze a string in a way that **strtok** does not support, you'll be able to write it.

lexi.cpp

```cpp
#include <iostream>
#include <string.h>
using namespace std;

int get_a_string(char *buffer, char *s, int start);

char strs[10][100];

int main() {
    int i;
    int n;
    int pos = 0;
    char buffer[200];

    cout << "Enter strings, separated by commas,";
    cout << endl << "and press ENTER: ";
    cin.getline(buffer, 199);
```

▼ *continued on next page*

```
        for (i = 0; i < 10; i++) {
            pos = get_a_string(buffer, strs[i], pos);
            if (pos == -1)
                break;
        }
        if (i == 11)
            n = 10;
        else
            n = i;

        cout << n << " strings were read." << endl;
        for (int i = 0; i < n; i++)
            cout << strs[i] << endl;

        return 0;
    }

// Get-a-string function.
// Starting at position "start," read next substring
//    from buffer into target string s.
//    Return position of first unread character;
//    return -1 if there are no characters to read.
//
int get_a_string(char *buffer, char *dest, int pos) {
    int i = pos, j = 0;

    // "Consume" initial comma and blank space(s).

    while (buffer[i] == ',' || buffer[i] == ' ')
        i++;

    // Return -1 if at end of buffer.

    if (buffer[i] == '\0')
        return -1;

    // Read characters into target string, until
    //    comma or end-of-string encountered.

    while (buffer[i] != ',' && buffer[i] != '\0')
        dest[j++] = buffer[i++];
```

```
// Terminate target string and return position
//   of first unread character.

dest[j] = '\0';
return i;
}
```

How It Works

This program has to do a number of things just right to avoid errors. It's easy enough to understand, however, if you look at each part of it carefully.

The first thing the program does, after the usual **#include** directives and declarations, is to declare an array of 10 strings, each of which can hold up to 100 bytes:

```
char strs[10][100];
```

It's important to declare the array this way. The following declaration, although it is allowed by the compiler (i.e., it's not syntactically wrong), would do the wrong thing.

```
char *strs[10];
```

This declaration would declare an array of 10 pointers, each of them having type **char***. The problem is that such a declaration allocates no space at all for the string data itself. We've seen this sort of declaration work fine when all the strings are initialized:

```
char *band[4] = {"John", "Paul", "George", "Ringo"};
```

Pointers are four bytes wide, so this declaration allocates 16 bytes (4 times 4) for the array. Because of the initializations on the right, the declaration also allocates just enough space for each of the strings "John", "Paul", etc., including a terminating null byte for each. None of those strings has any room to grow. And without the initialization, no room would be allocated for string data at all.

But the declaration of strs as a 10 by 100 array of **char** reserves 1,000 bytes—enough space for ten strings, each of which can store a maximum of 99 characters plus one for the terminating null.

After getting a line of input, the principal loop in **main** makes repeated calls to the get_a_string function—continuing to call it as long as there is another substring to read and no more than 10 substrings have been read.

```
for (i = 0; i < 10; i++) {
    pos = get_a_string(buffer, strs[i], pos);
```

```
    if (pos == -1)
        break;
}
```

The first statement within the body of the loop does the job of getting the next substring and copying it to the string array. The get_a_string function starts reading characters at the position indicated by pos, which is initialized to 0.

```
pos = get_a_string(buffer, strs[i], pos);
```

Each call to the get_a_string function returns the position of the first character not read. So, after the first call to this function, the string looks like this:

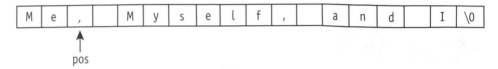

The value of pos, in this example, is therefore 2. (Remember that all arrays, including strings, are zero-based.) This value is fed back into pos to set up the *next* call to get_a_string, so that the function then reads characters starting at index 2. After this read, pos will be set to 10.

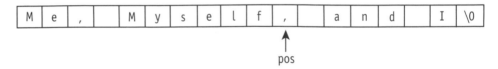

This process continues until there is no more data to read. If the function returns -1, that means there is no more input; the loop exits early:

```
    if (pos == -1)
        break;
```

As for the get_a_string definition, here is the function's mandate:

▶ Return -1 if there is nothing left to read;

▶ Otherwise, copy characters into the specified destination string and return the position of the first unread character.

The function has to accommodate several possibilities. After the first time the function is called, the new position will usually index a comma. This is because the function stops when it sees a comma, and doesn't read it.

Therefore, any given call to the function may have to read past an initial comma and leading spaces, if any. These are "consumed" (or "eaten," if you prefer), which means that they are read and ignored. If, after attempting to read commas and spaces, the function is at the end of the string, it returns immediately with a value of -1.

```
// "Consume" initial comma and blank space(s).

while (buffer[i] == ',' || buffer[i] == ' ')
    i++;

// Return -1 if at end of buffer.

if (buffer[i] == '\0')
    return -1;
```

The next step is easy: copy characters into the destination-string argument, s. Remember that j is the position to read characters to in the destination string, s; so j is initialized to 0. i is initialized to the value of the current-position indicator within the input string.

```
// Read characters into target string, until
//    comma or end-of-string encountered.

while (buffer[i] != "," && buffer[i] != '\0')
    dest[j++] = buffer[i++];
```

After the last cycle of this **while** loop, i points to the first unread character (either a comma or a terminating null), and j points to the end of the destination string. All that remains, then, is to terminate the destination string and returning the value of i:

```
dest[j] = '\0';
return i;
```

EXERCISES

Exercise 7.4.1.   Rewrite Example 7.4 so that it uses blank spaces as delimiters; that is, it starts reading a new substring after each series of one or more blank spaces. This is an easy exercise if you understand the example, because you only have to change two lines in the function get_a_string; the rest of the program remains exactly the same. (Hint: one of these changes is to alter the conditions under which the function stops reading characters into a substring.)

Exercise 7.4.2.   Rewrite the example so that the get_a_string function uses only two arguments: a starting address to read characters from in the input string, and (as before) the address of the destination string. The function should return the address of the first unread character. Or, if no string was read, it should return a null pointer, as follows:

```
return (char*) 0;
```

This version of the example uses essentially the same logic, but by using a starting address—rather than a combination of array address and starting-position index—it reduces the number of arguments. The get_a_line function should have the following declaration:

```
char *get_a_string(char *start_addr, char *dest);
```

The function definition itself can use either array indexing or the direct-pointer reference technique described in Chapter 6.

The New C++ String Class

Recent versions of C++ support a new, easier-to-use string type. Because this type is an extended type defined by the standard library, it is, technically speaking, a class. The concept of a *class* is something that we'll return to—with a vengeance—in Chapter 10.

✱   **A class is a data type defined by the program or by a library.**

✱   **In C++, such types look and act just like intrinsic data types (int, double, etc.) and can have operations defined for them.**

For the rest of the chapter, I refer to this new type (or rather, this class) simply as **string**. The **string** type hides most of the details of handling character data.

The old string type hides none of the details; it is just a pointer to an array of **char**. For convenience, I refer to these old-style strings as **char*** strings.

There are two reasons I've waited until now to present this easier-to-use **string** class:

▶ Not all C++ compilers come with library support for the new **string** class. If your compiler lacks this support, you need to know how to work with old-style **char*** strings. (Note: Chapter 15 explains how to define your own String class, which has many of the features presented here.)

▶ The use of **char*** strings can't be avoided altogether. String constants (that is, string literals) still have **char*** type. You can't perform any of the extended **string** operations on a **char*** string without involving a **string** variable.

With these caveats in mind, let's proceed to the subject of the **string** class.

Include String-Class Support

To use the new **string** type, the first thing you need to do is to turn on support for it by using an #include <string> directive. This is not exactly the same directive that enables string support in the function library.

```
#include <string>        // Support new string class
```

In constrast, the following directive turns on support for functions that work with old-style **char*** strings:

```
#include <string.h>      // Support old-style functions:
                         //  strcmp, strlen, etc.
```

What a difference the .h makes! By the way, you can include support for *both* libraries at the same time, if you want. You would probably do this rarely, of course, because the **string** class usually makes old-style string functions support unnecessary.

```
#include <string>        // Support new string class
#include <string.h>      // Support old-style functions
```

As with **cin** and **cout**, the name **string** must be qualified with the **std** prefix, unless you include the following statement, which recognizes all names in the **std** namespace:

```
using namespace std;
```

You can choose not to include this statement, but in that case, the new type must be referred to as **std::string**. (Likewise, **cin** and **cout** would have to be referred to as **std::cin** and **std::cout**.)

Declare and Initialize Variables of Type string

Once you have turned on support for the **string** class, it's easy to use it to declare variables.

```
string a, b, c;
```

This statement creates three variables having **string** type. Already, this should strike you as simpler than using C-style strings. You can declare these variables without worrying about how much space they need.

You can initialize the strings in a number of ways. Here's how to initialize them upon declaration:

```
string a("Here is a string."), b("Here is another.");
```

You can also use the assignment operator (=) to set their values.

```
string a, b;
a = "Here is a string."
b = "Here is another."
```

You can also combine the declaration and assignment steps. The effect is the same as initialization.

```
string a = "Here is a string. ";
```

Note that you have to use string constants ("Here is a string.", "Here is another.") to initialize these variables. As I mentioned earlier, string constants are old-style **char*** strings. You convert them by assigning them to variables having **string** type.

Working with Variables of Type string

The **string** class works as you'd probably expect—especially if you've worked with any version of Basic. Unlike old-style **char*** strings, you don't need to call a function to copy or compare contents.

For example, assume you have the following strings:

```
string cat("Persian");
string dog("Dane");
```

You can freely assign new string data to these variables, without worrying about capacity issues. The string named dog, for example, automatically grows as needed.

```
dog = "Persian";
```

You can compare contents by using the test-for-equality operator (==). With the **string** class, this comparison does what you'd expect; it evaluates to **true** if the contents are the same. (To perform such a comparison with two **char*** strings, you'd need to call **strcmp**.)

```
if (cat == dog)    // This condition is now TRUE
    cout << "cat and dog have the same name.";
```

To copy from one **string** variable to another, use the assignment operator (=). With the string class, assignment is defined so that it does what you'd expect: copy the contents from one string to another.

```
string country = dog;     // Copy string contents.
```

As in Basic, you can concatenate strings by using the addition operator (+):

```
string str = a + b;
```

You can even embed string constants in this kind of operation:

```
string str = a + " " + b;
```

However, the following statement does not compile.

```
string str = "The dog " + "is my friend.";  // ERROR!
```

The problem is that although the addition sign (+) is supported as a concatenation operator between two **string** variables, or between a **string** variable and a **char*** string, it is not supported between two **char*** strings.

Remember that use of the **string** class does not change the nature of all strings in C++; it creates a new class that has extended operations defined for it. Constants are still simple, null-terminated arrays of **char**.

Input and Output

Variables of type **string** work smoothly with **cin** and **cout**, just as you'd expect.

```
string prompt = "Enter your name: ";
string name;
cout << prompt;
cin >> name;
```

Use of **cin** in this context has the same drawback that it does with old-style, **char*** strings: characters are returned from the keyboard up until the first whitespace character (such as a space or a tab).

You can use the **getline** function to put an entire line of input into a **string** variable. This version is a global rather than a member function.

```
getline(cin, name);
```

In contrast to the earlier version of **getline**, this version does not require you to enter a maximum number of characters to read. There is no need for a maximum number, because the string will be exactly as big as it needs to be to contain any line of input.

Example 7.5. *Building Strings with the string Type*

This example performs the same action as Example 7.1, except that it uses **string** variables.

buildstr2.cpp

```cpp
#include <iostream>
#include <string>
using namespace std;

int main() {
    string str, name, addr, work;

    // Get three strings from the user.

    cout << "Enter name and press ENTER: ";
    getline(cin, name);
    cout << "Enter address and press ENTER: ";
    getline(cin, addr);
    cout << "Enter workplace and press ENTER: ",
    getline(cin, work);

    // Build the output string, and then print it.

    str = "\nMy name is " + name + ", " +
          "I live at " + addr +
          ",\nand I work at " + work + ".\n";

    cout << str;

    return 0;
}
```

How It Works

If anything, this version of the program is a good deal easier to write than the version in Exercise 7.1. The first difference is the **include** directive, which must refer to <string>, not <string.h>.

```cpp
#include <string>
using namespace std;
```

The **using namespace** statement, as usual, enables you to refer to **std** symbols (such as **cin**, **cout**, and also **string**) without a **std** pefix.

For the rest, things get easier. This version of the program declares four string variables without worrying about how much space to reserve. Remember that these strings automatically grow or contract in storage capacity, as needed.

```
string str, name, addr, work;
```

Likewise, the program then calls the **getline** function, without needing to specify maximum number of characters to read.

```
cout << "Enter name and press ENTER: ";
getline(cin, name);
cout << "Enter address and press ENTER: ";
getline(cin, addr);
cout << "Enter workplace and press ENTER: ",
getline(cin, work);
```

Finally, the program builds the string. This is easy to do, because the addition operator (+) is supported for the **string** class, giving a concise way to represent string concatenation.

```
str = "\nMy name is " + name + ", " +
      "I live at " + addr +
      ",\nand I work at " + work + ".\n";
```

Finally, the constructed string is printed, just as in the other version.

```
cout << str;
```

EXERCISES

Exercise 7.5.1.   Get three pieces of information from the user: a dog's name, its breed, and its age. Then print a sentence that uses this information.

Exercise 7.5.2.   Rewrite one of the Card-Dealing programs in Chapter 5 by using the **string** class. (Hint: to declare an array of **string**, treat it just like an array of any other fundamental data type. You'll still need to allocate enough space for array members, but each string is treated as a unit. No pointer syntax is required. Treat an array of **string** like a simple array of **int** or **double**.)

Other Operations on the string Type

The new **string** type wouldn't be too useful if you couldn't access string contents. Fortunately, you can index individual characters with the same syntax used to access characters of **char*** strings.

```
string[index]
```

For example, the following code prints out individual characters of a string, one to a line. (Admittedly, this isn't something you'd do very often in a real program, but it does demonstrate the power of the feature.)

```
#include <string>
using namespace std;
//...
string dog = "Mac";
for (int i = 0; i < dog.size(); i++)
    cout << dog[i] << endl;
```

When run, this code prints:

```
M
a
c
```

As with **char*** strings (or for that matter, any array in C++), string variables use zero-based indexing. This is why the initial setting for i is 0.

The loop condition depends on the length of the string. With a **char*** string, you'd find this length by calling the **strlen** function:

```
char doggy[] = "Sam";
```

```
int length = strlen(doggy);
```

With the **string** type, you find the length by calling the **size** member function:

```
string dog = "Napoleon";
```

```
int length = dog.size();
```

Because the **string** type is a C++ class, it is designed to be used with member functions rather than standard function calls. Syntactically, there's little new about member-function calls other than the fact that they use the *object.function* syntax. The syntax for getting the length of a string is simple.

```
string.size()
```

By using the index operator ([]) and the **size** member function, you can perform many operations on **string** variables. For example, the following code converts the characters in a string to all-uppercase.

```
#include <string>
#include <ctype.h>
using namespace std;
```

```
//...
string name = "Grandmaster Trash";
for (int i = 0; i < name.size(); i++)
    name[i] = toupper(name[i]);
```

Note ▶ Technically, a **string** variable is a simple object and not an array. The reason that a **string** variable supports indexing is that the brackets ([]) are defined as an operator for the type. In effect, indexing is simulated. Do not assume that you can treat a **string** variable the same way you'd treat an array in all contexts; in particular, the name of a **string** variable does not equate to the address of the first character.

In addition to the **size** function, the string class supports a number of other useful member functions. Here is a summary of some of the functions that are most commonly used.

Table 7.3: Member Functions of the String Class

FUNCTION (WITH SYNTAX)	ACTION
string.**assign**(*string2*, *start*, *num*)	Get the substring in *string2* starting at position *start* and *num* characters long; then copy this data into *string*.
string.**empty**()	Return **true** if *string* has zero length, **false** otherwise.
string.**find**(*substring*, *start*)	Search for first occurrence of *substring* within *string*; start the search at position *start*.
string.**insert**(*start*, *substring*)	Insert the contents of *substring* into *string*; insert at position *start*.
string.**replace**(*start*, *num*, *newstring*)	Replace the substring within *string*—starting at position *start* and *num* characters long—with the contents of *newstring*.
string.**swap**(*string2*)	Swap the contents of *string* and *string2*.

Chapter 7 *Summary*

Here are the main points of Chapter 7:

▶ Text characters are stored in the computer according to their ASCII codes. For example, the string "Hello!" is represented by the byte values 72, 101, 108, 108, 111, 33, and 0 (for the terminating null).

▶ Every string in C and C++ must have a terminating null—a 0 byte value. This enables string-handling functions to determine where the string ends. When you declare a string literal such as "Hello!", C++ automatically allocates space for this terminating null along with the other characters.

▶ The current length of a string (determined by searching for the terminating null) is not the same as the amount of total storage reserved for the string. The following declaration reserves 10 bytes of storage for str, but initializes it so that its current length is only six. The string will have three unused bytes as a result, enabling it to grow later on if needed.

```
char str[10] = "Hello!";
```

▶ Library functions such as **strcpy** (string copy) and **strcat** (string concatenation) can alter the length of an existing string. When you perform these operations, it's important that the string have enough space reserved to accommodate the new string length.

▶ The **strlen** function gets the current length of the string.

▶ Include the string.h file to provide type information for string-handling functions.

```
#include <string.h>
```

▶ If you try to increase the length of a string without having the necessary space reserved, you'll overwrite another variable's data area, creating hard-to-find bugs.

```
char str[] = "Hello!";
strcat(str, " So happy to see you.");   // ERROR!!!!
```

▶ To ensure that you don't copy too many characters to a string, you can use the **strncat** and **strncpy** functions.

```
char str[100];
strncpy(str, s2, 99);
strncat(str, s2, 99 – strlen(str));
```

▶ The stream operator (>>), used with the **cin** object, provides only limited control over input. When you use it to send data to a string address, it only gets the characters up to the first white space (blank, tab, or newline).

▶ To get a full line of input, use the **cin.getline** function. The second argument specifies the maximum number of characters to copy to the string (not counting the terminating null).

```
cin.getline(input_string, max);
```

▶ An expression such as `'A'` represents a single integer value (after translation into ASCII code); an expression such as `"A"` represents an array of **char** and is therefore translated into an address.

▶ Recent versions of C++ support a new **string** class, which is similar to the **char*** string type but is easier to use. You can declare **string** variables without worrying about how much string space they need. To switch on support for this class, use the `#include <string>` directive.

```
#include <string>
using namespace std;

string str;
```

▶ Assigning to a **string** variable causes string data to be copied (similar in effect to the **strcpy** function). The test-for-equality operator (−−) causes string contents to be compared (similar to the **strcmp** function).

```
string dog = "Red Rover";
if (dog == "Red Rover")
    cout << "The strings have same contents.";
```

▶ You can access individual characters within a **string** variable by using brackets, just as you would with a **char*** variable. But bear in mind that **string** variables are not true arrays. The **size()** member function gets the current length of string data.

```
if (int i = 0; i < dog.size(); i++)
    cout << dog[i] << endl;
```

▶ Remember that string constants have the old-style **char*** type. Operations are defined between **char*** and **string** objects, but not between two **char*** objects.

Files: Electronic Storage

So far, the programs in this book have performed calculations and printed results. That's a good start, but it only takes you so far in the real world.

Most practical applications (reservation systems, database systems, spreadsheets, and even games) store and retrieve persistent information. This is data that hangs around after the program ends, and even after the computer is turned off.

In contrast, main memory ("RAM") is certainly a kind of storage, but it's not persistent. As soon as the computer loses power, all the data in memory is lost forever (which is why you kick yourself if you don't save to disk in Word often enough). But even if main memory were more permanent—even if it didn't zero out when the computer shuts down—main memory is too precious a resource to be dedicated to persistent records.

So when you need a receptacle in which to place data for later use, put it in disk files.

Introducing File-Stream Objects

As you've used **cin** and **cout** (console input and output), you've already made use of objects. Now it's time to introduce a few more objects.

C++ provides classes of file-stream objects that support the same set of function calls and operators that **cin** and **cout** do. (Actually, they support a superset.) In object-oriented lingo, we'd say these objects support the same interface as **cin** and **cout**.

The terms *file* and *stream* are closely related. A stream is anything to which you can read or write data. The term evokes a picture of an endless flow of data like a small river, and although not all streams are endless, it's a useful image.

The term *stream* refers to all kinds of data i/o channels—console as well as to disk files—whereas a *file stream* refers only to disk files.

File-stream objects come in several types:

▶ File-input objects, which can be used just like **cin**.

▶ File-output objects, which can be used just like **cout**.

▶ File-input/output objects, which support the capabilities of both. (This is required for random access, presented in the last two sections of this chapter.)

File streams can also use text mode or binary mode. I'll start with text mode, because it's the easiest to understand.

Writing to a text file involves a few simple steps. The first step is to turn on support for file-stream operations by using the following **#include** directive:

```
#include <fstream>
```

This enables support for file-stream operations.

The second step is to create a file-stream object. I've chosen the name "fout" for convenience, but you could choose any name you want (such as "MyStupid-File," "RoundFile," or whatever). When you create this object, initialize it by specifying the name of the disk file to write to. Here, I've specified an output file named output.txt.

```
ofstream fout("output.txt");  // Open disk file
                              // output.txt
```

The object has type **ofstream**. When you open file streams, you can use the following types:

▶ **ofstream**, for file-output streams

▶ **ifstream**, for file-input streams

▶ **fstream**, a generic file stream (to which you have to specify input, output, or both when you open it—more on that later).

After the object is successfully created, you can write to it just as you would write to **cout**. This is the third and final step.

```
fout << "This is a line of text.";
```

For example, you could create the following variation on Example 1.2, writing to the disk file output.txt instead of to the console.

```
#include <fstream>
// ...
```

```
ofstream fout("output.txt");  // Open disk file
                              // output.txt
fout << "I am Blaxxon," << endl;
fout << "the cosmic computer.";
```

Conceptually, here's how to think of the action of the stream operator <<
when used with a file-stream object:

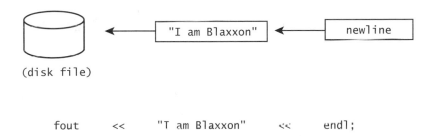

(disk file)

But unlike **cout**, file-stream objects are not unique. You can have multiple file-
stream objects—one for each file you want to interact with.

```
ofstream  out_file_1("memo.txt");
ofstream  out_file_2("messages.txt");
```

There's another difference between console and disk-file objects. When you
are done reading or writing to a file, it's a good idea to call the **close** function.
This causes the program to give up access to the file so someone else can use it.
C++ will close the file for you when the program exits successfully, but it's not a
bad idea to do it yourself.

```
out_file_1.close();
out_file_2.close();
```

How to Refer to Disk Files

In the last section I showed how you can create a file object by specifying the file's
name. If successful, this declaration *opens* the file for output, meaning you can
then write to it; it also gives you exclusive access.

```
ofstream fout("output.txt");
```

But where is the file located? If you searched the computer, where would you
find it?

By default, the file referred to is in the current directory—the directory from
which you run the program. (Or to use Windows or Macintosh lingo, this is
the current *folder*.) But you can, if you want, specify a complete path name,

optionally including a drive letter. This is all part of the complete file name—or more precisely, the *file specification,* a term used in reference manuals.

For example, you can open a file in the root directory of C: drive.

```
ofstream fout("c:\\output.txt");
```

The string literal here uses the C++ backslash notation. In the previous chapter, I explained that the backslash character has a special meaning in C++ programs: for example, \n represents a newline and \t represents a tab. To represent the backslash itself, use two in a row. So, the string `c:\\output.txt` in a C++ program code names this file

```
c:\output.txt
```

When you enter `c:\\output.txt` into program code, C++ does not put two backslashes in a string. Rather, it puts a single backslash for each occurrence of \\; C++ merely *interprets* \\ in program code as representing a single backslash, just as it interprets \n to mean a newline.

As another example, the following statement creates a file-stream output object located in the c:\programs\text directory:

```
ofstream fout("c:\\programs\\text\\output.txt");
```

This opens the file

```
c:\programs\text\output.txt
```

Example 8.1.   *Write Text to a File*

The example in this section does about the simplest thing you can do with a text file: open it, write a couple of lines of text, and exit.

The program prompts the user for the name of a file to write to. As a user, you enter the exact file name, including drive letter and complete path if desired. Do not use two backslashes to represent one: that is only a notational convention within C++ program code and has no affect on the user or on how strings are stored generally.

For example, you might enter:

```
c:\documents\output.txt
```

Note ▶   This program will replace whatever file you specify, destroying its old contents. Therefore, when you run it, be careful not to enter the name of an existing file unless you don't mind losing that file's contents.

Here's the program.

```
writetxt.cpp

    #include <iostream>
    #include <fstream>
    using namespace std;

    int main() {
        char filename[81];

        cout << "Enter a file name and press ENTER: ";
        cin.getline(filename, 80);
        ofstream file_out(filename);
        if (! file_out) {
            cout << "File " << filename;
            cout << " could not be opened.";
            return -1;
        }
        cout << "File " << filename << " was opened.";
        file_out << "I am Blaxxon," << endl;
        file_out << "the cosmic computer." << endl;
        file_out << "Fear me.";
        file_out.close();
        return 0;
    }
```

After running this program, you'll probably want to view its contents, to verify that the program wrote the text successfully. You can use any text editor or word processor to do that. (Or, if you are inside an MS-DOS Command shell, you can use the TYPE command.)

Note ▶ Once again, bear in mind that if you run this program and give it the name of an existing file, the program will quite happily overwrite that file. So, be careful!

How It Works

The beginning of the program turns on support for the iostream and fstream portions of the C++ library.

```
    #include <iostream>
    #include <fstream>
    using namespace std;
```

There is only one function, **main**. The first thing it does is to prompt for a file name.

```
char filename[81];

cout << "Enter a file name and press ENTER: ";
cin.getline(filename, 80);
```

Then it creates a file object, file_out.

```
ofstream file_out(filename);
```

This statement attempts to open the file named by the user. If the attempt to open the file was unsuccessful, a null value is placed in file_out. This value can this be tested in an **if** statement. (Remember that a null, or zero, value equates to false in this context.).

If the file was not successfully opened, the program prints an error message and exits. Remember that the logical negation operator (!) reverses the true/false value.

```
if (! file_out) {
    cout << "File " << filename;
    cout << " could not be opened.";
    return -1;
}
```

Why would the attempt to open the file ever fail?

There are a couple of things that could go wrong. The most obvious possibility is that the user did not enter a valid file specification. Another is that the user attempted to open a file that has been given read-only privileges by the operating system, and so cannot be overwritten.

If the file was successfully opened, the program proceeds to write several text strings and then close the stream.

```
cout << "File " << filename << " was opened.";
file_out << "I am Blaxxon," << endl;
file_out << "the cosmic computer." << endl;
file_out << "Fear me."
file_out.close();
return 0;
```

EXERCISES

Exercise 8.1.1.   Rewrite Example 8.1 so that it prompts for directory location and file name separately, rather than expecting both in one input line. (Hint: use two strings and use the **strcat** function to join them.)

Exercise 8.1.2. Write a program that lets the user enter any number of lines of text, one at a time. In effect, this creates a primitive editor that permits text entry but no editing of a line of text after it's been entered. Set up a loop that doesn't terminate until the user presses ENTER without typing any text (a zero-length string).

Alternatively, you can recognize a special code (for example, "@@@") to terminate the session. You can then use the **strcmp** ("string compare") function to determine if a line of text signals the "exit" condition.

```
if (strcmp(input_line, "@@@"))
    break;
```

Remember to print a short prompt before each line of text, such as:

```
Enter (@@@ to exit)>>
```

Hint: to write this program, prompt the user for an entire line of input (use the **getline** function) and then write this input to the file.

Example 8.2. *Display a Text File*

After you create and write to a file, you'll want to be able to view it. You can already do that with a variety of applications (such as Notepad in the Windows environment). You can also create your own programs for viewing a file.

Writing a complete, full-service text editor is beyond the scope of this book. But the examples in this chapter cover some of the basic elements. The main thing any word processor or text editor does is open a file, read lines of text, let the user manipulate those lines of text (which, after all, are just strings), and then write out the changes.

This example displays 24 lines of text at a time, asking the user whether or not to continue. The user can print another 24 lines or quit.

readtxt.cpp

```cpp
#include <iostream>
#include <fstream>
using namespace std;

int main() {
    int c;   // input character
    int i;   // loop counter
    char filename[81];
    char input_line[81];
```

readtxt.cpp, cont.

```
        cout << "Enter a file name and press ENTER: ";
        cin.getline(filename, 80);

        ifstream file_in(filename);

        if (! file_in) {
            cout << "File " << filename;
            cout << " could not be opened.";
            return -1;
        }

        while (1) {
            for (i = 1; i <= 24 && ! file_in.eof(); i++) {
                file_in.getline(input_line, 80);
                cout << input_line << endl;
            }
            if (file_in.eof())
                break;
            cout << "More? (Press 'Q' and ENTER to quit.)";
            cin.getline(input_line, 80);
            c = input_line[0];
            if (c == 'Q' || c == 'q')
                break;
        }
        return 0;
    }
```

How It Works

This example is similar to Example 8.1 but is a little more involved, mainly because it checks a couple of different conditions to determine if it should keep reading more lines.

After determining if the file stream was successfully opened (and exiting if it wasn't), the program sets up an infinite loop that exits when either of the following conditions are true:

▶ The end of the file is reached.

▶ The user indicates that he or she does not want to continue.

Here's the main loop in skeletal form:

```
while (1) {
    // ...
}
```

Within this main loop, the program reads up to 24 lines—less if the end of the file is reached first. The easy way to implement this is to use a **for** loop with a complex condition:

```
for (i = 1; i <= 24 && ! file_in.eof(); i++) {
    file_in.getline(input_line, 80);
    cout << input_line << endl;
}
```

The loop continues only as long as i is less than or equal to 24, and the end-of-file condition is not detected. The expression

```
file_in.eof()
```

returns true if the end of the file has been reached. Logical "not" (!) reverses this condition, so that ! `file_in.eof()` returns true only as long as there is more data to read.

The rest of the main loop checks to see if it should continue; if not, it breaks out of the loop and the program ends.

```
if (file_in.eof())
    break;
cout << "More? (Press 'Q' and ENTER to quit.)";
cin.getline(input_line, 1);
c = input_line[0];
if (c == 'Q' || c == 'q')
    break;
```

EXERCISES

Exercise 8.2.1.   Alter the example so the user can optionally enter a number in response to the "More?" prompt. The number determines how many lines to print at a time instead of 24. (Hint: use the **atoi** library function to convert string input to integer; if the value entered is greater than 0, modify the numbers of lines to read.)

Exercise 8.2.2.   Alter the example so that it prints the contents of the file in all-uppercase letters. You may find it helpful to copy some of the code from Exercise 7.3 on page 178.

Text Files vs. "Binary" Files

So far, we've used files as streams of text; you read and write to these files as you would the console. If you view the file with a text editor—or send the file contents directly to the console—you'll see the contents in human-readable form.

For example, when you write the number "255" to a text file, the program writes the ASCII character codes for "2", "5", and "5".

```
file_out << 255;
```

But there's another way to write data to a file: write the values directly. Instead of writing the ASCII character codes for the characters making up the string "255", you'd write the value 255 itself. If you then tried to view the file with a text editor, you wouldn't see the numerals "255". Instead, the text editor would try to show you ASCII code 255, which is not a printable character.

Programming manuals talk about two kinds of files:

▶ Text files, which you read and write to as you would the console. Usually, every byte written to a text file is the ASCII code of a printable character.

▶ So-called binary files, which you read and write to using the actual numeric values of the data. With this approach, ASCII codes are not involved.

This second technique may sound simpler, but, paradoxically, it's not. To view such a file in a meaningful way, you need an application that understands what the fields of the file are supposed to be and how to interpret them. Are a group of bytes to be interpreted as integer, floating-point, or string data? And where does one group of bytes start and another begin? In the case of strings, you're still writing ASCII character codes, of course. But otherwise, binary files do not involve ASCII codes.

When you create a file-stream object, you can specify text mode (the default) or binary mode. The mode setting itself changes one important detail:

✳ **In text mode, each newline character (ASCII 10) is translated into a carriage return-linefeed pair during a write operation.**

Let's consider why the translation is necessary for text mode.

Early in the book—as far back as Chapter 1—the examples used newline characters. These can be printed separately or embedded in the strings themselves.

```
char *msg_string = "Hello\nYou\n";
```

Strings use a single byte (ASCII code 10) to indicate a newline. But when the string is printed on the console, two operations need to be performed: print a carriage return (ASCII code 13), which moves the cursor to the beginning of the line, and print a linefeed (ASCII code 10).

When a string is written to the console, each newline in memory is translated into a carriage return-linefeed pair. For example, here's what the string `Hello\nYou\n` looks like when stored in main memory and what it looks like when written to the console.

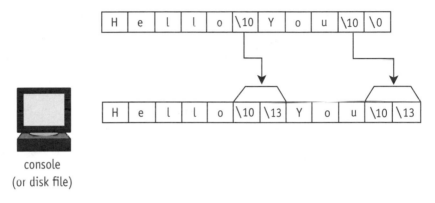

console
(or disk file)

Okay, you say. So this translation must be done when printing strings on the console. But is it necessary for text files as well?

Yes, and for a good reason. Data sent to a text file must have the same format as data sent to the console. This allows C++ to treat all streams of text (whether console or on disk) exactly the same way. Only the destination changes.

But with a binary file, it's important that no translation be performed. The value 10 may occur in the middle of a numeric field, and it must not be interpreted as a newline. If you translated this value wherever you found it, you'd likely create many errors.

There's another difference—probably the most important—between text-mode and binary-mode operations. It concerns the choices you make as a programmer.

▶ If a file is opened in text mode, you should use the same operations used for communicating with the console; these involve the stream operators (<<, >>) and the **getline** function.

▶ If a file is opened in binary mode, you should transfer data only by using the **read** and **write** member functions. These are direct read/write operations.

In the next section, I discuss these two functions.

Interlude

Are "Binary Files" Really More Binary?

The reason people use the term "binary file" is because with such a file, if you write the byte value 255, you're actually writing the binary expansion of 255, shown here as a string of 1s. This is because, ultimately, *all* data is stored as binary.

11111111

The use of the term "binary" is in some ways misleading. If you write "255" as text, you're still writing binary data—except that now each of these binary values is an ASCII character code. Conceptually, programmers tend to think of this as "text" format as opposed to "binary," because a text editor displays the file as text and does not trouble you with binary representation.

Incidentally, here's how "255" is actually written in text mode.

00110010   00110101   00110101

This binary sequence represents the numbers 50, 53, and 53, which in turn are the ASCII codes for the numerals "2", "5", and "5". When this data is sent to the console, all you see is the string of digits "255."

But the important point here is that this is text, as opposed to binary, mode—because while working in text mode you don't care about the underlying binary representation. All you care about is the fact that the file is seen as a stream of text characters. So, even though ultimately everything is binary, you should just think of this mode as "text mode."

Throughout this chapter, I adopt the standard term "binary file" to mean a file in which data isn't interpreted as ASCII character codes (unless it is string data to begin with). That's all the term means, really. As I've mentioned, large parts of such a file may not be readable by a text editor, whereas with a text file, everything should be readable as text, because all the data in a text file is interpreted as a series of ASCII characters.

Introducing Binary Operations

When working with binary files, you read and write data directly to the file, rather than translating data into text representations—which is what the stream operators (<< and >>) do.

Suppose you have the following data declarations. The variables declared occupy 4, 8, and 16 bytes respectively.

```
int n = 3;
double amount = 215.3
char *str[16] = "It's C++."
```

The following statements write the values of n, amount, and str directly to the file. Assume that binfil is a file-stream object successfully opened in binary mode.

```
binfil.write(reinterpret_cast<char*>(&n), sizeof(n));
binfil.write(reinterpret_cast<char*>(&amount),
   sizeof(amount));
binfil.write(str, sizeof(str));
```

Here's what the data looks like after being written. (The actual binary representations use strings of 1s and 0s, but I've translated these to make them more readable.)

4 bytes	8 bytes	16 bytes
3	215.3	"It's C++!"

To properly read this file, you need to know how to read these three fields. That's not as simple as it sounds. In actuality, the lines between different fields are invisible; in fact, they don't even exist, except in the mind of the programmer. (Remember, data on a computer—including disk files—is nothing but a series of bytes containing binary numbers.)

There is nothing in the file itself that tells you where one field begins and another starts. With a text file, you can always read a field by reading to the next newline or whitespace; but you can't do that with a binary file.

Therefore, when you read a binary file, you have to know what kind of data to expect. In the example code just shown, the data had this structure: an **int**, a **double**, and a 16-byte array of **char**, in that order. You could therefore read the data correctly by following this procedure:

1 Read four bytes directly into an integer variable.

2 Read eight bytes directly into a **double** variable.

3 Read 16 bytes into a string.

That's exactly what the following lines of code do.

```
binfil.read(reinterpret_cast<char*>(&n), sizeof(n));
binfil.read(reinterpret_cast<char*>(&amount),
   sizeof(amount));
binfil.read(str, 16);
```

The order that these reads are done in is critical. If, for example, you tried to read the **double** (floating-point) field first, the results would be garbage—because integer data and floating-point have incompatible formats.

Binary reads require a lot more precision than reading streams of text. With text files, a string of digits such as "12000" can be read either as an integer or floating-point, because the text-to-numeric conversion functions know exactly how to interpret such a string. But a direct binary read performs no conversions of any kind. Copying an eight-byte double directly to a four-byte integer creates a bad situation for your program. For one thing, it overwrites memory, creating a difficult-to-trace bug.

You perform input/output to a binary file by using the **read** and **write** functions. These functions each take two arguments: a data address and a number of bytes.

```
fstream.read(addr, number_of_bytes);    // Read data
                                         // into addr
fstream.write(addr, number_of_bytes);   // Write data
                                         // from addr
```

The first argument is a data address in memory: In the case of the **read** function, this is a destination to read the file's data into. In the case of the **write** function, this is a source address telling where to get the data from. (That data is then written to the file.)

In either case, this first argument must have the type **char***, so you need to pass an address expression (a pointer, array name, or an address obtained with "&"). You also need to change the type by using a data cast, unless the address type is already **char***.

This operation requires a special kind of data cast, which converts from one pointer type (**int***) to another (**char***). Because the cast changes the way the data pointed to is interpreted, it is called **reinterpret_cast**, as opposed to **static_cast**.

```
binfil.read(reinterpret_cast<char*>(&n), sizeof(n));
```

This statement may be easier to understand if you grasp that the following expression takes the address of the variable n, but converts the address to type **char***.

```
reinterpret_cast<char*>(&n)
```

In the case of string data, you don't need to use the **char*** cast, because the first argument already has that type.

```
binfil.write(str, sizeof(str));
```

The **sizeof** operator is helpful here for specifying the second argument. It returns the size in bytes of the type, variable, or the array specified.

Example 8.3. *Random–Access Write*

This next example writes binary data to a file. As I mentioned, the key to managing binary files is to pick a format and stick to it. In effect, data fields are differentiated not by a newline or whitespace (as in a text file) but by program behavior. In other words, you have to write your programs so that they know the correct data format to use before performing a read or a write.

The programs in this section and the next view a file as a series of fixed-length records, in which each record stores two pieces of data:

▶ a string field 20 bytes in length (19 characters maximum, plus one byte for a terminating null)

▶ an integer

The fact that this fixed pattern is used over and over again, throughout the file, makes it easy to use binary operations. We have a simple, consistent file format and stick to it.

This example supports *random access*, meaning that the user can go directly to any record, specified by number. The user does not have to read data sequentially (as is the case, for example, with a text file), starting at the beginning of the file and reading or writing each record in sequence.

If the user writes to an existing record number, that record is overwritten. If the user writes to a record number beyond the current length of the file, the file is automatically extended in length as needed.

```
writebin.cpp

    #include <iostream>
    #include <fstream>
    using namespace std;

    int get_int(int default_value);
    char name[20];

    int main() {
        char filename[81];
        int n;
        int age;
        int recsize = sizeof(name) + sizeof(int);

        cout << "Enter file name: ";
        cin.getline(filename, 80);
```

```
      // Open file for binary read and write.

      fstream  fbin(filename, ios::binary | ios::in |
        ios::out);
      if (!fbin) {
          cout << "Could not open file " << filename;
          return -1;
      }

  //  Get record number to write to.

      cout << "Enter file record number: ";
      n = get_int(0);

      // Get data from end user.

      cout << "Enter name: ";
      cin.getline(name, 19);
      cout << "Enter age: ";
      age = get_int(0);

      // Write data to the file.

      fbin.seekp(n * recsize);
      fbin.write(name, 20);
      fbin.write(reinterpret_cast<char*>(&age),
        sizeof(int));
      fbin.close();
      return 0;
  }

// Get integer function
// Get an integer from keyboard; return default
//  value if user enters 0-length string.
//
int get_int(int default_value) {
    char s[81];

    cin.getline(s, 80);
    if (strlen(s) == 0)
        return default_value;
    return atoi(s);
}
```

How It Works

The concept of *record* is at the heart of this example. A record is a data format—usually containing more than one field—that is repeated throughout a file, giving uniformity to the file's structure. No matter how long the file grows, it remains easy to find a record by using its record number.

Note ▶ Whenever you use records in an array or a binary file, the natural way to implement them is to use a C structure or C++ class. I spend a lot of time on classes starting in Chapter 10. The example in this chapter uses a simple record (or class) structure without the class syntax. But be patient; we'll get to that syntax in due time.

One of the first things the program does is to calculate this length:

```
int recsize = sizeof(name) + sizeof(int);
```

You can use this length information to go to any record. For example, record number 0 is at offset 0 in the file, record number 1 is at offset 24, and record number 2 is at offset 48, and so on.

offset: 0		20	24		44	48
	char * 20	int		char * 20	int	
rec.#: 0			1			2

The program opens the file by specifying several mode flags: **ios::binary**, **ios::in**, **ios::out**. The latter two cause the file stream to support both input and output. It's necessary to open in joint input/output mode to enable random access of records.

```
fstream  fbin(filename, ios::binary | ios::in |
   ios::out);
```

If the file was opened successfully, the program proceeds to get a record number from the user.

```
cout << "Enter file record number: ";
n = get_int(0);
```

The **get_int** function, also defined in the code, uses the technique for getting an integer described in the previous chapter. (The argument, by the way, specifies the default value to use if the user presses ENTER without typing anything.)

The program then gets the data to write to the specified record.

```
cout << "Enter name: ";
cin.getline(name, 80);
cout << "Enter age: ";
age = get_int(0);
```

Moving to the location of the specified record is just a matter of multiplying the number by the record size (recsize, equal to 24) and then moving to that offset. The **seekp** member function performs this move.

```
fbin.seekp(n * recsize);
```

The program then writes the data and closes.

```
fbin.write(name, 20);
fbin.write(reinterpret_cast<char*>(&age),
    sizeof(int));
fbin.close();
```

EXERCISES

Exercise 8.3.1. Write a program similar to Example 8.3 that writes records to a file, in which each contains the following information: model, a 20-byte string; make, another 20-byte string; year, a five-byte string; and mileage, an integer.

Exercise 8.3.2. Revise Example 8.3 so that it prompts the user for a record number, then prompts the user for the rest of the data and repeats. To exit, the user enters -1.

Example 8.4. *Random–Access Read*

Of course, the program in Example 8.3 isn't very useful unless you have a way of reading the data placed there. A text editor can't view the file in a satisfactory way—although it can display the portions of the file containing strings.

The program in this section reads data by using the same record format used in the last section: 20-byte string followed by a four-byte integer. The code is similar to that of Example 8.3, except for a few key statements.

readbin.cpp

```
#include <iostream>
#include <fstream>
using namespace std;
```

```cpp
int get_int(int default_value);
char name[20];

int main() {
    char filename[81];
    int n;
    int age;
    int recsize =  sizeof(name) + sizeof(int);


    cout << "Enter file name: ";
    cin.getline(filename, 80);

    // Open file for binary read write access.

    fstream  fbin(filename, ios::binary | ios::in |
      ios::out);
    if (!fbin) {
        cout << "Could not open file " << filename;
        return -1;
    }

    // Get record number and go to record.

    cout << "Enter file record number: ";
    n = get_int(0);
    fbin.seekp(n * recsize);

    // Read data from the file.

    fbin.read(name, 20);
    fbin.read(reinterpret_cast<char*>(&age),
      sizeof(int));

    // Display the data and close.

    cout << "The name is: " << name << endl;
    cout << "The age is: " << age <<endl;
    fbin.close();
    return 0;
}
```

▼ continued on next page

readbin.cpp, cont.

```cpp
// Get integer function
// Get an integer from keyboard; return default
//   value if user enters 0-length string.
//
int get_int(int default_value) {
    char s[81];

    cin.getline(s, 80);
    if (strlen(s) == 0)
        return default_value;
    return atoi(s);
}
```

How It Works

Most of this program does the same thing as Example 8.3. As before, the program gets a record number and then moves to the appropriate offset (after multiplying by the size of each record):

```cpp
fbin.seekp(n * recsize);
```

The first statements that differ from those in Example 8.3 read data from the file into the variables name and age. These are nearly the same as corresponding write statements in the other example; in fact, the arguments are the same.

```cpp
fbin.read(name, 20);
fbin.read(reinterpret_cast<char*>(&age),
    sizeof(int));
```

Once data is read into the two variables—name and age—the program prints the data, closes the file, and it's done.

```cpp
cout << "The name is: " << name << endl;
cout << "The age is: " << age << endl;
fbin.close();
```

EXERCISES

Exercise 8.4.1.   Write a program similar to Example 8.4 that reads records from a file, in which each contains the following information: model, a 20-byte string; make, another 20-byte string; year, a five-byte string; and mileage, an integer.

Exercise 8.4.2.   Revise Example 8.4 so that it prompts the user for a record number, then prints the data at that record and repeats. To exit, the user enters –1.

Exercise 8.4.3.   Revise the example further so that it performs both random-access read and write. Once this is completed, you'll have one program that can handle all input/output operations for files observing this format.

You'll need to present a command to the user by printing a menu of options:

1 Write a record

2 Read a record

3 Exit

The main loop of the program should do the following: print the menu, carry out a command, and exit if option 3 is chosen. Then repeat.

Chapter 8 *Summary*

Here are the main points of Chapter 8:

▶ To switch on file-stream support from the C++ standard library, use this **#include** directive.

```
#include <fstream>
```

▶ File-stream objects provide a way to communicate with files. To create a file-output stream, use an **ofstream** type declaration. For example:

```
ofstream fout(filename);
```

▶ You can then write to the stream as you'd write to **cout**:

```
fout << "Hello, human.";
```

▶ To create a file-input stream, use an **ifstream** declaration. A file-input stream supports the same operations that **cin** does, including the **getline** function.

```
ifstream fin(filename);

char input_string[81];
fin.getline(input_string, 80);
```

▶ If the file can't be opened, the file-stream object gets set to a null (zero). You can test the object in a condition; if the value is zero, there was an error, and the program should react as appropriate.

```
if (! file_in) {
    cout << "File " << filename;
    cout << " could not be opened.";
```

```
        return -1;
    }
```

▶ After you're done working with a file-stream object (regardless of mode), it is good programming practice to close it. This frees up the file so it can be accessed by other programs.

```
        fout.close();
```

▶ Files can be opened in either text mode or binary mode. In text mode, you read and write to a file just as you would the console. In binary mode, you use member functions to read and write data directly (without translating it into text representation.) To open a file stream in binary random-access mode, use the flags **ios::in**, **ios::out**, and **ios::binary**.

▶ Random-access mode means that you can go directly to any position in the file, without erasing portions of the file that you skipped over. You can read any portion of the file and overwrite any existing portions without affecting the rest. If you move beyond the file's current length and write data, the file is automatically extended.

▶ Use the **seekp** member function to move the file position. The function takes an argument giving an offset (in bytes) from the beginning of the file.

```
        fbin.seekp(offset);
```

▶ The **read** and **write** functions each take two arguments: a **char*** data address and the number of bytes to copy.

```
        fstream.read(addr, number_of_bytes);
        fstream.write(addr, number_of_bytes);
```

▶ With the **read** function, the address argument specifies a destination; the function reads data from the file into this location. With the **write** function, the address argument specifies a source; the function reads data from that source into the file.

▶ Because the type of the address argument is **char***, you need to apply a data cast if it is not a string. Use the **sizeof** operator to determine the number of bytes to read or write.

```
        binfil.write(reinterpret_cast<char*>(&n),
          sizeof(n));
        binfil.write(reinterpret_cast<char*>(&amount),
          sizeof(amount));
        binfil.write(str, sizeof(str));
```

Some Advanced Programming Techniques

9

With the ability to process data, print and analyze strings, and access disk files, you're on your way. You have the tools to write some serious C++ programs. But there are some other tricks to point out before I leave the basics and focus on object orientation.

These advanced features help you save time and put extra functionality in your program. One of these features—function overloading—has important ties to object orientation. But you can start using it right away, without having to understand any of the conceptual framework of objects and classes (which I'll get into in the next chapter).

We start with the topic of command-line arguments, a feature that can be used to improve the programs in Chapter 8.

Command-Line Arguments

All the programs in Chapter 8 operate on files, and the first thing that each of these programs does (after declaring variables) is prompt the user for a file name.

```
cout << "Enter a file name and press ENTER: ";
cin.getline(filename, 80);
```

This works, but it's not the ideal solution. Anyone using the DOS command line—or another command-line based system—would almost always prefer to enter the file name along with the name of the program. For example:

```
readtxt  output.txt
```

It's faster and easier to use the program this way, rather than having to wait for it to load and then prompt you.

You can implement this behavior by using the *command-line argument* feature of C++. The first thing you do is to define **main** differently:

```
int main(int argc, char *agrv[]) {
    // ...
}
```

The two arguments to **main**—argc and argv—supply information about what the user entered on the command line.

▶ argc gives the total number of command-line arguments entered by the user, including the program name itself. So for the following command line, argc returns the value 2.

```
readtxt   output.txt
```

▶ argv is an array of strings that contains all arguments on the command line, starting with the program name. In the example just shown, argv[0] points to readtxt and argv[1] points to output.txt.

You can treat the members of argv as you would any strings, except they should be considered read-only: you can't grow them, and you shouldn't try to copy data to them. But you can freely print them or copy their data to other strings.

For example, to print the first two command-line arguments (including, remember, the program name), you could use this code:

```
cout << argv[0] << endl;
cout << argv[1] << endl << endl;
cout << "argc is equal to " << argc;
```

which, in the example shown above, would produce

```
readtxt
output.txt

argc is equal to 2
```

As another example, consider this command line for a program named "copyfile":

```
copyfile  file1.txt  file2.txt
```

Here's how argc and argv would work in this case:

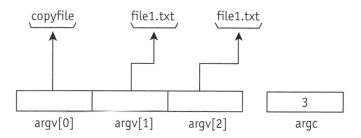

So you could do the following:

```
cout << argv[0];    // Print "copyfile"
cout << argv[1];    // Print "file1.txt"
cout << argv[2];    // Print "file2.txt"
cout << argc;       // Print "3"
```

Example 9.1. ### *Display File from Command Line*

This example is a variation on Example 8.2 that does one thing differently: it uses a filename specified on the command line, if any; otherwise, it prompts for a filename as in Example 8.2.

In the code that follows, I've highlighted the lines that are different from Example 8.2. The rest of the code is the same.

```
readtxt2.cpp

    #include <iostream>
    #include <fstream>
    #include <string.h>
    using namespace std;

    int main(int argc, char *argv[]) {
        int c;   // input character
        int i;   // loop counter
        char filename[81];
        char input_line[81];

        if (argc > 1)
            strncpy(filename, argv[1], 80);
        else {
```
▼ *continued on next page*

```
        cout << "Enter a file name and press ENTER: ";
        cin.getline(filename, 80);
    }

    ifstream file_in(filename);

    if (! file_in) {
        cout << "File " << filename;
        cout << " could not be opened.";
        return -1;
    }

    while (1) {
        for (i = 1; i <= 24 && ! file_in.eof(); i++) {
            file_in.getline(input_line, 80);
            cout << input_line;
        }
        if (file_in.eof())
            break;
        cout << endl;
        cout << "More? (Press 'Q' and ENTER to quit.)";
        cin.getline(input_line, 80);
        c = input_line[0];
        if (c == 'Q' || c == 'q')
            break;
    }
    return 0;
}
```

With this version of the program, you can use the command line to enter commands like this:

```
readtxt2  output.txt
```

Alternatively, you can just enter the name of the program and let the program prompt you for the name of the file to display.

```
readfile2
```

How It Works

Only a few lines in this program are different from Example 8.2; this section describes each of those lines.

One of the files the program includes is string.h, to enable string-handling functions. You'll see in a moment why this is necessary.

```
#include <string.h>
```

Another difference is the argument list for **main**, which is not empty:

```
int main(int argc, char *argv[]) {
```

The program has one other difference from Example 8.2. The first thing the program does is check the value of argc. If argc is greater than 1, that means the user provided a command-line argument (beyond the program name itself), so the program copies that argument to filename string. Command-line arguments beyond argv[1], if any, are ignored.

```
if (argc > 1)
    strncpy(filename, argv[1], 80);
```

If argc is not greater than 1, that means the user did not enter a filename on the command line. The program therefore prompts for the filename, as in Example 8.2.

```
else {
    cout << "Enter a file name and press ENTER: ");
    cin.getline(filename, 80); ·
}
```

EXERCISES

Exercise 9.1.1.   Alter Exercise 9.1 so it requires the user to enter the filename on the command line. In other words, the syntax of the program requires:

```
readtxt3 filename
```

If the user enters more or fewer command-line arguments, print an error message and quit.

Exercise 9.1.2.   Write a program that does nothing except print all the command-line arguments, each on a separate line.

Function Overloading

Natural languages—particularly English—often employ a word to mean a number of different things depending on the context. Think of how many meanings there are for the word "fair." You can go *to* the fair, enjoy fair weather, and notice all the fair-haired people at the fair.

In computer-programming terminology, we could say this is an example of *overloading*—loading a word with multiple meanings.

C++ uses overloading as well. But rather than providing a source of confusion or amusement, overloading in C++ is useful and precise. You can reuse a function name to work with different types of data.

Consider the swap function. As with all C++ functions, swap must be declared with definite type information.

```
void swap(int *p1, int *p2);
```

This is an unfortunate limitation. The swap function had to be defined to work on one type of data: in this case, pointers to **int**. But you might want swap to work on other kinds of data.

One solution—the solution you'd have to use with C, Basic, and most non-object-oriented languages—is to write a different version of the function for each type of data, adopting a naming convention so you never reuse the exact same name.

```
void swap_int(int *p1, int *p2);
void swap_dbl(double *p1, double *p2);
void swap_ptrs(char **p1, char **p2);
```

This solution works, but C++ provides a better solution. C++ lets you reuse the one name—swap—with different kinds of data, relying on the type information in the argument list to keep the versions separate. The name "swap" is reused—that is to say, *overloaded*—for programmer convenience.

```
void swap(int *p1, int *p2);
void swap(double *p1, double *p2);
void swap(char **p1, char **p2);
```

Note ▶ The version of swap shown here for the **char*** types does not transfer string data; it only swaps the values of two **char*** pointers themselves. For example, p1 and p2 point to two strings. After the swap(&p1, &p2) function call, p1 points to the string that p2 formerly pointed to, and vice versa.

How does the C++ compiler keep all these functions straight? Simple: it looks at arguments involved in a function call. Because each variable has a specific type, it's always possible for C++ to know which version of swap to use.

Again, for each version of the function, there must be a separate declaration and a separate definition. Here are two definitions for swap.

```
void swap(int *p1, int *p2) {
    int temp = *p1;
    *p1 = *p2;
    *p2 = temp;
}

void swap(double *p1, double *p2);
    double temp = *p1;
    *p1 = *p2;
    *p2 = temp;
}
```

Interlude

Overloading and OOPS

Function overloading is related to one of the deepest ideas in object-oriented programming systems (OOPS): the idea that a data type dictates how a function or operator behaves.

A closely related idea is that of *operator overloading*. An operator (such as + or −) can be applied to any number of different data types, and the operator will do the correct thing for the types involved—presuming the supporting code exists. (Chapter 13 describes how to write these operator functions for your own types.)

An elementary example of operator overloading comes from the core language. Adding two integers and adding two floating-point numbers require different machine instructions. The C++ compiler executes different low-level routines depending on the types in an expression such as:

```
a + b
```

With function overloading, you can change the types of variables without necessarily changing the function name. The function call will do the right thing . . . because (presumably) you've programmed multiple versions of the function to work with different types. In the swap example, imagine you've declared a and b as integers:

```
int a, b;
//...
swap(&a, &b);
```

▼ *continued on next page*

Interlude

▼ *continued*

If you then change the types of a and b to **double**, the call to swap still works. The C++ compiler executes a call to a different version of the function.

Once again, the idea is one deeply ingrained in object orientation: *the type of the data involved dictates the behavior of the function.*

Yet overloading is not a full implementation of this idea. As you'll learn in upcoming chapters, type information may be known imperfectly at compile time. In some cases, you may only know the general type of the argument— you may know only that it observes some general interface—and in that case, function overloading is insufficient. That's where polymorphism and virtual functions come into play. I'll have more to say about these concepts in Chapter 17.

Example 9.2. *Printing Different Types of Arrays*

Here's a simple example that uses function overloading. The program prints three kinds of arrays, each time calling a function named print_array.

```cpp
print_arrs.cpp

    #include <iostream>
    using namespace std;

    void print_arr(int *arr, int n);
    void print_arr(double *arr, int n);
    void print_arr(char **arr, int n);

    int a[] = {1, 1, 2, 3, 5, 8, 13};
    double b[] = {1.4142, 3.141592 };
    char *c[] = {"Inken", "Blinken", "Nod" };


    int main() {
        print_arr(a, 7);
        print_arr(b, 2);
        print_arr(c, 3);
        return 0;
    }
```

```cpp
void print_arr(int *arr, int n) {
    for (int i = 0; i < n; i++)
        cout << arr[i] << " ";
    cout << endl;
}

void print_arr(double *arr, int n) {
    for (int i = 0; i < n; i++)
        cout << arr[i] << " ";
    cout << endl;
}

void print_arr(char **arr, int n) {
    for (int i = 0; i < n; i++)
        cout << arr[i] << endl;
}
```

How It Works

This example is a straightforward use of function overloading. The first thing it does (after the **#include** directives) is declare all the different versions of the function print_arr.

```cpp
print_arr(int *arr, int n);
print_arr(double *arr, int n);
print_arr(char **arr, int n);
```

The program then declares three kinds of arrays:

```cpp
int a[] = {1, 1, 2, 3, 5, 8, 13};
double b[] = {1.4142, 3.141592 };
char *c[] = {"Inken", "Blinken", "Nod" );
```

From within main, the program then uses the same function name—print_arr—to print all these arrays.

```cpp
print_arr(a, 7);
print_arr(b, 2);
print_arr(c, 3);
```

Finally, the program defines the versions of print_arr.

EXERCISE

Exercise 9.2.1. Write two versions of a generic get_number function, so get_number can be used to get either an integer or floating-point number, as desired. As with the get_int and get_dbl examples in Chapter 7, the function should take a numeric argument that specifies the default value. Given this call:

```
get_number(0)
```

the function should return an integer value, whereas

```
get_number(0.0)
```

should return a value of type **double**. Remember that C++ notation recognizes any constant expression with a decimal point as a floating-point expression with **double** type. Therefore, all you have to do is overload two versions of the function in which one takes and returns an **int**, and the other takes and returns a **double**.

The do-while Loop

Here are the control structures I've introduced so far. There are three of them (or four if you consider that the **if** statement has two versions).

```
if (condition)
    statement
```

```
if (condition)
    statement
else
    statement
```

```
while (condition)
    statement
```

```
for (initializer; condition; increment)
    statement
```

Remember, any instance of *statement* in any of these structures can be replaced with a compound statement, consisting of one or more statements between a pair of braces ({}).

```
{ statements }
```

In addition to these statements, I also demonstrated the use of **break** and **return** statements to transfer control out of a loop or function.

With this syntax, you have all the tools you need to control C++ programs. These are sufficient for creating any kind of program flow you're ever likely to need. Technically, you could get away with just the **if** and **while** statements.

There are also a couple of other control structures which, while not strictly necessary, are often helpful. One of these is the **do-while** statement, which has this syntax:

```
do statement
while (condition);
```

This control structure is similar to the ordinary **while** statement. The difference is that with this version of **while**, the statement is guaranteed to be executed at least once, before the condition is evaluated.

I've already shown an example where this would have been helpful. Example 5.5 used the following code inside a larger loop:

```
i++;                     // Advance to next card
while (card_drawn[i])    // Skip past cards
    i++;                 //  already drawn.
```

Clearly, in this fragment, the statement i++; is executed at least once, and then it may be executed again. This makes the code fragment a perfect candidate for the use of **do-while**. You can rewrite the code this way:

```
do i++;                      // Advance to next card
while (card_drawn[i]);       //  while current card has
                             //   been drawn
```

This code fragment, while more compact, tends to be more difficult to read. It's customary to use the compound-statement version of **do-while**, substituting {*statements* } for the single *statement*.

```
do {
    i++;                         // Advance to next card
} while (card_drawn[i]);  //  while current card has
                             //   been drawn
```

This is more readable, don't you think?

The action of **do-while** can be expressed in terms of simple **if** and **goto** statements, reflecting the actual logic of the machine code that the compiler generates. Here's what the **do-while** statement does:

```
top_of_loop:
    statement
    if (condition) goto top_of_loop;
```

The switch-case Statement

Rounding out the control structures supported in C++ is the **switch** statement. As with the **do-while** statement, the **switch** statement is not strictly necessary, but it can in some cases make for more concise and readable code.

One of the most common patterns you see in programming is a series of **if-else** statements that test a single value against a series of target values. For example, the following code fragment prints one, two, three, and so on, depending on the value of x:

```
if (x == 1)
    cout << "one";
else if (x == 2)
    cout << "two";
else if (x == 3)
    cout << "three";
//...
```

You can also write this as a **switch** statement:

```
switch(x) {
    case 1:
        cout << "one";
        break;
    case 2:
        cout << "two";
        break;
    case 3:
        cout << "three";
        break;
    //...
}
```

Technically, the **switch** statement has a simple syntax.

```
switch (value) {
    statements
}
```

To make the statements useful, you need to include labeled statements. Labels can have either of these special forms within a **switch** statement:

```
case target_value: statement
```

```
default: statement
```

Here's how the **switch** statement works:

1 The *value* after the **switch** keyword is evaluated.

2 If there is a **case** statement label that matches this value, then control is transferred to the labeled statement.

3 If no **case** statement label matches the value, and there is a **default** label, then control is transferred to the statement labeled as **default**.

Once control is transferred to a labeled statement, it continues to proceed in a forward direction as normal, unless a **break** statement is encountered, in which case control is transferred to the end of the **switch** statement. This is why each **case** statement block needs to be terminated by **break**, unless you want control to fall through to the next case.

```
case 1:
    cout << "one";
    break;
```

Multiple Modules

In Chapter 4, I mentioned that the use of multiple functions in your program enables you to adopt a division-of-labor approach that makes large projects more doable. The division of labor improves even more when you use multiple modules.

What do I mean by *module*? Well, consider the way all the programs have been created in this book: there is one source file (a .cpp file), which is translated into one object file containing machine code (an .o file) and then linked into an executable (an .exe file).

Can you create a program from more than one source file? Yes. The key to doing that is the use of functions. A single function cannot span more than one source file. You can, however, place individual functions in different source files.

Here's a simple example. This program has four functions: **main**, calc, get_int, and get_dbl. These could all be put in one source file, but for the sake of illustration, I've put the function definitions into two separate files, mod1.cpp and mod2.cpp. These are shown on the top of page 232.

Each of the two source files (.cpp files) is a separate module.

This example also illustrates the use of an include file, myproj.h. (In fact, this is a good illustration of why include files are useful in general.) Assume that any of the three functions other than **main**—these are calc, get_int, and get_dbl—may be called by a function in another module. To enable such calls, you need to put function declarations at the beginning of each source file.

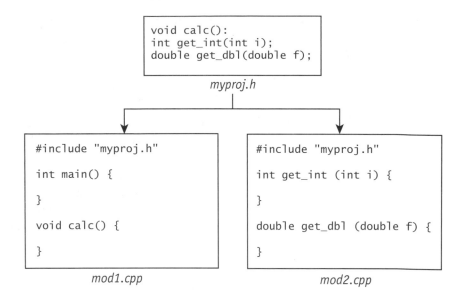

```
void calc():
int get_int(int i);
double get_dbl(double f);
```

myproj.h

```
#include "myproj.h"

int main() {

}

void calc() {

}
```

mod1.cpp

```
#include "myproj.h"

int get_int (int i) {

}

double get_dbl (double f) {

}
```

mod2.cpp

These declarations need to be included in every file:

```
void calc();
int get_int(int);
double get_dbl(double);
```

This can get a little confusing, so remember these rules:

1 Each function is defined in exactly one place—that is, in one source file. For instance, in the current example, the function calc is defined in mod1.cpp.

2 But every source file needs a declaration (that is, a prototype) of this function in order to support calls to it. Otherwise, the function is invisible and cannot be called.

The C++ compiler will look for the definition of each prototyped function in the source file; if it cannot find the definition, the compiler will assume the function is defined in another module.

When you have many modules, you may find that putting all of these declarations at the beginning of every module is time-consuming and error-prone. A better practice is to place all your function declarations in a central file—an include file—and then use an **#include** directive.

Using an include file may seem indirect, but it offers advantages. All the prototypes of the common functions are maintained in this one place, making changes easier.

You can share data variables in the same way, but variables are assumed to be private to the module in which they're created—unless an **extern** declaration is added to each file (or to the include file). For example, the following declaration states that variables a, b, and c are declared somewhere in the program, possibly (though not necessarily) in another module.

```
extern int a, b, c;
```

The variables have to be defined somewhere, of course—meaning that each has to be created in one and only one module (just as each function has to be defined in only one module). You create a variable by using a standard variable declaration, optionally with initialization.

```
int a = 0, b = 0, c = 1;
```

I don't use multiple modules in this book for the most part, because it represents overkill for short examples. But for really large software projects, the use of multiple modules offers huge advantages:

▶ Probably the biggest single advantage is that multiple modules support multiple programmers. Each programmer can work on his own module. If there were just one module, only one programmer could be writing code at any given time. The others would have to stare out the window.

▶ The multimodule approach provides yet another way to logically subdivide the program. Functions that specialize in number crunching can be placed in one module, while another module specializes in user-interface functions. This extends the division-of-labor approach that functions make possible.

▶ You can control the degree of communication among modules. You can, for example, declare a global variable or a function without declaring it in the include file. In that case, it's private to its own module. The name can be referred to by functions within the module, but not by anything outside.

The last advantage just described has a connection to object-oriented programming. In older languages such as C, the use of separate modules was the only way to create groups of symbols (that is, functions and variables) in which some were private and some were public.

This is useful for large, complex projects. A programmer has responsibility for implementing public items but the programmer can also write his or her own support functions, not intended to be used by anyone else. The private portion of the module is protected from the outside, so that the programmer never need worry about other programmers calling these private functions (or referring to private data) and in the process making all kinds of assumptions about how they work.

The public/private distinction is a way of achieving *encapsulation*—something I'll explore much more in upcoming chapters. The important point is this:

Encapsulation is one of the major benefits of C++ classes. If you understand how this works with modules, you'll find C++ classes easier to understand.

Once you've written all the code, each of the modules can be compiled and then linked together. If you set up a project correctly from within your development environment, this process of compiling and linking is automated for you.

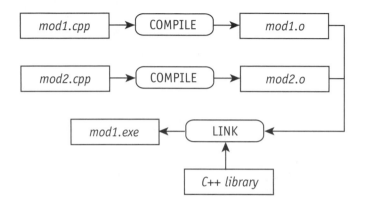

Exception Handling

Exception handling is a sophisticated way to respond to errors at runtime. C++ gurus sometimes put great emphasis on exception handling—it's an excellent technique for recovering from errors cropping up in the middle of complex programs. In commercial software, it's practically a necessity.

But for short programs, exception-handling is at best optional—if not outright overkill. If you have short programs plagued by runtime errors, you might consider adding exception handling. But in general, this feature is useful only after you start developing complex programs that involve many function calls.

With that caveat in mind, the next several sections present C++ exception handling, starting with the more basic concepts.

Say Hello to Exceptions

In Chapter 1, I stated that there are two basic kinds of errors you have to worry about as a programmer, and that these errors are different because each kind requires a different response. To recap, there are:

▶ *Syntax errors,* which require you to fix your code before you can successfully compile your program.

▶ *Program-logic* errors, which are discovered only after you have compiled the program and tested it.

There's also a third kind of error—although it's related to the second category. This third kind of error is special because of its effect on the program.

This third category is that of runtime errors, or *exceptions*. The term "exception" refers to an occurrence at runtime that is "exceptional" because it interrupts the normal flow of the program. Such an occurrence demands immediate handling and usually involves an error. The program must respond to the situation, exit, or do both.

Examples of exceptions include but are not limited to:

▶ Attempt to divide by zero.

▶ Use of a null pointer in an expression that requires a valid pointer.

▶ Failure to allocate requested memory.

▶ Arithmetic overflow during a calculation.

The basic problem posed by exceptions is this: when one of these situations occurs in your program, you want the program to handle the situation smoothly and then make an intelligent decision as to whether to continue operation or not. Sometimes, you can respond to an exception by printing an "Operation not supported" message and then continuing. Or, you may choose to terminate the program smoothly, after closing system resources and printing a user-friendly message. The default behavior—which is not desirable, especially in commercial software—is to terminate abruptly.

Handling Exceptions: A First Attempt

In a small program—let's say one that involves few function calls—you can check for error conditions and handle them where you find them.

For example, you can protect the greatest-common-factor function (gcf) by looking for a zero divisor and handling the problem on the spot. Detecting this condition yourself prevents abrupt, ugly termination with an error message that you didn't choose.

Here's how the gcf function (from Chapter 4) might appear if you add error-handling code.

```
int gcf(int a, int b) {
    if (b == 0) {
        cout << "ERROR! Attempt to divide by zero." <<
            endl;
        return -1;
    }
    if (a % b == 0)
```

```
        return b;
    else
        return gcf(b, a % b);
}
```

What should happen after the error is detected? The approach here is to return an error code -1. But this approach has problems. First, -1 might be a value legally returned by gcf during its normal operation; -1 therefore conflicts with a normal return value. There may be, in fact, no return value that is eligible to serve as the error signal.

Second, if the function is called in the middle of a complex program, the error code needs to be "propagated upward" with one function after another returning the error code until the error is finally communicated back to the main function.

You don't want to write such error-propagation code. In a complex program, that would be a major headache.

An alternative approach is to respond by terminating the program on the spot by calling the **exit** function. Now, no error signal needs to be propagated, because the program just exits.

```
int gcf(int a, int b) {
    if (b == 0) {
        cout << "ERROR! Attempt to divide by zero."
          << endl;
        exit(-1);
    }
    if (a % b == 0)
        return b;
    else
        return gcf(b, a % b);
}
```

This approach may work fine for small programs. But it has a drawback in complex software: it doesn't enable you to centralize your error handling in one place. Instead, with this approach, error handling must be sprinkled throughout the code. There are other problems, too. This approach is inflexible and doesn't give other parts of the program a chance to respond.

Introducing try-catch Exception Handling

Recent versions of C++ (specifically, all versions that are ANSI-compliant) support the **try**, **catch**, and **throw** keywords for handling exceptions. The use of these keywords is sometimes called *structured* exception handling, because it provides a more sophisticated and structured approach to dealing with exceptions than the methods in the previous section. Mostly though, people just refer to this feature of C++ as "exception handling."

The most important feature of C++ exception handling is that it protects not just a block of code, but all functions called by this block, and all functions called by functions called by this block, and so on.

This aspect of exception handling cannot be emphasized enough. It's as though the general of an army broadcast a command to all his troops that certain issues are to be brought to his immediate attention, bypassing the regular chain of command. Even the lowest private is given a direct channel to the general when he finds what the general is looking for. In a similar way, exception handling enables you to centralize all your error handling, bypassing intermediate functions and freeing you from having to write error-propagating code.

The syntax involves the **try** and **catch** keywords: one **try** block followed by any number of **catch** blocks. In the simple case (shown here), there is just one **catch** block.

```
try {
    try_statements
}
catch (type argument) {
    catch_statements
}
```

When this structure is encountered, the *try_statements* are executed unconditionally; that is, the *try_statements* are always executed—unless, of course, an exception is raised.

If an exception is raised—either by the *try_statements* themselves or by a function called during execution of these statements—such an exception may be caught and handled by the **catch** block.

The action of the **catch** block is as follows: if the type of the exception raised matches the specified *type*, then control is transferred to the **catch** block. If the type does not match, then the argument of the next **catch** block is checked, and so on, until the list of **catch** blocks is exhausted. If no block of code catches the exception, the program terminates.

The items in parentheses following **catch** may include *type argument* or *type* by itself. The *argument* is optional.

This syntax is challenging at first, but an example should help clarify. Assume the program encounters the following statements:

```
try {
    open_files();
    read_files();
    process_data();
```

```
    }
    catch (int err) {
        error_handler_1();
    }
    catch (double err) {
        error_handler_2();
    }
```

The program executes the statements inside the **try** block unconditionally. These statements call three functions—open_files, read_files, and process_data. Several things may happen during execution of these functions. First, the program may run normally. In that case, neither of the **catch** blocks is executed. But suppose an exception occurs. In that case, if the exception has type **int**, error_handler_1 is called. If the exception has type **double**, error_handler_2 is called.

These rules raise an obvious question: what type can an exception have?

The answer is that an exception can have most any type. It can be an intrinsic type, such as **int**, **double**, or **char**. It can also have a user-defined type; this includes the **string** type introduced at the end of Chapter 7 as well as a type defined with the **class** keyword (which I introduce in Chapter 11).

If you raise the exception yourself, you determine its type. This is what the **throw** keyword does.

> **throw** *exception_object*;

The action of this statement is to raise an exception. The normal flow of program control is interrupted. The exception must be caught by an appropriate **catch** block. If the exception is not caught, the program terminates.

For example, the following statement raises an exception and gives it type **int**:

```
    throw 12;            // Raise exception with err no. 12
```

There's a subtle but crucial point regarding exception types. The type of an exception is determined programmatically: *it isn't necessarily related to the nature of the exception*. For example, an exception of type **int** doesn't necessarily mean that there was a problem with integers, and an exception of type **double** doesn't necessarily mean that there was a problem with floating-point math.

Exceptions themselves don't really have a type, anyway. It is more correct to say that what is thrown (and caught) is an exception *object,* which is a packet of data that may include information about the exception.

Some kinds of exceptions are raised automatically by the system; these cause exception objects to be thrown with the special **exception** type. You can catch these exceptions by using this **exception** type.

```
try {
//...
}
catch(exception &e) {
    cout << "EXCEPTION RAISED: " << e.what() << endl;
}
```

The **what** member function of the **exception** class returns error-message text.

Example 9.3. *Exception Handling with GCF*

This example, when run, finds the greatest common factor of the pair 12 and 18, and of the pair 125 and 45. Then it attempts a function call that would result in division by 0. The error condition is detected in the gcf function, but it is handled in **main**.

```
gcf_except

    #include <iostream>
    using namespace std;

    int gcf(int a, int b);

    int main() {
        try {
            cout << "gcf(12, 18) = " << gcf(12, 18) << endl;
            cout << "gcf(125, 45) = " << gcf(125, 45) << endl;
            cout << "gcf(5, 0) = " << gcf(5, 0) << endl;
            return 0;
        }
        catch (int err) {
            cout << "EXCEPTION RAISED! " << endl;
            cout << "Error num: " << err << endl;
            return err;
        }
    }

    int gcf(int a, int b) {
        if (b == 0)
            throw 1;
```

▼ *continued on next page*

gcf_except, cont.

```
        if (a % b == 0)
            return b;
        else
            return gcf(b, a % b);
    }
```

How It Works

Most of this example is similar to Example 4.3. There are three important differences:

▶ Except for the **catch** block, all the statements in **main** are placed in a **try** block. These statements are executed unconditionally, unless and until an exception is raised.

▶ A **catch** block is used to handle any exception having **int** type.

▶ The gcf function tests whether 0 is passed to the b argument; if it is, the function raises an exception and gives it **int** type.

The use of the **int** type is somewhat arbitrary. The **int** type is useful, however, for sending back an error code. Remember that the type of the exception object is just a way of communicating information from one part of the program to another.

The gcf function tests whether 0 is passed to the b argument. If it is, the code raises an exception to prevent division by 0.

```
        if (b == 0)
            throw 1;
```

This exception is raised as an integer (in this case, the number 1). Control is immediately transferred away, as the program looks for the appropriate **catch** block. The exception is caught by the **catch** block in **main**, which handles any exception having **int** type. The following block is therefore executed.

```
    catch (int err) {
        cout << "EXCEPTION RAISED! " << endl;
        cout << "Error no. " << err << endl;
        return err;
    }
```

The last thing this code does is return (out of **main**), passing the value of the error code back to the operating system.

One of the most important features of this example is that the code that raises the exception is in a different function from the code that handles it. This is the whole point of C++ exception handling. An exception raised in a particular function can be handled by a **try-catch** block in either the same function or anywhere above it in the function-call hierarchy.

EXERCISE

Exercise 9.3.1.   If your compiler supports the **string** type described at the end of Chapter 7, then revise the example so that it passes an exception object using the **string** type instead of **int**. You may find this type of exception more useful, because you can pass back an error message.

Note: you can convert a **char*** string to a **string** object on the fly by using code such as the following:

```
throw string("Division by error.");
```

Interlude | **Can I Use Multiple try-catch Blocks?**

You can use **try-catch** blocks as often as you want. It's even possible for every function to have its own **try-catch** block. Doing that would defeat the purpose of exception-handling, however. The advantage of C++ exception handling is that it enables you to centralize error-handling in a few places.

It may often happen that an exception is raised by a function deep in the function-call hierarchy; in other words, **main** calls a function that calls a function that calls a function, etc. . . . that finally calls the current function. If an exception is raised, the system will look up through the function-call hierarchy to find a matching **catch** block.

If there are multiple **try-catch** blocks in the function-call hierarchy, control is transferred to the nearest such block. For example, a **try-catch** block in the current function, or its immediate caller, takes precedence over a **try-catch** block that is all the way "up the line" in **main**.

By analogy, a private who has standing orders from his sergeant will go to the sergeant before going to the general. If there are no orders from his sergeant, he will go up the line until he finds an officer who will respond.

This mechanism makes for maximum flexibility. The **main** function can set general error-handling procedures, but as other functions are called, they can add to or modify error-handling behavior as appropriate.

Chapter 9   *Summary*

Here are the main points of Chapter 9:

▶ To access command-line arguments, declare **main** with two arguments of its own, argc and argv:

```
int main(int argc, char *argv[]) {
// ...
}
```

▶ argc contains the number of command-line arguments entered by the user, including the program name itself.

▶ argv is an array of pointers to strings, in which each string contains a command-line argument, starting with the program name. For example:

```
cout << argv[0];    // Print program name.
cout << argv[1];    // Print next item on cmd line.
cout << argv[2];    // Print next item after that.
```

▶ Function overloading lets you write multiple versions of the same function, using the type of arguments to differentiate between them. For example, you can have different versions of the swap function:

```
void swap(int *p1, int *p2) {
    int temp = *p1;
    *p1 = *p2l;
    *p2 = temp;
}

void swap(double *p1, double *p2);
    double temp = *p1;
    *p1 = *p2l;
    *p2 = temp;
}
```

▶ The compiler determines exactly what function to call by checking the type of the arguments at compile time. In this example, the types of a and b determine which version of swap to use.

```
swap(a, b);
```

▶ Although, by definition, function overloading reuses a function name, it has the effect of creating distinct functions. Each of these functions requires a separate declaration and definition. Despite their sharing of a name—and the fact that they may do similar things—the functions are really separate from one another.

▶ The **do-while** loop has the following syntax. This control structure is similar to **while**, except the statement is guaranteed to be performed at least once before the condition is evaluated.

```
do statement
while (condition);
```

▶ Use of the compound-statement syntax is particularly helpful with the **do-while** statement. For example:

```
do {
    i++;
} while (card_drawn[i]);
```

▶ If you have more than one function or global data declaration, you can subdivide your program into multiple source files. Each of these source files is a *module*.

▶ Among other advantages, the use of multiple modules enables you to have more than one programmer at a time working on a large programming project.

▶ A function can call a function defined in another module, but only if the called function is prototyped. For this reason, the common practice is to place prototypes for all the common functions at the beginning of each and every module. For example:

```
void calc();
int get_int(int);
double get_dbl(double);
```

▶ A convenient approach to managing the prototypes for common functions is to put them into a single file, called an "include" file. That file can then be read into each source file with the help of the **#include** directive.

```
#include "myproj.h"
```

▶ Variables to be shared throughout a multiple-module program need to be given an **extern** declaration in each module. In addition to the **extern** declarations, each variable also needs to be defined—in one and only in one module—by the use of a standard variable declaration.

▶ Exception handling is a technique enabling you to centralize handling of run-time errors. It tends to be most useful in complex software. The **try** keyword defines a block of statements executed unconditionally. The **catch** block or blocks following a **try** block can handle an exception that is raised—either by the statements in the **try** block or by a function called during execution of these statements. One of the great advantages of this feature—particularly for complex programs—is that it frees you from having to write code that "propagates an error" from a low-level function all the way back up to **main**.

▶ Some kinds of exceptions are raised automatically (and thrown as objects having the special type **exception**). However, you can also raise exceptions yourself by using the **throw** keyword. You can give these exceptions any valid type.

10 Getting Yourself Object Oriented

The most important development in the world of programming the last fifteen years has been the development of object-oriented programming systems (OOPS). It's the principal feature that makes C++ different from its predecessor, C.

Books on programming sometimes go overboard in the claims made for object-oriented programming: it will solve every programming problem you've ever had, it will freshen your breath, it will make you more popular, it will improve the economy . . . you get the idea.

But OOPS doesn't always make a large difference in small programs. It's just another set of tools—tools useful for organizing large amounts of code into logical chunks. Some true believers claim it provides better techniques for modeling objects in the real world, and there's some truth in that idea. It is good at creating objects that interact with a complex system—such as a network or graphical user-interface.

*Nevertheless, if you've been following the rest of the chapters of this book, you've already been using objects—notably, the **cin** and **cout** objects (for console input and output), and file-stream objects. That's just the beginning.*

Why Get Object Oriented?

It's safe to say that one of the biggest causes of programming errors is having too many interconnections between different parts of a program.

The problem occurs when a great deal of data is shared among all functions of the program (typically the case in large projects). One function assumes that a certain variable has a steady value, but another function changes it. I showed an example of this in Chapter 4, in which one little variable, i, causes a major error if it's made global.

245

So how can you limit access to global variables? In large projects, a kind of anarchy exists. Local data is private (thank goodness), but all functions have access to all global variables in the program, or at least in the same module.

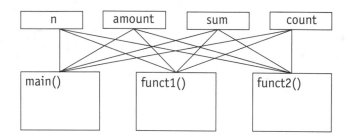

Object-oriented programming brings order to this chaos. Instead of giving all functions unlimited access to global data, you develop *classes,* in which access to certain data is privileged. Only functions of the class can access class data. (Actually, you can choose to make each data field public or private, but assume for now that you'd just make it private.)

Suppose you've designed a Circle object that provides certain services to the user of that object: you can move, resize, or redraw the circle. These are implemented as functions that need access to a common pool of data, such as the position and extent of the circle, but you don't want to give anything outside the class the ability to reach in and change the data directly.

You can achieve this by putting related functions and data into a common class. Anyone can call the Circle functions, but the data inside can't be accessed by anything outside.

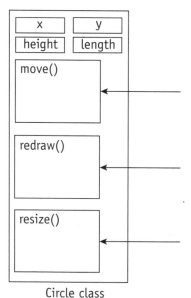

Circle class

This important feature of object-oriented programming is called *encapsulation*—a fancy word for hiding the details.

A String Parser

In Chapter 7, I used a get_a_string function to parse a string: each call to the function read up to the next comma and put the result in a destination string.

```
for (i = 0; i < 10; i++) {
    pos = get a string(buffer, strs[i], pos);
    if (pos == -1)
        break;
}
```

This code is not the easiest to understand, and it requires the caller of the function to declare and maintain an extra variable pos.

It would be nice if you could instead use an object that maintained its own data. All you'd have to do is create the object and then call one of three functions to do the work:

FUNCTION	DESCRIPTION
get(char *s)	Get next substring and place in destination string s. Return true if there's data to read, false otherwise.
more()	Return true if there's data to read, false otherwise.
reset()	Reset current-position indicator to beginning of string buffer.

Conceptually, you could think of the object's class as shown at the top of page 248.

The awkward get_a_string loop shown earlier could then be replaced with this more elegant code:

```
i = 0;
while (parser.more())
    parser.get(strs[i++]);
```

Or you could make use of the "get" function's return value (which is true if there's more of the input string left) to write even more concise code:

```
i = 0;
while (parser.get(strs[i]))
    i++;
```

10

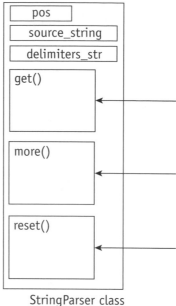

StringParser class

The use of this parser object makes only a modest improvement to your code. But it begins to suggest the flavor of object-oriented programming. The important point: You can hide the details.

Note ▶ Most of this same functionality is provided by the standard C++ library function, **strtok**. However, that solution is less object-oriented; for one thing, it can only be used on one string at a time, unlike the StringParser object described in Chapter 14 of this book. Beyond that, StringParser is an effective example, even though most of its functionality duplicates the **strtok** function.

Objects vs. Classes

So what's a class and what's an object? How are they different?

A class is a unit of program organization: it contains code and type information for one user-defined type. You declare a class by defining all its components—these include *data members,* which make up the contents of the class, and *member functions,* which define what objects of the class do.

Once you've declared a class (or included a class declaration someone else wrote), you can create one or more objects. An object is an instance of one class. This is a one-to-many relationship.

The cardinal rules are:

* **A class is a user-defined data type, which can have both data and function code.**

* **An object is an instance of a type, of which you can have any number.**

The main thing to remember is that a class is a user-defined type. As an analogy, there is one **int** type; but you can have any number of **int** variables. There's a similar relationship between classes and objects. For any given class, you can declare any number of objects.

Another Example: The Fraction Class

On one level, the use of objects is really about using the language to extend the notion of data type. You can use C++ to define fundamental new types, which syntactically, work much the same way as standard types, such as **int**, **char**, **float**, and **double**.

An example is a hypothetical Fraction class. One limitation of the floating-point types (**float**, **double**) is that they cannot hold most fractional quantities with absolute precision. No matter how many places of precision you have, you'll never be able to represent the quantity 1/3 exactly in a binary (or for that matter, in a decimal) system. Even if you had a hundred-thousand places of precision to the right of the decimal point, there would always be some error, however small!

By using the techniques in this book, you can create a true Fraction data type (some people might call this a "rational number" type), which holds the ratio of any two integers with absolute precision.

You'd first declare the class and then declare Fraction objects, just as you would other kinds of data.

```
Fraction a, b, c;
```

You can also initialize these objects as you declare them. The twist here is that you initialize an object by using an argument list. This is one of a very few ways in which classes and objects look different, syntactically, from an intrinsic C++ type (such as **int**).

```
Fraction a(1, 2);     // a = 1/2
Fraction b(1, 3);     // b = 1/3
```

You can also define operator functions for your classes to make objects of that class work with any C++ operator you wish. With a numeric class such as Fraction, it's common to make the class support basic numeric operations (+, -, *, /), assignment (=), and the stream operator (<<) for use with **cout** and other file-output streams.

```
Fraction a(1, 2);    // a = 1/2
Fraction b(1, 3);    // b = 1/3
Fraction c;


c = a + b;           // c = 1/2 + 1/3
cout << c;           // Print "5/6".
```

This may look like magic, but in C++ it works.

Object Creation and Destruction

Data protection is no small matter in complex programs, or even in medium-sized programs that interact with something complex, such as Microsoft Windows. In the case of the Fraction class, you can add it to your project without any concern over whether the rest of the program could inadvertently alter Fraction data. A class creates a separate namespace.

Yet C++ classes do even more than that. The process of object creation, initialization, and destruction is automated for you. You can even design multiple ways to let the user create and initialize an object. For example, in the case of the string-parser class:

```
// Create a parser with no initial values.
//   (Initialize later.)

StringParser parser1;

// Specify input string, use default delimiter (",").

StringParser parser2("Me, Myself, and I");

// Specify both input string and delimiter.

StringParser parser3("I:Thee:Thou", ":");
```

For each kind of argument list, the class must define a separate *constructor*. As you'll see in Chapter 12, constructors make liberal use of C++ function overloading, which is one reason why overloading is important in C++.

Sometimes special actions need to be taken when an object is created or destroyed. In addition to initialization, constructors can perform whatever housekeeping operation you need, such as allocating memory or opening a file. Likewise, *destructors* can perform any cleanup needed as an object goes away.

Inheritance, or Subclassing

Believe it or not, most of the object-oriented features described so far are actually doable in the old C language—albeit with a good deal more work (principally through the use of separate modules)—with a couple of exceptions:

▶ Operator functions are not supported in most languages. Many programmers do not consider this a fatal flaw, however; you can do anything by calling member functions instead of using operators. Operator overloading is a nice bonus, but it's not essential to everyone.

▶ Object creation, destruction, and initialization cannot be automated in a traditional language. The user of a C user-defined type (a structure) has to explicitly call any functions needed for creation and destruction. For example, you'd have to create a Circle structure and then call an Init_Circle function. Again, this is not fatal, simply an inconvenience.

We come now to a feature of C++ classes that is not supported by traditional languages such as C at all . . . this feature is *inheritance,* or more formally, *subclassing.* Let me explain why it can be useful.

There are no magic formulas for producing reusable code. Your functions, modules, and classes will be reusable only if you put in enough functionality while making them flexible enough to be used in many situations.

Inheritance addresses the flexibility issue. As an analogy, consider that automobile dealers thrive on the selling of options . . .

"Oh, that's a very nice car, but if we could just add air conditioning and a sunroof."

"Yes, sir! And I'll sell them to you at my cost—plus a small fee."

There are also features called "after-market," in which an owner adds things to the car that the manufacturer doesn't even know about. My point is this: *with serious purchases, a user is more likely to be satisfied if he or she can customize the object to suit personal needs.*

Similarly, a class is more likely to be useful if users of that class can add whatever features they want, including abilities that the original writer of the class never thought of.

Inheritance makes this easy—in some ways. With the Fraction class, you might find the class useful but might need another capability: for example, the ability to automatically get the equivalent floating-point value of the fraction (or rather, its nearest approximation). To do this, you'd need to declare a new class and add just the one new function.

```
class FloatFraction : public Fraction {
public:
```

10

```
        double get_float();
};
```

Then you'd provide a function definition. (For now, don't worry about the syntax—I'll cover it in the next chapter.)

```
double FloatFraction::get_float() {
    double x = get_num();
    double y = get_den();
    return x / y;
}
```

I'm assuming here that the get_num and get_den functions return a Fraction object's numerator and denominator, respectively. Given the availability of these functions, the get_float function is easy to write, as you can see.

But that's the rub. To write really useful extensions to an existing class, you need to know how to make things work inside that class—you may need to get in and muck around. And if someone else wrote the class, they may have to expose much of the class's internal structure to make you truly able to customize it. This goes a bit against the spirit of encapsulation, or data hiding.

All the same, inheritance can be useful. In this section, you've seen how a few lines of code created a new class that does everything the Fraction class did, but more besides. Now you can declare FloatFraction objects and use the new function get_float:

```
FloatFraction a;
a.set(3, 4);                // a = 3/4
cout << a.get_float();      // Print "0.75"
```

Creating Shared Interfaces

Inheritance is not only important in itself, but also as the only way in C++ to realize a feature considered truly essential to object-oriented programming: shared interfaces.

The term *interface* has many meanings. In this context, I mean a set of services (or functions) that different objects are free to respond to in their own way.

This is a subtle but crucial point. An object's class defines all its function code—so, all objects of the same class share identical behavior. But objects of *different but related* classes can define their own responses to a common interface.

For example, assume you have a general Shape class that defines several functions: move, redraw, and resize (just three, to keep this simple). The Shape class itself has no function-definition code; it's being used as a common interface (an *abstract class,* to use C++ terminology). The only thing the interface does is establish type information for each function.

The important point here is that different subclasses (such as Circle, Square, and Polygon) all support the same three functions—but each subclass responds to those functions with different behavior.

And this is crucial, in turn, because it enables someone to call a general Shape function (such as redraw) without necessarily having to know in advance what the resulting behavior will be.

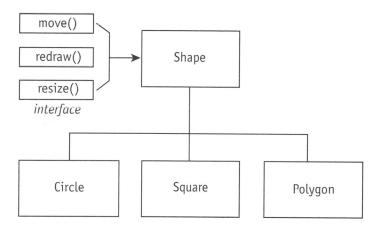

Now, the beauty of this system is that you can use a pointer to the general type (Shape) to call any of these services. The exact type of the object can be determined later, at runtime.

```
pShape->redraw();
```

This is C++ notation for:

```
(*pShape).redraw();
```

In other words: Get the object pointed to by pShape, and then send that object a message: "Draw yourself!"

But if all the program has is a pointer to the *general* type (Shape), how does the right function code for the *specific* type (for example, Circle or Square) get executed? That's the subject of the next section.

Polymorphism: True Object Independence

In describing how shared interfaces work, I've finally come to *polymorphism.* This is the most abstract concept in this book, but it's the one that many people consider the most important.

And this is true despite the fact that in a small-to-medium-sized program, you may not ever get into a practical situation involving polymorphism at all. But with any code that interacts with a larger, more complex system (say, Microsoft Windows or a network), polymorphism is critical; it's implicit in everything you do.

Do you wonder why programmers refer to languages such as C++ as being *object* oriented rather than class oriented? There's a reason for this. What object-oriented programming is really about, ultimately, is making the main program give up control to an object. Another way of stating this is to say:

✳ **The knowledge of how to carry out an action (also called a function or service) resides in the object itself, not in the user of that object.**

This is the essence of polymorphism, which—more literally—means that the implementation of a single function can take many different shapes.

Why is this so important? Well, consider for a moment how things are done in traditional programming. You could create a user-defined type of sorts—in the C language, you'd do that with a **struct** declaration, listing a number of public data fields. One of these fields could contain in integer indicating the object's specific type: for example, circle, square, or polygon.

Now, each of these specific kinds of shapes has to be drawn differently. So the user of the Shape type would have to check the object's specific type and take a different action depending on this value.

```
if (the_shape.type == CIRCLE)
    draw_circle(the_shape);
else if (the_shape.type == SQUARE)
    draw_square(the_shape);
else if (the_shape.type == POLYGON)
    draw_polygon(the_shape);
//...
```

Or, using the **switch case** syntax introduced in Chapter 9:

```
switch(the_shape.type) {
    case CIRCLE:
        draw_circle(the_shape);
        break;
    case SQUARE:
        draw_square(the_shape);
        break;
    case POLYGON:
        draw_polygon(the_shape);
        break;
    //...
```

If there are many of these subtypes, this block of code requires lots of work to write. But there's another, much more fundamental, problem. The user of the Shape type must know, *in advance,* all the subtypes that will ever be supported. Once this code is written and compiled, that list of subtypes is closed. New types cannot be added without going back and rewriting the main program.

And, no matter how many cases of subtypes you try to accommodate, there is one rather serious limitation: *New types cannot be added in the future . . .* not without rewriting and recompiling the program that uses the object.

As the inventor of a new subtype of object, you don't want to have to say to your users, "You can add this new subtype, but you'll have to go back, rewrite, and recompile all the code that refers to it, adding extra case-logic throughout your entire program."

And it gets worse. You might be providing a service over a network or interacting with an interface such as Microsoft Windows. And then it won't be possible to have the user of an object rewrite and recompile the code *at all.* You can't ask Microsoft to create a new version of Windows, for example, every time you write a new Windows application. Windows has to be able to send general messages, such as "redraw yourself, " without knowing in advance what all the possible responses might be.

Polymorphism and Virtual Functions

A limited kind of polymorphism can be achieved with function overloading and operator overloading. This is not a true solution, but it suffices in some cases. For example, one of the nice features of C++ is that you can define a new object type (a class) and also define how it supports the stream operator (<<) used with output streams such as **cout**.

```
Fraction fract1(1, 2);
cout << fract1;                  // Print "1/2"
```

At first glance, **cout** would seem to be polymorphic; that is, you can use it to print an endless variety of types. Because you can define a << operator function for each new type you create, you can always make the following statement work for any class of object:

```
cout << my_object;
```

The limitation here is that C++ must be able to determine that object's exact type at compile time. True polymorphism is not achieved. If the program is passed a pointer to a general object type across a network, for example, the **cout** object will not know how to print it. The following statement does not resolve the operation correctly:

```
cout << *pObject;      // Print what kind of object???
```

There is a way to resolve this situation. You can create a general "printable object" type that interacts correctly with **cout** (as well as any other output stream, by the way).

The solution in this and all similar cases involves the use of virtual functions. The beauty of the **virtual** keyword is that it makes a function in your program, as well as all the code that calls it, do everything correctly. Everything is handled for you, so that a call to a virtual function looks just like a call to any other member function.

What the **virtual** keyword says is this: "No matter how you got a reference or a pointer to an object, let the object itself decide how to carry out the function call." This means that the address of the object's implementation of that function is looked up at runtime. This is called *late binding,* because the actual function address is not resolved until just before the function is called.

And that's the essence of objects in C++. Despite the fact that heavy tomes are written on the subject, it's really just about creating data objects that know how to provide a set of services—in which the knowledge of how to carry out these services resides in the objects themselves.

It's almost as though each object acts as a miniature computer—an independent entity—that maintains its own data, as well as sending and receiving messages and responding appropriately. The main program never needs to tell the object how to do its job.

Interlude

Polymorphism and Traditional Languages

I stated that polymorphism is essential in writing a Windows application or providing a service across a network. Lots of people have, in the past, written such applications without access to an object-oriented language. But I stand by my statement.

In a traditional language such as C, there is a way of producing a polymorphic effect, although it is cumbersome, error-prone, and less elegant than the C++ approach.

The C technique registers a *call-back function:* this involves giving the object user (or, in the case of Windows, the application manager) the address of one or more functions. Using this address, the user of the object then makes an indirect function call at runtime, causing control to transfer to a function you have supplied.

The effect, at the machine-code level, is the same as employing a virtual function. What then is the disadvantage of the C-language approach?

Interlude

▼ *continued*

Actually, there are two:

▶ As with many object-oriented features, you can simulate the same effects in C, but it's a lot more work. In this case, the extra work involves registering the address of one or more functions, as well as making indirect function calls (requiring pointer syntax). Virtual functions are definitely easier to use.

▶ The C-language approach provides much less type checking. There's nothing to stop you from passing a function with an incorrect argument list. The C++ approach is much more rigorous, as it enforces strict type checking for all the functions. C++ also requires a class to implement *all* the functions in the interface, if it's going to support the interface at all.

The general situation with non-object-oriented languages such as C is this: yes, you can create graphical applications, network solutions, and applications for a graphical user interface such as the Macintosh or Microsoft Windows. But C++, with its ability to define independent objects, is better suited to these tasks.

What about Reusability?

Some people contend that the main motivation for object-oriented programming is that it provides the best support for writing reusable code.

This is not a claim to be lightly dismissed. As I mentioned in Chapter 4, a major goal in the history of programming techniques has been to make it easy to reuse old code for new purposes—so that programmers don't have to write the same instructions or statements over and over again.

Actually, the basic tool in this regard is the use of functions. The existence of the C++ standard library is a testament to that fact. You don't have to ever write the instructions to calculate a square root, for example. All you have to do is call the **sqrt** function:

```
#include <math.h>

double sq2 = sqrt(2);
```

Not only does the **sqrt** function save the time required to write square-root code, it also saves the time required to *learn how to do it yourself*. It's not just the sheer labor of writing the **sqrt** function code that is provided; it's also the exper-tise. If you had to write the function yourself, you'd likely have to go look up an algorithm for finding square roots. (Similarly, when you purchase a car, you're not just buying a hunk of tin; you're acquiring the benefits of centuries of engi-neering knowledge.)

By analogy, all progress in human industry is founded on this premise: the preexistence of old tools enables you to build ever more advanced tools, because (so the old saw goes) you don't have to reinvent the wheel each time.

The idea of reusable code certainly did not originate with OOPS. But OOPS does attempt to take the reusability you get with functions and extend it.

Here's how objects can potentially make your code more reusable:

▶ A class is a convenient way of packaging closely related code and data. The ability to hide much of the class is helpful in making it reusable, because that prevents errors due to name conflicts, as well as errors due to other programmers refer-ring to class internals they have no business messing with.

▶ Inheritance (subclassing) helps makes classes more reusable by allowing the users of a class to customize it. Unfortunately, this feature runs a bit counter to the goal of data hiding (encapsulation), because the more open you make a class, the less you protect its internals.

▶ The development of shared interfaces offers the possibility of making code more reusable by adopting standard sets of services. Ideally, you create a situation in which many service providers and many service clients can interact through a common set of functions. Because the interfaces are polymorphic, client soft-ware can even get a pointer to a new type of object at runtime and make good use of it—even though this new type didn't even exist when the client software was created.

The last advantage is potentially the most exciting one. Development of stan-dard interfaces means that new software can constantly be developed and inter-act smoothly with old software—all without requiring things to be rewritten and rebuilt. (Avoiding such rewriting is, in fact, the very goal of reusability.)

But development of standards is a human project, requiring documenta-tion, careful planning, and—if I may borrow a term from religion—*evangelism*. Object-oriented programming provides some useful tools, but they have to be applied with care and planning. Nothing in life is guaranteed.

Chapter 10 *Summary*

Here are the main points of Chapter 10:

▶ One of the major problems in software development has always been the complex interactions between all the functions in a program and all its global data. One of the major design goals of object-oriented programming is to reduce the amount of universally accessible global data.

▶ Instead, closely related data and functions are grouped together in a *class*. You can then make the data private to that class. (Or, as you'll see in the next chapter, you can make as many fields private as you choose) This hiding of parts of the class is called *encapsulation*.

▶ A function defined inside a class is called a *member function*.

▶ A data field of a class is called a *data member*.

▶ A class, as mentioned above, is a unit of code that defines a new type.

▶ Each instance of a class is an *object*. The relation of classes to objects is like that between the **int** type and individual **int** variables. For example, if Fraction has been defined as a class, you can declare any number of Fraction variables. These are objects.

```
Fraction f1, f2, f3;
```

▶ When you define a new class, you can subclass an existing class (also called *inheriting* from that other class). The existing class is referred to as the *base class*. This feature is potentially a great timesaving device, because general class features already defined don't need to be defined again. Essentially, you create a subclass based on an old class, and declare only the features that are new.

```
class FloatFraction : public Fraction {
public:
    double get_float();
};
```

▶ Probably the most important aspect of subclassing is that it is the only way in C++ to define shared interfaces. An interface, in this context, is a standard set of services—provided as a collection of functions that can be called by the user of the class.

▶ An inheritance hierarchy—in which each of any number of subclasses inherit from a common interface (abstract class)—enables C++ to enforce type checking for all the functions and arguments. But each subclass is free to respond to a function call in its own way.

10

▶ Calls to class functions under these conditions are *polymorphic,* as long as the functions are declared **virtual**. Polymorphism means "many forms": a single function call may have many different implementations.

▶ Critical to the idea of polymorphism in C++ is this principle: No matter how you get a reference or pointer to an object, the right function code gets executed, although you may not know the object's exact type. This is because knowledge of how to provide a service resides in each object, not in the code that uses it.

▶ Object-oriented programming can help encourage the development of reusable code, but in the end, it is only a set of tools. Most of the work in making code reusable requires human effort.

The Fraction Class

Some people talk about object orientation as though it were easy: You wave the magic wand of C++ and your troubles disappear. But writing a useful class requires thought and planning. To be reusable—to offer so much that other programmers will make use of it—requires that you place serious functionality into the class.

But the good news is that once you develop, write, and test a class that truly meets your needs, you've created a strong addition to the C++ language. Alternatively, you can use classes and objects as a way to package code and data together.

Because the task of writing a real class is involved, I'm going to focus mainly on a single class over the next several chapters: the Fraction class, which (when done) will meet a practical need, by providing a new way to store and operate on numbers.

Point: A Simple Class

Before we get to the Fraction class, let's look at a simpler class. But first, here's the general syntax of the C++ class keyword.

```
class class_name {
    declarations
};
```

Except when you write a subclass, the syntax is no more complicated than this. The declarations can include data declarations, function declarations, or both. Here's a simple example that only involves data declarations.

```
class Point {
    int x, y;            // private -- may not be accessed
};
```

But members are private by default, which means that they cannot be accessed. This first attempt at declaring a Point class is therefore not useful. To be of any use at all, the class needs to have at least one public member.

```
class Point {
public:
    int x, y;
};
```

This is better. Now the class can actually be used. Given a class declaration for Point, you can declare individual Point objects, such as pt1.

```
Point pt1;
```

You can then assign values to individual data fields (called data members):

```
pt1.x = 1;
```

In this example, which includes no function members, you can think of the Point class as simply a collection of data fields. Each item declared with Point type has an x and y member, and because these are integers, you can use them just as you would any integer variable.

```
cout << pt1.y + 4;     // Print sum of two integers.
```

Before we leave the simple version of the Point class, there's an aspect of syntax worth commenting on. A class declaration ends with a semicolon.

```
class Point {
public:
    int x, y;
};
```

When you're starting to write C++ code, the semicolon is an easy thing to get tripped up on. A class declaration *requires* a semicolon after the closing brace (}), whereas a function definition *rejects* that same use of a semicolon (i.e., you'd get a syntax error).

Keep in mind this cardinal rule:

✱ A class, data, or data-member declaration always ends with a semicolon, without exception. This is true even when there is a closing brace (}).

So class declarations place a semicolon after the closing brace, whereas function definitions do not.

Interlude

For C Programmers: Structures and Classes

In C++, the **struct** and **class** keywords are equivalent, except that members of a **struct** are public by default. But both keywords create classes in C++. (This means that the general term "class" and the keyword **class** are not precisely coextensive.)

In C, when you declare a **struct** type, you have to reuse the **struct** keyword whenever you invoke the structure as a type name. For example:

```
struct Point pt1, pt2, pt3;
```

But this is never necessary in C++. Once Point is declared as a new type (with either **struct** or **class**), you can use it directly. So after you port C-language code to C++, you can replace the data declaration above with:

```
Point pt1, pt2, pt3;
```

The treatment of **struct** in C++ arises from the need for backward compatibility. C code often makes liberal use of **struct**:

```
struct Point {
    int x, y;
};
```

The C language has no **public** or **private** keyword, and the user of a **struct** type must be able to access all members. Therefore, to maintain compatibility, **struct** members had to be public by default. At the same time, a design goal was to make C structures easy to extend. You can therefore add function members to **struct** types if you choose.

Does C++ even need a **class** keyword? Technically, no. But **class** performs a self-documenting function, as the purpose of a class is usually to add function members. It's also good discipline to have class members be private by default. In object orientation, making a member public ought to happen only as a deliberate choice.

Private: Members Only (Protecting the Data)

In the previous section, the Point class permitted direct access to its data members, because they were declared public.

What do you do when you want to prevent direct access of the data members? You might, for example, want to ensure that data assigned to the two members (x, y) is in a particular range. The way to do that in C++ is to prevent direct access to these data members, and require the user of the class to call certain functions.

The following version of Point prevents access to x and y from outside the class, but permits indirect access through several member functions.

```
class Point {
private:              // Data members (private)
    int x, y;
public:               // Member functions
    void set(int new_x, int new_y);
    int get_x();
    int get_y();
};
```

This class declaration is still fairly simple. You'll note that it declares three public member functions—set, get_x, and get_y—as well as two private data members. Now, after declaring Point objects, you can only manipulate values by calling one of the public functions:

```
Point point1;
point1.set(10, 20);
cout << point1.get_x() << ", " << point1.get_y();
```

This prints:

```
10, 20
```

If you try to data members directly, the compiler flags that attempt as an error:

```
point1.x = 10;            // ERROR!
```

The three function members don't write themselves, of course; they have to be defined somewhere in the program. The function definitions can go any-where—they can even be placed in a separate module, or compiled and then added to the standard C++ library. In any case, type information must be given for the functions . . . but the class declaration provides the function prototypes. It's only necessary, therefore, for the class declaration to appear before code that uses the class.

The `Point::` prefix clarifies the scope of these definitions, so the compiler knows that they apply to functions declared in the Point class. This is important, because every class can have its own function named `set`, and you can also have a global function named `set`.

```
void Point::set(int new_x, int new_y) {
    x = new_x;
    y = new_y;
}

int Point::get_x() {
    return x;
}

int Point::get_y() {
    return y;
}
```

The `Point::` scope prefix is applied to the function name. The return type (**void** or **int**, as the case may be) still appears in its normal position, at the beginning of the first line of the definition.

The syntax for member-function definitions can be summarized as:

```
type class_name::function_name (argument_list) {
    statements
}
```

Given these functions, you have control over the data. You can, for example, rewrite the Point::set function so negative input values are converted to positive.

```
void Point::set(int new_x, int new_y) {
    if (new_x < 0)
        new_x *= -1;
    if (new_y < 0)
        new_y *= -1;
    x = new_x;
    y = new_y;
}
```

Here, I'm using the multiplication-assignment operator (`*=`); `new_x *= -1` has the same effect as `new_x = new_x * -1`.

Although function code *outside the class* cannot refer directly to private data members x and y, function definitions *of* the class can refer to class members without qualification, whether they are private or not. For example, this statement sets a new value for class member x.

```
x = new_x;
```

Conceptually, you can visualize the Point class this way. Every Point object (that is, variable declared with the Point class name) shares this same structure.

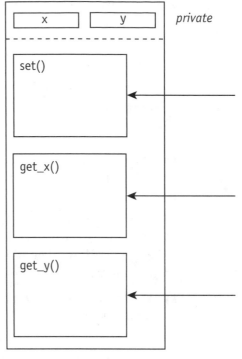

Point class

Example 11.1. *Testing the Point Class*

Once you create the Point class, you can use the name "Point" just as you would any standard type name—int, float, double, and so on. There is no need to qualify references to "Point" with any other keyword.

The following program performs some simple tests on the Point class, using it to set and get some data. Code that's new is in bold; the rest is existing code from the chapter.

```cpp
Point1.cpp

    #include <iostream>
    using namespace std;

    class Point {
    private:              // Data members (private)
        int x, y;
```

11

Point1.cpp, cont.

```cpp
public:                 // Member functions
    void set(int new_x, int new_y);
    int get_x();
    int get_y();
};

int main() {
    Point pt1, pt2;

    pt1.set(10, 20);
    cout << "pt1 is " << pt1.get_x();
    cout << ", " << pt1.get_y() << endl;
    pt2.set(-5, -25);
    cout << "pt2 is " << pt2.get_x();
    cout << ", " << pt2.get_y() << endl;
    return 0;
}

void Point::set(int new_x, int new_y) {
    if (new_x < 0)
        new_x *= -1;
    if (new_y < 0)
        new_y *= -1;
    x = new_x;
    y = new_y;
}

int Point::get_x() {
    return x;
}

int Point::get_y() {
    return y;
}
```

How It Works

This is a simple example. The Point class must be declared first, so it can be used by **main**. Given this declaration, main can declare a couple of different objects of Point type:

```cpp
Point pt1, pt2;
```

The set, get_x, and get_y functions can then be applied to both pt1 and pt2. These three statements call Point functions through the object p1:

```
pt1.set(10, 20);
cout << "pt1 is " << pt1.get_x();
cout << ", " << pt1.get_y() << endl;
```

And these next three statements call Point functions through the object p2:

```
pt2.set(-5, -25);
cout << "pt2 is " << pt2.get_x();
cout << ", " << pt2.get_y() << endl;
```

EXERCISES

Exercise 11.1.1. Revise the set function so it establishes an upper limit of 100 for values of x and y; if a value greater than 100 is entered, it is reduced to 100. Revise **main** to test this behavior.

Exercise 11.1.2. Write two new functions for the Point class: set_x and set_y, which set the individual values x and y. Remember to reverse the negative sign, if any, as is done in the set function.

Introducing the Fraction Class

One of the best ways to think about object orientation is to consider it a way to define new data types. A class is an extension to the language itself. A good example is a Fraction class (which could also be called a "rational number" class) that stores two numbers, representing the numerator and the denominator, respectively.

The Fraction class is useful if you ever need to store numbers such as 1/3 or 2/7, and you need to store them precisely. You can even use the class to store dollars-and-cents figures such as $1.57.

Note ▶ With dollars and cents, the issue is not about units, but about storing multiples of 1/100 without error in a binary system. 0.5 can be stored precisely as a binary floating point (because 1/2 is a power of 2), but 0.51 cannot be, because 1/10 and 1/100 are not powers of two. If you write simple tests involving such figures in a C++ program, a **double** initialized to 0.51 will *seem* to work correctly at first, and maybe for some time thereafter. But there is a tiny degree of error lurking just beneath the surface, and eventually these errors accumulate into larger errors.

In creating the Fraction class, it becomes especially important to restrict access to the data members, for several reasons. For one thing, you should never allow a 0 denominator, because the ratio 1/0 is not a legal operation in mathematics.

And even with legal operations, it's important to simplify ratios so there's a unique expression of every rational number. For example, the following ratios:

3/3   2/4   6/2   -1/-1   2/-1

These should simplify into:

1/1   1/2   3/1   1/1   -2/1

In the next few sections, I'll develop functions that automatically handle all this work. For the user of the finished Fraction class, the beauty of it is that all the details of working with fractions are hidden. If the class is written correctly, programmers who have never seen the source code can use the class to create any number of Fraction objects, and operations such as the following will do the right thing "automagically."

```
Fraction a(1, 6);    // a = 1/6
Fraction b(1, 3);    // b = 1/3

if (a + b == Fraction(1, 2))
    cout << "1/6 + 1/3 equals 1/2";
```

This full version of the Fraction class will take a few chapters to develop. Let's start with the simplest possible version.

```
class Fraction {
private:
    int num, den;       // Numerator and denominator.
public:
    void set(int n, int d);
    int get_num();
    int get_den();
private:
    void normalize();   // Put fraction into standard
                        // form.
    int gcf(int a, int b);   // Greatest Common Factor.
    int lcm(int a, int b);   // Lowest Common
                             // Denominator.
};
```

This class declaration has three parts:

▶ Private data members. These are num and den, which store the numerator and denominator, respectively. (You may recall from school that in the fraction 1/3, for example, 1 is the numerator and 3 is the denominator.)

▶ Public function members. These provide indirect access to class data.

▶ Private function members. These are support functions we'll make use of later in the chapter. For now, they just return zero values.

With these functions declared, you can use the class to do simple operations, such as these:

```
Fraction fract;
fract.set(1, 2);
cout << fract.get_num();
cout << "/";
cout << fract.get_den();
```

So far, this isn't very interesting, because the class does nothing more sophisticated than the Point class. But it's a place to start.

You can visualize the Fraction class this way.

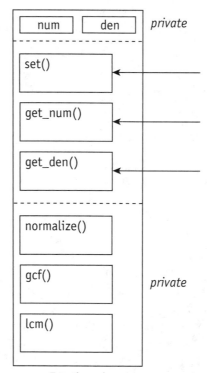

Fraction class

As always, functions declared in the class—whether public or private—have to be defined somewhere. The class declaration provides a series of function prototypes, so aside from the class and the function definitions, these functions do not need to be declared anywhere else.

```
void Fraction::set(int n, int d) {
    num = n;
    den = d;
}

int Fraction::get_num(){
    return n;
}

int Fraction::get_den(){
    return d;
}

// TO BE DONE...
// These remaining functions are syntactically
//   correct, but don't do anything useful yet. We'll
//   fill them in later.

void Fraction::normalize(){
    return;
}

int Fraction::gcf(int a, int b){
    return 0;
}

int Fraction::lcm(int a, int b){
    return 0;
}
```

Inline Functions

Three of the functions in the Fraction class do simple things: set or get data. Even in more sophisticated versions of the class, these functions won't get complicated. They are therefore good candidates for *inlining*.

When a function is inlined, the compiler treats a call to the function differently from an ordinary function call. The call does not transfer control to a new program location. Instead, the compiler replaces the function call with the body of the function. For example, suppose that the set function is inlined, as follows:

```
void set() {num = n; den = d;}
```

Now, whenever the following statement is encountered in program code:

```
fract.set(1, 2);
```

the compiler inserts the machine instructions for the set function. The result is essentially the same as if the following C++ code were inserted into the program:

```
{fract.num = 1; fract.den = 2;}
```

And if the get_num function is inlined, the expression

```
fract.get_num()
```

is replaced with a machine instruction or two that gets the value of fract.num. But in this last case, you may wonder: Why write a get_num function at all, if it is just going to be replaced by a reference to fract.num? Why not just let num be a public member?

The answer is that by having a get_num function, you control access to the num data member, even though the function is inline. If num were made a public data member, the user of the Fraction class could both read and write the value of num directly—which would violate our concept of the class.

You can make functions inline by placing their function definitions in the class declaration itself. Remember that no semicolon follows the end of a function definition.

The altered lines below are in bold.

```
class Fraction {
private:
    int num, den;        // Numerator and denominator.
public:
    void set(int n, int d) {num = n; den = d;
                            normalize();}
    int get_num()  {return num;}
    int get_den()  {return den;}
private:
    void normalize();    // Put fraction into standard
                         // form.
    int gcf(int a, int b);   // Greatest Common Factor.
    int lcm(int a, int b);   // Lowest Common
                             // Denominator.
};
```

Because the three private functions are not inlined, their function definitions still need to be included separately in the code:

```
void Fraction::normalize(){
    return;
}

int Fraction::gcf(int a, int b){
    return 0;
}

int Fraction::lcm(int a, int b){
    return 0;
}
```

What is the advantage of making a function inline? Simple. If the action of the function amounts to only a few machine instructions (such as moving data from a particular memory location to another), then you can improve the efficiency of the program by writing it as an inline function. A true function call involves a certain amount of overhead at runtime (consisting of several machine instructions), and when the action of the function amounts to less work than this overhead, it ought to be inlined.

But functions that have more than a few simple statements should not be inlined. Remember that wherever there is an inline-function call, the compiler places the entire body of the function into the code; so if an inline function is called often, the program ends up taking up more space than it needs to. Inline functions also have some additional restrictions that do not apply to other functions. They cannot use recursion, for example.

The three support functions—normalize, gcf, and lcm—are going to get longer, so we won't make those inline.

Find the Greatest Common Factor

All the actions inside the Fraction class, described in the next few chapters, rest on two concepts in number theory: greatest common factor (GCF) and lowest common multiple (LCM).

I first described a greatest-common-factor function in Chapter 4. As you may recall, the greatest common factor is the largest number that evenly divides two other numbers. For example:

NUMBERS	GREATEST COMMON FACTOR
12, 18	6
12, 10	2
25, 50	25
50, 25	25
20, 21	1

The gcf function of Chapter 4 makes use of modular division (%), which divides one integer by another and returns the remainder. The full solution uses an elegant recursive algorithm.

```
int gcf(int a, int b) {
    if (a % b == 0)
        return b;
    else
        return gcf(b, a % b);
}
```

We can almost use this function as is, and plug it into the Fraction class as a needed support function.

But there is a problem: this version of the gcf function assumes that the inputs are both positive integers. We needed to consider, for a moment, what might go wrong.

First, what happens if one of the arguments is 0?

If you experiment with different values, you'll find that a value of $a = 0$ causes no problem. A value of $a = 0$ and $b = 5$, for example, produces a result of 5. This is because the terminating case is immediately reached. 0 % 5 produces 0 (since dividing 0 by any other number produces no remainder). Therefore, the function successfully returns 5.

But a value of $b = 0$ causes the function to attempt division by zero; this causes a runtime error that stops the program.

But when we write normalize—another Fraction class support function—in an upcoming section, we will ensure that a and b are properly adjusted before gcf is ever called. The normalize function will adjust any fraction that has 0 in it by changing the fraction to 0/1. The bottom line is that (because of how the rest of the code is written) the argument to b will never be 0.

Note ▶ Remember that one of the main purposes of object-oriented programming is to control access to functions. By making gcf private, we have ensured that only Fraction-class support functions can ever call gcf; through careful programming, therefore, we can make sure that 0 is never passed to b.

Another concern is: what happens if negative numbers are passed? If you experiment with different values, you'll find that the use of negative signs doesn't change the absolute value of the result; gcf(25, 35) produces 5, but so does gcf(25, -35). There is one problem, however: the sign of the result becomes difficult to predict.

For the purposes of this class, it's easier to produce correct results if we express all denominators and common multiples as positive numbers. We can do this in the gcf function by always returning a positive number for the terminal case.

```
int gcf(int a, int b) {
    if (a % b == 0)
        return abs(b);
    else
        return gcf(b, a % b);
}
```

Here, I've put in bold the one expression that changes from the first version of gcf. It's a simple change, replacing b with abs(b). The **abs** function is a C++ standard library function that returns the absolute value of a number. The absolute value is always non-negative.

Find the Lowest Common Multiple

Once the gcf function is defined, the rest of the Fraction class is not difficult to write. Another support function that will prove useful is a function that gets the lowest common multiple. This function will make use of the gcf function.

The LCM is the lowest number which is a multiple of both of two inputs. This is the converse of the GCF. So for example, the LCM of 200 and 300 is 600. The greatest common factor, meanwhile, is 100.

The trick in finding the LCM is to first isolate the greatest common factor, and then multiply by this factor only once. Because otherwise, when you multiply A and B, you are implicitly including the same factor twice. The common factor must therefore be removed from A and from B.

In other words, for two inputs A and B, isolate the GCF. Divide A by this number and divide B by this number. Then multiply by GCF one time.

The formula is:

$n = GCF(a, b)$
$LCM(A, B) = n * (a / n) * (b / n)$

The second line simplifies to:

$LCM(A, B) = (a / n) * b$

The LCM function is now easy to write.

```
int lcm(int a, int b) {
    return (a / gcf(a, b)) * b;
}
```

You can easily verify that this works. For example, take the case of 200 and 300. The greatest common factor is 100. The LCM formula therefore produces a result of 600:

LCM = 200 / 100 * 300 = 2 * 300 = 600.

And 600 is in fact the lowest common multiple of 200 and 300. You can try this on any number of other pairs. The function is correct.

Example 11.2. *Fraction Support Functions*

Now that we know how to write the gcf and lcm functions, it's an easy matter to add that code to the Fraction class. Here is the code for a first working version of the class. I've also added code for the normalize function, which simplifies fractions after each operation.

Code that is new or altered from earlier versions is in bold.

Fract1.cpp

```
#include <stdlib.h>

class Fraction {
private:
    int num, den;       // Numerator and denominator.
public:
    void set(int n, int d) {num = n; den = d;
                            normalize();}
    int get_num()  {return num;}
    int get_den()  {return den;}
private:
    void normalize();   // Put fraction into standard
                        // form.
    int gcf(int a, int b);  // Greatest Common Factor.
    int lcm(int a, int b);  // Lowest Common
                            // Denominator.
};
```

11

```cpp
// Normalize: put fraction into a standard form, unique
//   for each mathematically different value.
//
void Fraction::normalize(){

    // Handle cases involving 0

    if (den == 0 || num == 0) {
        num = 0;
        den = 1;
    }

    // Put neg. sign in numerator only.

    if (den < 0) {
        num *= -1;
        den *= -1;
    }

    // Factor out GCF from numerator and denominator.

    int n = gcf(num, den);
    num = num / n;
    den = den / n;
}

// Greatest Common Factor
//
int Fraction::gcf(int a, int b) {
    if (a % b == 0)
        return abs(b);
    else
        return gcf(b, a % b);
}

// Lowest Common Multiple
//
int Fraction::lcm(int a, int b){
    return (a / gcf(a, b)) * b;
}
```

How It Works

First, the stdlib.h file is included to support the **abs** function used in the Fraction::gcf definition.

```
#include <stdlib.h>
```

The code for the gcf and lcm functions can be copied from the previous two sections, with one change. The function heading must use the `Fraction::` prefix before the name. Note that this only has to be done in the heading:

```
int Fraction::gcf(int a, int b) {
    if (a % b == 0)
        return abs(b);
    else
        return gcf(b, a % b);
}
```

When the function calls itself in the recursive function call

```
return gcf(b, a % b);
```

it's not necessary to use the `Fraction::` prefix. That's because, inside a class function, the scope of that class is assumed.

Similarly, when the Fraction::lcm function calls gcf, class scope is again assumed. In other words, Fraction::lcm is assumed to be calling Fraction::gcf.

```
int Fraction::lcm(int a, int b){
    return (a / gcf(a, b)) * b;
}
```

In general, every time the C++ compiler comes across a variable or function name, it looks for the declaration of that name in this order:

▶ Within the same function (in the case of local variables)

▶ Within the same class (if the function is a member function)

▶ If no declaration is found at the function or class level, the compiler looks for a global declaration.

The normalize function is the only new code here. The first thing the function does is to handle cases involving zero. A denominator equal to 0 is an illegal value, so the fraction is changed to 0/1. In addition, all values with numerator equal 0 are equivalent:

```
0/1    0/2    0/5    0/-1    0/25
```

These are all put in the standard form 0/1.

One of the main goals of the Fraction class is to ensure that all mathematically equal values are represented in exactly the same way. (This will make things easier when it's time to implement the test-for-equality operator.) One problem is posed by negative numbers. These two expressions represent the same value:

-2/3   2/-3

As do these:

4/5   -4/-5

The easiest solution is to test the denominator; if it's less than 0, reverse the sign of both the numerator and denominator. This takes care of both of the problematic cases above in one fell swoop.

```
if (den < 0) {
    num *= -1;
    den *= -1;
}
```

The rest of the function is straightforward: find the greatest common factor and then divide both the numerator and denominator by this amount.

```
int n = gcf(num, den);
num = num / n;
den = den / n;
```

For example, take the fraction 30/50. The greatest common factor is 10. The normalize function executes the necessary division and produces 3/5.

The normalize function is important for more than one reason. First, as I mentioned earlier, it's important that equivalent values be expressed exactly the same way. Second, when we start defining arithmetic operations for the Fraction class, large numbers can accumulate for the numerator and denominator. To avoid overflow errors at runtime, it's important to simplify Fraction expressions whenever there's an opportunity.

EXERCISES

Exercise 11.2.1.   Are there any combination of values for the fraction numerator and denominator that will cause errors, or does the definition of the class anticipate all possible problems?

Exercise 11.2.2.   Rewrite the normalize function so it uses the division-assignment operator (/=). Remember that this operation:

a /= b

is equivalent to

```
a = a / b
```

Example 11.3.   ## Testing the Fraction Class

Once you have completed a class declaration, you need to test it by using it to declare one or more objects and then use the objects. The following code enables the user to enter values for a fraction and then read the values after the fraction is simplified. The loop repeats operations any number of times.

Fract2.cpp

```cpp
#include <stdlib.h>
#include <iostream>
using namespace std;

class Fraction {
private:
    int num, den;        // Numerator and denominator.
public:
    void set(int n, int d) {num = n; den = d;
                            normalize();}
    int get_num()  {return num;}
    int get_den()  {return den;}
private:
    void normalize();    // Put fraction into standard
                         // form.
    int gcf(int a, int b);   // Greatest Common Factor.
    int lcm(int a, int b);   // Lowest Common
                             // Denominator.
};

int main() {
    int a, b;
    char str[81];
    Fraction fract;
    while (1) {
        cout << "Enter numerator: ";
```

```
            cin >> a;
            cout << "Enter denominator: ";
            cin >> b;
            fract.set(a, b);
            cout << "Numerator is   " << fract.get_num()
                << endl;
            cout << "Denominator is " << fract.get_den()
                << endl;
            cout << "Do again? (Y or N) ";
            cin >> str;
            if (!(str[0] == 'Y' || str[0] == 'y'))
                break;
    }
}


// -------------------------------------------------
// FRACTION CLASS FUNCTIONS

// Normalize: put fraction into a standard form, unique
//   for each mathematically different value.
//
void Fraction::normalize(){

    // Handle cases involving 0

    if (den == 0 || num == 0) {
        num = 0;
        den = 1;
    }

    // Put neg. sign in numerator only.

    if (den < 0) {
        num *= -1;
        den *= -1;
    }

    // Factor out GCF from numerator and denominator.
```

▼ *continued on next page*

Fract2.cpp, cont.

```
        int n = gcf(num, den);
        num = num / n;
        den = den / n;
    }

    // Greatest Common Factor
    //
    int Fraction::gcf(int a, int b) {
        if (a % b == 0)
            return abs(b);
        else
            return gcf(b, a % b);
    }

    // Lowest Common Multiple
    //
    int Fraction::lcm(int a, int b){
        return (a / gcf(a, b)) * b;
    }
```

How it Works

The most important thing to notice about this function is that the class declaration must come first, before the class or its functions are referenced in **main**. After the class is declared, the functions (including **main**) can be placed in any order.

A common practice is to put class declarations, along with any other needed declarations and directives, into a header file. You could certainly take that approach here. Assuming that the name of this header file was Fraction.h, you'd need to add the following to a program that used the Fraction class:

```
#include "Fraction.h"
```

Function definitions that are *not* inlined must be placed somewhere in the program . . . or else they must be separately compiled and linked into the project.

The third line of **main** creates an uninitialized Fraction object:

```
Fraction fact;
```

Other statements in **main** then set the Fraction object and read back its value. Note that the call to the set function assigns values, but it also calls the normalize function, which causes the fraction to be simplified as appropriate.

```
        fract.set(a, b);
        cout << "Numerator is    " << fract.get_num()
          << endl;
        cout << "Denominator is " << fract.get_den()
          << endl;
```

EXERCISE

Exercise 11.3.1. Write a program that uses the Fraction class by setting a series of values by calling the set function: 2/2, 4/8, -9/-9, 10/50, 100/25. Have the program print out the results and verify that each fraction was correctly simplified.

Interlude | ## A New Kind of #include?

In the last example, you may note that I introduced new syntax for the **#include** directive. Remember that to turn on support for an area of the C++ library, the preferred method is to use angle brackets:

```
    #include <iostream>
```

But to include declarations from your own project files, you need to use quotation marks:

```
    #include "Fraction.h"
```

Why the difference? These two forms of the **#include** directive do almost the same thing, but with the quote-mark syntax, the C++ compiler is directed to first look in the current directory, and only secondly to look in the standard include-file directory (which, for example, is set in an MS-DOS system through the use of the INCLUDE environment variable).

Depending on what version of the C++ compiler you have, you could probably use the quote-mark syntax (that is, the second form) for both library files and project files. But that is not a good idea; to be compatible with standards to be enforced by all future versions of C++, you should stick to the standard practice of using angle brackets to turn on features of the C++ standard library.

Example 11.4. *Fraction Arithmetic: add and mult*

The next step in creating a working Fraction class is to add some simple arithmetic functions, add and mult. These functions will not by themselves implement operators for the class; however, after you add these to the class, true operator functions will be easy to write.

Addition is the hardest, but you may recall the technique from grade school. Consider addition of two fractions:

```
A/B + C/D
```

The trick is to first find the lowest common denominator (LCD)—by finding the lowest common multiple between B and D:

```
LCD = LCM(B, D).
```

Fortunately, we have a convenient utility function, lcm, to do just that. Then A/B has to be converted to a fraction that uses this LCD:

```
A    *    LCD/B
--        -----
B    *    LCD/B
```

We then get a fraction in which the denominator is LCD. Similarly for C/D:

```
C    *    LCD/D
--        -----
D    *    LCD/D
```

After these multiplications are performed, the two fractions will have a common denominator (LCD) and they can be added together. The resulting fraction is:

```
(A * LCD/B)  + (C * LCD/D)
-------------------------
            LCD
```

The algorithm is therefore:

Calculate LCD from LCM(B, D)
Set Quotient1 to LCD/B
Set Quotient2 to LCD/D
Set numerator for the new fraction to A * Quotient1 + C * Quotient2
Set denominator for the new fraction to LCD.

Multiplication is easier:

Set numerator for the new fraction to A * C.
Set denominator for the new fraction to B * D.

With these algorithms in hand, we can now go ahead and write code that declares and implements the two new functions, as well as tests the class. As before, the lines that are bold represent new or altered lines; everything else is the same as in the last example.

Fract3.cpp

```cpp
#include <iostream>
using namespace std;

class Fraction {
private:
    int num, den;       // Numerator and denominator.
public:
    void set(int n, int d)
        {num = n; den = d; normalize();}
    int get_num()  {return num;}
    int get_den()  {return den;}
    Fraction add(Fraction other);
    Fraction mult(Fraction other);
private:
    void normalize();   // Put fraction into standard
                        // form.
    int gcf(int a, int b);  // Greatest Common Factor.
    int lcm(int a, int b);  // Lowest Common
                            // Denominator.
};

int main() {
    Fraction fract1, fract2, fract3;

    fract1.set(1, 2);
    fract2.set(1, 3);
    fract3 = fract1.add(fract2);
    cout << "1/2 plus 1/3 = ";
    cout << fract3.get_num() << "/" <<
      fract3.get_den();
}

// ------------------------------------------------
// FRACTION CLASS FUNCTIONS

// Normalize: put fraction into a standard form, unique
//  for each mathematically different value.
//
void Fraction::normalize(){
```

▼ *continued on next page*

```cpp
    // Handle cases involving 0

    if (den == 0 || num == 0) {
        num = 0;
        den = 1;
    }

    // Put neg. sign in numerator only.

    if (den < 0) {
        num *= -1;
        den *= -1;
    }

    // Factor out GCF from numerator and denominator.

    int n = gcf(num, den);
    num = num / n;
    den = den / n;
}

// Greatest Common Factor
//
int Fraction::gcf(int a, int b) {
    if (a % b == 0)
        return abs(b);
    else
        return gcf(b, a % b);
}

// Lowest Common Multiple
//
int Fraction::lcm(int a, int b){
    return (a / gcf(a, b)) * b;
}

Fraction Fraction::add(Fraction other) {
    Fraction fract;
    int lcd = lcm(den, other.den);
    int quot1 = lcd/den;
    int quot2 = lcd/other.den;
```

```
        fract.set(num * quot1 + other.num * quot2, lcd);
        fract.normalize();
        return fract;
    }

    Fraction Fraction::mult(Fraction other) {
        Fraction fract;
        fract.set(num * other.num, den * other.den);
        fract.normalize();
        return fract;
    }
```

How It Works

The add and mult functions apply the algorithms that I described earlier. They also use a new type signature: each of these functions takes an argument of type Fraction and also returns a value of type Fraction. Consider the type declaration of the add function.

<u>Fraction</u> <u>Fraction::add</u> (<u>Fraction</u> other);

   ①   ②   ③

Each occurrence of Fraction in this declaration has a different purpose.

1 The use of Fraction at the beginning of the declaration indicates that the function returns an object of type Fraction.

2 The name prefix Fraction:: indicates that the add function is declared within the Fraction class.

3 Within the parentheses, Fraction indicates that there is one argument, other, which has type Fraction.

Though these three uses of Fraction often go together, they are not logically required to do so. For example, you could have a function that takes an argument of type **int**, returns a Fraction object, but is not declared within the Fraction class. The declaration would look like this:

```
Fraction my_func(int n);
```

Because the `Fraction::add` function returns an object of type Fraction, it must first create a new object.

```
Fraction fract;
```

The function then applies the algorithm I described earlier:

```
int lcd = lcm(den, other.den);
int quot1 = lcd/den;
int quot2 = lcd/other.den;
fract.set(num * quot1 + other.num * quot2, lcd);
```

Finally, after setting the values for the new Fraction object (fract), the function returns this object.

```
return fact;
```

The basic procedure is essentially the same for the mult function.

EXERCISES

Exercise 11.4.1.   Rewrite **main** so it adds any two fractions input and prints the results.

Exercise 11.4.2.   Rewrite **main** so it multiplies any two fractions input and prints the results.

Exercise 11.4.3.   Write an add function for the Point class introduced earlier. The function should add the x values to get the new value of x, and it should add the y values to get the new value of y.

Exercise 11.4.4.   Write sub and div functions for the Fraction class, along with code in **main** to test these functions. (The algorithm for sub is similar to that for add, although you can write an even simpler function by multiplying the numerator of the argument by -1 and then just calling the add function.)

Chapter 11   *Summary*

Here are the main points of Chapter 11:

▶ A class declaration has this form:

```
class class_name {
    declarations
};
```

▶ In C++, the **struct** keyword is syntactically equivalent to the **class** keyword, with one important difference: members of a class declared with **struct** are public by default; members of a class declared with **class** are private by default.

▶ Because members of a **class** type are private by default, you need to use the **public** keyword to declare at least one member public. Every member following **public:** is affected by the keyword, up until the end of the function or the next occurrence of **private**. For example:

```
class Fraction {
private:
    int num, den;
public:
    void set(int n, int d);
    int get_num();
    int get_den();
private:
    void normalize();
    int gcf(int a, int b);
    int lcm(int a, int b);
};
```

▶ Class declarations and data member declarations end with a semicolon (even after a closing brace) without exception.

▶ Once a class is declared, you can use it as a type name, just as you would **int**, **float**, **double**, and so on. So if Fraction has been declared as a class, you can declare a series of Fraction objects:

```
Fraction a, b, c, my_fraction, fract1;
```

▶ Functions of a class can refer to other members of a class (whether private or not) without qualification.

▶ Every member function must be defined somewhere.

▶ To place a member-function definition outside the class declaration, use this syntax:

```
type class_name::function_name (argument_list)
    statements
}
```

▶ If you place a member-function definition inside the class declaration, the function is inline, which means that there is no function-call overhead. Instead, the machine instructions that implement the function are placed right into the body of the rest of the code.

▶ The class declaration must precede use of the class. The function definitions can be placed anywhere in the program (or even in a separate module).

▶ Functions (whether they are member functions or not) can use classes as argument types and also as return types. If a function has a class for its return type, that means it must return an object. To do this, it must first create an object by declaring it as a local variable. Then it must return that variable.

Constructors:
If You Build It . . .

One of the themes in this book is that object orientation is a way to create a fundamental new data type. I'll focus on that idea for several chapters.

But I haven't yet come through on this promise—that you can make classes as convenient as standard data types. One of the most convenient features of types such as **int**, **float**, **double**, and so on is that you can initialize them as you declare them. (C++ is somewhat more liberal than C in this regard; you can initialize with any value, not just constants.)

You're about to see how easy it is to support initialization for objects, as well. Welcome to the craft of C++ construction.

Introducing Constructors

The term *constructor* is just C++-speak for an initialization function. By "initialization function," I mean a function that tells the compiler how to interpret declarations such as this:

```
Fraction a(1, 2);    // a = 1/2
```

Given what you've seen of the Fraction class, you'd probably guess this declaration ought to have the same effect as these statements:

```
Fraction a;
a.set(1, 2);
```

And in fact, in this chapter, we're going to make the class behave precisely that way. But the computer has no way of guessing this is what you want to do, no matter how obvious it may seem. You have to tell the computer how to carry out initializations. This is what constructors are for.

A constructor is a special member function (and as such, it must be declared inside the class). It has this syntax:

```
class_name(argument_list) {
    statements
}
```

This makes for an odd-looking function. There is no return type (not even **void**)! The class name, in a sense, is the return type—or rather, what replaces the return type. The role of the constructor is to create an object of this class.

Here's an example of how a constructor might be declared (that is, proto-typed).

```
Fraction(int n, int d);
```

Within the context of the class, the declaration looks like this:

```
class Fraction {
public:
// ...
    Fraction(int n, int d);
// ...
};
```

This is only a declaration, of course. Like any function, the constructor needs to be defined somewhere. You can place the definition outside the class declaration, in which case you have to use a `Fraction::` prefix to clarify scope:

```
Fraction::Fraction(int n, int d) {
    set(n, d);
}
```

A constructor defined outside of the declaration has this syntax:

```
class_name::class_name(argument_list) {
    statements
}
```

The first use of *class_name* is in the name prefix (*class_name*::), which states that this function is part of the class (or rather, it has class scope). The second use of *class_name* in this sequence is the name of the function itself. This may appear confusing, at first, but remember that a constructor's name is always the name of its class.

You can also inline the constructor. The definition of this particular construc-tor is brief, so it's a good candidate for inlining.

```
class Fraction {
public:
// ...
    Fraction(int n, int d) {set(n, d);}
// ...
};
```

Multiple Constructors (Overloading)

Function overloading—the reuse of the same function name in different contexts—turns out to be critical for writing constructors. As you may recall from Chapter 9, you can use the same function name to create several different functions, letting the C++ compiler rely on the types of the argument lists to differentiate them.

For example, you can declare several constructors for the Fraction class—one with no arguments, another with two, and a third with just one argument.

```
class Fraction {
public:
// ...
    Fraction();
    Fraction(int n, int d);
    Fraction(int n);
// ...
};
```

Any or all of these can be defined as inline functions.

And you could create a much longer list of constructors than these if you wanted. For example, you could write a constructor that took one string argument, in addition to the constructor that takes one integer argument. The compiler is able to know, from context, which of these to apply.

```
    Fraction(int n);
    Fraction(char *str);
```

In the case of the Fraction class, however, it's really only necessary to have two constructors: one that takes two integer arguments and one that takes no arguments at all. This later constructor is called the default constructor, and it's important enough to merit its own discussion—which I go into in the next section.

The Default Constructor . . . and a Warning

Every time you write a class (unless it's a trivial class that requires no constructors at all), you should always write a default constructor—that's the constructor with no arguments.

There's a very good reason for this general rule. It's because of the following feature of the C++ language, which can take you by surprise:

If you write no constructors, the compiler automatically supplies a default constructor for you. But if you write any constructors at all, the compiler does not supply a default constructor.

Okay, that's a strange but critical point. Let me go over it again, slowly. First of all, let's say you define a class without any constructors.

```
class Point {
private:
    int x, y;
public:
    set(int new_x, int new_y);
    int get_x();
    int get_y();
};
```

Because you wrote a class with no constructors, the compiler obliges you by automatically supplying one: a default constructor. That's the constructor with no arguments. Because this constructor is supplied for you, you can go ahead and use the class to declare objects.

```
Point a, b, c;
```

So far, so good: if you write no constructors, an automatic one is supplied for you, so that the user of the class can declare objects. But look what happens as soon as you do define a constructor.

```
class Point {
private:
    int x, y;
public:
    Point(int new_x, int new_y) {set(new_x, new_y);}
    set(int new_x, int new_y);
    int get_x();
    int get_y();
};
```

Given this constructor, you can now declare objects this way:

```
Point a(1, 2), b(10, -20);
```

But now, you get an error if you try to declare objects with no arguments!

```
Point c;      // ERROR! No more default constructor
```

What happened? The problem is the behavior I mentioned earlier. If you define *any constructors at all,* then the compiler does not supply a default constructor for you. The automatic default constructor, which you had been relying upon, is rudely yanked away!

When you first start writing classes, this quirky behavior of the compiler can surprise you. You go along using a class without explicitly writing constructors, letting users of the class declare objects this way:

```
Point a, b, c;
```

But this innocent-looking code breaks as soon as you write a constructor other than the default constructor.

To avoid this problem, always write a default constructor of your own, rather than depending on the compiler. This default constructor you write can be as simple as you like. In fact, it can have zero statements.

```
Point() { }
```

The behavior of the compiler-supplied default constructor is to set all data members to zero. This puts null bytes in all **char** string positions (if the string data is contained directly inside the class), and sets all pointers to null values (meaning they point nowhere). This is fine for many classes, but is incorrect for the Fraction class. That's another reason to write a default constructor—to make sure it does the right thing.

Interlude

Is C++ Out to Trick You with the Default Constructor?

It may seem strange that C++ operates this way: lulling you into a false sense of security by supplying a default constructor (again, that's the constructor with no arguments) and then yanking it away as soon as you write any other constructor.

Admittedly, this is weird behavior. It's one of the quirks that C++ has because it has to be both an object-oriented language and a language designed to be backwardly compatible with C (although not totally, because C permits some loose declarations that C++ doesn't allow).

▼ *continued on next page*

▼ *continued*

Interlude

The **struct** keyword, in particular, causes some quirkiness. C++ treats a **struct** type as a class (as I've mentioned), but it also has to work so that C code, such as the following, still compiles successfully in C++:

```
struct Point {
    int x, y;
};

struct Point a;
a.x = 1;
```

The C language has no **public** or **private** keyword, so this code can only compile if the **struct** keyword (unlike the **class** keyword) creates a type in which all members are public by default. Another problem is that the C language has no concept of a constructor; so if this code is to compile in C++, the compiler must automatically supply a default constructor, enabling statements such as the following to compile:

```
struct Point a;
```

This, by the way, is equivalent in C++ to:

```
Point a;
```

Therefore, to be backward-compatible with C, C++ had to supply an automatic default constructor. However, if you write any constructor at all, it's assumed that you are writing original code in C++ and that you know all about member functions and constructors.

In that case, your excuse—that you don't know about constructors—is gone, and C++ assumes that you ought to be able to write all the member functions you need, including the default constructor.

Example 12.1. *Point Class Constructors*

This example revisits the Point class from the previous chapter and adds a couple of simple constructors—the default constructor and a constructor taking two arguments. It then tests these in a simple program.

Point2.cpp

```cpp
#include <iostream>
using namespace std;

class Point {
private:                // Data members (private)
    int x, y;
public:                 // Constructors
    Point() {}
    Point(int new_x, int new_y) {set(new_x, new_y);}

// Other member functions

    void set(int new_x, int new_y);
    int get_x();
    int get_y();
};

int main() {
    Point pt1, pt2;
    Point pt3(5, 10);

    cout << "The value of pt1 is ";
    cout << pt1.get_x() << ", ";
    cout << pt1.get_y() << endl;

    cout << "The value of pt3 is ";
    cout << pt3.get_x() << ", ";
    cout << pt3.get_y() << endl;
    return 0;
}

void Point::set(int new_x, int new_y) {
    if (new_x < 0)
        new_x *= -1;
    if (new_y < 0)
        new_y *= -1;
    x = new_x;
    y = new_y;
}
```

▼ *continued on next page*

Point2.cpp, cont.

```
int Point::get_x() {
    return x;
}

int Point::get_y() {
    return y;
}
```

How It Works

The extensions to the class declaration here are minor. Two lines in the declaration add the constructors. Because they are written as inline functions, no other extensions to the class code are needed.

```
public:                 // Constructors
    Point() {}
    Point(int new_x, int new y) {set(new_x, new_y);}
```

Note that the two constructors are declared in the public section of the class. If they were declared private, then they wouldn't be accessible to the user of the Point class, and so the whole point (as it were) would be lost.

The default constructor may look a little strange at first. This definition includes no statements, so in effect it does nothing.

```
    Point() {}
```

The code in **main** makes two uses of the default constructor (for pt1 and pt2) and one use of the other constructor (for pt3).

```
    Point pt1, pt2;
    Point pt3(5, 10);
```

EXERCISES

Exercise 12.1.1.   Add code to the two constructors of the Point class, to report their use. The default constructor should print "Using default constructor" and the other should print "Using (int, int) constructor." (Tip: if you want to keep these functions inline, you can have the function definitions span multiple lines if you need to.)

Exercises 12.1.2.   Add a third constructor that takes just one integer argument. This constructor should set x to the argument specified, and set y to 0.

Example 12.2. *Fraction Class Constructors*

This example is slightly different from Example 12.1, because the default constructor for the Fraction class has to do a little more. If the constructor contains no statements, members are initialized to 0. This is not acceptable behavior, because the denominator (as I explained in the previous chapter) cannot be set to 0, ever. The default constructor here therefore sets the fraction to 0/1.

As always, code that is bold represents lines that are new or altered. Everything else is unchanged from the last version of the Fraction class in Chapter 11.

Fract4.cpp

```cpp
#include <iostream>
using namespace std;

class Fraction {
private:
    int num, den;       // Numerator and denominator.
public:
    Fraction() {set(0, 1);}
    Fraction(int n, int d) {set(n, d);}

    void set(int n, int d) {num = n; den = d;
                            normalize();}
    int get_num()  {return num;}
    int get_den()  {return den;}
    Fraction add(Fraction other);
    Fraction mult(Fraction other);
private:
    void normalize();   // Put fraction into standard
                        // form.
    int gcf(int a, int b);  // Greatest Common Factor.
    int lcm(int a, int b);  // Lowest Common
                            // Denominator.
};

int main() {
    Fraction f1, f2;
    Fraction f3(1, 2);

    cout << "The value of f1 is ";
```
▼ *continued on next page*

```
        cout << f1.get_num() << "/";
        cout << f1.get_den() << endl;

        cout << "The value of f3 is ";
        cout << f3.get_num() << "/";
        cout << f3.get_den() << endl;
        return 0;
}


// ---------------------------------------------------
// FRACTION CLASS FUNCTIONS

// Normalize: put fraction into a standard form,
//   unique for each mathematically different value.
//
void Fraction::normalize(){

    // Handle cases involving 0

    if (den == 0 || num == 0) {
        num = 0;
        den = 1;
    }

    // Put neg. sign in numerator only.

    if (den < 0) {
        num *= -1;
        den *= -1;
    }

    // Factor out GCF from numerator and denominator.

    int n = gcf(num, den);
    num = num / n;
    den = den / n;
}

// Greatest Common Factor
//
int Fraction::gcf(int a, int b) {
    if (a % b == 0)
```

12

Fract4.cpp, cont.

```cpp
            return abs(b);
        else
            return gcf(b, a % b);
    }

    // Lowest Common Multiple
    //
    int Fraction::lcm(int a, int b){
        return (a / gcf(a, b)) * b;
    }

    Fraction Fraction::add(Fraction other) {
        Fraction fract;
        int lcd = lcm(den, other.den);
        int quot1 = lcd/den;
        int quot2 = lcd/other.den;
        fract.set(num * quot1 + other.num * quot2, lcd);
        fract.normalize();
        return fract;
    }

    Fraction Fraction::mult(Fraction other) {
        Fraction fract;
        fract.set(num * other.num, den * other.den);
        fract.normalize();
        return fract;
    }
```

How It Works

If you followed Example 12.1, this example is straightforward. The only twist is that the default constructor needs to set the denominator value to 1 rather than leaving it at 0.

```cpp
    Fraction() {set(0, 1);}
```

This example, by the way, demonstrates a good reason for writing a default constructor: letting each member get set to 0 (depending on the particular class) may not always be an acceptable result.

The code in **main** makes three uses of constructors. The declarations of f1 and f2 invoke the default constructor. The declaration of f3 invokes the other constructor.

EXERCISES

Exercise 12.2.1. Rewrite the default constructor so that instead of calling set(0, 1), it sets the data members, num and den, directly. Is this more or less efficient? Is it necessary to call the normalize function?

Exercise 12.2.2. Write a third constructor that takes just one **int** argument. Respond by setting num to this argument and by setting den to 1.

Reference Variables and Arguments (&)

Before you proceed to learn about the other special constructor (called the *copy constructor*), it's necessary to take a detour to learn about C++ references.

This subject is probably new to you if you're a C programmer. The good news is that references make certain things easier to program, not harder. And as you'll see in the next section, it turns out to be necessary for doing certain things in C++.

Simply stated, a reference in C++ provides the behavior of a pointer without the pointer syntax. That's an important point, so let me state it again.

✳ **A reference variable, argument, or return value behaves like a pointer, but it removes the need for pointer syntax.**

The most direct way to manipulate a variable, of course, is to do so directly:

```
int n;
n = 5;
```

Another way to manipulate a variable—as you may recall from Chapter 6—is to use a pointer.

```
int n, *p;
p = &n;        // Let p point to n.
*p = 5;        // Set the THING p POINTS TO, to 5.
```

Here, p points to n, so setting *p to 5 has the same effect as setting n to 5.

A reference does much the same thing, although it avoids the pointer syntax. First, you declare a variable (n) and a reference to it (r).

```
int n;
int &r = n;
```

You may object that the ampersand (&) is exactly the same character used for the address operator. That's correct. The difference here is that the ampersand is being used in a declaration. Given this context, the ampersand creates a reference variable r that refers to the variable n. This means that changes to r cause changes to n:

```
r = 5;        // This has the effect of setting n to 5.
```

This operation has the same effect of using pointer p to set the value of n, but with r, no "at" operator (*) was involved. Recall that manipulation through p required this operator:

```
*p = 5;
```

Unlike pointer variables, the target of a reference variable can only be set once, during initialization.

Simple reference variables—interesting though they might be—are little used in C++. Much more useful are reference arguments. Remember the swap function from Chapter 6, which required pointers? You can do the same thing, with less syntax, by using reference arguments.

```
void swap_ref(int &a, int &b) {
    int temp = a;
    a = b;
    b = temp;
}
```

This example may seem to violate what I said in Chapter 6—about how such an example requires pointers—but of course it doesn't at all, because reference arguments produce pointer behavior without involving pointer syntax. The arguments a and b are not *copies* of the function inputs, but *references* to them. At runtime, the program uses pointers, but that fact is hidden from the source code.

Therefore, the function behaves as if it were written this way:

```
void swap_ptr(int *a, int *b) {
    int temp = *a;
    *a = *b;
    *b = temp;
}
```

There is also a difference in how these functions are called, because the compiler checks the argument types. (It's possible to fool the compiler, by the way, by using multiple modules and changing header information, but why would you want to?) You call the reference version of swap this way:

```
int big = 100;
int little = 1;
swap_ref(big, little);    // swap using references
```

The call to swap_ref implicitly passes addresses, although that's not reflected in the source code. So you don't use the address operator (&), even though addresses are actually being passed.

But you'd call the pointer version of swap the following way. Notice that the use of the address operator (&) is required with the pointer version.

```
int big = 100;
int little = 1;
swap_ptr(&big, &little);    // swap using pointers
```

The Copy Constructor

Earlier I introduced a special constructor: the default constructor. The other special constructor is the *copy constructor*.

The copy constructor is special for two reasons: First, this constructor gets called in a number of common situations, whether you're aware of its existence or not.

Second, if you don't write one, the compiler automatically supplies one for you. The compiler is more forgiving with this constructor than it is with the default constructor. It doesn't yank the automatic copy constructor away just because you decided to write constructors of your own.

Here are the situations in which the copy constructor is automatically called:

▶ When the return value of a function has class type. (We've already seen this in the case of the add and mult functions from Chapter 11.) The function creates a copy of the object and hands this back to the caller.

▶ When an argument has class type. A copy of the argument is made and then passed to the function.

▶ When you use one object to initialize another. For example.

```
Fraction a(1, 2);
Fraction b(a);
```

The copy constructor is not called when a pointer to an object is passed. It's only called when a new copy of an existing object needs to be made.

The syntax for the copy constructor declaration is:

```
class_name(class_name const &source)
```

The **const** keyword is new here. This keyword ensures that the argument cannot be altered by the function—which makes sense, because making a copy of something should never corrupt the original.

The other thing that's new about this syntax is the use of a reference argument. The use of this argument means that the function actually gets a pointer, even though the source code does not use pointer syntax.

Here's an example for the Point class. First, the copy constructor has to be declared in the class declaration.

```
class Point {
//...
public:                    // Constructors
    Point(Point const &src);
//...
};
```

Because the function definition was not inlined, it must be given a definition outside the class declaration.

```
Point::Point(Point const &src) {
    x = src.x;
    y = src.y;
}
```

Why write a copy constructor at all if the compiler supplies one for you? Actually, in this case—and even in the case of the Fraction class—it isn't really necessary. The behavior of the compiler-supplied copy constructor is to perform a member-by-member copy of each of the data members.

In Chapter 14, I show an example of a class (namely, the String class) that needs to have a programmer-defined copy constructor to work correctly.

Interlude

The Copy Constructor and References

One of the main reasons that C++ needs to support references is so that you can write a copy constructor. Without this syntax, the task would be impossible. Consider what would happen if you declared a copy constructor this way:

```
Point(Point const src)
```

The compiler doesn't allow this, and a little reflection shows why. When an argument such as src is passed to a function, a copy of that object must be made and placed on the stack. But that would mean that for the copy constructor to work, it would have to make a copy of an object—so, in effect, it would need to call itself! This would lead to an infinite regress, and so it would be totally unworkable.

▼ *continued on next page*

Interlude

▼ *continued*

What if the copy constructor were declared this way?

```
Point(Point const *src)
```

There's nothing syntactically wrong with such a declaration, and in fact it's a valid constructor. The problem is that it can't be used as a *copy* constructor because the syntax of this declaration implies that a pointer, not an object, is the argument.

Using a reference enables you to write a member function that works correctly as a copy constructor. Syntactically, the argument is an object, not a pointer. However, because the implementation of the call involves pointers (that is, a pointer is passed under the covers), no infinite regress occurs.

```
Point(Point const &src)
```

Example 12.3.   ## *Fraction Class Copy Constructor*

The following code shows the Fraction class, revised to include a programmer-defined copy constructor. This example prints a message every time the copy constructor is called.

As always, code that's placed in bold represents lines that are new or altered from previous versions of Fraction class code.

Fract5.cpp

```cpp
#include <iostream>
using namespace std;

class Fraction {
private:
    int num, den;       // Numerator and denominator.
public:
    Fraction() {set(0, 1);}
    Fraction(int n, int d) {set(n, d);}
    Fraction(Fraction const &src);

    void set(int n, int d) {num = n; den = d;
                                normalize();}
    int get_num()  {return num;}
```

Fract5.cpp, cont.

```cpp
        int get_den()  {return den;}
        Fraction add(Fraction other);
        Fraction mult(Fraction other);
private:
    void normalize();    // Put fraction into standard
                         // form.
        int gcf(int a, int b);  // Greatest Common Factor.
        int lcm(int a, int b);  // Lowest Common
                                // Denominator.
};

int main() {
    Fraction f1(3, 4);
    Fraction f2(f1);

    Fraction f3 = f1.add(f2);

    cout << "The value of f3 is ";
    cout << f3.get_num() << "/";
    cout << f3.get_den() << endl;
    return 0;
}

// ------------------------------------------------
// FRACTION CLASS FUNCTIONS

Fraction::Fraction(Fraction const &src) {
    cout << "Now executing copy constructor." << endl;
    num = src.num;
    den = src.den;
}

// Normalize: put fraction into a standard form,
//   unique for each mathematically different value.
//
void Fraction::normalize(){

    // Handle cases involving 0

    if (den == 0 || num == 0) {
        num = 0;
```

▼ continued on next page

```
        den = 1;
    }

    // Put neg. sign in numerator only.

    if (den < 0) {
        num *= -1;
        den *= -1;
    }

    // Factor out GCF from numerator and denominator.

    int n = gcf(num, den);
    num = num / n;
    den = den / n;
}

// Greatest Common Factor
//
int Fraction::gcf(int a, int b) {
    if (a % b == 0)
        return abs(b);
    else
        return gcf(b, a % b);
}

// Lowest Common Multiple
//
int Fraction::lcm(int a, int b){
    return (a / gcf(a, b)) * b;
}

Fraction Fraction::add(Fraction other) {
    Fraction fract;
    int lcd = lcm(den, other.den);
    int quot1 = lcd/den;
    int quot2 = lcd/other.den;
    fract.set(num * quot1 + other.num * quot2, lcd);
    fract.normalize();
    return fract;
```

Fract5.cpp, cont.

```
    }

Fraction Fraction::mult(Fraction other) {
    Fraction fract;
    fract.set(num * other.num, den * other.den);
    fract.normalize();
    return fract;
}
```

How It Works

There's little that's new in this example. All it does is print a message when the copy constructor is called. This doesn't really represent new functionality, because if you don't write a copy constructor the compiler automatically supplies one for you.

The compiler-supplied copy constructor does exactly what this version does, except for printing the message.

```
Fraction::Fraction(Fraction const &src) {
    cout << "Now executing copy constructor." << endl;
    num = src.num;
    den = src.den;
}
```

When you run the program, you'll see that it makes repeated calls to the copy constructor. The following statement, obviously, results in one call to this constructor:

```
Fraction f2(f1);
```

But this next statement results in three calls to the copy constructor: once when the object f2 is passed as an argument, once when the new object is passed back as a return value, and once again when that object is copied to f3.

```
Fraction f3 = f1.add(f2);
```

That's a lot of copying—probably more than you want. Some of the copying can be eliminated simply by making the add function take a reference argument, as is done for the copy constructor itself. That's a task we'll take up in the next chapter.

EXERCISES

Exercise 12.3.1. Rewrite the Fraction copy constructor as an inline function. Do not include the statement that prints a message.

Exercise 12.3.2. Instead of setting num and den separately, make a call to the set function. Is this more or less efficient? Explain why.

Chapter 12 *Summary*

Here are the main points of Chapter 12:

▶ A constructor is simply an initialization function for a class. It has this form:

```
class_name(argument_list)
```

▶ If a constructor is not inlined, the constructor's function definition has this form:

```
class_name::class_name(argument_list {
    statements
}
```

▶ You can have any number of different constructors. They have the same function name (which is the name of the class). The only requirement is that each constructor must be uniquely identified by number or type of arguments.

▶ The default constructor is the constructor with no arguments at all. It has this declaration:

```
class_name()
```

▶ The default constructor is called when an object is declared with no argument list. For example:

```
Point a;
```

▶ If you declare no constructors, the compiler automatically supplies a default constructor for you. This automatic constructor sets all data members to zero (pointers are set to null). However, if you write any constructors at all, the compiler does not supply a default constructor.

▶ So, to program defensively, always write a default constructor. It can include zero statements if you wish. For example:

```
Point a() {}
```

▶ In C++, a reference is a variable or argument declared with the ampersand (&). The result is that pointers are used at runtime, but no pointer syntax is involved. The program appears to be passing a value, even though it's actually passing a pointer.

▶ A class's copy constructor is called whenever an object needs to be copied. This includes situations in which an object (not a pointer to that object) is passed to a function or in which the function returns an object as its return value.

▶ The copy constructor uses a reference argument, as well as the **const** keyword, which prevents changes to an argument. The copy constructor has this syntax:

```
class_name(class_name const &source)
```

▶ If you do not write a copy constructor, the compiler always supplies one for you. It carries out a simple member-by-member copy.

Operator Functions: Doing It with Class

After reading Chapter 12, you know how to write classes (object types) that work just like standard data types, right?

Well, almost. One of the most important features of a standard data type such as **int**, **float**, **double**, *and even* **char**, *is that you can perform operations on them. In fact, without these operators, it would be difficult to perform any calculations in C++ at all.*

C++ lets you define how to perform these same operations (such as +, -, *, and /) on objects of your own classes. You can also define how a test-for-equality is carried out, letting you determine whether two quantities are equal.

The benefit of this C++ capability is that it enables you to declare new classes that, for nearly all intents and purposes, work just like fundamental data types.

Introducing Class Operator Functions

The basic syntax for writing class operator functions is simple, and once you grasp it, you'll be able to use as many operators as you want.

return_type **operator@(***argument_list***)**

In applying this syntax, you replace the symbol @ with a valid C++ operator, such as +, -, *, and /. You are not limited to these four; in fact, any operator symbol supported for C++ standard types can be used here. Normal associativity and precedence rules are enforced, as appropriate, for the symbol. (See Appendix A.)

You can define an operator function as either a member function or a global (that is, nonmember) function.

▶ If you declare an operator function as a member function, then the object through which the function is called corresponds to the left operand.

▶ If you declare an operator function as a global function, then both operands correspond to an argument.

This makes a lot more sense with examples. Here's how the addition and subtraction (+ and -) operator functions can be declared as part of the Point class:

```
class Point {
//...
public:

    Point operator+(Point pt);
    Point operator-(Point pt);
};
```

Given these declarations, you can apply operators to a Point object:

```
Point point1, point2, point3;
point1 = point2 + point3;
```

The compiler interprets this statement by calling the **operator+** function through the left operand—point2 in this case. The right operand—point3 in this case—becomes the argument to the function. You can visualize the relationship this way:

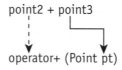

What happens to point2? Is its value ignored? No. The function treats point2 as "this object" so that unqualified use to x and y refer to *point2's* copy of x and y. You can see how this works in the function definition:

```
Point Point::operator+(Point pt) {
    Point new_pt;
    new_pt.x = x + pt.x;
    new_pt.y = y + pt.y;
    return new_pt;
}
```

Unqualified use of data members x and y refer to values in the left operand (point2 in this case). The expressions pt.x and pt.y refer to values in the right operand (point3 in this case).

The operator functions here are declared with Point return type, which means they return a Point object. This makes sense: if you add two points together, you should get another point; and if you subtract a point from another, you should get another point. But C++ allows you to specify any valid type for the return-value type of an operator function.

The argument list can contain any type as well. Overloading is permitted here: you can declare an operator function that interacts with the **int** type, another that interacts with the **double** type, and so on.

In the case of the Point class, it might make sense to permit multiplication by an integer. The declaration of the operator function would look like this:

```
Point operator*(int n);
```

The function definition might reasonably look like this:

```
Point Point::operator*(int n) {
    Point new_pt;
    new_pt.x = x * n;
    new_pt.y = y * n;
    return new_pt;
}
```

Again, the function returns a Point object, although you could have it return any type of value that you chose.

As a contrasting example, you could create an operator function that calculates the distance between two points and returns a floating-point (**double**) result. For this example, I've chosen the % operator, but you can choose any other binary operator defined in C++. (See Appendix A.) The important point here is that you can choose any return type that would be appropriate for the operation you're performing.

```
#include <math.h>

double Point::operator%(Point pt) {
    int d1 = pt.x - x;
    int d2 = pt.y - y;
    return sqrt((double) (d1 * d1 + d2 * d2));
}
```

Given this function definition, the following code would correctly print out the distance between points (20, 20) and (24, 23) as 5.0.

```
Point pt1(20, 20);
Point pt2(24, 23);
cout << "Distance between points is : " << pt1%pt2;
```

Operator Functions As Global Functions

In the previous section, I stated that you can declare operator functions as global functions. There is a disadvantage to doing things this way. You no longer have all the relevant functions centered in the class declaration. But in some cases (which I'll discuss in a moment), it turns out to be necessary to use this approach.

A global operator function is declared outside of any class. The types in the argument list determine what kinds of operands the function applies to. For example, the Point class addition-operator function can be rewritten as a global function. Here's the declaration (prototype), which should appear before the function is called:

```
Point operator+(Point pt1, Point pt2);
```

Here's the function definition:

```
Point operator+(Point pt1, Point pt2) {
    Point new_pt;
    new_pt.x = pt1.x + pt2.x;
    new_pt.y = pt1.y + pt2.y;
    return new_pt;
}
```

You can visualize a call to this function this way:

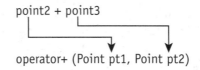

Now both operands are interpreted as function arguments. The left operand (point2 in this case) gives its value to the first argument, pt1. The right argument (point3) gives its value to the second argument, pt2. There is no concept of "this object," and all references to Point data members must be qualified.

That can create a problem. If the data members are not public, this function cannot access them. One solution is to use function calls, if available, to get access to the data.

```
Point operator+(Point pt1, Point pt2) {
    Point new_pt;
    int a = pt1.get_x() + pt2.get_x();
    int b = pt1.get_y() + pt2.get_y();
    new_pt.set(a, b);
    return new_pt;
}
```

But that's not a pretty solution, and with some classes, it may not even work. For example, you might have a class in which the private data members are completely inaccessible, but you still want to be able to write operator functions. A better solution is to declare a function as a *friend function,* which means that the function is global, but it has access to private members of the class.

Here, the function is declared as a friend to the Point class.

```
class Point {
//...
public:

    friend Point operator+(Point pt1, Point pt2);
};
```

Now the function definition has direct access to all Point class members, even if they are private.

```
Point operator+(Point pt1, Point pt2) {
    Point new_pt;
    int a = pt1.x + pt2.x;
    int b = pt1.y + pt2.y;
    new_pt.set(a, b);
    return new_pt;
}
```

Sometimes it's necessary to write an operator functions as a global function. In a member function, the left operand is interpreted as "this object" in the function definition. But what if the left operand does not have an object type? What if you want to support an operation like this?

```
point1 = 3 * point2;
```

The problem here is that the left operand has **int** type, not Point type. But you can't write new operations for **int**, as if it were a class. The only way to support the operation is to write a global function.

```
Point operator*(int n, Point pt) {
    Point new_pt;
    new_pt.x = pt.x * n;
    new_pt.y = pt.y * n;
    return new_pt;
}
```

As before, to gain access to private data members, the function may need to be made a friend of the class:

```
class Point {
//...
public:

    friend Point operator*(int n, Point pt);
};
```

You can visualize the call to this function this way:

Improve Efficiency with References

The obvious way to implement operations on objects is to use simple object types (classes) as arguments. But as Chapter 12 pointed out, every time an object is passed or returned as a value, a call to the copy constructor is issued.

Moreover, whenever an object is created, the program must request memory from the system to create a new object. This all goes on under the covers, but it still affects program efficiency.

You can make your programs more efficient by writing classes in such a way that they minimize object creation. There's an easy way to do that: use reference types.

Here's a Point-class add function, along with an addition-operator (+) function that calls it, written without use of reference types.

```
class Point {
//...
public:

    Point add(Point pt);
    Point operator+(Point pt);
};

Point Point::add(Point pt) {
    Point new_pt;
    new_pt.x = x + pt.x;
    new_pt.y = y + pt.y;
    return new_pt;
```

```
}

Point Point::operator+(Point pt)
    return add(pt);
}
```

This is the obvious way to write these functions, but look how much an expression such as pt1 + pt2 results in the creation of new objects:

▶ The right operand is passed to the operator+ function. A copy of pt2 is made and passed to this function.

▶ The operator+ function calls the add function. Now *another* copy of pt2 must be made and passed along.

▶ The add function creates a new object, new_pt. This calls the default constructor. When that function returns, the program makes a copy of new_pt and passes it back to its caller (the operator+ function).

▶ The operator+ function returns to its caller, requiring yet another copy of new_pt to be made.

That's a lot of copying! Five new objects are created, involving one call to the default constructor and four calls to the copy constructor. This is inefficient behavior.

Note ▶ In these days of super-fast CPUs, you may object that efficiency is not a factor. With a class as simple as Point, it may take thousands of repeated operations (or even millions!) to experience a noticeable time delay when you do something inefficient. However, you can never be sure of how a class will be used. When there's an easy way to make your code more efficient, you ought to take advantage of it.

You can eliminate two of these copy operations by using reference arguments. Here is the revised version, with altered lines in bold.

```
class Point {
//...
public:

    Point add(const Point &pt);
    Point operator+(const Point &pt);
};

Point Point::add(const Point &pt) {
    Point new_pt;
```

```
        new_pt.x = x + pt.x;
        new_pt.y = y + pt.y;
        return new_pt;
    }
```

Point Point::operator+(const Point &pt)
```
        return add(pt);
    }
```

One of the benefits of using reference types such as Point& is that the implementation of the function calls change, but no other change is required in the source code. Remember, when you pass a reference, the function gets a reference to the original data—but without pointer syntax.

I also use the **const** keyword here; this keyword prevents changes to the argument being passed. When the function got its own copy of the argument, it couldn't alter the value of the original copy no matter what it did. But a reference argument, like a pointer, has the potential to alter the original copy. The **const** keyword restores data protection, so that the function can't accidentally alter the value of an argument.

The change eliminates two instances of object copying. But each time one of these functions returns, it makes a copy of an object. You can cut down on this copying by making one or both of the functions inline. The `operator+` function, which does nothing more than call the add function, is a good candidate for inlining.

```
    class Point {
    //...
    public:

        Point add(const Point &pt);
        Point operator+(const Point &pt) {return add(pt);}
    };
```

When the `operator+` function is inlined in this manner, operations such as `pt1 + pt2` are translated directly into calls to the add function.

Example 13.1. *Point Class Operators*

You now have all the tools you need to write efficient and useful operator functions for the Point class. The following code shows a complete declaration of the Point class, along with code that tests it by declaring and operating on objects.

Code brought over from Chapter 12 is left in normal font. New or altered lines are in bold.

Point3.cpp

```cpp
#include <iostream>
using namespace std;

class Point {
private:                // Data members (private)
    int x, y;
public:                 // Constructors
    Point() {}
    Point(int new_x, int new_y) {set(new_x, new_y);}
    Point(const Point &src) {set(src.x, src.y);}

// Operations

    Point add(const Point &pt);
    Point sub(const Point &pt);
    Point operator+(const Point &pt) {return add(pt);}
    Point operator-(const Point &pt) {return sub(pt);}

// Other member functions

    void set(int new_x, int new_y);
    int get_x() const {return x;}
    int get_y() const {return y;}
};

int main() {

    Point point1(20, 20);
    Point point2(0, 5);
    Point point3(-10, 25);
    Point point4 = point1 + point2 + point3;

    cout << "The point is " << point4.get_x();
    cout << ", " << point4.get_y() << "." << endl;

    return 0;
}

void Point::set(int new_x, int new_y) {
    if (new_x < 0)
```

▼ *continued on next page*

Point3.cpp, cont.

```
            new_x *= -1;
        if (new_y < 0)
            new_y *= -1;
        x = new_x;
        y = new_y;
    }

    Point Point::add(const Point &pt) {
        Point new_pt;
        new_pt.x = x + pt.x;
        new_pt.y = y + pt.y;
        return new_pt;
    }

    Point Point::sub(const Point &pt) {
        Point new_pt;
        new_pt.x = x - pt.x;
        new_pt.y = y - pt.y;
        return new_pt;
    }
```

How It Works

This example adds a series of member functions to the Point class.

```
Point add(const Point &pt);
Point sub(const Point &pt);
Point operator+(const Point &pt) {return add(pt);}
Point operator-(const Point &pt) {return sub(pt);}
```

The add and sub functions carry out point addition and subtraction operations, so that you can write statements like this:

```
Point point1 = point2.add(point3);
```

This statement adds point2 and point3 together to produce a new Point object. The operator+ function is an inline function that translates expressions such as the following into calls to the add function:

```
Point point1 = point2 + point3;
```

Because this function is inline, and because it uses a reference argument (const Point &), there is minimum overhead involved. The expression point2

+ `point3` is translated into a call to the operator+ function, which in turn calls the add function.

The `add` function, in turn, creates a new point (new_pt), initializing it by adding the coordinates of "this object" to the coordinates of the object argument. "This object" is the object through which the function call is made—in other words, point2 in the expression below:

```
point2.add(point3);
```

The operator- and sub functions work in a similar manner.

This example also adds the **const** keyword to the declarations of the get_x and get_y functions. The keyword is added just after the rest of the declaration, but before the opening brace ({). In this context, the **const** keyword says, "The function agrees not to change any data member, or call any member function other than another **const** function."

```
int get_x() const {return x;}
int get_y() const {return y;}
```

This is a useful change to make, for several reasons. It prevents accidental changes to data members, it allows the functions to be called by other **const** functions, and it allows the functions to be called by functions that have agreed not to alter a Fraction object (because they have a **const** Fraction argument).

EXERCISES

Exercise 13.1.1.   Write a test to see how many times the default constructor and the copy constructor are called. (Hint: insert statements that send output to **cout**; you can span multiple lines if needed, as long as the function definitions are syntactically correct.) Then run the program as is and also run it with the reference arguments (const Point &) changed back to ordinary arguments (Point). How much more efficient is the former approach?

Exercise 13.1.2.   Write and test an expanded Point class that supports multiplication of a Point object by an integer. Use global functions, aided by **friend** declarations, as described in the previous section.

Example 13.2.   *Fraction Class Operators*

This example uses techniques similar to those in Example 13.1, to extend basic operator support to the Fraction class. As before, the code uses reference arguments (`const Fraction &`) for efficiency.

Fract6.cpp

```cpp
#include <iostream>
using namespace std;

class Fraction {
private:
    int num, den;        // Numerator and denominator.
public:
    Fraction() {set(0, 1);}
    Fraction(int n, int d) {set(n, d);}
    Fraction(const Fraction &src);

    void set(int n, int d) {num = n; den = d;
                            normalize();}
    int get_num() const {return num;}
    int get_den() const {return den;}
    Fraction add(const Fraction &other);
    Fraction mult(const Fraction &other);
    Fraction operator+(const Fraction &other)
        {return add(other);}
    Fraction operator*(const Fraction &other)
        {return mult(other);}

private:
    void normalize();   // Put fraction into standard
                        // form.
    int gcf(int a, int b);  // Greatest Common Factor.
    int lcm(int a, int b);  // Lowest Common
                            // Denominator.
};

int main() {
    Fraction f1(1, 2);
    Fraction f2(1, 3);

    Fraction f3 = f1 + f2;

    cout << "1/2 + 1/3 = ";
    cout << f3.get_num() << "/";
    cout << f3.get_den() << "." << endl;
```

Fract6.cpp, cont.

```cpp
        return 0;
    }

    // --------------------------------------------------
    // FRACTION CLASS FUNCTIONS

    Fraction::Fraction(Fraction const &src) {
        num = src.num;
        den = src.den;
    }

    // Normalize: put fraction into a standard form,
    //   unique for each mathematically different value.
    //
    void Fraction::normalize(){

        // Handle cases involving 0

        if (den == 0 || num == 0) {
            num = 0;
            den = 1;
        }

        // Put neg. sign in numerator only.

        if (den < 0) {
            num *= -1;
            den *= -1;
        }

        // Factor out GCF from numerator and denominator.

        int n = gcf(num, den);
        num = num / n;
        den = den / n;
    }

    // Greatest Common Factor
    //
    int Fraction::gcf(int a, int b) {
```

▼ *continued on next page*

Fract6.cpp, cont.

```
        if (a % b == 0)
            return abs(b);
        else
            return gcf(b, a % b);
    }

    // Lowest Common Multiple
    //
    int Fraction::lcm(int a, int b){
        return (a / gcf(a, b)) * b;
    }

    Fraction Fraction::add(const Fraction &other) {
        Fraction fract;
        int lcd = lcm(den, other.den);
        int quot1 = lcd/den;
        int quot2 = lcd/other.den;
        fract.set(num * quot1 + other.num * quot2, lcd);
        fract.normalize();
        return fract;
    }

    Fraction Fraction::mult(const Fraction &other) {
        Fraction fract;
        fract.set(num * other.num, den * other.den);
        fract.normalize();
        return fract;
    }
```

How It Works

The add and mult functions are taken from previously existing code in the Fraction class. All I've done is change the type of the argument, so that each of these functions use reference arguments, providing a more efficient implementation.

```
    Fraction add(const Fraction &other);
    Fraction mult(const Fraction &other);
```

When the declarations of these functions change, the function definitions must change as well, to reflect the altered argument type. But this change only affects the function heading (shown in bold below). The rest of the definitions stay the same.

```
Fraction Fraction::add(const Fraction &other) {
    Fraction fract;
    int lcd = lcm(den, other.den);
    int quot1 = lcd/den;
    int quot2 = lcd/other.den;
    fract.set(num * quot1 + other.num * quot2, lcd);
    fract.normalize();
    return fract;
}

Fraction Fraction::mult(const Fraction &other) {
    Fraction fract;
    fract.set(num * other.num, den * other.den);
    fract.normalize();
    return fract;
}
```

For explanations of how these functions work, you may want to review Chapter 11.

In any case, the Fraction class operator functions do nothing more than call the appropriate member function (add or mult, as the case may be) and return the value. For example, when the compiler sees the expression

```
f1 + f2
```

it translates this expression by making the following function call:

```
f1.operator+(f2)
```

The Fraction class operator+ function is an inline function defined as follows:

```
Fraction operator+(const Fraction &other)
    {return add(other);}
```

The function call is therefore translated, finally, as:

```
f1.add(f2)
```

Multiplication operations are handled the same way.

The statements in the main function test the operator-function code by declaring fractions, adding them, and printing the results.

```
Fraction f1(1, 2);
Fraction f2(1, 3);
```

```
Fraction f3 = f1 + f2;

cout << "1/2 + 1/3 = ";
cout << f3.get_num() << "/";
cout << f3.get_den() << "." << endl;
```

EXERCISES

Exercise 13.2.1.   Revise the main function in Example 13.1 so that it prompts for a series of fraction values, exiting the input loop when 0 is entered for a denominator. Make the program track of the sum all the fractions entered and print the result.

Exercise 13.2.2.   Write an `operator-` function (subtraction) for the Fraction class.

Exercise 13.2.3.   Write an `operator/` function (division) for the Fraction class.

Working with Other Types

Thanks to overloading, you can write many different functions for each operator, in which each function works on different types. For example, you can write several versions of `operator+` that deal with the Fraction class:

```
class Fraction {
//...
public:
    operator+(const Fraction &other);
    friend operator+(int n, const Fraction &fr);
    friend operator+(const Fraction &fr, int n);
}
```

Each of these functions (which have to be defined somewhere, by the way) deals with a different combination of **int** and Fraction operands, enabling you to support expressions like this:

```
Fraction fract1 = 1 + Fraction(1, 2) + Fraction (3, 4)
    + 4;
```

But there's a much easier way to support operations with integers. All you really need is a function that converts integers to Fraction objects. If such an operation were in place, you'd only need to write one version of the operator+ function. In an expression such as the following, the compiler would convert the number 1 into Fraction format and then call the `Fraction::operator+` function to add two fractions.

```
Fraction fract1 = 1 + Fraction(1, 2);
```

It turns out that such a conversion function is easy to write—it's supplied by the Fraction constructor that takes a single **int** argument! This is a simple constructor, and it can be made an inline function for efficiency.

```
Fraction(int n) {set(n, 1);}
```

Given this declaration, all the operations declared for two Fraction objects are automatically extended to include operations involving a Fraction object and an integer.

The Class Assignment Function (=)

When you write a class, the C++ compiler is friendly enough to automatically supply three special member functions for you. I've introduced two of these so far.

▶ The default constructor. The behavior of the automatic (compiler-supplied) version is to initialize each member to zero. Note that the compiler yanks this constructor away if you write any constructors of your own . . . so to be safe, you should always write your own default constructor, even if it does nothing.

▶ The copy constructor. The behavior of the automatic version is to perform a simple member-by-member copy of the source object.

▶ The assignment operator function (=). This is the new one.

The assignment operator function is special because the compiler supplies one if you don't. That's why we've been able to do operations such as this one:

```
Fraction f1;
f1 = f2 + f3;
```

The default behavior of the operator= function is similar to the copy constructor: it also performs a simple member-by-member copy. This may lead you to the question: Is the assignment operator function *the same thing* as the copy constructor?

No, it's not, although it's easy to get that idea. In both cases, all the values in one object are (by default) copied to another. The difference is that the copy constructor initializes a new object, while the assignment operator copies values to an *existing* object. In some cases (for example, classes that involve a memory request or file open), the copy constructor may need to carry out more work than the assignment operator function.

When you write your own assignment operator function, use the following syntax:

```
class_name &operator=(const class_name &source_arg)
```

This declaration has an interesting twist: it is similar to the copy constructor, but the operator= function must return a reference to an object of the class, as well as take a reference argument.

Here's what the operator= function might look like for the Fraction class:

```
class Fraction {
//...
public:
    Fraction &operator=(const Fraction &src) {
        set(src.num, src.den);
        return *this;
    };
};
```

This code involves the use of a new keyword, **this**. I explain the use of the **this** keyword and other mysteries of the assignment operator function in the next chapter.

In the meantime, it's enough to know that for a class like this one, you don't need to write an assignment operator function at all. The default behavior is quite adequate here, and the compiler always supplies this operator function if you don't.

The Test-for-Equality Function (==)

The test-for-equality operator is another matter. The compiler does not automatically supply an operator== function for your class, so the following code (for example) does not work if you don't write the required function:

```
Fraction f1(2, 3);
Fraction f2(4, 6);

if (f1 == f2)
    cout << "The fractions are equal.";
else
    cout << "The fractions are not equal.";
```

What this code should do, of course, is to print the message stating that the fractions are equal, even though different numbers (2/3 versus 4/6) are entered in each case.

Will the operation work correctly if you simply compare the numerators and denominators (num and den)? Yes, given the way we've constructed this class. We've written this class so that after values are set, a Fraction is reduced to a unique mathematical expression (for example, converting -10/-20 into 1/2).

Therefore, writing a test for equality (`operator==`) is easy. If the numerator and denominators are both equal, then the fractions are equal.

```
int Fraction::operator==(const Fraction &other) {
    if (num == other.num && den == other.den)
        return true;
    else
        return false;
}
```

This function definition can be streamlined by just returning the result of the condition itself.

```
int Fraction::operator==(const Fraction &other) {
    return (num == other.num && den == other.den);
}
```

The function definition is now short enough that inlining is appropriate.

```
class Fraction {
//...
public:
    int operator==(const Fraction &other) {
        return (num == other.num && den == other.den);
    };
};
```

Use of a reference argument type (const Fraction &) results in more efficient program behavior, by the way, which is why it is used here.

Interlude

What about the Boolean Type (bool)?

The most up-to-date versions of C++ include support for the specialized Boolean type, **bool**. This type is equivalent to the **int** type except for one important difference: Although you can assign any values you want to a **bool** value, **bool** values are automatically converted to true (1) if they are non-negative.

▼ continued on next page

Interlude

▼ *continued*

It's good programming practice to take advantage of the **bool** type in this situation if it's supported by your version of the compiler. A **bool** value is one intended to hold either a true or false value, so the type performs a self-documenting function.

The **bool** version of the function looks the same but has the **bool** return type. Nothing else needs to be changed.

```
public Fraction {
    //...
public:
    bool operator==(const Fraction &other) {
        return (num == other.num && den == other.den);
    };
};
```

A Class "Print" Function

Just one more touch is necessary before we can finally get a version of the Fraction class that is reasonably complete. It's a bother to have to keep writing essentially the same lines of code every time we want to print the contents of a fraction:

```
cout << f3.get_num() << "/";
cout << f3.get_den() << "." << endl;
```

If you've been following the chapter up till now, you've probably noticed that the example code has needed to include similar statements over and over again. Eliminating the need to keep reentering these statements is what reusability is all about.

The obvious way to handle this is to write a function. But since each class has its own data format, each should ideally have its own "print" function. You can even name a member function "print," because it is not a reserved word in C++.

```
void Fraction::print() {
    cout << num << "/";
    cout << den;
};
```

But as good as this solution is, it is far from being the best. A more object-oriented solution takes advantage of the fact that **cout** is an object. The ideal "print" function would interact with **cout** (as well as all other **ostream** objects, such as output files).

Best of all would be a solution that treats Fraction like any other fundamental data type (as I've been promising in this chapter). This is what you ought to be able to do:

```
cout << fract;
```

The way to support such statements is to write an operator<< function that interacts with **cout**'s parent class, **ostream**. The function must be a global function, because the left operand is an object of **ostream** class and we don't have access to updating or altering **ostream** code.

The function should be declared as a friend of the Fraction class, so that it has access to private members.

```
class Fraction {
//...
public:
    friend ostream &operator<<(ostream &os, Fraction
        &fr);
};
```

Notice that the function returns a reference to an **ostream** object. This is necessary so that statements such as the following work correctly:

```
cout << "The value of the fraction is " << fract <<
    endl;
```

Finally, here is a working definition for the operator<< function.

```
ostream &operator<<(ostream &os, Fraction &fr) {
    os << fr.num << "/" << fr.den;
    return os;
}
```

The beauty of this solution is that it correctly directs the Fraction display to be sent to any **ostream** object specified. This includes file-stream objects, as well as **cout**. For example, if outfile is a text-file output object, you can use it to print a fraction to the file.

```
outfile << fact;
```

Example 13.3. *The Completed Fraction Class*

Although you can add many more extensions to the Fraction class (especially support for subtraction and division, which were specified earlier as an exercise), the class is getting reasonably complete. In this example, I give it in a form that's powerful enough to be widely useful.

Note that you don't need to include all this code in every program that uses the class. The stand-alone class functions (those not inlined) can be placed in their own module, where they only have to be compiled once. The resulting object file (.o file) can then be linked into any project that needs it. You would also need to place the class declaration in its own header file (Fract.h) and then place the following statement at the beginning of any program that uses the class.

```
#include "Fract.h"
```

Here is the complete version of the Fraction class, along with code to test it. As before, only code that is new is shown in bold here.

Fract7.cpp

```cpp
#include <iostream>
using namespace std;

class Fraction {
private:
    int num, den;      // Numerator and denominator.
public:
    Fraction() {set(0, 1);}
    Fraction(int n, int d) {set(n, d);}
    Fraction(int n) {set(n, 1);}
    Fraction(const Fraction &src);

    void set(int n, int d) {num = n; den = d;
                            normalize();}
    int get_num() const {return num;}
    int get_den() const {return den;}
    Fraction add(const Fraction &other);
    Fraction mult(const Fraction &other);
    Fraction operator+(const Fraction &other)
        {return add(other);}
    Fraction operator*(const Fraction &other)
        {return mult(other);}
    int operator==(const Fraction &other);
    friend ostream &operator<<(ostream &os, Fraction
      &fr);
```

Fract7.cpp, cont.

```cpp
private:
    void normalize();    // Put fraction into standard
                         // form.
    int gcf(int a, int b);  // Greatest Common Factor.
    int lcm(int a, int b);  // Lowest Common
                            // Denominator.
};

int main() {
    Fraction f1(1, 2);
    Fraction f2(1, 3);

    Fraction f3 = f1 + f2 + 1;

    cout << "1/2 + 1/3 + 1 = " << f3 << endl;
    return 0;
}

// --------------------------------------------------
// FRACTION CLASS FUNCTIONS

Fraction::Fraction(Fraction const &src) {
    num = src.num;
    den = src.den;
}

// Normalize: put fraction into a standard form,
//   unique for each mathematically different value.
//
void Fraction::normalize(){

    // Handle cases involving 0

    if (den == 0 || num == 0) {
        num = 0;
        den = 1;
    }

    // Put neg. sign in numerator only.
```

▼ *continued on next page*

```cpp
        if (den < 0) {
            num *= -1;
            den *= -1;
        }

        // Factor out GCF from numerator and denominator.

        int n = gcf(num, den);
        num = num / n;
        den = den / n;
    }

    // Greatest Common Factor
    //
    int Fraction::gcf(int a, int b) {
        if (a % b == 0)
            return abs(b);
        else
            return gcf(b, a % b);
    }

    // Lowest Common Multiple
    //
    int Fraction::lcm(int a, int b){
        return (a / gcf(a, b)) * b;
    }

    Fraction Fraction::add(const Fraction &other) {
        Fraction fract;
        int lcd = lcm(den, other.den);
        int quot1 = lcd/den;
        int quot2 = lcd/other.den;
        fract.set(num * quot1 + other.num * quot2, lcd);
        fract.normalize();
        return fract;
    }

    Fraction Fraction::mult(const Fraction &other) {
        Fraction fract;
        fract.set(num * other.num, den * other.den);
```

Fract7.cpp, cont.

```cpp
        fract.normalize();
        return fract;
}

int Fraction::operator==(const Fraction &other) {
        return (num == other.num && den == other.den);
}

// ------------------------------------------------
// FRACTION CLASS FRIEND FUNCTION

ostream &operator<<(ostream &os, Fraction &fr) {
        os << fr.num << "/" << fr.den;
        return os;
}
```

13

How It Works

This example adds just a few more capabilities to the Fraction class:

▶ A constructor that takes a single **int** argument.

▶ An operator function that supports the test-for-equality operator (==).

▶ A global function that supports printing Fraction objects to an **ostream** object such as **cout**.

The new constructor is simple, so it can be inlined (defined in the class declaration). As I mentioned earlier, one of the benefits of this constructor is that it defines how to convert an integer value to a Fraction object, wherever such conversion is required. So, given this constructor, you don't need to add a bunch of additional functions that tell how to operate on integer arguments; instead, the program automatically converts integers to Fraction objects as needed.

```cpp
        Fraction(int n) {set(n, 1);}
```

The action of this function is to use whatever number is specified as numerator and use 1 for the denominator. This means that 1 is converted to 1/1, 2 is converted to 2/1, 5 is converted to 5/1, and so on.

That action suits the mathematics of the situation perfectly. When the integer 5 is converted into 5/1, for example, it retains precisely the same value, but is in Fraction format. This is exactly the desired behavior.

The other new extensions to the Fraction class incorporate code introduced in previous sections. First, the class declaration is expanded so that it declares two new functions:

```
int operator==(const Fraction &other);
friend ostream &operator<<(ostream &os, Fraction
    &fr);
```

The first function here, `operator==`, is a true member function of the Fraction class; it is identified outside the class as `Fraction::operator==`, to clarify its scope. Because it's a member function, it's called through a particular object.

```
int Fraction::operator==(const Fraction &other) {
    return (num == other.num && den == other.den);
}
```

Remember, unqualified references to num and den here refer to members of "this object"—in other words, the left operand. The expressions `other.num` and `other.den` refer to values of the right operand.

The declaration of the `operator<<` function indicates that it's a global function, but also a friend of the Fraction class. It can therefore access private data (specifically, num and den). This is an overloaded function. The compiler depends on the argument list to uniquely identify it. Again, here is the definition.

```
ostream &operator<<(ostream &os, Fraction &fr) {
    os << fr.num << "/" << fr.den;
    return os;
}
```

EXERCISES

Exercise 13.3.1.   Alter the operator<< function of Exercise 13.4 so that it prints numbers in the format "(n, d)", where n and d are the numerator and denominator (num and den members), respectively.

Exercise 13.3.2.   Write greater-than (>) and less-than (<) functions, and revise the main function of Exercise 13.4 to test these functions. For example, test whether 1/2 + 1/3 is greater than 5/9. (Hint: remember that A/B is greater than C/D if A * D > B * C.)

Exercise 13.3.3. Write an `operator<<` function for sending the contents of a Point object to an ostream object (such as **cout**). Assume the function has been declared as a friend function of the Point class. Write the function definition.

Chapter 13 *Summary*

Here are the main points of Chapter 13:

▶ An operator function for a class has the following declaration, in which @ stands for any valid C++ operator.

> *return_type* **operator@(***argument_list***)**

▶ An operator function may be declared as a member function or a global function. If it is a member function, then (for a binary operator) there is one argument. For example, the `operator+` function for the Point class could have this declaration and definition:

```
class Point {
//...
public:
    Point operator+(Point pt);
};

Point Point::operator+(Point pt) {
    Point new_pt;
    new_pt.x = x + pt.x;
    new_pt.y = y + pt.y;
    return new_pt;
}
```

▶ Given this code, the compiler now knows how to interpret the addition sign when applied to two objects of the class.

```
point1 + point2
```

▶ When an operator function is used this way, the left operand becomes the object through which the function is called, and the right operand is passed as an argument. Thus, in the `operator+` definition above, unqualified references to x and y refer to the values of the left operand.

▶ Operator functions can also be declared as global functions. For a binary operator, the function has two arguments. For example:

```
Point operator+(Point pt1, Point pt2) {
    Point new_pt;
    new_pt.x = pt1.x + pt2.x;
    new_pt.y = pt1.y + pt2.y;
    return new_pt;
}
```

▶ One drawback of writing the operator function this way is that it loses access to private members. To prevent this problem, declare the global function as a friend of the class. For example:

```
class Point {
//...
public:
    friend Point operator+(Point pt1, Point pt2);
};
```

▶ If an argument takes an object but does not need to alter it, you can often improve the efficiency of a function by revising it to use a reference argument—for example, changing an argument of type `Point` to type `const Point&`.

▶ A constructor with one argument provides a conversion function. For example, the following constructor enables automatic conversion of integer data into Fraction class format.

```
Fraction(int n) {set(n, 1);}
```

▶ If you don't write an assignment operator function (=), the compiler automatically supplies one for you. The behavior of the compiler-supplied version is to perform a simple member-by-member copy.

▶ The compiler does not supply a test-for-equality function (==), so you need to write your own if you want to be able to compare objects. It's a good idea to use the **bool** return type, if your compiler supports it; otherwise, use **int** return type for this function.

▶ The best way to write a "print" function for a class is to write a version of the `operator<<` function that is a global function but (as a friend) has access to private data of the class. The first argument should have **ostream** type, so that the stream operator (<<) is supported for **cout** and all other classes that share

ostream as a base class. You should first declare this function as a friend to your class. For example:

```
class Point {
//...
public:
  friend ostream &operator<<(ostream &os, Fraction
    &fr);
};
```

▶ In the function definition, the statements should write data from the right operand (`fr` in this case) to the **ostream** argument. Then the function should return the **ostream** argument itself. For example:

```
ostream &operator<<(ostream &os, Fraction &fr) {
    os << fr.num << "/" << fr.den;
    return os;
}
```

What's "new": The StringParser Class

One of the themes of this book is that there's nothing magic about classes and object-oriented programming. Contrary to what some books may tell you, a class is not useful just because it's a class—any more than a tool consisting of random pieces of metal stuck together is useful. A class becomes useful when it provides a set of related services that solve common programming problems.

One of the most common tasks in programming is to get input and analyze it. This chapter features a class—the StringParser class—that breaks an input string into a series of substrings, each containing a word.

Note ▶ Most of the functionality of this class is also provided by the **strtok** library function . . . but it's useful to know how to write the class. One thing that's not possible with the **strtok** library function is the ability to scan more than one string at a time; with the object-oriented approach, that's not a problem.

In the process of discussing this class, the chapter also discusses the **new** keyword, one of the most important keywords in C++ for working with classes. The use of this keyword lets you get memory and, in effect, allocate new variables whenever you need to.

The "new" Operator

Up till now, I've described pointer operations in two familiar steps: allocate data by declaring a variable, and then assign its address to a pointer. For example:

```
int n;
int *p = &n;
```

This procedure is perfectly fine for simple programs. But C++ provides a way to combine these actions into one step, and (as I'll show in this chapter), this approach is sometimes the only one that works. It involves the use of the **new** keyword, which has this syntax:

new *type*

When C++ evaluates this expression, it allocates a new data item with the specified type and returns a pointer to the item. That means you can write statements like this:

```
int *p;
p = new int;
```

Or you can combine these two statements into one.

```
int *p = new int;
```

The effect of this statement is to create an unnamed integer variable, accessible only through a pointer, p.

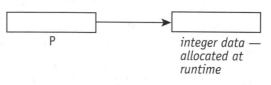

```
int *p = new int;
```

By using the pointer, you can (as usual) manipulate the value of the integer and use it in expressions.

```
*p = 5;
*p = *p + 1;
cout << "The value of the integer is " << *p;
```

But what's the purpose of creating an integer accessible only through a pointer? Why not just use an ordinary integer declaration as before?

```
int n;
```

What's gained here is that the integer value (again, accessible only through p) is not declared in the program. It's created on the fly. The integer value is allocated in the middle of program execution; it is not allocated (like most variables) when the program is loaded into memory.

This gives the program freedom to create new data space—in effect, creating new variables—whenever it needs to.

The **new** operator has a counterpart, an operator that gives back the memory that **new** requested. This is the **delete** operator, which has the syntax:

    delete *pointer*;

This syntax describes a statement, in which *pointer* is an address expression. The effect of the statement is to destroy the item pointed to by *pointer*, giving back the memory used by it to the operating system.

The following example code does these three things: 1) create integer storage on the fly; 2) use a pointer to manipulate the integer; and 3) release the memory occupied by that integer back to the operating system.

```
int *p = new int;
*p = 5;
*p = *p + 3;
cout << "The value of the integer is " << *p;
delete p;
```

Again, is it really useful to have to go through these extra steps (allocating and releasing memory)? Maybe not in this case, but stayed tuned.

Objects and "new"

So far, I've said little about an important concept in object orientation: *pointers to objects*. This concept turns out to be critical in the more advanced concepts in object orientation.

When a program interacts with other programs in a graphical user interface or network environment, it usually passes or receives pointers to objects. In the previous chapter, I showed that passing around objects can be inefficient: each time an object is copied, new data is allocated and a call to the copy constructor is made. If an object is passed around repeatedly, the constant making of new copies results in a great deal of extra work.

To minimize this inefficiency, systems applications and libraries usually pass around pointers to objects. Typically, a program creates an object and then gives a pointer to the object to another program.

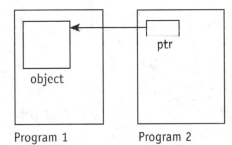

Program 1   Program 2

There are other advantages to using pointers to objects as well, as you'll see in Chapter 17. A pointer to an object can have a general pointer type (it can be a pointer to an abstract class, or interface), while the object has a more specific type. It's this fact that gives object orientation its special flexibility. But more about that later.

The **new** operator works with object types (classes) as well as fundamental data types. In fact, **new** was added mainly to work with classes, although it can prove very useful for working with types such as **int** and **double**.

For example, you can use **new** to allocate a Fraction object and get a pointer to it.

```
Fraction *pFract = new Fraction;
```

This statement creates a Fraction object and calls the default constructor, since no arguments are specified. But you can specify arguments here, just as you would if you declared a Fraction object as a variable in the program.

```
Fraction *pFract = new Fraction(1, 2);  // Init to 1/2
```

The syntax for using **new** to allocate an object with an argument list is:

new *class_name(argument_list)*

This expression allocates an object of the specified class, calls the appropriate constructor (as determined by *argument_list*), and returns the address of the object.

Once you have a pointer to an object, how do you use it? How do you refer to the object's members? The obvious way is to dereference the pointer and then access a member. For example:

```
Fraction *pFract = new Fraction(1, 2);
cout << "The numerator is " << (*pFract).get_num();
```

This operation—dereferencing a pointer and then accessing members of the object pointed to—is so common that C++ supplies a special operator just to make for more concise code. Here's the syntax.

pointer->member
pointer->member()

This syntax describes access to a data member and a function member, respectively. These two expressions are equivalent to:

*(*pointer).member*
*(*pointer).member()*

The example shown earlier, using a pointer to call get_num, can be rewritten as:

```
cout << "The numerator is " << pFract->get_num();
```

Here's another example, which calls the object's set function to assign new values to the fraction.

```
pFract->set(2, 5);    // Set fraction pointed to,
                      //  assigning the value 2/5.
```

Allocating Array Data

So far, I've shown how to dynamically allocate memory at runtime—to ask for more memory than the program originally required. This sounds good, but when is it of practical value?

A simple, and rather common, case is this: what if you need to allocate space for an array, but you don't know ahead of time how big to make the array? One obvious solution is just to use arrays so big that you don't think they'll be exceeded, and hope that nothing goes wrong (and in fact I've used an approach like that earlier in the book, for strings). But this clearly isn't the best possible approach. It's error prone.

C++ enables you to declare a memory block at runtime by using the **new** operator with this syntax:

new *type*[*size*]

This expression allocates *size* elements, in which element has the specified *type*; then it evaluates the address of the first element. The *type* can be either a standard type (**int**, double, **char**, and so on) or a class. The value *size* is an integer.

This version of **new** returns a pointer to indicated *type*, just like the other versions of **new**. For example:

```
int *p = new int[50];
p[0] = 1;
p[9] = 100;
```

An important aspect of this syntax is that the specified size need not be a constant. You can determine the memory needs at runtime. An obvious application of this feature is to ask the user how big to make an array.

```
int n;
cout << "How many elements?";
cint >> n;
int *p = new int[n];
```

This is a useful technique and I use it in the next example.

When you use the **new** operator in any of its forms, you take responsibility for creating and releasing memory. Therefore, by the end of the program, you should use the **delete** operator to destroy any new memory objects you've created. If you have allocated a memory block using the syntax in this section, release that block by using the following statement:

```
delete [] pointer;
```

Interlude

Dealing with Problems in Memory Allocation

When you use the **new** operator, the program makes a request to the operating system, asking for memory. The system responds by checking available memory and seeing if there is space available.

With today's modern computer platforms, large amounts of memory are usually available. Unless you are making exceptionally large memory requests, you can generally expect to always get the memory you need. Still, it is possible that the memory may not be available, so programs need to plan for this possibility.

If the memory requested is not available, the **new** operator returns a null pointer. You can test for this possibility, and take the appropriate action.

```
int *p = new int[1000];
if (!p) {
    cout << "Insufficient memory.";
    exit(0);
}
```

Another problem that can occur is due to *memory leaks*. When you successfully request memory with **new**, the operating system reserves the memory block until it is released with **delete**. If you then end the program without releasing all your dynamically allocated memory blocks, then the system loses some memory every time you run the program. Eventually, your computer has a great deal less usable memory.

The computer isn't losing physical memory, of course, and rebooting restores memory completely. But users should not have to do that, at least not very often.

To avoid that problem, make sure you use **delete** to release any dynamically allocated memory before the program ends. Some programming systems—such as Java and Microsoft Visual Basic—have a process called a garbage collector, which runs in the background, finding memory blocks no longer in use and deleting them. C++ does not have such a feature, in part because it takes up processor cycles and because, as with C, it assumes that you know what you are doing.

Example 14.1. *Dynamic Memory in Action*

This example shows a simple use for dynamic memory: allocating an array with the size requested by the user. This array is then used to hold values input by the user, then print them, total them, and print out the average.

```cpp
new1.cpp

#include <iostream>
using namespace std;

int main() {
    int sum = 0;
    int n;
    int *p;

    cout << "Enter number of items: ";
    cin >> n;

    p = new int[n];      // Allocate n integers

    for (int i = 0; i < n; i++) {
        cout << "Enter item #" << i << ": ";
        cin >> p[i];
        sum += p[i];
    }
    cout << "Here are the items: ";
    for (int i = 0; i < n; i++)
        cout << p[i] << ", ";
    cout << endl;
    cout << "The total is: " << sum << endl;
    cout << "The average is: " << (double) sum / n
      << endl;

    delete [] p;         // Release n integers.

    return 0;
}
```

14

How It Works

The most interesting feature of this example is that it uses the **new** operator to dynamically request memory. First, the program prompts the user for a number:

```
cout << "Enter number of items: ";
cin >> n;
```

Having gotten a value for n, the program then allocates space for n elements.

```
p = new int[n];      // Allocate n integers
```

The pointer p (which was previously declared as type **char***), contains the address of the first element. You can use it as a base address for indexing, just as you'd use an array name. The rest of the code proceeds to do just that, up until the final statement, which uses the **delete** [] syntax to release all the elements allocated with new.

```
delete [] p;       // Release n integers.
```

Note that the brackets ([]) are required here because the memory block was created to have multiple elements. Otherwise, the simpler form of delete would suffice.

EXERCISE

Exercise 14.1.1.   Revise Exercise 14.1 so that it creates an array of floating-point numbers (type **double**). Note that most variables should change to use base type **double**, although n should still be an integer.

Design for a Parser (Lexical Analyzer)

The whole point of a programming tool, of course, is to solve practical problems. The benefit of the **new** operator is that it lets you creates data structures on an ad hoc basis—creating them as the need arises. Let's see how this might work within a useful class.

Note ▶   Most of the functionality of the class developed here (StringParser) is provided by the **strtok** ("string tokenizer") function from the C++ standard library, although that provides a less object-oriented approach. The real purpose of describing the StringParser class is to illustrate certain programming techniques for writing classes.

At the beginning of the chapter, I mentioned that one of the most common programming tasks is parsing—or rather, lexical analysis. You can see this in the conjunction with the Fraction class.

You may want to prompt the user to give input in this form:

```
3/4
```

Instead of having to pull this string apart and trying to decide where one substring begins and another ends, it would be nice to have an object that does it for you.

Specifically, you'd create an object by specifying two strings.

```
StringParser parser("3/4", "/");
```

The first string contains the data to be analyzed—this is typically an input string. The second string is the delimiter string—it contains characters to be used to distinguish one substring (or "word") from another. Any one of these characters can serve to show where one substring ends and another begins. For example, given this statement:

```
StringParser parser("3/4/55@10", "/@");
```

the parser object will recognize the substrings "3", "4", "55", and "10".

Getting back to the original example, suppose that input_string contains the string data "3/4" and the parser is created by this statement:

```
StringParser parser(input_string, "/");
```

Now we should be able to extract the substrings "3" and "4" just by calling a get function:

```
char *p1, *p2;
p1 = parser.get();
p2 = parser.get();
```

The advantage of this approach is that all you have to do is to say "get the next string" (which is what the "get" function does). You don't have to worry about maintaining a current-position indicator within input_string. This is a good example of one of the major reasons you use classes: to shield data.

Of course, we're not shielding that much data: just the current-position indicator, along with the input string and delimiter string—which, although specified, only have to be specified once. A really powerful class might be one which hides many pieces of data. Or, it might be one (such as the String class we'll consider in the next section) that has only one piece of data but manipulates it in complex ways.

But let's get back to the StringParser class. The get function creates a brand-new, null-terminated string, and returns a pointer to that string: These two lines of code create two strings.

```
p1 = parser.get();
p2 = parser.get();
```

Where does the string data get allocated? With the **new** operator, of course (which you'll see when I show the implementation of the class). Because new string data is created through the use of this operator, the data must eventually be released, or you risk creating memory holes as I described earlier in the Interlude, "Dealing with Problems in Memory Allocation."

```
delete [] p1;
delete [] p2;
```

Because the get function returns a new string each time it's called and doesn't keep track of it internally, it's the caller's responsibility to use **delete** to release the string space.

Note ▶ You may already see that there are some problems with this approach. The get function returns a pointer to a spanking brand-new string, and you don't have to worry about how it allocates space for the string. But now the responsibility for destroying the string rests squarely on the user of the object. It might be better (and in fact it probably is) to have the get function copy string data to an *existing* string that the caller has allocated space for. That is left as an exercise in an upcoming section.

Sometimes, of course, you just want to get a substring long enough to convert it to a number. We can add that capability as well by creating a get_int function.

```
int d = parser.get_int();
int n = parser.get_int();
```

This turns out to be easy to implement, as you'll see. The get_int function need only call the **get** function (assuming one is available) and then call the **atoi** library function, which reads string data to produce an integer.

The class also needs to supply an "Is there more?" function, which returns true (1) if the end of the string has not been reached. Here's how you might use this function, called **more**, together with the **get** function, in a program.

```
#include <iostream>
using namespace std;
//...
char *p[10];
for (int i = 0; parser.more() && i < 10; i++)
    p[i] = parser.get();

for (int j = 0; j < i; j++) {
```

```
        cout << p[j] << endl;
        delete [] p[j];
    }
```

The declaration sets up an array of ten pointers, each of which has type **char***: Note that no actual string data is allocated here—just the pointers—because the string data will be supplied by the parser object. Pointers in this array just store the addresses.

```
    char *p[10];
```

The first loop uses the parser object. The loop calls the more function inside the loop condition and it calls the get function to retrieve a new string during each cycle of the loop. These two member functions are easy to use.

```
    for (int i = 0; parser.more() && i < 10; i++)
        p[i] = parser.get();
```

The second loop prints out all the strings, so you can see that the class functions are working correctly. Note that `delete []` must be used once for each pointer returned to destroy the strings before the program ends.

Let's summarize all the functions that the StringParser class should support. First, it needs to support a couple of constructors.

Table 14.1: StringParser Supported Constructor Functions

FUNCTION CALL	DESCRIPTION
StringParser(input_str, delimiter_str)	Set the input string and delimiter string to the specified values.
StringParser(input_str)	Set the input string to the specified value and use a default delimiter string of ",".

The class should also support these other member functions.

Table 14.2: StringParser Supported Member Functions

FUNCTION CALL	DESCRIPTION
get()	Find the next substring. Create a new string and copy the contents of the substring to this new string.
get_int()	Return the value of the next substring converted to its face value as an integer. (For example, return the value 5 if the next substring is "5".)
more()	Return true as long as there is more data remaining in the input string.
reset()	Reset the internal current-position indicator to the beginning of the input string.

Only one thing more is necessary to begin writing and testing the class: algorithms for each of these functions.

The get function is likely to be the most challenging to write. Complicating matters is the fact that the get function can be approached more than one way. For example, one of the things that the function has to do is to "consume" the delimiter characters—this means to read past them without copying them into a destination string. Should delimiters (if any) be consumed before or after a substring is read?

I use the following algorithm for the get function.

Allocate new string data.
While the current character is a delimiter,
    Ignore this character and advance the current position.
While the current character is not a delimiter and not a null,
        Copy this character to the new string, and
        Advance the current position.
Append a null to the new string.
Return a pointer to the new string.

The get_int function is a simpler matter, because it reuses the get function to do most of its work. Here is all the function has to do:

Call the get function to retrieve the next substring.
Set n equal to the integer value of this substring by calling atoi.
Destroy the new string (releasing its memory).
Return n.

The last two functions are simpler. The more function has only to do the following:

Return false (0) if the current position is a null (indicating the end of the string).
Otherwise, return 1.

Simplest of all is the reset function:

Set the current position to 0.

The class also needs to keep track of private data: the input string, delimiter string, and the current-position indicator, pos. Here is the design of the class summarized visually:

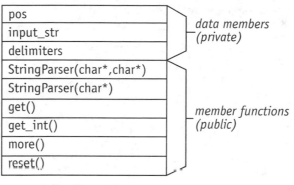

StringParser class

Example 14.2. *The StringParser Class*

This section implements the StringParser class and tests it. When run, the program prints this prompt:

```
Enter input line:
```

As the user, you respond by entering any characters you want. You can include any number of slashes (/) and commas (,); these, if included, determine where substrings are. For example, suppose you enter the following line:

```
2/3/35//5,1,,,,22
```

The program responds by printing:

```
2
3
35
5
1
22
```

You can see that a series of delimiters (,,,,) is treated the same as a single delimiter (,). This is by design. It's quite possible to write the class functions differently, so that a series of delimiters cause the program to read in a series of empty strings.

You may note that there is no default constructor for the StringParser class. This is also by design. A parser object that was not initialized with an input string would not be useful.

parse1.cpp

```cpp
#include <iostream>
#include <stdlib.h>
#include <string.h>
using namespace std;

class StringParser {
private:
    int pos;
    char *input_str;
    char *delimiters;

public:
    StringParser(char *inp, char *delim)
        {input_str = inp; delimiters = delim; pos = 0; }

    StringParser(char *inp)
        {input_str = inp; delimiters = ","; pos = 0; }

    char *get();
    int get_int();
    int more()   {return input_str[pos] != '\0'; }
    void reset() {pos = 0;}
};

int main() {
    char input_str[100];
    char *p;

    cout << "Enter input line: ";
    cin.getline(input_str, 99);

    StringParser parser(input_str, "/,");

    while (parser.more()) {
        p = parser.get();   // Get ptr to newly
                            // allocated string
        cout << p << endl;  // Print it
        delete [] p;        // Release string memory
    }
```

```
        return 0;
}

// ----------------------------------------------
// STRINGPARSER CLASS FUNCTIONS

char *StringParser::get() {
    int j = 0;
    char *new_str;
    new_str = new char[100];

    // Consume initial delimiters, if any

    while (strchr(delimiters, input_str[pos]))
        pos++;

    // Copy characters as long as none is a
    //  delimiter or end of string (null)

    while (input_str[pos] != '\0' &&
            ! strchr(delimiters, input_str[pos]))

        new_str[j++] = input_str[pos++];

    // Finish string and return it.

    new_str[j] = '\0';
    return new_str;
}

int StringParser::get_int() {
    char *p = get();
    return atoi(p);
    delete [] p;
}
```

14

How It Works

The first thing the program does is include a number of files. Support for iostream must be included, as usual, in order to use **cin** and **cout**. The files stdlib.h and string.h must be included to support the **atoi** and **strchr** library functions, respectively, which are used by the StringParser class.

```
#include <iostream>
#include <stdlib.h>
#include <string.h>
```

The main function tests the StringParser class by using an object to analyze an input line entered by the user.

```
cout << "Enter input line: ";
cin.getline(input_str, 99);

StringParser parser(input_str, "/,");

while (parser.more()) {
    p = parser.get();      // Get ptr to newly
                           // allocated string
    cout << p << endl;     // Print it
    delete [] p;           // Release string memory
}
```

The StringParser class declares three private members: pos, input_str, and delimiters. Note that the last two are only pointers, not string arrays. They could be implemented as string arrays, in which case data would have be copied by calling the **strcpy** function rather than simply storing an address (as is done here). The code here makes the simplifying assumption that the original string data (that is, the input line) will not be destroyed before the class is done using it. But be careful: if input_str goes out of scope before the parser object does, the object would have a pointer to invalid data.

```
int pos;
char *input_str;
char *delimiters;
```

The class declares all the functions described earlier in this chapter. Most of these are fairly short, so I choose to inline them.

```
StringParser(char *inp, char *delim)
    {input_str = inp; delimiters = delim; pos = 0;}
```

```
StringParser(char *inp)
    {input_str = inp; delimiters = ","; pos = 0;}

char *get();
int get_int();
int more()   {return input_str[pos] != '\0';}
void reset() {pos = 0;}
```

The get function is the real workhorse of this class, of course, and it is not inlined, because it includes too much code. The first thing the get function does is to allocate a new string. The size 100 is arbitrary, and I picked it because I don't expect it to be exceeded. That can be a poor assumption in certain situations, of course, and there are ways of addressing that limitation, which I mention later.

```
new_str = new char[100];
```

The next thing the get function does is to "consume" any delimiters it might find. This is necessary because the previous get operation, if any, leaves the current position indexing a delimiter character. (During the first call to get, there probably won't be any delimiter characters at the beginning of the string, in which case this code does nothing.)

```
while (strchr(delimiters, input_str[pos]))
    pos++;
```

This statement involves a call to the **strchr** library function, which returns a null value if the character specified by the second argument cannot be found in the first argument, a string. If the character *can* be found in the first argument (delimiters), **strchr** returns a non-null value and so the expression is considered "true." Basically, this code says:

While input_str[pos] matches one of the characters in the delimiters string,
    Increment pos.

The variable pos, of course, is the current-position indicator, and input_str[pos] is therefore the "current character."

The next thing the function does is to read characters into the new string as long as the current character is *not* a delimiter and not a null-terminator.

```
while (input_str[pos] != '\0' &&
        ! strchr(delimiters, input_str[pos]))

    new_str[j++] = input_str[pos++];
```

Finally, the function terminates the new string and returns it.

```
new_str[j] = '\0';
return new_str;
```

Improving the Code

There's at least one gaping flaw in the StringParser code: it assumes that each substring will never exceed more than 99 characters. If it does, the `get` function will exceed the size of the dynamically allocated string (new_str) and cause difficult-to-debug errors as the get function overwrites areas of memory that it shouldn't.

As a C++ programmer, you should be forever vigilant against this kind of disruption. If there's any possibility that a loop or a function will overwrite areas of memory that it shouldn't, you should act to prevent it.

One obvious solution is to prevent writing to the new string after 99 characters have been written. The problematic code is:

```
while (input_str[pos] != '\0' &&
        ! strchr(delimiters, input_str[pos]))

    new_str[j++] = input_str[pos++];
```

You can solve the problem by inserting an **if** condition in the middle of the statement. Here I put the new code in bold:

```
while (input_str[pos] != '\0' &&
        ! strchr(delimiters, input_str[pos]))

    if (j < 100)
        new_str[j++] = input_str[pos++];
```

A more versatile solution is to determine ahead of time how much space will be needed for new_str. This involves more work on the part of the `get` function, of course, but it's made relatively easy by use of the **strcspn** library function.

This function returns the index of the first character in s1 (the first argument specified) that matches any character in the second argument. If no characters match, it returns the index of the terminating null in s1.

```
int substring_size = strcspn(input_str + pos,
    delimiters);
char *new_str = new char[substring_size];
```

To work correctly, this code should be placed just after the loop that consumes initial delimiter characters.

EXERCISES

Exercise 14.2.1. Revise Example 14.2 so that it makes calls to the get_int function rather than the get function. This means, by the way, that only numbers will be read, but it simplifies some of the code in the main function.

Exercise 14.2.2. In the StringParser class, add a get_dbl function that reads a floating-point number and returns a value of type **double**. (Hint: this code is similar to get_int, but calls **atof** instead of **atoi**.)

Exercise 14.2.3. Rewrite the get function so that it copies the substring to an existing string, which must be specified as an argument. The declaration of the get function changes to:

```
get(char *dest);
```

The responsibility for allocating string data (to hold the substrings) shifts to the user of the object. You need to revise the main function so that it declares space to hold this destination string.

Exercise 14.2.4. Add a set_size function to the StringParser class, so that the user of the object can specify a maximum number of substring characters to read. Alter the get function as needed so it uses this setting.

Chapter 14 *Summary*

Here are the main points of Chapter 14:

▶ The **new** operator dynamically allocates new memory at runtime. It has the following syntax, which describes an expression returning a pointer to the requested memory. This pointer has type *type*.

```
new type
```

▶ If the type is an object type (that is, a class), you can optionally specify arguments, to invoke the desired constructor.

```
new type(argument_list)
```

▶ You can also use **new** to specify a series of items (memory block). As with the other versions of **new**, this syntax describes an expression that returns a value of type *type*.

```
new type[number_of_elements]
```

▶ Before the program ends, it is your responsibility to release any dynamically allocated memory. To delete a single item created with **new**, use this statement:

```
delete pointer;
```

▶ To delete a memory block (of whatever size) created with **new**, use this statement:

```
delete [] pointer;
```

▶ Here's a brief example that uses **new** and **delete**.

```
Fraction *pFract = new Fraction[10];
//...
delete [] pFract;
```

▶ The -> operator makes it easier to work with pointers to objects. For example:

```
pFract->set(1, 2);
```

This is equivalent to:

```
(*pFract).set(1, 2);
```

What's "this": The String Class

As you get deeply into the fine art of writing classes, you'll sooner or later have to confront issues related to resource management.

To be more specific: when certain kinds of objects come into existence, the program code must ask the system to allocate some resource. The most common kind of resource is memory. As you'll see in this chapter, resource management creates some special problems that, fortunately, C++ has specific language features to handle.

This chapter shows how to write a high-level String class, which gives a simple but thorough demonstration of resource-management issues.

The purpose of this class, like most classes, is to hide details. The String class frees users of the class from the problems of allocating and releasing memory for strings. In short, the String class encapsulates **char** arrays and operations on them, making a string look—to the class user—like a simple data type rather than the complex structure that it is.

Note ▶ The String class presented here is a simpler version of the **string** class presented at the end of Chapter 7. If your compiler includes library for the string class, you don't need to use the class defined here, but this class is still a very useful example of some important aspects of object-oriented programming in C++. In particular, this chapter uses a String class to illustrate use of **this** keyword, destructors, and deep copying.

Introducing the String Class

C and C++ programmers have a love/hate relationship with C-style strings . . . okay, it's a relationship that might be better described as one that ranges from hate to "putting up with grudgingly."

On the plus side, C-style (that is to say, null-terminated) strings provide direct access to data and don't impose any hidden overhead. What you see is what you get.

But when working with this data type, you need to watch out for all kinds of errors, which (beginning in Chapter 7) I've tried to steer you past. Most of these problems are related to the issue of space allocation; if you don't allocate enough space to hold the string data, you can end up overwriting other areas of memory, causing difficult-to-track-down bugs, which in turn can cause you many frustrating hours trying to fix your programs. And that's not good.

A C/C++ string is a composite data type, meaning that it's made up of a series of elements.

```
char name[] = "C++ Without Fear";
```

What this statement creates is not a single piece of data, but rather an array of 17 elements (including 16 spaces for the string data and another for the terminating null).

It would be nice to have a String data type in which you could treat strings as individual objects, not worrying about their internal details. It would be really nice if the whole process of allocating, destroying, and reallocating string-data space were entirely automated, so that you never again had to worry about whether you had allocated enough space.

Then you could create and manipulate strings like this:

```
String str1, str2, str3;
str1 = "To be, ";
str2 = "or not to be.";
str3 = str1 + str2;
```

This chapter demonstrates how to implement these features, and a lot more.

Introducing Class Destructors

We'll look first at a simple version of the String class, which automates the basic tasks of creation and destruction. Before that, however, I need to introduce a new piece of syntax, the destructor. This is a member function with the following declaration:

```
~class_name()
```

In other words, the destructor for a class has a syntax similar to that for a constructor, except for the tilde (~) at the beginning of the name—and the fact that the argument list must be blank.

For example, the Fraction class might have a destructor declared as follows:

```
class Fraction {
//...
public:
    ~Fraction();
};
```

But I didn't introduce the use of destructors earlier—and for a good reason. It wasn't needed.

The purpose of a class's destructor is to clean up resources just before an object is destroyed. This happens whenever an object is explicitly destroyed when you use any form of **delete**:

```
Fraction *pF = new Fraction;
//...
delete pF;      // Destroy object pointed to by pF.
```

An object is also destroyed when it's declared as a variable and then goes out of scope.

```
void aFunction() {
//...
    Fraction fract1(1, 2);    // Object fract1 created.
    cout << fract1 + 1;
}                             // Object fract1 destroyed.
```

So what happens when an object is destroyed? Often, nothing happens. The memory occupied by the object is released and thereby made available for other data items. Just before that happens, the class destructor, if any, is called.

With the Fraction class, for example, there's nothing to do. Upon destruction, Fraction data members—specifically, num and den—simply go away. There are no additional system resources that have to be closed or released.

But the String class is another matter. The String class needs to contain a single data member—a pointer to string data.

```
class String {
private:
    ptr;
//...
};
```

All the String constructors, as you'll see, allocate the actual string data—which the data member, ptr, points to—over and above the memory occupied by the object itself. The destructor has the job of releasing this string data.

```
~String() {delete [] ptr;}
```

Without this destructor, use of the String class would cause continual memory leaks . . . which might not seem like a problem at first, but any program foolish enough to use such class would eat away at memory—until after a while the user found that he or she didn't have enough memory to do anything and had to reboot. Poorly written classes can cause very frustrated, angry users. And that's not a good thing.

Example 15.1. *A Simple String Class*

In this section, I show the simple version of the String class that I promised. This version has enough functionality to be at least somewhat useful. It includes two constructors, one destructor, and a test-for-equality (==) operator function.

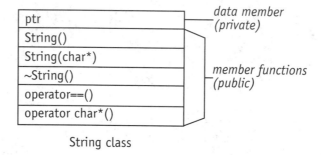

String class

Here is the code that implements and tests this class.

```
string1.cpp

#include <iostream>
#include <string.h>
using namespace std;

class String {
private:
    char *ptr;
public:
    String();
    String(char *s);
    ~String();

    int operator==(const String &other);
    operator char*() {return ptr;}
};
```

string1.cpp, cont.

```cpp
int main() {
    String a("STRING 1");
    String b("STRING 2");
    cout << "The value of a is: " << endl;
    cout << a << endl;
    cout << "The value of b is: " << endl;
    cout << b;
}

// --------------------------------
// STRING CLASS FUNCTIONS

String::String() {
    ptr = new char[1];
    ptr[0] - '\0';
}

String::String(char *s) {
    int n = strlen(s);
    ptr = new char[n + 1];
    strcpy(ptr, s);
}

String::~String() {
    delete [] ptr;
}

int String:: operator==(const String &other) {
    return (strcmp(ptr, other.ptr) == 0);
}
```

How It Works

Looked at from one angle, the class is extremely simple. It only contains one data member, ptr.

```cpp
private:
    char *ptr;
```

This member is made private because it will be set and reset by class functions that allocate memory blocks. It's important that code outside the class not be allowed to change this pointer.

All the complexity of the class stems from its behavior. The most important principle of this class is that every time string data is assigned to a String object, string data must be allocated for it and ptr must be assigned the address of the data.

This is true even if *an empty string* is assigned to a String object. This is why the default constructor must allocate one byte of string data and copy a null terminator.

```
String::String() {
    ptr = new char[1];
    ptr[0] = '\0';
}
```

Simply assigning a null value (address = 0) to ptr would be inadequate here. You'll often want to use a String object where a C/C++ string (**char***) is valid; in those cases, you'll need to pass an empty string, and that means a string of one byte in which that byte contains a null terminator.

The String(char*) constructor is less mysterious: obviously, it must copy string data from the **char*** argument. The constructor allocates enough bytes to hold all the string data; this length is determined by using the **strlen** function. The constructor must also allocate one additional byte to hold the terminating null (since the **strlen** function itself does not count the terminator).

```
String::String(char *s) {
    int n = strlen(s);
    ptr = new char[n + 1];
    strcpy(ptr, s);
}
```

The destructor, as I mentioned in the previous section, must release the string data before the object is destroyed.

```
String::~String() {
    delete [] ptr;
}
```

The `operator==` function is easy to write, although you need to note that simply comparing ptr values would not produce correct results:

```
// INCORRECT VERSION - TOO RESTRICTIVE!
```

```
int String:: operator==(const String &other) {
    return (ptr == other.ptr);
}
```

The problem with this version of **operator==** is that it returns true (1) only if the current object and the other object (the object corresponding to the right operand) point to the same area of memory. But suppose two string objects each point to a string "cat" but that each has its own copy of that string. That's the case here:

```
String str1("cat");
String str2("cat");
```

If the two strings have identical *contents*, the function should return true, even if the strings are located at different memory locations. That's why simply comparing two pointers for equality is too restrictive a test.

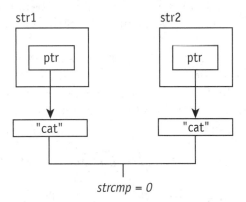

strcmp = 0

The solution is to call the **strcmp** library function. This function takes two string addresses and performs a comparison between the two strings pointed to. It returns 0 if the two strings have the same contents. That's what you want in this case.

```
int String:: operator==(const String &other) {
    return (strcmp(ptr, other.ptr) == 0);
}
```

The main function performs a simple test of String functions. The first two statements inside of **main** invoke the String(char*) constructor.

```
int main() {
    String a("STRING 1");
    String b("STRING 2");
    cout << "The value of a is: " << endl;
    cout << a << endl;
    cout << "The value of b is: " << endl;
```

```
        cout << b;
    }
```

Note that the string objects (a and b) are "printable"—that is, they can be given to **cout** as output by using the stream operator, <<.

And you can do this marvelous action because the String class declares a **char*** conversion function. With this function declared, you can use a String object wherever data of type **char*** is expected.

```
operator char*() {return ptr;}
```

The conversion function responds by returning the address of the string data, which is contained in the data member ptr.

EXERCISES

Exercise 15.1.1.   Rewrite the main function in Exercise 15.1 so that it uses and tests the default constructor for the String class.

Exercise 15.1.2.   Write `operator>` and `operator<` functions for the String class. (Hint: the **strcmp** function returns a value greater than or less than zero, respectively, if the first string comes later or earlier in alphabetical sequence. Thus, the string "abc" is "less than" the string "xyz.")

"Deep" Copying and the Copy Constructor

So far, the String class works, but frankly, it's a little dull. In fact, if you couldn't add any more functionality to it, you'd have little reason to replace the standard C/C++ **char*** type, with all its drawbacks.

The class becomes more useful when we can use it to copy one String object to another. However, this is where things begin to become a little complicated.

The obvious way to copy one object to another is just to do what the automatic (compiler-supplied) copy constructor does: perform a simple member-by-member copy. The value of ptr is copied directly, so that the new object points to the same memory location that the first object points to. This is a *shallow copy*.

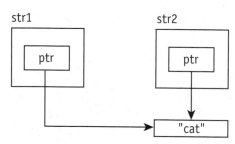

This works fine in some cases, but there is a problem: what if something happens to the string data that str2 points to? In particular, if str2 subsequently goes out of scope or is deleted for some reason, the object str1 becomes invalidated as well.

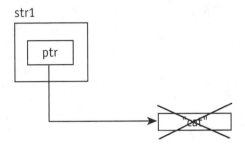

This, in fact, is just what happens if you attempt to assign a new string to str1 in the following code:

```
String str1("Hello.");
str1 = "cat";
```

If you add this code to Example 15.1 right now, you'll find that it doesn't successfully put the string "cat" into the object variable str1—at least not reliably. On my computer, it ends up erasing the value of str1, so that it appears to contain an empty string. You get unsatisfactory results if you then print the value of str1.

```
cout << str1;
```

Why is this? Well, consider what happens when the program executes the statement

```
str1 = "cat";
```

By default, the compiler supplies an assignment-operator function of type `operator=(const String&)`, which copies from one object of the same type to another. Therefore, to assign from the string "cat", the compiler interprets this statement as if it were written this way:

```
str1 = String("cat");
```

The program does two things:

1 It calls the `String(char*)` constructor to create a temporary String object.

2 It calls the `operator=(const String&)` function to assign from one String object to another.

At first glance, this ought to work. But consider how the compiler-supplied version of the assignment-operator function does: it does a simple member-by-member copy. The value of the ptr data member is assigned the value of the ptr in the temporary String object; this, in turn, means that the two objects point to the same address in memory.

But the temporary String object is quickly thrown away, as soon as the statement is finished execution. The destructor is called for the temporary String object, and the string-data memory is given back. What happens then? The data member `str1.ptr` is left pointing to a deleted area of memory!

So, to avoid these problems, use a *deep copy*. This is an approach to copying an object that reconstructs its entire contents rather than simply copying values. In the case of the String class, this means giving the destination object its own copy of the string data.

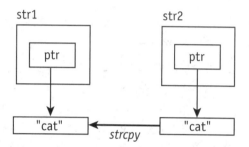

We can start by making the copy constructor use the deep-copy technique. The code here makes use of the **strlen** library function (which gets the current length of a string, up to but not including its null terminator) and the **strcpy** function (which copies string data from one area of memory to another).

```
String::String(const String &src) {
    int n = strlen(src.ptr);
    ptr = new char[n + 1];
    strcpy(ptr, src.ptr);
}
```

A correctly written assignment-operator function will use similar code. First, however, you need to understand another C++ keyword: **this**.

The "this" Keyword

The **this** keyword seems, at first glance, a strange critter. Some programmers use it frequently, but others may never use it, except in the case of the assignment operator—in which case it is required, as you'll see.

Simply stated, the **this** keyword is a pointer to the current object—the object through which a member function is called. The **this** keyword is meaningful only inside a class's member functions.

When a member function is called, the C++ compiler actually passes a hidden argument, which is—you guessed it—the **this** pointer. Consider the following call to a Fraction class member function.

```
fract1.set(1, 3);
```

Although this is not reflected in the source code, the function call is translated into this form:

```
Fraction::set(&fract1, 1, 3);
```

In other words, a pointer to fract1 is passed as the hidden first argument. That argument is accessible within the member function as **this**.

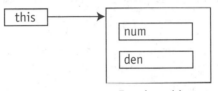

Fraction object

Once again, here's the definition of the Fraction class `set` function.

```
void set(int n, int d)
    {num = n; den = d; normalize();}
```

The function behaves as if it were written this way:

```
void set(int n, int d)
    {this->num = n; this->den = d; normalize();}
```

And, in fact, you *can* write the set function that way. It's not necessary, however, because unqualified references to a data member are assumed to be references through the **this** pointer. In most cases, using the **this** pointer to refer to data members, though legal, is unnecessary.

Incidentally, the call to normalize passes a hidden **this** pointer, although (once again) the hidden argument is not reflected in source code.

```
normalize(this);
```

That's actually not a legal statement, because the **this** pointer, though passed as an argument, must remain hidden. It is legal to write the call in the following way, although (as with the data members) this usage is unnecessary.

```
this->normalize();
```

Revisiting the Assignment Operator

Now, what does the **this** pointer have to do with the assignment-operator function? To understand the answer, you first need to review how assignments work in C++. Remember that the assignment operator (=) produces an expression just like any other and must produce a value, although it has an important side effect (that of setting the value of the left operand).

The value produced by an assignment expression (for example, x = y) returns the value that was assigned—in other words, the new value of the left operand. This value can then be reused in a larger expression. For example, consider this expression:

```
x = y = 0;
```

This statement is equivalent to the following, in which the expression y = 0 returns the new value of y (which is 0) and passes it along:

```
x = (y = 0);
```

The statement therefore assigns 0 to both x and y.

In C++, assignment-operator functions must therefore produce a value: namely, that of the left operand. In a class operator function (you'll recall) the left operand is the object through which the function was called.

But how does an object return itself? That's right; it uses the **this** pointer. By applying the indirection operator (*) to **this**, you get not a pointer to the current object, but the object itself.

In other words, this statement

```
return *this;
```

says, "Return myself!"

This may be a complex train of logic, but all you really have to do is remember one cardinal rule:

> **In the definition of any assignment-operator function (=), the last statement should be "return *this".**

That's all you really have to remember about the **this** keyword. The keyword can also be useful, on occasion, when an object needs to call a global function and explicitly pass a pointer to itself. But mostly, you'll use it in assignment-operator functions.

To simplify matters, let's first create a cpy function that copies string data from a **char*** argument. This function releases the current string-data memory, allocates enough memory for the new string and then does the copying by calling **strcpy**.

```
void String::cpy(char *s) {
    delete [] ptr;
    int n = strlen(s);
    ptr = new char[n + 1];
    strcpy(ptr, s);
}
```

Now it's an easy matter to write an assignment-operator function.

```
String& String::operator=(const String &src) {
    cpy(src.ptr);
    return *this;
}
```

Notice that the function returns a reference to a String object (type "String&") rather than a String object itself. This return type prevents an unnecessary use of the copy constructor. Remember that use of a reference passes along a pointer (under the covers), but avoids pointer syntax.

You can just as easily write an assignment-operator function that takes a **char*** argument. Although adding this function to the class isn't strictly necessary (because one of the constructors provides a conversion from the **char*** type), it makes evaluation of some expressions more efficient.

```
String& String::operator=(char *s) {
    cpy(s);
    return *this;
}
```

Both of these functions are short enough to be inlined.

Note ▶ If you compare the definitions of the copy constructor (see page 379) and the assignment-operator function (which calls the cpy member function), you'll see that they do similar things. There is an important difference, however: the cpy member function assumes that the current object has already been created and initialized. It therefore uses the **delete** operator to free the memory currently pointed to by ptr. The copy constructor makes no such assumption, since the object is new.

Writing a Concatenation Function

The String class is getting to be a lot more useful. The same string, for example, can repeatedly be assigned different values, without your having to worry about exceeding the amount of space reserved for the string. Here, str1 is first assigned a shorter string ("the") and then is assigned a larger string ("the cat").

```
String str1, str2, str3;
str1 = "the";
cout << str1 << endl;
str1 = "the cat";
cout << str1 << endl;
str2 = "the cat";
if (str1 == str2)
    cout << "str1 and str2 hold the same data." << endl;
```

But we can make the String class even better than that. What you'd really like to do perhaps is to be able to write statements like this:

```
String a("the ");
String b("end.");
String c = "This is " + b + c;
```

This requires writing an `operator+` function for the String class. To make things easier, let's start by writing a cat (short for "concatenation") member function. Writing the `operator+` function will then be a breeze.

The basic problem to solve here—as with most String member functions—is just how much string space to allocate. That's not too difficult, fortunately, because all you have to do is use the **strlen** library function to determine string lengths, and then add them.

The algorithm for the `cat` function is therefore:

Set N to the length of the current string plus the length of the string data to be added.

Allocate a new **char** memory block of size N+1, and set a pointer P1 to point to this block.

Copy current string data to this memory block (pointed to by P1) and then concatenate the new string data onto the old.

Delete the old memory block pointed to by ptr.

Set data member ptr to the same address as P1.

This algorithm is designed so that the old memory block (pointed to ptr) is not deleted until its data is copied to the memory block. That means you can't use the **delete** operator right away, and you have to temporarily store the new address in another pointer: P1.

Here is the C++ code that implements this algorithm.

```
void String::cat(char *s) {

    // Allocate sufficient room for new string data.
```

```
    int n = strlen(ptr) + strlen(s);
    char *p1 = new char[n + 1];

    // Copy data to this new memory block.

    strcpy(p1, ptr);
    strcat(p1, s);

    // Release old memory block and update ptr.

    delete [] ptr;
    ptr = p1;
}
```

Writing the **operator+** function is now an easy task. A call to the cat function does most of the work.

```
String String::operator+(char *s) {
    String new_str(ptr);
    new_str.cat(s);
    return new_str;
}
```

This is a pretty simple function, thanks to the existence of the cat member function. But notice that unlike some of the other operator functions in the String class, this function cannot return a reference. That's because the + operator creates a new object—which is not equal to either of the operands—and the entire object (not just a reference) must be returned to the caller of the function.

The relevant rule is:

> When a member function needs to return an existing object (as in an assignment-operator function), a reference return type is sufficient. But returning a reference is insufficient when a function needs to return a new object.

Example 15.2. *The Complete String Class*

It's easy now to present a fairly complete String class, although there is lots of room for you to add functionality of your own. To complete the String class, we need only add the member functions described in the last several sections.

As usual, the lines that are in bold contain statements that have been added to the previous example, Example 15.1.

string2.cpp

```cpp
#include <iostream>
#include <string.h>
using namespace std;

class String {
private:
    char *ptr;
public:
    String();
    String(char *s);
    String(const String &src);
    ~String();

    String& operator=(const String &src)
        {cpy(src.ptr); return *this;}

    String& operator=(char *s)
        {cpy(s); return *this;}

    String operator+(char *s);
    int operator==(const String &other);
    operator char*() {return ptr;}

    void cat(char *s);
    void cpy(char *s);
};

int main() {
    String a, b, c;
    a = "I ";
    b = "am ";
    c = "so ";
    String d = a + b + c + "very happy!\n";
    cout << d;
    return 0;
}

// ----------------------------------
// STRING CLASS FUNCTIONS
```

```cpp
String::String() {
    ptr = new char[1];
    ptr[0] = '\0';
}

String::String(char *s) {
    int n = strlen(s);
    ptr = new char[n + 1];
    strcpy(ptr, s);
}

String::String(const String &src) {
    int n = strlen(src.ptr);
    ptr = new char[n + 1];
    strcpy(ptr, src.ptr);
}

String::~String() {
    delete [] ptr;
}

int String::operator==(const String &other) {
    return (strcmp(ptr, other.ptr) == 0);
}

String String::operator+(char *s) {
    String new_str(ptr);
    new_str.cat(s);
    return new_str;
}

// cpy -- Copy string function
//
void String::cpy(char *s) {
    delete [] ptr;
    int n = strlen(s);
    ptr = new char[n + 1];
    strcpy(ptr, s);
}
```

▼ continued on next page

string2.cpp, cont.

```
// cat -- Concatenate string function
//
void String::cat(char *s) {

    // Allocate sufficient room for new string data.

    int n = strlen(ptr) + strlen(s);
    char *p1 = new char[n + 1];

    // Copy data to this new memory block.

    strcpy(p1, ptr);
    strcat(p1, s);

    // Release old memory block and update ptr.

    delete [] ptr;
    ptr = p1;
}
```

How It Works

All the functions in this example have been described in previous sections, so I won't devote space to explaining them here. There is one aspect of this example, however, that merits a little more discussion. You may notice that there is only one version of the operator+ function.

```
String String::operator+(char *s) {
    String new_str(ptr);
    new_str.cat(s);
    return new_str;
}
```

This function assumes that the right operand has type **char***. It therefore supports operations like this one:

```
String a("King ");
String b = a + "Kong";
```

But how does the class support operations like the following, in which both operands are String objects?

```
String a("King "), b("Kong");
String b = a + b;
```

The answer is that although the class does not directly support the + operation between two String objects, the handy conversion function comes to the rescue here.

```
operator char*() {return ptr;}
```

The class knows how to convert a String object into a **char*** type, whenever such a conversion would supply the only way to legally evaluate an expression. In the "Kong" expression above, the object b is converted into a **char*** string, and the statement is executed as if it were written this way:

```
String b = a + "Kong";
```

We therefore can get away with having just one operator+ function.

There's still a limitation with the way this function is written. Because the operator+ function is a member function, and not a global function, a String object must appear as the right operand. This means you can't execute statements such as the following:

```
String b = "My name is " + a + "Kong.";
```

The only way to support such statements—in which a **char*** string appears as the left operand in the leftmost addition (+)—is to rewrite the operator+ function as a global friend function. This is left as an exercise.

EXERCISES

Exercise 15.2.1. Rewrite the operator+ function as a global friend function, as just suggested. Review Chapter 13 if you need to. (Hint: no real change has to be made to the code other than the way the function is declared.)

Exercise 15.2.2. In all the member functions that have a **char*** argument, change them to use an argument of **const char*** type. Does the code in the main function still work?

Exercise 15.2.3. Add a convert-to-integer function that calls the **atoi** library function to convert the face value of the digits in the string (if any) to an integer. Also write a convert-to-double function that calls the **atof** library function. (Note: remember to include the file stdlib.h.)

Exercise 15.2.4. Write a String(int n) constructor that initializes the string data by including n spaces, where n is the integer specified. Write an operator= (int n) function that does a similar kind of assignment.

Exercise 15.2.5.   Write an `operator[]` function for the String class, so that you can simulate array-indexing directly, and not have to extract a **char*** string to gain access to individual characters. This function should return a reference to a **char**, so that you can use array-indexing to get an l-value (that is, an expression that can appear on the left of an assignment).

This function should have the following declaration:

```
char& operator[](const int i);
```

Chapter 15 *Summary*

Here are the main points of Chapter 15:

▶ A class destructor is called just before an object is destroyed. Writing a destructor is useful when an object has ownership of memory or some other system resource that needs to be closed. A destructor has the following declaration:

```
~class_name()
```

▶ A destructor is called when an object is explicitly destroyed by use of the **delete** operator or when the object goes out of scope.

▶ A *shallow copy* is a simple member-to-member copy between one object and another. For simple classes, this is often enough.

▶ A *deep copy* reconstructs the contents of one object and replicates them in another. This kind of copying—which requires the author of a class to write a copy constructor and an assignment-operator function—is often necessary for classes that manipulate system resources, such as memory or file access.

▶ The **this** keyword can be used in a class member function: it's translated into a pointer to the current object (that is, the object through which the function was called).

▶ Within a member function, unqualified references to a member are equivalent to references through the **this** pointer. For example, within the String class, a call to the normalize function is equivalent to:

```
this->normalize();
```

▶ All versions of the assignment-operator function should end by returning a reference to the current object.

```
return *this;
```

▶ Member functions that return an existing object should have a reference return type (such as String& instead of String). For example, all assignment-operator functions should return a reference.

```
String& String::operator=(const String &src) {
    cpy(src.ptr);
    return *this;
}
```

▶ Member functions, such as operator+, that return a brand-new object should not have a reference return type. Instead, they create a new object, set its values, and then return it.

```
String String::operator+(char *s) {
    String new_str(ptr);
    new_str.cat(s);
    return new_str;
}
```

15

Inheritance: What a Legacy

One of the most distinctive features of classes is subclassing, in which one class inherits the members of a previously defined class. This feature is important for several reasons.

The first reason is that subclassing lets you customize existing software. You can take a class someone else has created and add new features of your own. You can also overwrite any and all existing features of the class. Classes are therefore extensible and reusable (and that's the last you'll see of annoying buzzwords in this chapter, I promise).

This sounds wonderful . . . and sometimes it really is, but (for technical reasons I'll cover in this chapter) things are not always that easy. For one thing, you have to revise all the constructors.

Subclassing is also important for reasons having to do with an inheritance hierarchy *and creation of* interfaces, *which I'll talk about more in Chapter 17. (Oops— there are two more buzzwords. Sorry. But I promise to stick to English as much as possible.)*

Subclassing for Fun and Profit

A subclass has all the members of another class (called the *base class*), along with any new members you specify. Here's the syntax for declaring a subclass.

```
class class_name : public base_class {
    declarations
};
```

The *class_name* in this context specifies the new class. It inherits all the members of the base class (except for constructors—more about that later).

The *declarations* are a combination of data members, member functions, or both—just as in a standard class declaration. These declarations represent new members that are added to the existing members (inherited from the base class).

The *declarations* can also specify one or more members that are already declared in the base class. With this technique, a declaration of an existing base-class member is *overridden* and therefore ignored in favor of the new declaration.

Generally, to avoid confusion, you should use the override feature only to provide new definitions for existing functions. This is an important programming technique that will come center stage in Chapter 17.

Here's an example that creates a new class based on the Fraction class.

```
class FloatFraction : public Fraction {
public:
    double get_float();
};
```

This code illustrates a simple idea: it declares the FloatFraction class as a subclass of the previously existing Fraction class, meaning that each FloatFraction object has all the members declared in the Fraction class. In addition, each FloatFraction object has get_float, a member function.

Once this class is declared, you can use it as a type name just like any other class.

```
FloatFraction f1;
f1.set(1, 4);
cout << "The decimal representation is "
  << f1.get_float();
```

Assuming the get_float function is defined properly, this code should print out the result "0.25".

Here's an example that creates a new class based on the String class. This example is a little more complex.

```
class ExtString : public String {
private:
    int nullTerminated;
public:
    int length;
    int isNullTerminated()
      {return nullTerminated != 0;}
};
```

This code declares the class ExtString as a subclass of the String class; it therefore includes String-class members. In addition, it includes nullTerminated, a private data member. Because this member is private, code defined outside the class cannot refer to it, but outside code can access the two public members: length, a data member, and isNullTerminated, a function.

Here's another example involving inheritance from the Fraction class—but this time through an intermediate class (FloatFraction).

```
class ProperFraction : public FloatFraction {
public:
    int get_whole();
    int get_num();                  // OVERRIDDEN FUNCTION!
    void pr_proper(ostream &os);
};
```

The base class here is FloatFraction. ProperFraction is a kind of "grandchild" class that contains every member of FloatFraction and, by extension, every member of the Fraction class as well (because FloatFraction is itself a subclass of Fraction).

These declarations create a hierarchy, in which ProperFraction is an indirect subclass of Fraction.

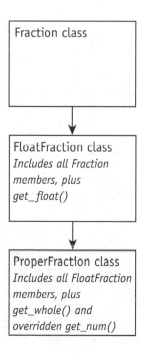

Fraction class

FloatFraction class
Includes all Fraction members, plus get_float()

ProperFraction class
Includes all FloatFraction members, plus get_whole() and overridden get_num()

Finally, here is another class that inherits directly from the Fraction class.

```
class FractionUnits : public Fraction {

public:
    String units;
};
```

The String class is involved in the FractionUnits declaration, but not as a base class or subclass. You can say that each FractionUnits object *has* a String object and it is *a kind of* FloatFraction—that is, it is a more specialized kind of Fraction object.

Look at it this way: when A is a subclass of B, you can say that A is a more specialized kind of B. Dog is a subclass of Mammal, which is a subclass of Animal, and so on. At the same time, the Dog class *contains* the class Teeth, the class Tail, and so on.

```
class Dog : public Mammal {
public:
    Teeth dog_teeth;
    Tail dog_tail;
//...
};
```

Interlude

Why "public" Base Classes?

In the syntax I showed earlier for declaring subclasses, you should notice the use of the **public** keyword, to qualify the base class: In this context, the keyword specifies the *base-class access level*.

```
class class_name : public base_class {
    declarations
};
```

Technically, you can omit the **public** keyword in favor of a straight declaration:

```
class FloatFraction : Fraction {
//...
};
```

The problem is that—as with class member declarations—the default base-class access level is **private**. And private access is usually not what you want in this context. Specifically, private base-class access says that all

Interlude

▼ *continued*

members inherited from the base class become private in the new class. So, for example, the get_num function would be inherited, but it would become private—and therefore not accessible to outside code.

```
FloatFraction aFract;
cout << aFract.get_num();  // Error! Not legal if
                           //  get_num is private.
```

In contrast, public base-class access says that all base-class members are inherited just as they are. This is almost always what you want, so it's wise to just get in the habit of putting **public** in front of the base-class name in the declaration.

The situations in which you'd benefit from having base-class access level other than **public** are probably not that common. This is one of those quirky aspects of C++ syntax (there are a couple of others) that isn't really useful to most people and whose origins are obscure. But fortunately, the solution is easy enough. Just put **public** in front of the base class.

Example 16.1. *The FloatFraction Class*

This next example marks a departure for this book. Instead of putting everything in one file, I assume that the source code is stored in a couple of separate files—in this case, Fract.h and Fract.cpp—which I include here for convenience.

First, here is the code that implements and tests the FloatFraction class itself. Note that it has an **#include** directive to bring in type information for the base class, Fraction.

FloatFract1.cpp

```
#include <iostream>
#include "Fract.h"
using namespace std;

class FloatFraction : public Fraction {
public:
 double get_float() {
   return (static_cast<double>(get_num())/get_den();}
};
```

▼ *continued on next page*

16

Floatfrac1.cpp, cont.

```
int main() {
    FloatFraction fract1;

    fract1.set(1, 2);
    cout << "Value of 1/2 is " << fract1.get_float()
      << endl;
    fract1.set(3, 5);
    cout << "Value of 3/5 is " << fract1.get_float()
      << endl;
    return 0;
}
```

This file is short, because it includes only the code needed for the subclass, FloatFraction. This class involves a good deal of C++ code, but that code is contained in the base class, Fraction. It is *reused* by the FloatFraction class.

The declaration of the Fraction class is placed in the file Fract.h.

Fract.h

```
#include <iostream>
using namespace std;

class Fraction {
private:
    int num, den;        // Numerator and denominator.
public:
    Fraction() {set(0, 1);}
    Fraction(int n, int d) {set(n, d);}
    Fraction(int n) {set(n, 1);}
    Fraction(const Fraction &src)
        {set(src.num, src.den);}

    void set(int n, int d) {num = n; den = d;
    normalize();}
    int get_num() const {return num;}
    int get_den() const {return den;}
    Fraction add(const Fraction &other);
    Fraction mult(const Fraction &other);
    Fraction operator+(const Fraction &other)
        {return add(other);}
```

Fract.h, cont.

```cpp
    Fraction operator*(const Fraction &other)
        {return mult(other);}
    int operator==(const Fraction &other);
    friend ostream &operator<<(ostream &os, Fraction
      &fr);

private:
    void normalize();   // Put fraction into standard
                        // form.
    int gcf(int a, int b);  // Greatest Common Factor.
    int lcm(int a, int b);  // Lowest Common
                            // Denominator.
};
```

The code that implements Fraction-class member functions (other than those that are inlined) is placed in the file Fract.cpp. Note that this file must be added to the current project. Look at the Project and File menus for your development environment, and look for an Add New Item command.

Fract.cpp

```cpp
#include "Fract.h"

// -----------------------------------------------
// FRACTION CLASS FUNCTIONS

// Normalize: put fraction into a standard form,
//  unique for each mathematically different value.
//
void Fraction::normalize(){

    // Handle cases involving 0

    if (den == 0 || num == 0) {
        num = 0;
        den = 1;
    }

    // Put neg. sign in numerator only.
```

16

▼ *continued on next page*

```cpp
        if (den < 0) {
            num *= -1;
            den *= -1;
        }

        // Factor out GCF from numerator and denominator.

        int n = gcf(num, den);
        num = num / n;
        den = den / n;
    }

    // Greatest Common Factor
    //
    int Fraction::gcf(int a, int b) {
        if (a % b == 0)
            return abs(b);
        else
            return gcf(b, a % b);
    }

    // Lowest Common Multiple
    //
    int Fraction::lcm(int a, int b){
        return (a / gcf(a, b)) * b;
    }

    Fraction Fraction::add(const Fraction &other) {
        Fraction fract;
        int lcd = lcm(den, other.den);
        int quot1 = lcd/den;
        int quot2 = lcd/other.den;
        fract.set(num * quot1 + other.num * quot2, lcd);
        fract.normalize();
        return fract;
    }

    Fraction Fraction::mult(const Fraction &other) {
        Fraction fract;
        fract.set(num * other.num, den * other.den);
```

Fract.cpp, cont.

```
        fract.normalize();
        return fract;
    }

    int Fraction::operator==(const Fraction &other) {
        return (num == other.num && den == other.den);
    }

    // -------------------------------------------------
    // FRACTION CLASS FRIEND FUNCTION

    ostream &operator<<(ostream &os, Fraction &fr) {
        os << fr.num << "/" << fr.den;
        return os;
    }
```

Note ▶ If you are using Microsoft Visual Studio, remember that each and every .cpp file needs to start with the directive `#include <stdafx.h>`. Make sure you insert this directive at the beginning of Float.cpp as well as every other .cpp file.

How It Works

The notable thing about this example is how short the code in the file Float-Fract1.cpp is.

This subclass adds only one function, get_float. The function definition (which is so short it can be inlined) employs one trick: the code recasts the data type of the expression get_num before the division takes place. Doing this causes the program to use floating-point division and produce a floating-point result.

```
        double get_float() {
            return static_cast<double>(get_num())/get_den();}
```

In looking at this function definition, you may wonder: why does the code use the get_num and get_den functions to get the values of num and den, respectively? Aren't these members, and therefore, can't their values be accessed directly?

If you were writing code for the Fraction class itself, that would be true. But this is not Fraction class code—it is FloatFraction code. And num and den, which are private members, cannot be accessed directly by other classes . . .

including Fraction's own subclasses! Therefore, FloatFraction code is forced to use get_num and get_den to get the values of these members.

The main function takes advantage of the new FloatFraction member function (get_float) as well as an inherited member function (set).

```
fract1.set(1, 2);
cout << "Value of 1/2 is " << fract1.get_float()
  << endl;
fract1.set(3, 5);
cout << "Value of 3/5 is " << fract1.get_float()
  << endl;
```

EXERCISES

Exercise 16.1.1. Alter Example 16.1 so that it includes a set_float member function in the FloatFraction class. The function should take an argument of type **double**, and use it to set the values of num and den. One way to do this is to (1) multiply the value by 100 and then round to an integer, (2) set num to this value, (3) set den to 100, and (4) call normalize. Note: if you use the **set** function to do steps (2) and (3), step (4) is carried out automatically. Hint: to round to an integer, use an **int** data cast:

```
new_value = static_cast<int>(value * 100.0);
```

Exercise 16.1.2. Write a constructor for the FloatFraction class that takes a single argument of type **double**. This should be easy if you've completed Exercise 16.1.1.

Problems with the FloatFraction Class

Creating a subclass is *almost* as easy as I made it look in the previous section. Unfortunately, as soon as you do some experimenting with FloatFraction objects, you'll quickly see that the class has limitations.

For example, the following innocent-looking code does just what you'd want it to do, given a complete Fraction class:

```
Fraction f1(1, 2);
f1 = f1 + Fraction(1, 3);
if (f1 == Fraction(5, 6))
    cout << "1/2 + 1/3 = 5/6";
```

But if you use the FloatFraction class—which, according to what I've said, ought to support everything the Fraction class does—each of these statements produces errors.

```
FloatFraction f1(1, 2);              // Error!
f1 = f1 + FloatFraction(1, 3);       // Error!
if (f1 == FloatFraction(5, 6))       // Error!
    cout << "1/2 + 1/3 = 5/6";
```

There are two sources of problems in the current version of the FloatFraction class, each of which is fairly easy to correct.

▶ One problem is that subclasses do not inherit constructors.

▶ Another source of problems is that many Fraction class functions return objects (or take arguments) of type Fraction, not FloatFraction.

Let's consider each of these in turn. The issue with constructors is so significant that it deserves to be another cardinal rule:

✱   **A subclass does not inherit constructors. (Therefore, do not rely on the constructors of the base class.)**

It may seem unfair of C++ not to let constructors be inherited, but this exception makes a certain amount of sense. What if you have a subclass that added one or more data members to the base class? For example:

```
class FloatFraction2 : public Fraction {
public:
    double float_amt;
    int whole;
};
```

The Fraction constructors set the values of num and den by calling the set function, which also calls the normalize function to adjust those two values as needed. But what, in this case, should be done with the new data members float_amt and whole?

The philosophy of C++ is that you should write your own constructors, even when creating a subclass, and that you ought to initialize each member. Because a base-class constructor may not be adequate (because it cannot possibly initialize the new members), C++ takes the view that you should write an entirely new group of constructors for each subclass.

There are some exceptions even to *that* rule, however. I've noted in other chapters that the compiler supplies three special member functions if the author of the class does not supply them. The situation becomes a little more complicated with subclasses, but similar rules apply. Each of these functions ends up using the base class.

16

Default Constructors for Subclasses

The compiler automatically supplies a default constructor if the author of the class writes no constructors at all for *that particular class*. Because the current version of the FloatFraction class contains no constructor declarations of its own, the compiler supplies a default constructor.

The general rule for an automatic default constructor (taking subclasses into account) is that first it calls the default constructor of the base class. It then zeroes out each of the new data members in the subclass.

Note ▶ If a member is itself an object, then (in this situation) that object's own default constructor is called.

Copy Constructors for Subclasses

As I described earlier, the compiler supplies an automatic copy constructor if the class code itself does not declare one. This compiler-supplied version first calls the base-class copy constructor. It then performs a straight member-by-member copy of each of the new data members.

Assignment Function for Subclasses

You may be able to guess what this does: the automatic assignment function (supplied by the compiler if you don't write one) first calls the base-class assignment function. It then performs a straight member-by-member copy of each of the new data members.

Add the Missing Constructors

The missing constructors for the FloatFraction class are easy to supply. They need do no more than the corresponding Fraction constructors do.

```
FloatFraction() {set(0, 1);}
FloatFraction(int n, int d) {set(n, d);}
FloatFraction(int n) {set(n, 1);}
FloatFraction(const FloatFraction &src)
    {set(src.get_num(), src.get_den());}
```

To produce this code, I copied and pasted the Fraction constructors and changed each occurrence of "Fraction" to "FloatFraction"—which is easy to do with a word processor or text editor.

I also had to make one other change. You'd like to keep the definition of the copy constructor simple, so that it looks like this:

```
FloatFraction(const FloatFraction &src)
    {set(src.num, src.den);}    // ERROR! Private!
```

The problem is that num and den are private members—of the Fraction class. This means they are not accessible from other classes, not even subclasses of Fraction! (That's a problem I'll revisit in this chapter.) Consequently, in Float Fraction code, you need to use the public functions get_num and get_den.

Resolving Type Conflicts with the Base Class

If you do serious experimentation with the FloatFraction class, you'll find that most of the operations don't work. The set function is an important exception; it is about the only inherited function that does work.

But C++ is not being as unreasonable as it first might appear. For example, consider how the `Fraction::add` function is declared.

```
Fraction add(const Fraction &other);
```

This function is fully inherited and supported in the FloatFraction class. But look at what the function does: it takes an argument of type Fraction (not Float-Fraction) and returns an argument of type Fraction (again, not FloatFraction).

Consequently, you *can* use the add function in statements like this:

```
Fraction f1, f2;
FloatFraction ff;
f1 = ff.add(f2);
```

This code uses all the types correctly, because it takes pains to use the Fraction class to pass and receive values. But its usefulness is limited.

What you'd really like to do—but currently cannot—is to create expressions that mix FloatFraction objects with other FloatFraction objects:

```
FloatFraction f0, f1, f2;
f1 = f0.add(f2);
```

Fortunately, there is an easy solution to this category of problems. All you need to do is add another constructor: a converter from the Fraction class.

```
FloatFraction(Fraction fract)
    {set(fract.get_num(), fract.get_den());}
```

Now, all these problems go away. The add function returns an object of type Fraction, but that value is easily converted back to FloatFraction type. This approach works so well because FloatFraction contains no new data members, so nothing else needs to be done to make operations from the Fraction class work correctly. But (as you'll see in the Example 16.4, later in the chapter) if there are new data members involved, you may need to override some of the Fraction member functions.

Example 16.2. ## The Completed FloatFraction Class

To make the FloatFraction class work the way we'd expect it to, it's necessary to supply all the needed constructors, as well as to supply a constructor of type FloatFraction(Fraction). Here's the completed code.

```cpp
FloatFract2.cpp

#include <iostream>
#include "Fract.h"
using namespace std;

class FloatFraction : public Fraction {
public:
    FloatFraction() {set(0, 1);}
    FloatFraction(int n, int d) {set(n, d);}
    FloatFraction(int n) {set(n, 1);}
    FloatFraction(const FloatFraction &src)
        {set(src.get_num(), src.get_den());}
    FloatFraction(const Fraction &src)
        {set(src.get_num(), src.get_den());}

    double get_float() {
      return static_cast<double>(get_num())/get_den();
    }
};

int main() {
    FloatFraction f1(1, 2), f2(1, 3), f3;

    f3 = f1 + f2;
    cout << "Value of f3 is " << f3 << endl;
    cout << "Float value of f3 is " << f3.get_float()
      << endl;
    return 0;
}
```

How It Works

This example should be straightforward. The revised declaration for Float-Fraction includes all the needed constructors, so declarations such as the following are now fully supported:

```
FloatFraction f1(1, 2), f2(1, 3), f3;
```

The class also includes the constructor that converts from Fraction to Float-Fraction:

```
FloatFraction(const Fraction &src)
        {set(src.get_num(), src.get_den());}
```

Because of this last constructor, all the operations declared in the Fraction class now work smoothly with the FloatFraction class—it's no longer a problem that the `operator+` function returns a Fraction object, for example, because this object is converted back to FloatFraction type as needed. Therefore, the following statement works without a hitch:

```
f3 = f1 + f2;
```

EXERCISES

Exercise 16.2.1.   Revise the main function in Example 16.2 so that it demonstrates successful use of the test-for-equality operator (==) as well as addition and multiplication.

Example 16.2.2.   Answer the question: given this completed version of FloatFraction, can you freely mix FloatFraction and Fraction objects in all contexts?

Example 16.3. *The ProperFraction Class*

This section demonstrates how inheritance can be extended by creating the subclass of a subclass. It isn't always necessary to write classes in this manner; you can instead subclass the same base class directly, any number of times (creating a "flat" hierarchy of classes.) But it's useful to know that a subclass can in turn become a base class for some other subclass.

Each time you subclass, and create another level in hierarchy, you add more abilities and/or more capacity to hold data. As I suggested earlier—with the Dog/Mammal/Animal bit—a subclass should ideally be considered a more specialized version of the base class. This is a cardinal rule:

✳   **Generally you should subclass an existing class to add more specialized abilities or qualities to that class.**

Again, if A is a subclass of B, A should be considered *a kind of* B, just as Dog is *a kind of* Mammal.

But to be candid, that's all part of the theoretical framework of object orientation. Sometimes you subclass because that's the easiest way to get something to work. Assume for the sake of argument that you already have the FloatFraction class declared, and you want to add some more functions to produce the ProperFraction class. This example shows how you can subclass FloatFraction, which itself is a subclass of Fraction.

PropFract1.cpp

```cpp
#include <iostream>
#include "Fract.h"
using namespace std;

class FloatFraction : public Fraction {
public:
    FloatFraction() {set(0, 1);}
    FloatFraction(int n, int d) {set(n, d);}
    FloatFraction(int n) {set(n, 1);}
    FloatFraction(const FloatFraction &src)
        {set(src.get_num(), src.get_den());}
    FloatFraction(const Fraction &src)
        {set(src.get_num(), src.get_den());}

    double get_float() {
      return static_cast<double>(get_num())/get_den();
    }
};

class ProperFraction : public FloatFraction {
public:
    ProperFraction() {set(0, 1);}
    ProperFraction(int n, int d) {set(n, d);}
    ProperFraction(int n) {set(n, 1);}
    ProperFraction(const ProperFraction &src)
        {set(src.Fraction::get_num(), src.get_den());}
    ProperFraction(const FloatFraction &src)
        {set(src.Fraction::get_num(), src.get_den());}
```

```cpp
    ProperFraction(const Fraction &src)
        {set(src.Fraction::get_num(), src.get_den());}


    void pr_proper(ostream &os);
    int get_whole();
    int get_num();              // OVERRIDDEN FUNCTION!
};

int main() {
    ProperFraction f1(1, 2), f2(5, 6), f3;

    f3 = f1 + f2;
    cout << "Value of f3 is ";
    f3.pr_proper(cout);
    cout << endl;
    cout << "Float value of f3 is " << f3.get_float()
      << endl;
    return 0;
}

// PROPERFRACTION FUNCTIONS
//-------------------------------------------------

// Print Proper Fraction function:
// Using the output stream (os) specified, print an
//  object in the form "1 1/2"
//
void ProperFraction::pr_proper(ostream &os) {
    if (get_whole() != 0)
        os << get_whole() << " ";
    os << get_num() << "/" << get_den();
}

// Get Whole function
// Return whole-number portion by using integer
// division.
//
int ProperFraction::get_whole() {
```

▼ continued on next page

PropFract1.cpp, cont.

```
        int n = Fraction::get_num();
        return n / get_den();
    }

    // Get Numerator function (OVERRIDDEN)
    // Return numerator for a proper fraction, by using
    //  modulus (remainder) division.
    //
    int ProperFraction::get_num() {
        int n = Fraction::get_num();
        return n % get_den();
    }
```

How It Works

This example introduces a couple of new twists:

▶ The get_num function, which is one of the most commonly used functions from the Fraction class, is overridden in the ProperFraction class. This complicates matters, forcing you to specify which version of the get_num function to use.

▶ The inheritance scheme is a little more complicated. To ensure all the class operations work correctly, you need to supply a conversion from the Fraction class as well as from the immediate base class, FloatFraction.

The get_num function is overridden here because this function should behave differently. Here's how the class is intended to work: Suppose an object stores the value 5/2; this is equivalent to the proper fraction 2 1/2. For a Fraction object, the following code should print "5/2".

```
Fraction fract(5, 2);
cout << fract.get_num() << "/";
cout << fract.get_den();
```

But for a ProperFraction object, the same code should print "1/2". That's because it's part of the following statements, which print "2 1/2".

```
ProperFraction fract(5, 2);
cout << fract.get_whole() << " ";
cout << fract.get_num() << "/";
cout << fract.get_den();
```

In a proper fraction, which isolates the integer portion, the numerator should be output as 1, not 5.

A ProperFraction object stores data internally exactly as a Fraction object does. Assume you set them the same way:

```
Fraction fract1(5,2);
ProperFraction fract2(5, 2);
```

Both the ProperFraction object and the Fraction object store a value of 5 for num and 2 for den. The difference in these objects is in how they behave when a user of the object gets a value. If you call the get_num function, the Fraction object returns 5, while the ProperFraction object should return 1.

The get_num function therefore needs to behave differently.

Complicating things further is the fact that in order to implement Proper-Fraction's version of the get_num function, you need a way to get the value of num directly. But the only way to do that is to call the original version of get_num, which has been overridden!

Fortunately, C++ provides a simple solution: even when you've overridden a member, you can always refer to the base-class version by using the scope operator (::). By using this notation, you can call the original version of get_num.

```
int ProperFraction::get_num() {
    int n = Fraction::get_num();
    return n % get_den();
}
```

This works even though Fraction is an *indirect* base class of ProperFraction.

The rest of the code is fairly straightforward. Constructors need to be provided for the ProperFraction class, including constructors that convert from the immediate base class FloatFraction and its base class, Fraction.

```
ProperFraction() {set(0, 1);}
ProperFraction(int n, int d) {set(n, d);}
ProperFraction(int n) {set(n, 1);}
ProperFraction(const ProperFraction &src)
    {set(src.Fraction::get_num(), src.get_den());}
ProperFraction(const FloatFraction &src)
    {set(src.Fraction::get_num(), src.get_den());}
ProperFraction(const Fraction &src)
    {set(src.Fraction::get_num(), src.get_den());}
```

Again, it's necessary to use the scope operator (::) to specify the base-class version of get_num.

EXERCISES

Exercise 16.3.1. Write an `operator<<` function that works with the ProperFraction class, enabling you to print to **cout** (and other output streams) directly. Review the coding techniques in Chapter 13 as needed. Remember that this function needs to be a global function declared as a friend.

```
ProperFraction pf;
//...
cout << pf << endl;
```

Exercise 16.3.2. Write a constructor for the ProperFraction class that takes three **int** arguments—w, n, and d—representing whole-number portion, numerator, and denominator, respectively. For example, you could initialize an object to 4 2/3 by using the inputs 4, 2, and 3.

```
ProperFraction pf(4, 2, 3);
```

Private and Protected Members

Throughout much of this chapter, the problem of accessing num and den has complicated things. The subclasses FloatFraction and ProperFraction do inherit the two data members, num and den. However, because these members are private, they are not accessible in code (except, of course, in the code of the Fraction class itself). Even subclass code cannot refer to private members. They are there, but invisible.

Consequently, in the subclass function-definition code, you have to resort to the get_num and get_den functions to get at the values of num and den. Matters become more complicated, as we've seen, when one of these functions (get_num) is overridden. Things would be easier if subclasses could refer to num and den directly. Then this function:

```
int ProperFraction::get_num() {
    int n = Fraction::get_num();
    return n / get_den();
}
```

could be rewritten this way:

```
int ProperFraction::get_num() {
    return num / den;
}
```

This function would then be so short it could be inlined:

```
int get_num() {return num / den;}
```

It would seem to make sense to let subclasses refer to num and den, wouldn't it? The ideal arrangement might be to let subclass code access the data, while restricting access from code that is neither Fraction-class code nor that of any subclass.

There is a way to do that. C++ supports a third access level—protected—which is midway between private and public. If num and den had been given this access level (through the use of the **protected** keyword), then all the subclasses could refer to them directly.

```
class Fraction {
protected:
    int num, den;       // Numerator and denominator.
    //...
```

Notably, members declared with **protected** still have restricted access. Only the Fraction class itself and its (direct or indirect) subclasses can refer to protected members.

So, isn't the solution to alter the Fraction class declaration in this way?

Maybe, but in some cases that isn't possible. If the Fraction class has already been compiled and given to you by another programmer, you may not be able to alter the class. In that case, you have to work around the limitations of private data as best you can.

Another, deeper question is: *should* class members be declared protected rather than private? Although it's usually clear what should be public, the decision to make something protected or private is not always obvious. When you declare something private, you're saying you don't want anyone to alter it or pay attention to it (not even yourself) when writing a subclass. It probably makes sense, for example, to make the support functions (lcd, gcf) private, because no one should really mess with these. They are called only by the normalize function, and that's really the only function that should use it.

Other members might be made protected. The normalize function itself is probably a good candidate, since this function is useful generally. And authors of a subclass would find it useful to refer to the data members, num and den, as we've seen.

But problems could arise if the author of a subclass tried to set num and den directly rather than relying on the "set" function. So, it may make sense to keep num and den private, depending on how much you trust the people who might try to write a subclass.

Here's a summary of the three access levels in C++.

16

Table 16.1: Access Levels in C++

ACCESS LEVEL	DESCRIPTION
public	The member can be accessed by any function, whether part of the class or not.
protected	The member can be accessed by a function only if it is a member of the class or of a subclass.
private	The member can be accessed by a function only if it is a member of the class.

Example 16.4.   *Contained Members: FractionUnits*

I end this chapter with a variation that contains a new data member, `units`. The new data members added by a subclass can have any valid type, and here I'm using an object type—that is, another class. As I stated earlier, this other type— String—is not part of the class hierarchy but is *contained* in the class that uses it.

As I've done in the last couple of examples, I assume that all the code for the base class, Fraction, is placed into the files Fract.h and Fract.cpp, which need to be added to the project. Here I assume the same thing for the String class, which should be supported by the files StringClass.h and StringClass.cpp. To run the next example, first create these files from the code in Chapter 15. Alternatively, you can use the built-in C++ **string** class; see the note after the end of this code listing.

FractionUnits1.cpp

```
#include <iostream>
#include <string.h>
#include "Fract.h"
#include "StringClass.h"
using namespace std;

class FractionUnits : public Fraction {
public:
    String units;

    FractionUnits() {set(0, 1);}
    FractionUnits(int n, int d) {set(n, d);}
    FractionUnits(int n) {set(n, 1);}
```

FractionUnits1.cpp, cont.

```cpp
        FractionUnits(const Fraction &src)
            {set(src.get_num(), src.get_den());}
        FractionUnits(const FractionUnits &src)
            {set(src.get_num(), src.get_den());
              units = src.units;}

        // OVERRIDDEN FUNCTIONS

        FractionUnits add(const FractionUnits &other);
        FractionUnits operator+(const FractionUnits
        &other)
            {return add(other);}
        int operator--(const FractionUnits &other);

        friend ostream &operator<<(ostream &os,
          FractionUnits &fr);
};

int main() {
    FractionUnits f1(1, 2), f2(4, 3);
    f1.units = "feet";
    f2.units = "feet";
    FractionUnits f3 = f1 + f2;
    cout << "The length of the item is " << f3 << endl;
    return 0;
}

// FRACTIONUNIT FUNCTIONS
//---------------------------------------------

FractionUnits FractionUnits::add(const FractionUnits
  &other) {
    FractionUnits fr = Fraction::add(other);
    if (units == other.units)
        fr.units = units;
    return fr;
}

int FractionUnits::operator==(const FractionUnits
  &other) {
```

▼ *continued on next page*

FractionUnits1.cpp, cont.

```
        return Fraction::operator==(other) && units ==
        other.units;
    }

    ostream &operator<<(ostream &os, FractionUnits &fr) {
        os << fr.get_num() << "/" << fr.get_den();
        if (strlen(fr.units) > 0)
            os << " " << fr.units;
        return os;
    }
```

Note ▶ If your compiler supports the new **string** class, you can run this example
by (1) replacing `#include "StringClass.h"` with `#include <string>`,
(2) declaring units with the **string** class rather than String, and (3) in the
`operator<<` function, calculating the length of the string by using `fr.unit.
size()` rather than `strlen(fr.units)`.

How It Works

As with the other examples in this chapter, the FractionUnit class declares its
own constructors (because, remember, constructors are not inherited).

```
        FractionUnits() {set(0, 1);}
        FractionUnits(int n, int d) {set(n, d);}
        FractionUnits(int n) {set(n, 1);}
        FractionUnits(const Fraction &src)
            {set(src.get_num(), src.get_den());}
        FractionUnits(const FractionUnits &src)
            {set(src.get_num(), src.get_den());
            units = src.units;}
```

In addition, the class overrides several functions. The purpose of the
FractionUnit class is to let the user of the class store the name of some sort of
units (for example, "feet", "inches", "pounds", or "meters"). It declares a new data
member—`units`—and makes it public so that the user of a FractionUnits
object can set this member directly.

The class implements certain behavior that makes working with units easier.
(This is a fundamental concept in object orientation, of course: data structures
and behavior should be designed and built together.)

▶ When you add two objects containing the same kind of units, those units should be preserved. For example, adding 1/2 inches to 1/3 inches should produce 5/6 inches. The add and operator+ functions are therefore overridden.

▶ When you compare two FractionUnits objects, they should be considered equal only if they have the same units. For example, 1/4 feet is equal to 1/4 feet but not to 1/4 miles. The operator== function is therefore overridden.

▶ When you print a FractionUnits object to the console, it should print the units, if any. For example,

```
FractionUnits fr(1, 2);
fr.units = "miles";
cout << fr;
```

In summary, the class needs to override the add, operator==, and operator+ functions, and to support a new version of the operator<< function.

```
FractionUnits add(const FractionUnits &other);
FractionUnits operator+(const FractionUnits &other)
    {return add(other);}
int operator==(const FractionUnits &other);
```

The function definitions here use base-class code as much as possible, observing the object-oriented principle that reuse is a good thing. For example, the overridden add function calls the base-class version (Fraction::add) to do most of the work.

```
FractionUnits FractionUnits::add(const FractionUnits
    &other) {
    FractionUnits fr = Fraction::add(other);
    if (units == other.units)
        fr.units = units;
    return fr;
}
```

The operator+ function is an interesting case here. Although the inline definition would seem to do exactly what the Fraction class version does, it actually doesn't. Both versions call the add function—but each calls the version of the add function *defined in its own class*. If this function were not overridden, operator+ would call Fraction::add, not FractionUnits::add.

```
FractionUnits operator+(const FractionUnits &other)
    {return add(other);}
```

Finally, although the operator<< function is not, technically speaking, overridden (since it is not a member function), for the code provides a version

16

that interacts with the FractionUnits class. Because of function overloading, this code does not create conflicts with the Fraction class version of `operator<<`.

```
friend ostream &operator<<(ostream &os,
    FractionUnits &fr);
```

EXERCISE

Exercise 16.4.1.   Implement multiplication for the FractionUnits class by overriding the `mult` and `operator*` functions. Any combination of units should be allowed. If one object contains units having string s and the other is an empty string, the units should be set to s. If one contains string s1 and the other contains string s2, the resulting units should be `s1 * s2`. For example, `1/2 feet` multiplied by `3/4 sec` should yield `3/8 feet * sec`.

Chapter 16   *Summary*

Here are the main points of Chapter 16:

▶ To declare a subclass of an existing class, use this syntax:

```
class class_name : public base_class {
    declarations
};
```

▶ The **public** keyword in this context is not required by the syntax, but it is strongly recommended (particularly when you are first learning C++). If the base-class has **private** access level, then all members in the base class become private when they are inherited by the subclass.

▶ All the members of a base class are inherited by the subclass (except for constructors).

▶ The declarations in the subclass may specify new members—which become members of the class along with inherited members—as well as existing members of the base class. Doing the latter *overrides* the base-class declaration. Generally, it only makes sense to override member functions in order to provide different behavior.

▶ By default, the name of a class member refers to the version in *that specific class*, so (for example) if "foo" is an overridden function, the use of "foo" refers to the new version, not that of the base class. However, you can choose to specify the base-class version by using the scope operator (::). For example, in the following definition, the get_num function defined in the ProperFraction class calls the version defined in Fraction (the base class).

```
int ProperFraction::get_num() {
    int n = Fraction::get_num();
    return n % get_den();
}
```

▶ Remember, constructors are not inherited by subclasses. Each subclass must declare its own.

▶ As always, the compiler supplies an automatic version of the default constructor, copy constructor, and the operator= function, as described in previous chapters. For subclasses, each of these compiler-supplied functions calls the base-class version. For example, the default constructor calls the base-class default constructor and then sets each new member of the subclass to a zero or null value. (But note: as always, the compiler supplies the default constructor only if you write no constructors at all.)

▶ It's often helpful to write a constructor that converts an object of the base class into an object of the subclass. This can solve type conflicts when member functions are inherited. For example:

```
class FloatFraction : public Fraction {
public:
//...
    FloatFraction(const Fraction &src)
        {set(src.get_num(), src.get_den());}
```

▶ Private members of a base class are inherited by a subclass but are not accessible in subclass code. To declare members accessible by code in any and all subclasses—but not by code outside the class hierarchy—declare them as **protected**. (These members are also accessible by code in indirect subclasses down through any number of generations.)

```
protected:
    int num, den;
```

▶ Classes (subclasses as well as ordinary classes) can contain objects as members—which means that one class can contain instances of another.

16

Polymorphism: Object Independence

17

To be most useful, objects need independence. Each should act as though it were a miniature computer that can send and respond to messages. As long as a new object type uses the appropriate interface, you should be able to plug it into existing software.

Literally, polymorphism means "many forms." On the most basic level, it means the ability to implement the same operation multiple ways. Stated that way, it's trivial. But the real point is this: without changing anything about the code that uses an object, you can substitute another object type and the program will still work.

Consider an analogy. Your word processor can successfully interact with any kind of printer you purchase. You can even, five years from now, remove an old printer and hook up a printer which today doesn't even exist. The people who write word processors today don't need to know about all the types of printers that will be developed in the future.

That's the reason for polymorphism: to make software objects work like pieces of hardware, which can work together and be interchanged as needed. Old software can smoothly connect to ever newer software . . . and that's what reusability is all about.

A Different Approach to the FloatFraction Class

Understanding polymorphism begins with understanding virtual functions and when you need them. I'll start with a programming problem that demonstrates the simple use of virtual functions.

The FloatFraction class of Chapter 16 produced a floating-point (**double**) value "on the fly"—that is, it calculated the floating-point value whenever the user of the object asked for that value by calling get_float.

That's a valid technique and is often quite sufficient. But calculating the floating-point value takes up valuable processor time. You might want to avoid this calculation, by instead using a persistent floating-point value. This is a superior way to do things if the client code (the code using the class) refers to the floating-point value many times a second and you want to make those references more efficient.

To implement this technique, you'd do the following:

▶ Declare a new data member, float_val, which stores the floating-point value for the class. This makes the floating-point value persistent, so it's never recalculated except when necessary.

▶ Override the normalize function so it calculates the floating-point value in addition to performing its other tasks. Doing this, of course, assumes you have access to the normalize function, so assume that normalize was originally declared with the **protected** keyword.

The beauty of this strategy is its simplicity. Overriding the normalize function is a comprehensive way to make sure that float_val (the data member) is calculated only as needed.

The Fraction class code, as well as the code of all subclasses, always assigns data values by calling the set member function, which in turn calls normalize after setting the values of num and den. Therefore, all you have to do is override normalize to ensure that float_val is recalculated whenever there are new values.

Here is the overridden version of normalize:

```
void FloatFraction::normalize() {
    Fraction::normalize();
    float_val = static_cast<double>(get_num()) /
        get_den();
}
```

That's all that has to be done inside this function definition. Notice that you don't have to rewrite normalize in its entirety . . . most of the work is done by calling the base-class version Fraction::normalize. The only new line of code is the one that sets the value of the data member float_val.

Unfortunately, there's a problem. There are now *two* versions of normalize—Fraction::normalize and FloatFraction::normalize. Which version does the set function call? To review, here is the definition of set in the Fraction class:

```
void set(int n, int d)
    {num = n; den = d; normalize();}
```

You might think that the call to normalize would call whatever version was defined in the class of the current object (that is, the object through which the function was called). You might think that, but you'd be wrong.

When the C++ compiler read in the definition of set in the Fraction class, it had to make a decision then and there (at compile time) about how to call the function. And to do that, it had to fix the function address. The `set` function might as well have been written this way:

```
void set(int n, int d)
     {num = n; den = d; Fraction::normalize();}
```

Consequently, the set function will never call the overridden version of normalize. And if you have ideas about overriding the set function itself, think again; for the set function needs access to two private variables—num and den—and subclasses do not have this access. A subclass, therefore, cannot successfully override the set function.

What you'd like instead would be a way to make a flexible function call—a call to a function whose actual address is not determined until runtime. (This is called *late binding*.) In that case, the call to normalize would in effect say "call *this object's* implementation of normalize." Then the call to normalize would automatically do the right thing. In a subclass such as FractionUnits, the `set` function would call the new version of normalize, not the old.

This would be a flexible way of calling a function . . . a call to an as-yet-to-be-determined function address . . . you might even say it was a call to a *virtual* function.

Virtual Functions to the Rescue!

The solution, therefore, is to make the normalize function a virtual function. And there's a way to do that—use the **virtual** keyword.

This may not always be possible after the fact, of course. For everything to work correctly, you would need (at this point) to go back and alter Fraction class code. In that code, the normalize function must be made **protected**, and declared **virtual** as well.

This is easy to do if you have the option of rewriting the Fraction class. Precede the function declaration with **protected:** and place the **virtual** keyword at the beginning of the function declaration.

```
class Fraction {
//...
protected:
    virtual void normalize();      // Put into standard
                                   // form.
//...
};
```

Other than the revisions described in the previous section, this is the only change that has to be made. Once a function is declared virtual, it is virtual forever in all contexts and in all subclasses. You never have to use the **virtual** keyword again with that function.

Better yet, you call a virtual function exactly the same way you'd call any other. Under the covers, C++ has to use a special procedure to call a virtual function. But this is invisible in the C++ source code.

There are a few restrictions.

▶ You can only make member functions virtual.

▶ Inline functions cannot be made virtual.

▶ Constructors cannot be made virtual, although—paradoxically—destructors can be.

Which functions should you make virtual? Why not just make all eligible functions virtual? Actually, there's a performance penalty paid whenever a virtual function is called—but it's a slight one. Therefore, a good general guideline is this:

✳ **Any member function that might be overridden by a subclass should be declared virtual.**

It's legal for a subclass to override a function that is not virtual, but doing so creates a risk that in certain contexts the right function might not get called (as we saw with normalize in the previous section). If you think a member function might be overridden, make it virtual.

Interlude

What Is the Virtual Penalty?

Although it's not necessary to know how virtual function calls are implemented by C++, it's useful to understand something about the trade-off: virtual functions are more flexible, but there is a small penalty to be paid. If you're really sure that a certain function will never be overridden, there is no point in making it virtual, especially if you want your programs to be as efficient as possible.

The penalty, however, is small one, particularly when one considers the impressive speed and memory capacity of today's computers. There are actually two penalties, which are closely linked: a performance penalty and a space penalty.

Interlude

▼ *continued*

When a C++ program executes a standard function call, it does what I outlined in Chapter 4: it temporarily transfers control of the program to a specific address and returns when the function is done. This is a simple action you can visualize this way:

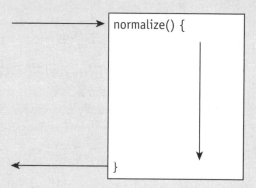

Execution of a virtual function is more involved. Each object contains a hidden "vtable" pointer that points to a table of all the virtual functions for its particular class. For example, all objects of class FloatFraction contain a vtable pointer to the table of virtual functions for FloatFraction. (If a class has no virtual functions at all, by the way, its objects don't need to have a vtable pointer, and that saves some space.)

To call a virtual function, the program uses the vtable pointer to make an indirect function call. This process, in effect, looks up the correct function address at runtime. (Remember, this is done under the covers and so is completely invisible to the C++ source code.) You can visualize the action this way:

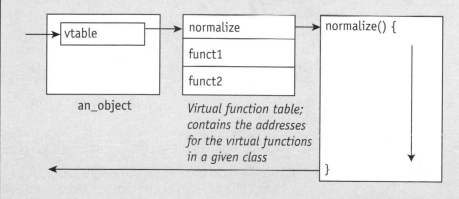

an_object

*Virtual function table;
contains the addresses
for the virtual functions
in a given class*

▼ *continued on next page*

17

Interlude

▼ *continued*

Because each object contains a vtable pointer, you can say that *the knowledge of how to carry out an action is built into the object itself,* as I stated at the beginning of the chapter. The vtable pointer enables each individual object to have this "knowledge," because it points to function implementations specific to its own class.

Clearly there are some penalties, however slight. The performance penalty arises from the slightly greater time required to make an indirect function call compared to a direct one (although that difference is measured in microseconds). The space penalty arises from the bytes taken up by the vtable pointer and the table itself (although that's a trivial amount of space in terms of today's memory capacities). The moral: make a function virtual if there's any chance it will be overridden. The cost is slight.

Example 17.1. *The Revised FloatFraction Class*

This next example demonstrates the FloatFraction class. The code here presumes that Fraction function-definition code is contained in the file Fract.cpp (which must be added to any project that uses the Fraction class). While I don't list Fract.cpp here, I do list Fract.h to show changes that need to be made to the Fraction class declaration.

Here's the new version of FloatFraction, which contains a new data member float_val and overrides the normalize function. Lines that have been added or changed from the earlier version of FloatFraction (from Chapter 16) are in bold.

FloatFract3.cpp

```cpp
#include <iostream>
#include "fract.h"
using namespace std;

class FloatFraction : public Fraction {
public:
    double float_val;

    FloatFraction() {set(0, 1);}
    FloatFraction(int n, int d) {set(n, d);}
    FloatFraction(int n) {set(n, 1);}
    FloatFraction(const FloatFraction &src)
```

FloatFract3.cpp, cont.

```cpp
            {set(src.get_num(), src.get_den());}
        FloatFraction(const Fraction &src)
            {set(src.get_num(), src.get_den());}

        void normalize();    // OVERRIDDEN
};

void FloatFraction::normalize() {
    Fraction::normalize();
    float_val = static_cast<double>(get_num()) /
      get_den();
}

int main() {
    FloatFraction fract1(1, 4), fract2(1, 2);

    FloatFraction fract3 = fract1 + fract2;
    cout << "1/4 + 1/2 = " << fract3 << endl;
    cout << "Floating pt value is = "
      << fract3.float_val;
}
```

Here is the revised version of the file Fract.h, which contains the Fraction class declarations. The one line that needs to be altered is in bold.

Fract.h

```cpp
    #include <iostream>
    using namespace std;

    class Fraction {
    private:
        int num, den;       // Numerator and denominator.
    public:
        Fraction() {set(0, 1);}
        Fraction(int n, int d) {set(n, d);}
        Fraction(int n) {set(n, 1);}
        Fraction(const Fraction &src) {set(src.n, src.d);}
```

▼ continued on next page

17

Fract.h, cont.

```
        void set(int n, int d) {num = n; den = d;
                                 normalize();}
    int get_num() const {return num;}
    int get_den() const {return den;}
    Fraction add(const Fraction &other);
    Fraction mult(const Fraction &other);
    Fraction operator+(const Fraction &other)
        {return add(other);}
    Fraction operator*(const Fraction &other)
        {return mult(other);}
    int operator==(const Fraction &other);
    friend ostream &operator<<(ostream &os, Fraction
        &fr);

protected:
    virtual void normalize();    // Put into standard
                                 // form.
private:
    int gcf(int a, int b);  // Greatest Common Factor.
    int lcm(int a, int b);  // Lowest Common
                                 // Denominator.

};
```

How It Works

This program follows the strategy outlined earlier. The floating-point value is made persistent and is only recalculated as needed.

```
class FloatFraction : public Fraction {
public:
    double float_val;
//...
```

The key to this example is the overridden normalize function. The new version of normalize recalculates the value of float_val, so that float_value is always updated whenever changes are made to the object.

```
void FloatFraction::normalize() {
    Fraction::normalize();
```

```
float_val = static_cast<double>(get_num()) /
    get_den();
}
```

The set function is inherited from the base class (Fraction) and it makes the call to normalize.

```
void set(int n, int d)
    {num = n; den = d; normalize();}
```

This function correctly calls the new version of normalize (FloatFraction::normalize) even though it is a Fraction member function which *knows nothing about the existence of any subclasses!* This works because normalize is declared with the **virtual** keyword in the Fraction class. And that keyword says, in effect, "Don't determine which version of this function to call until runtime."

```
protected:
    virtual void normalize();    // Put into standard
                                 // form.
```

Note that if this function had been declared **protected** and **virtual** in the beginning, there would be no need to alter or recompile it now.

The main function tests the FloatFraction class by declaring FloatFraction objects and then accessing the new member float_val.

```
FloatFraction fract1(1, 4), fract2(1, 2);

FloatFraction fract3 = fract1 + fract2;
cout << "1/4 + 1/2 = " << fract3 << NL;
cout << "Floating pt value is = "
    << fract3.float_val;
```

This code should print the value 0.75 if everything works correctly.

Improving the Code

Although I made float_val a public member, that wasn't necessarily the best approach. Providing public access to float_val has some of the same drawbacks that providing public access to num and den would have. It's fine to let users of the class get the value of float_val directly, but errors can result if they're allowed to manipulate the value. This is another case where data access ought to be controlled, and that's one of the principal uses of member functions.

But you'd like to get the value without that costly function-call overhead. The solution is to inline the function, just as is done for get_num and get_den.

Here is the complete revised version of FloatFraction with the altered lines in bold.

FloatFract2.cpp

```cpp
#include <iostream>
#include "fract.h"
using namespace std;

class FloatFraction : public Fraction {
private:
    double float_val;

public:
    FloatFraction() {set(0, 1);}
    FloatFraction(int n, int d) {set(n, d);}
    FloatFraction(int n) {set(n, 1);}
    FloatFraction(const FloatFraction &src)
        {set(src.get_num(), src.get_den());}
    FloatFraction(const Fraction &src)
        {set(src.get_num(), src.get_den());}

    double get_float(); {return float_val;}
    void normalize();   // OVERRIDDEN
};

void FloatFraction::normalize() {
    Fraction::normalize();
    float_val = (double) get_num) / get_den;
}

int main() {
    FloatFraction fract1(1, 4), fract2(1, 2);

    FloatFraction fract3 = fract1 + fract2;
    cout << "1/4 + 1/2 = " << fract3 << endl;
    cout << "Floating pt value is = "
      << fract3.get_float();
}
```

EXERCISE

Exercise 17.1.1.   In the overridden version of normalize (FloatFraction::normalize), add the following statement:

```
cout << "I am now in FloatFraction::normalize!" << endl;
```

When printed, this message tells you that the overridden version of normalize is being executed rather than the base-class version. Rebuild and rerun the program, noting how many times the message is printed. Then, alter Fract.h by removing the **virtual** keyword from the declaration. What you should find is that the message is not printed, verifying that the use of **virtual** is necessary to get the right implementation to execute. (You should also find that float_val member contains garbage.)

"Pure Virtual" and Other Arcane Matters

With any luck, I've convinced you that virtual functions matter. The issue is that of always getting the right implementation to execute even when the function is overridden.

Remember, you can choose to execute the base-class version of a function by specifying it in code, if that's what you want.

```
Fraction::normalize();
```

But if you don't make this specification, then presumably you want an object to execute its *own* version of a function, not that of a base class. And that's when virtual functions are necessary. It's a matter of getting function calls to "do the right thing" even though the base class has no knowledge of how a subclass might choose to implement a function.

The implications of this ability go further than you might suspect. Inheritance hierarchies are deeply ingrained in development systems such as Microsoft Foundation Classes (used with Visual C++) and the Java library. (Though not the same as C++, Java is a language closely based on C++ concepts and shares much of its syntax.)

Virtual functions are critical to all such inheritance hierarchies. In a system such as Visual C++, Java, or even Visual Basic, you subclass a general Form, Window, or Document class to create your own form, window, or document. The operating system calls on this object to perform certain tasks—Repaint, Resize, Move, and so on. These actions are all implemented as virtual functions (although that may not be obvious in Visual Basic). The use of virtual functions is what ensures *your* functions are called using *your* implementation of *your* code.

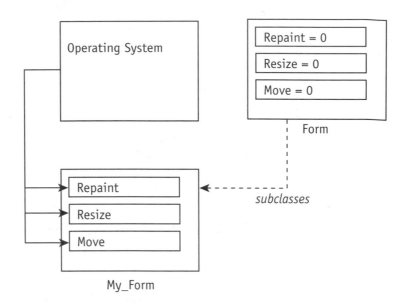

Central to this idea is the concept of *interface*, which is explicitly a part of the Java language but is implemented through class inheritance in C++.

Before discussing interfaces, I first need to talk about a strange concept: *pure virtual functions*. A pure virtual function is one that has no implementation at all—at least, not in the base class. You indicate a pure virtual function by using the notation "= 0". For example, a class might define normalize as follows:

```
class Number {
protected:
    virtual void normalize() = 0;
};
```

Here, the normalize function is pure virtual. The declaration has no function definition.

What is the point of such declarations? Well, it all has to do with abstract classes, which I describe next.

Abstract Classes and Interfaces

An abstract class is a class that has one or more pure virtual functions—that is, virtual functions without implementations. That's the case with the Number class in the last section.

An important rule is that abstract classes cannot be *instantiated*. This intimidating word simply means that you can't use the class to declare objects.

```
Number a, b, c; // ERROR! Number is an abstract class,
                //   because it has a pure virtual funct.
                // Therefore, a, b, & c cannot be
                // created.
```

But an abstract class can be useful as a general pattern for its subclasses. Suppose you have an inheritance hierarchy for Windows development, and that this hierarchy includes an abstract Form class. You can subclass this to create individual, concrete forms.

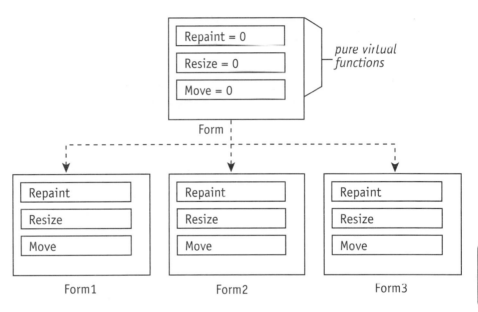

Before you can use a subclass to instantiate (that is, create) objects, it must provide function definitions for all the pure virtual functions. A class that leaves even one of these functions unimplemented is abstract, and therefore cannot be used to instantiate objects.

All this is useful in turn, because it gives you a way of specifying and enforcing a general set of services (which we might call an interface, even though this isn't Java). There are several important principles to be noted about interfaces:

▶ Each subclass is free to implement all these services (i.e., pure virtual functions) in any way it wants.

▶ Every service needs to be implemented, or the class cannot be instantiated.

▶ Every class must strictly observe type information—return type and the type of each argument. This gives the inheritance hierarchy discipline, so that actions that are obviously wrong (passing the wrong kind of data, for example) are flagged by the compiler.

The author of a subclass knows that he or she must implement the services defined in the interface—such as Repaint, Move, and Load—but within that mandate, he or she is free. And because all these functions are virtual, the correct implementation is always executed, no matter how an object is accessed.

The next section shows an example of how this is useful.

Why cout Is Not Truly Polymorphic

Let's go back to the case of **cout** and the stream operator (<<). As I noted in Chapter 10, this is a case that is almost—but not quite—polymorphic.

The virtue of using **cout** to print output (unlike C's **printf** function) is that this feature can be made to work with any class. For example, recall how it can be made to work with the Fraction class. Here is the function definition that supports this behavior.

```
ostream &operator<<(ostream &os, Fraction &fr) {
    os << fr.num << "/" << fr.den;
    return os;
}
```

So in theory one might say that for any given object the following statement can be made to work, for any type whatsoever:

```
cout << "The value of the object is " << an_object;
```

However—although this is not at first obvious—there is an important limitation to this claim I've just made. The function **cout** can work with an object only if its type is known at compile time. That means that the client code must know all about the object's type.

But isn't that always true? How can you even refer to an object whose type isn't fully defined?

Actually, it *is* possible to refer to an object whose type isn't fully defined. One way to do that is to use a **void** pointer, which is a pointer to an object of any type. But if you use such a pointer and dereference it, **cout** will not know how to print the object.

```
void *p = &an_object;
cout << *p;                    // ERROR! *p cannot be printed
```

Ideally, you ought to be able to do something like this. You ought to be able to use a dereferenced pointer to an object (that is, an expression such as *p) and have the object be printed in the correct format. Another way of saying that is: *the knowledge of how to print an object ought to be built into the object itself.*

And this is important, in turn, because of the possibilities of systems programming. You might get a pointer to a new type of object over the Internet or from another program. You'd like to know that as long as the object's class observes the appropriate interface, you could still print it in the correct format.

To do this, we can declare an abstract class named Printable, which declares a pure virtual function named print_me. In the next example, I will show how any class that subclasses Printable and implements this function can be correctly printed by **cout** (or any other **ostream** class), even if the stream is only given a general pointer.

Then the following statement will work, even though nothing at all may be known about the class of an_object beyond the fact it subclasses Printable.

```
Printable *p = &an_object

cout << *p;    // This will be printed in the correct
               //  format,as defined by the class of
               //  an_object.
```

There's an important rule that makes this code possible. An object of subclass type can be passed where a base-class object is expected. And a pointer to an object of subclass type can be passed to a pointer of base-class type. Or, to put it more simply:

✱ **Something specific (a subclass object or pointer) can always be passed to something general (a base-class object or pointer).**

The converse is not generally true (passing a base-class pointer to a subclass pointer) unless there is a conversion function to support it.

Example 17.2. ## *True Polymorphism: The Printable Class*

This next example demonstrates a way to work with **cout** (and other **ostream** classes) that is truly polymorphic. By observing a general interface—realized here as the abstract class Printable—you can correctly print any kind of object . . . even if the exact type of that object is not known at compile time.

That may, at first, seem impossible. But I mean exactly what I state. You can print an object without knowing its type, because you (that is, the client code) don't need to know how to print the object at all. The knowledge of how to be correctly printed is built into the object itself. All you have to know is that the object implements the appropriate interface.

Printme.cpp

```cpp
#include <iostream>
using namespace std;

class Printable {
    virtual void print_me(ostream &os) = 0;

    friend ostream &operator<<(ostream &os, Printable
      &pr);
};


// Operator<< function:
// All this does is cause the virtual function,
//  print_me, to be called.
//
ostream &operator<<(ostream &os, Printable &pr) {
    pr.print_me(os);
    return os;
};

// CLASSES SUBCLASSING PRINTABLE
//-------------------------------------------

class P_int : public Printable {
public:
    int n;

    P_int() {};
    P_int(int new_n) {n = new_n;}
    void print_me(ostream &os);
};

class P_dbl : public Printable {
public:
    double val;

    P_dbl() {};
```

Printme.cpp, cont.

```cpp
        P_dbl(double new_val) {val = new_val;}
        void print_me(ostream &os);
};

// IMPLEMENTATIONS OF PRINT_ME
//-------------------------------------

void P_int::print_me(ostream &os) {
    os << n;
}

void P_dbl::print_me(ostream &os) {
    os << "   " << val;
}

// MAIN FUNCTION
//-------------------------------------
int main() {
    Printable *p;
    P_int num1(5);
    P_dbl num2(6.25);

    p = &num1;
    cout << "Here is a number: " << *p << endl;
    p = &num2;
    cout << "Here is another:   " << *p << endl;
    return 0;
}
```

17

How It Works

The code in this example consists of three major parts:

▶ The abstract class Printable.

▶ The subclasses P_int and P_dbl, which contain an integer and floating point value, respectively, and which tell how to print the object.

▶ The main function, which puts all these classes to the test.

The Printable class is an abstract class, which you can also think of as an interface that defines a single service: the virtual function print_me.

```
class Printable {
    virtual void print_me(ostream &os) = 0;

    friend ostream &operator<<(ostream &os, Printable
        &pr);
};
```

The idea of the class is simple: subclasses of Printable implement the function print_me to define how they send data to an output stream (that is, to any object of the **ostream** class).

The Printable class also declares a global friend function. This function converts an expression such as this:

```
cout << an_object
```

into a call to the object's own print_me function.

```
an_object.print_me(cout)
```

Because print_me is virtual, the correct version of print_me is always called, no matter how the object is accessed. As the code in this example demonstrates, you can use a general pointer to an object.

```
Printable *p = &an_object;
//...
cout << *p;
```

Consequently, the object pointed to will be printed in the correct format for that object's class, even though the precise class may not be known at compile time. True polymorphism is achieved.

The actual implementations of print_me do little in this particular example, but that's not important. Integers and floating-point values are easily printed. I put in a small difference between them—printing a couple of extra spaces for the floating-point implementation—so that you can notice that a different version of print_me is being called.

```
void P_int::print_me(ostream &os) {
    os << n;
}

void P_dbl::print_me(ostream &os) {
    os << "  " << val;
}
```

Implementations of print_me for other classes can be much more interesting. Here, for example, is how you might implement print_me for the Fraction class:

```
void Fraction::print_me(ostream &os) {
    os << get_num() << "/" << get_den();
}
```

EXERCISE

Exercise 17.2.2.   Revise the Fraction class so it subclasses Printable and implements the print_me function. Then test the results by using code such as the following to print a Fraction object:

```
Fraction fract1(3, 4);
//...
Printable *p = &fract1;
cout << "The value is " << *p;
```

If all goes well, you should find that the Fraction object is printed in the correct format. (Hint: to ensure that the Printable class declaration isn't compiled twice, you may need to move the declaration of Printable to the beginning of the Fract.h file, which you then include. Also, remember to use the **public** keyword when subclassing.)

Alternatively, you can create a "wrapper" class for the Fraction class, similar to the wrapper classes for integers and floating-point numbers (Pr_int and Pr_dbl).

A Final Word (or Two)

When I was first learning about object-oriented programming way back in the 1980s, I developed the idea in my mind that object-oriented programming was all about creating individual, self-contained entities that communicate by sending messages to one another.

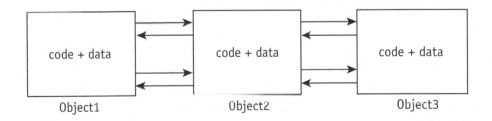

I still think that's not a bad way to get a handle on some of the major concepts. Individual, self-contained entities tend to shield their contents; they therefore have encapsulation—the ability to keep their data private.

I'm not sure how well inheritance is demonstrated by this model, although you can make it fit. If each of the individual objects is like a microprocessor or chip (to think of it all in hardware terms), then ideally you should be able to pop out a chip, make some modifications or improvements to it, and pop it back in.

Above all, the model of "independent entities sending messages to one another" is a good way of illustrating what polymorphism and virtual functions are all about.

Recall what I said a little earlier about the Printable interface in the introduction to Example 17.2. Here I paraphrase it in general terms:

*   **You can use an object without knowing its exact type or knowing the location of its function code, because the knowledge of how to perform the service is built into the object itself, not the user of that object.**

This principle is consistent with the idea of independent objects that communicate by sending messages. The user of an object doesn't need to tell that object how to do its job. What goes on inside another object is a mystery. You simply send a message, knowing the object will respond in some appropriate way.

In essence, objects—independent units of code and data—are liberated from slavish dependence on the internal structure of other objects.

But the result is not anarchy. Object-oriented programming systems enforce discipline in the area of type checking. If you want to support an interface, you have to implement all the services (i.e., virtual functions) of that interface, and you have to match the types in the argument lists exactly. The interfaces—the points at which different classes and objects can interact—are tightly controlled in object-oriented programming.

But as long as you observe the proper interface, you can implement a function in a way that had not yet been written at the time the client code was written. The following code will always work correctly—without being revised or recompiled—even if the specific type of an_object changes.

```
Printable = &an_object;
cout << *p;
```

Or better yet, p can point to an object supplied by another part of the system. The printing operation (cout << *p) will work, even though the program knows nothing at all about what p points to—other than the fact that the object pointed to implements the Printable interface.

A Final Final Word

But what does all this mean? Why does polymorphism matter? Is it because it contributes to code reuse? Well, yes. But I'm not sure that's the whole story.

Object-oriented programming is really about *systems* . . . graphical systems, network systems, and other aspects of the technology in which we daily become more enmeshed. Items in a graphical-user interface, or in a network, do act like independent objects sending messages to one another.

Traditional programming techniques were developed for a different world, a world in which it could be a triumph just to submit a stack of punch cards and see your program have a successful beginning, middle, and end, instead of gagging and puking. In this world, you assumed you were the only game in town and that you controlled everything. The world was limited, but it was simpler.

Today's software has become more complex as it has become richer. The success of Microsoft Windows, for example, stems in part from its rich set of components. And the component model is not as easy to implement with traditional programming techniques. Such systems need to be constructed in a way that permits existing software to hook up to ever newer components. And that's a need well served by polymorphism and independent objects.

Ultimately, this way of looking at things is closer to the reality of the great wide world. One of the exalted claims made for object orientation is that "it more closely models the real world." That's an inflated claim, to be sure, but one with a golden nugget of truth. We *do* live in a complex world. We *do* interact with things and people independent from ourselves. We do need to give others credit for having specialized knowledge that we don't have. Ironically, the real meaning of "object-oriented programming" is to treat data structures as *more* than mere objects—to treat them, in effect, as independent agents.

Functions are sometimes described as "subprograms" (and in fact, an earlier version of Microsoft Basic did use that terminology, until it was changed to "Sub procedure"). By comparison, an object is not merely an independent program, but an independent microcomputer, complete with its own internal state (data) and its own response code. Like the parts of a system, objects can send each other messages without understanding anything other than the connections (i.e., the interfaces). OOPS and polymorphism help liberate objects by making them independent.

And maybe, if we could liberate software objects, giving them the independence and freedom to do what each of them knows how to do best, we might feel more encouraged to liberate ourselves and each other.

Chapter 17 *Summary*

Here are the main points of Chapter 17:

▶ *Polymorphism* means that the knowledge of how to perform a service is built into the object itself, not the client code (that is, the code that uses it). Consequently, the resolution of a single function call or operation can take unlimited different forms. The object's type may change, resulting in a new response, even though the client code has not been altered or recompiled.

▶ Polymorphism is made possible by virtual functions.

▶ The address of a virtual function is not resolved until runtime. (This is also called *late binding*.) Consequently, the exact class of an object—as known at runtime—determines which implementation of a virtual function gets executed.

▶ To make a function virtual, precede its declaration in the class with the **virtual** keyword. For example:

```
protected:
    virtual void normalize();
```

▶ Once a function is declared virtual, it is virtual in all subclasses and in all contexts. You don't need to use the **virtual** keyword more than once per function.

▶ You cannot make a constructor or an inline function virtual.

▶ However, a destructor can be virtual.

▶ There is a small performance penalty and a small space penalty whenever a function is made virtual. However, these losses of efficiency are extremely minor in terms of today's powerful computers.

▶ As a general rule, any member function that might be overridden should be declared virtual.

▶ A *pure virtual function* has no implementation (that is, no function definition) in the class in which it is declared. You declare a pure virtual function by using the "= 0" notation. For example:

```
virtual void print_me() = 0;
```

▶ A class with at least one pure virtual function is an *abstract class*. Such a class cannot be used to instantiate objects. That is to say, it cannot be used to declare objects.

```
Number a, b, c;     // ERROR!
```

▶ Abstract classes are useful, however, as a means to create a general interface—a list of services that a subclass provides by implementing all the virtual functions.

▶ In the final analysis, polymorphism is a way of liberating objects from slavish dependence on one another (because the knowledge of how to perform a service is built into each individual object). It's ultimately this feature that gives object orientation its special flavor and makes it *object* oriented, not merely class oriented.

C++ Operators

Table A1 in this section lists C++ operators by precedence, associativity, description, and syntax. The precedence levels—to which I've assigned numbers—have no significance beyond the fact that all operators at the same level have equal precedence.

Association can be left to right or right to left. This difference matters when two operators are at the same level of precedence. For example, in the expression

    *p++

the * and ++ operators are at the same level of precedence (level 2), so the order of evaluation is determined by associativity—in this case right to left. The expression is therefore evaluated as if written this way:

    *(p++)

meaning that it is the pointer p itself (not what it points to) that gets incremented.

Note that level-2 operators in this table are unary operators, with only one operand. Most other operators are binary, with two operands. Some operators (such as *) have both a unary and binary version—which in some cases do very different things.

The items in the syntax column represent several kinds of expressions:

▶ *expr*—any expression

▶ *num*—any number (this includes items of type **char**)

▶ *int*—an integer

▶ *ptr*—a pointer (i.e., an address expression)

▶ *member*—a member of a class

▶ *lvalue*—an item that can legally appear on the left of an assignment; this includes a variable (but not one declared with **const**), an array element, a reference, or a fully dereferenced pointer. Constants are not lvalues.

435

Table A1: Table of C++ Operators

LEVEL	ASSOC.	OPERATOR	DESCRIPTION	SYNTAX
1	L-to-R	()	Call a function	*func(args)*
1	L-to-R	[]	Access array element	*array[int]*
1	L-to-R	->	Access class member	*ptr->member*
1	L-to-R	.	Access class member	*object.member*
1	L-to-R	::	Specify scope	*class::name* *:name*
2	*R-to-L*	!	Logical negation	*!expr*
2	*R-to-L*	~	Bitwise negation	*~expr*
2	*R-to-L*	++	Increment	*++num* *num++*
2	*R-to-L*	--	Decrement	*--num* *num--*
2	*R-to-L*	-	Change sign of	*-num*
2	*R-to-L*	*	Get contents at (dereference pointer)	**ptr*
2	*R-to-L*	&	Get address of	*&lvalue*
2	*R-to-L*	**sizeof**	Get size of data in bytes	**sizeof**(*expr*)
2	*R-to-L*	**new**	Allocate data object(s)	**new** *type* **new** *type[int]* **new** *type(args)*
2	*R-to-L*	**delete**	Remove data object(s)	**delete** *ptr* **delete** [] *ptr*
2	*R-to-L*	*cast*	Change data type	*(type) expr*
3	L-to-R	.*	Pointer-to-member (rarely used)	*obj.*ptr_mem*
3	L-to-R	->*	Pointer-to-member (rarely used)	*ptr->*ptr_mem*
4	L-to-R	*	Multiply	*num * num*
4	L-to-R	/	Divide	*num / num*
4	L-to-R	%	Modulus (remainder)	*int % int*
5	L-to-R	+	Add	*num + num* *ptr + int* *int + ptr*
5	L-to-R	-	Subtract	*num − num* *ptr − int* *ptr − ptr*
6	L-to-R	<<	Left shift (bitwise; also stream op)	*expr << int*
6	L-to-R	>>	Right shift (bitwise; also stream op)	*expr >> int*

Table A1: Table of C++ Operators (cont.)

LEVEL	ASSOC.	OPERATOR	DESCRIPTION	SYNTAX
7	L-to-R	<	Is less than?	$num < num$ $ptr < ptr$
7	L-to-R	<=	Is less than or equal?	$num <= num$ $ptr <= ptr$
7	L-to-R	>	Is greater than?	$num > num$ $ptr > ptr$
7	L-to-R	>=	Is greater than or equal?	$num >= num$ $ptr >= ptr$
8	L-to-R	==	Test for equality	$num == num$ $ptr == ptr$
8	L-to-R	!=	Test for inequality	$num != num$ $ptr != ptr$
9	L-to-R	&	Bitwise AND	int **&** int
10	L-to-R	^	Bitwise XOR (exclusive OR)	$int ^ int$
11	L-to-R	|	Bitwise OR	$int \| int$
12	L-to-R	&&	Logical AND	$expr$ **&&** $expr$
13	L-to-R	||	Logical OR	$expr \|\| expr$
14	R-to-L	?:	Conditional operator: evaluate *expr1*; if nonzero, evaluate and return *expr2*; otherwise, evaluate and return *expr3*.	$expr1$ **?** $expr2 : expr3$
15	R-to-L	=	Assign	$lvalue = expr$
15	R-to-L	+=	Add and assign	$lvalue += expr$
15	R-to-L	-=	Subtract and assign	$lvalue -= expr$
15	R-to-L	*=	Multiply and assign	$lvalue *= expr$
15	R-to-L	/=	Divide and assign	$lvalue /= expr$
15	R-to-L	%=	Modular divide and assign	$lvalue \%= int$
15	R-to-L	>>=	Right shift and assign	$lvalue >>= int$
15	R-to-L	<=	Left shift and assign	$lvalue <= int$
15	R-to-L	&=	Bitwise AND and assign	$lvalue$ **&=** int
15	R-to-L	^=	Bitwise XOR and assign	$lvalue ^= int$
15	R-to-L	|=	Bitwise OR and assign	$lvalue \|= int$
16	L-to-R	,	Join (evaluate both expressions and return *expr2*)	$expr1, expr2$

APPENDIX B

Intrinsic Data Types

Table B1 lists data types supported by all versions of C++, along with typical ranges. Although the C++ specification itself does not prescribe these ranges (it describes only the relationship among them), they are nearly universal on today's 32-bit systems. When 64-bit systems become standard, the ranges will need to be revised.

Unsigned types do not store negative numbers, but have a larger positive range. You can use the **unsigned** keyword by itself; it's interpreted as **unsigned int**.

The **int** type is a little peculiar; it represents the "natural" size of integers on any given computer, as **double** is the "natural" floating-point type. Expressions of smaller type are converted to one of these formats during integer or floating-point operations. There is rarely any reason to use smaller types (**short** or **float**), except when you are writing large numbers of data records to a file and storage is at a premium.

I use billion here in the American sense, to mean one thousand million (1,000,000,000).

Table B1: Data Types Supported by C++

TYPE	DESCRIPTION	TYPICAL RANGE
char	1-byte integer (used to hold an ASCII character value)	-128 to 127
unsigned char	1-byte unsigned integer	0 to 255
signed char	1-byte signed integer	-128 to 127
short	2-byte integer	-32,768 to 32,767
unsigned short	2-byte unsigned integer	0 to 65, 535
int	4-byte integer (but can be same as short on 16-bit systems)	Approx. ±2 billion (2×10^9)
unsigned int	4-byte unsigned integer (but can be same as unsigned short)	0 to approx. 4 billion
long	4-byte integer	Approx. ±2 billion

▼ *continued on next page*

Table B1: Data Types Supported by C++ (cont.)

TYPE	DESCRIPTION	TYPICAL RANGE
unsigned long	4-byte unsigned integer	0 to approx. 4 billion
float	Single-precision floating pt.	$\pm 3.4 \times 10^{38}$
double	Double-precision floating pt.	$\pm 1.8 \times 10^{308}$

Compilers that are fully compliant with ANSI C++ also support the following

Table B2: Data Types Supported by ANSI C++ Compliant Compilers

TYPE	DESCRIPTION	TYPICAL RANGE
bool	Boolean value	true (1) or false (0)
long double	Extra-wide double-precision	At least as great as **double**
wchar_t	Wide character	Same as **unsigned int**

Notes on **float** and **double** types:

▸ Values in **float** format can store the value 0.0 precisely. They can also store tiny values as close to zero as 1.175×10^{-38}.

▸ Values in **double** format can store the value 0.0 precisely. They can also store tiny values as close to zero as $2.225074 \times 10^{-308}$.

▸ Literal constants notated with a decimal point (such as 5.0) are automatically stored in **double** format. However, constants can be forced into **float** format by appending an "F" suffix. For example: "5.0F".

▸ You can optionally notate floating-point values by using scientific notation. For example:

```
3.5e4           // 3.5 times 10 to the 4th
                //  = 35000
2e-5            // 2.0 times 10 to the -5th
                //  = 0.00002
```

C++ Syntax Summary

This appendix, which summarizes the syntax of the C++ language, is intended as a quick reference. It is not intended as an absolutely exhaustive description of everything possible in C++, although on some points it comes close. Please refer also to Appendix A: Operators and Appendix B: Intrinsic Data Types.

Literal Constants

Literal constants in C++ can take several forms:

```
integer_number
floating_pt_number
'ASCII_symbol'
"literal_string"
{ constant, constant, ... }
```

The last form is recursive, so you can have aggregates within aggregates, which is meaningful when initializing a multidimensional array:

```
matrix[10][10] = {{1, 2, 3}, {4, 5, 6} };
```

This example initializes the first three elements in each of the first two rows of matrix. Other elements are left uninitialized.

Basic Expression Syntax

An expression in C++ is anything that has a value. (But note exception at the end of this section.) This covers a lot of ground: a numeral such as 5 is an expression, but so is x + 5 - sqrt(2.0). The important thing to understand about expressions is that a smaller expression may be part of a larger expression, to any degree of complexity desired by the programmer.

The other important thing to understand about expressions in C++ is that some expressions have one or more side-effects. For example:

```
x = 3 * --j
```

This is an expression with two side effects, since it changes the value of both x and j. This expression produces a value (namely, the value that was assigned to x). Therefore, it can be reused inside a larger expression. Like all expressions in C++, it does not become a statement until terminated by a semicolon:

```
x = 3 * --j;
```

A C++ expression may be a literal constant, a symbolic name (such as a variable), or expressions connected by operators. The latter case may involve either a binary or unary operator. The following are all expressions:

```
literal_constant
name
expression op expression
op expression
expression op
```

C++ also supports one trinary operator: the conditional operator. See page 437 for more information on this operator.

```
expression ? expression : expression
```

Expression syntax is recursive. With the building blocks of literal constants, symbolic names, and operators, you can build an expression of any size. For example:

```
b = (x + 24) / z * strlen("the pits")
```

Note ▶ Although, as a general rule, expressions always have a value, there are also **void** expressions, which are valid but do not have a value. The most common example is a call to a function with **void** return type.

Basic Statement Syntax

A statement in C++ is roughly analogous to a sentence in a human language. A statement may also be considered to be something like an instruction or command—except that it is possible for a statement to be the cause of many actions. About the only thing you can say absolutely about statements is that a series of one or more statements is required to form the body of a function definition—and such a definition, in turn, defines a task.

The most common form of a statement in C++ is an expression terminated by a semicolon:

```
expression;
```

It is also legal to have a statement with no expression (an empty statement), which is a no-op:

```
;
```

Any number of statements can be grouped together to form a compound statement (sometimes called a "statement block"). Remember that a compound statement is valid anywhere a single statement is valid.

```
{ statements }
```

Each of the control structures (covered in the next section) also defines a valid statement. Syntax for control structures includes one or two smaller statements; therefore, control structures can be nested to any level.

Control Structures

The **if** statement has two forms. The first form is:

```
if (condition_expr)
    statement
```

in which *condition_expr* is an expression. The program evaluates this expression, and if any nonzero value is returned, the condition is considered "true" and *statement* is therefore executed. (Boolean expressions such as a < b evaluate to 1 if true and 0 if false, so they behave as expected. Note that a == b, not a = b, is the test for equality.)

An **if** statement can also have an optional **else** clause.

```
if (condition_expr)
    statement
else
    statement
```

The standard **while** statement has the following syntax. If *condition_expr* evaluates to a nonzero value, *statement* is executed as in an **if** statement. But the process is repeated after each execution of *statement*. The loop finally breaks if *condition_expr* fails to be true (nonzero) when it is tested at the top of the loop.

```
while (condition_expr)
    statement
```

The **do-while** variation is similar, but it guarantees that the enclosed *statement* is executed at least once.

```
do
    statement
while (condition_expr);
```

The **for** statement provides a compact way of using three expressions to control execution of a loop.

```
for (init_expr; condition_expr; incr_expr)
    statement
```

This control structure is nearly identical to following **while** loop. Any and all of the three expressions may be omitted; the result in that case is a no-op, or (in the case of *condition_expr*) an unconditional result of "true" (i.e., the loop always executes).

```
init_expr;
while (condition_expr) {
    statement
    incr_expr;
}
```

The difference between these uses of **for** and **while** is that within the *statement,* the **continue** keyword causes a different effect. (See next section.) A **for** statement also permits use of *init_expr* to declare a variable "on the fly," which then becomes local to the **for** statement. For example:

```
for (int i = 0; i < ARRAY_LENGTH; i++)
    a[i] = i;
```

Finally, **switch-case** is an alternative to the use of nested **if-else**. The **switch** statement has this syntax:

```
switch (target_expr) {
    statements
}
```

Within the statements, you can place any number of statements labeled with the **case** keyword. A **case** statement has this syntax:

```
case constant: statement
```

It follows from the recursive nature of the syntax that a single statement may have many labels:

```
case 'a':
case 'e':
```

```
case 'i':
case 'o':
case 'u':
    cout < "is a vowel";
```

You can also include an optional **default** label.

default: *statement*

The action of **switch** is to evaluate the expression *target_expr*. Control is then transferred to the **case** statement, if any, whose *constant* value matches the value of *target_expr*. If none of these values match and there is a **default** label, control is transferred there. If there is no matching **case** and no **default** label, then control is transferred to the end of the **switch** statement (the first statement after the end of the block).

For example, the following example prints "is a vowel", "may be a vowel", or "is not a vowel", depending on the value of c.

```
switch (c) {
    case 'a':
    case 'e':
    case 'i':
    case 'o':
    case 'u':
        cout < "is a vowel";
        break;
    case 'y':
        cout < "may be a vowel";
        break;
    default:
        cout < "is not a vowel";
}
```

Once control is transferred to any statement within the block, execution continues normally, falling through to the next case unless a **break** statement is encountered.

Special Control Statements

Several special statements can affect action within a control structure. First, the **break** statement causes execution to break out of the nearest enclosing **while**, **for**, or **switch** statement. In all such cases, execution is transferred to the first statement after the end of the control structure (or, if the control structure is the last statement in a function, the function returns).

```
break;
```

The **continue** statement is legal within a **while** or **for** statement. The effect is to advance execution to the top of the next loop cycle; this means that execution of the current statement (or statement block) is suspended and the program proceeds to evaluate *condition_expr* again.

```
continue;
```

Within a **for** loop, **continue** causes the *incr_expr* (increment expression) to be evaluated before advancing to the top of the next loop cycle; this is the essential difference between **for** and **while** loops.

The **goto** statement causes unconditional transfer of control to a specified statement.

```
goto label;
```

The label, to be valid, must refer to a statement within the current function labeled as follows:

```
label: statement
```

Data Declarations

A data declaration is a statement that creates one or more data items (or *objects*). A data declaration can declare one item.

```
type  var_decl;
```

Or it can declare two or more items separated by commas.

```
type  var_decl, var_decl, ... ;
```

Each variable declaration (*var_decl*) can be as simple as a variable name:

```
variable
```

Or it can include an optional initializing expression. Unlike classic C, C++ does not require the initializing expression to be a constant.

```
variable = init_expr
```

In a declaration, the variable name can also be qualified with operators such as [], *, (), and &; these create arrays, pointers, pointers to functions, and references, respectively. To determine what kind of item has been declared, ask yourself what the item represents if it appears in executable code. For example, the data declaration

```
int **ptr;
```

means that **ptr, when it appears in code, is an item of type **int**; ptr itself is therefore a pointer to a pointer to an integer.

Function Declarations

Before a function can be called by another function, it must first be declared. It can be given a simple type declaration first (a prototype). The complete declaration—which includes the definition—can then be placed anywhere in the source file or defined in another module.

A function prototype has this syntax:

```
type function_name(argument_list);
```

The *type* indicates the type of value that function must return. A function can optionally have the special **void** type, indicating that it does not return a value.

The argument list contains one or more argument declarations separated by commas. The argument list may be left blank, indicating that the function has no arguments. (Unlike C, C++ does not permit the use of blank argument lists to mean an indeterminate list to be filled in later.)

Each entry in the argument list has the following form. Declaration syntax follows other details mentioned in the last section (with an optional initializing expression indicating a default value), except that each *type* and *var_decl* must be one-to-one.

```
type  var_decl
```

A more complete syntax for a function prototype is therefore:

```
type function_name(type var_decl, type var_decl, ...);
```

Syntax for a complete function declaration (including function definition) is the same, except that it includes one or more statements.

```
type function_name(argument_list) {
    statements
}
```

A function definition does not end with a semicolon (;) after the final closing brace. Also, note that names of arguments (but not types) can be omitted from a prototype—but not from a function definition.

Class Declarations

Once a class has been declared, the class name can be used directly as a type name, just like an intrinsic data type such as **int**, **double**, **float**, and so on. The basic syntax for a class declaration is:

```
class class_name {
    declarations
};
```

Unlike a function definition, a class declaration is always terminated by a semicolon (;) after the closing brace.

The *declarations* can include any number of data and/or function declarations. Within the declarations, the **public**, **protected**, and **private** keywords can occur, along with a colon (:), to indicate the access level of the declarations that follow it. For example, in the following class declaration, data members a and b are private; data member c, as well as function f1, are public.

```
class my_class {
private:
    int a, b;
public:
    int c;
    void f1(int a);
};
```

Within a class declaration, constructors and destructors have the following special declarations. You can have any number of constructors, differentiated by argument lists. You can have at most one destructor.

```
class_name (argument_list)          // Constructor
~class_name()                       // Destructor
```

The syntax for a subclass declaration includes the name of a base class. Although the use of **public** here is not syntactically required, it is strongly recommended (otherwise, inherited members become private).

```
class class_name : public base_class {
    declarations
};
```

Most versions of C++ also support multiple inheritance, in which you list more than one base class separated by commas. For example, to inherit from two classes:

```
class class_name : public base_class, public
base_class {
    declarations
};
```

Note ▶ The syntax given here applies to the **struct** and **union** keywords as well as to **class**. To declare a **struct** class, therefore, replace the **class** keyword with **struct**. A **struct** class is identical to one defined with **class**, except that members are public by default rather than private. Members of a **union** class are public by default, but, in addition, unions have other features that are outside the scope of this book. The basic idea of a union is that its members share the same starting address in memory; generally this means that only one member of the union is "in use" at any given time.

ASCII Codes

This table summarizes the first 127 standard ASCII codes. It does not cover extended ASCII codes (above 127 in value) or the wide (16-bit) character set. In this table, a two- or three-digit number specifies a numeric value; the box immediately to its right shows the corresponding character.

Some of these characters are special (unprintable) characters. They include:

NUL—null value

ACK—acknowledgement signal (used by network communications)

BEL—bell

BS—backspace

LF—linefeed

FF—form feed (new page)

CR—carriage return

NAK—no acknowledgement

DEL—delete

Table D1: ASCII Codes

00	NUL	26		52	4	78	N	104	h
01		27		53	5	79	O	105	i
02		28	FS	54	6	80	P	106	j
03		29	GS	55	7	81	Q	107	k
04		30	RS	56	8	82	R	108	l
05		31	US	57	9	83	S	109	m
06	ACK	32	space	58	:	84	T	110	n
07	BEL	33	!	59	;	85	U	111	o
08	BS	34	"	60	<	86	V	112	p
09		35	#	61	=	87	W	113	q
10	LF	36	$	62	>	88	X	114	r
11		37	%	63	?	89	Y	115	s
12	FF	38	&	64	@	90	Z	116	t
13	CR	39	'	65	A	91	[	117	u
14		40	(	66	B	92	\	118	v
15		41	)	67	C	93	]	119	w
16		42	*	68	D	94	^	120	x
17		43	+	69	E	95	_	121	y
18		44	,	70	F	96	`	122	z
19		45	–	71	G	97	a	123	{
20		46	.	72	H	98	b	124		
21	NAK	47	/	73	I	99	c	125	}
22	SYN	48	0	74	J	100	d	126	~
23		49	1	75	K	101	e	127	DEL
24		50	2	76	L	102	f		
25		51	3	77	M	103	g		

Common Library Functions

The C++ library is too large to be covered in a few pages. However, the most commonly used library functions fall into just a few categories: string functions, data-conversion functions, single-character functions, math functions, and (because they are used in this book) the randomization functions. This appendix provides a quick overview.

String Functions

To use these functions, include the file string.h. The functions apply to traditional C **char*** strings, but not to the new, automated C++ **string** class. The latter is described near the end of Chapter 7.

In the following Table E1, *s*, *s1*, and *s2* are null-terminated **char*** strings (actually, each of these arguments contain the address of the string); *n* is an integer; and *ch* is a single character. Except where otherwise noted, each of these functions returns the first string argument (which, as I've indicated, is an address).

Table E1: Common Library String Functions

FUNCTION	ACTION
strcat(*s1*, *s2*)	Concatenates the contents of *s2* onto the end of *s1*.
strchr(*s*, *ch*)	Returns a pointer to the first occurrence of *ch* in string *s*; returns NULL if *ch* cannot be found.
strcmp(*s1*, *s2*)	Performs a comparison between contents of *s1* and *s2*, returning a negative integer, 0, or a positive integer, depending on whether *s1* appears before *s2* in alpha order, is identical to *s2*, or appears later in alpha order.
strcpy(*s1*, *s2*)	Copies the contents of *s2* to *s1*, replacing existing contents.

▼ *continued on next page*

Table E1: Common Library String Functions (cont.)

FUNCTION	ACTION
strcspn($s1, s2$)	Searches $s1$ for occurrence of any character in $s2$; returns index of the first matching $s1$ character; returns the length of $s1$ if none found.
strlen(s)	Returns length of s (not including null byte).
strncat($s1, s2, n$)	Same action as **strcat**, but copies at most n characters.
strncmp($s1, s2, n$)	Same action as **strcmp**, but compares at most n characters.
strncpy($s1, s2, n$)	Same action as **strcpy**, but copies at most n characters.
strpbrk($s1, s2$)	Searches $s1$ for occurrence of any character in $s2$; returns a pointer to the first matching $s1$ character; returns NULL if none found.
strrchr(s, ch)	Same action as **strpbrk**, but searches $s1$ in reverse order.
strspn($s1, s2$)	Searches $s1$ for the first character that does not match any character in $s2$; returns index of this character; returns length of $s1$ if none found.
strstr($s1, s2$)	Searches $s1$ for the first occurrence of substring $s2$; returns a pointer to substring found within $s1$; returns NULL if not found.
strtok($s1, s2$)	Returns a pointer to the first token (substring) in $s1$, using delimiters specified in $s2$. Subsequent calls to this function, with NULL for the first argument, find the next token within the current string—that is, the previously set value of $s1$. Specifying a non-null value for $s1$ resets the tokenization process with a new string.

Data-Conversion Functions

To use these functions, include the file stdlib.h.

Table E2: Common Library Data-Conversion Functions

FUNCTION	ACTION
atof(s)	Reads the **char*** text string s as a floating-point digit string and returns the equivalent **double**. The function skips leading spaces and stops reading after the first character that doesn't form part of a valid floating-point representation (such as "1.5" or "2e12").
atoi(s)	Reads the **char*** text string s as an integer digit string and returns the equivalent **int**. The function skips leading spaces and stops reading after the first character that doesn't form part of a valid integer representation (such as "-33").

Single-Character Functions

To use any of the functions in this section, include the file ctype.h.

Each of the functions in this first subgroup tests a single character value (for example, 'X' or my_string[5]) and returns a Boolean result: true (1) or false (0).

The ctype.h file also includes declarations for the following two functions, each of which returns an **int** value containing an ASCII character.

Table E3a: Single-Character Functions

FUNCTION	ACTION
isalnum(*ch*)	Is the character alphanumeric (a letter or digit)?
isalpha(*ch*)	Is the character a letter?
iscntrl(*ch*)	Is the character a control character? (These include backspace, line-feed, form feed, and tab, among others; these are nonprintable characters that perform actions.)
isdigit(*ch*)	Is the character a digit in the range 0 through 9?
isgraph(*ch*)	Is the character visible? (This includes printable characters other than a space.)
islower(*ch*)	Is the character a lowercase letter?
isprint(*ch*)	Is the character printable? (This includes space characters.)
ispunct(*ch*)	Is the character a punctuation character?
isspace(*ch*)	Is the character a whitespace? (This includes tab, newline, and form feed, in addition to the simple space character.)
isupper(*ch*)	Is the character an uppercase letter?
isxdigit(*ch*)	Is the character a hexadecimal digit? This includes digits in the range 0 through 9, as well as A through E and a through e.

Math Functions

Table E3b: Single-Character Functions

FUNCTION	ACTION
tolower(*ch*)	Returns an uppercase character if *ch* is a lowercase letter; otherwise returns *ch* as is.
toupper(*ch*)	Returns a lowercase character if *ch* is an uppercase letter; otherwise returns *ch* as is.

To use these functions, include the file math.h.

Except where otherwise noted, each of these functions takes arguments of type **double** and returns a **double** result. All of these functions return their results; none of them alter an argument.

Note: in this list, I've omitted some of the more obscure and redundant math functions.

Table E4: Math Functions

FUNCTION	ACTION
abs(n)	Returns the absolute value of integer n. (Result has **int** type.)
acos(x)	Arc cosine of x.
asin(x)	Arc sine of x.
atan(x)	Arc tangent of x.
ceil(x)	Rounds x upward to nearest integer. (But result is still returned as a **double**).
cos(x)	Cosine of x.
cosh(x)	Hyperbolic cosine of x.
exp(x)	Raises the mathematical constant e to the power x.
fabs(x)	Returns the absolute value of x.
floor(x)	Rounds x downward to nearest integer. (But result is still returned as a **double**).
log(x)	Natural logarithm (base e) of x.
log10(x)	Logarithm (base 10) of x.
pow(x, y)	Raises x to the power y.
sin(x)	Sine of x.
sinh(x)	Hyperbolic sine of x.
sqrt(x)	Square root of x.
tan(x)	Tangent of x.
tanh(x)	Hyperbolic tangent of x.

Randomization

To use all these functions, you need to include the files stdlib.h and time.h.

Table E5: Randomization Functions

FUNCTION	ACTION
rand()	Returns the next number (an **int**) in the current random-number sequence. This sequence should first be set by calling **srand**. The number returned ranges in value between 0 and RAND_MAX (defined in stdlib.h).
srand(*seed*)	Takes the seed number—an **unsigned int**—to start the random-number sequence used for calls to **rand**.
time(NULL)	Returns system time. Calling this function is a good choice for getting the seed number to pass to **srand**. (Note: the **time** function also has other uses; these do not all involve a NULL argument.)

Glossary of Terms

This section reviews the terminology used in this book. For more complete discussions of the concepts, please see the Index.

abstract class—A class that cannot be used to create objects, but which may still be useful as a general pattern (i.e., interface) for other classes. An abstract class has at least one *pure virtual function*.

address—The numeric location of a piece of data or program code in memory. This location is often called a variable or function's "physical location" in memory—although opening up the computer to try to find this location is not recommended. Addresses, when displayed, are usually shown in hexadecimal (base 16) and aren't too meaningful except in the context of a program.

If everyone in the world lived on the same street, you could state your address as a single number (i.e., 12300 instead of "12300 Main Street," etc.). That's what a data or program address is: just a number that determines where a variable of a function is located.

ANSI—American National Standards Institute. ANSI C++ is the specification that C++ compilers need to support full, up-to-date, and correct versions of C++. ANSI C++ includes a number of features—such as exception-handling, templates, and the **bool** type—that were not present in the earliest versions of C++.

argument—A value passed to a function.

array—A data structure made up of multiple elements, in which each element has the same type. Individual elements are accessed through an index number. For example, an array declared as `int arr[5]` is an array of five **int** values (integers) accessed through the index numbers 0, 1, 2, 3, and 4. Index numbers in C-based languages run from 0 to n-1.

Not surprisingly, there is a close relationship between arrays and addresses, because they both use numbers to locate data. This relationship is especially close in C and C++.

459

associativity—The rule (either left-to-right or right-to-left) that determines how to evaluate an expression that combines two or more operators at the same level of precedence. For example, in the expression *p++, the operators associate left to right, so the expression is equivalent to *(p++).

base class—A class from which you inherit by declaring a subclass.

bit—A single digit stored in a computer's CPU or memory. Each bit has a value of 1 or 0.

Boolean—A true/false value or true/false operation. In full ANSI C++, the special type **bool** is supported. If this type is not available, you can use the **int** type to hold true/false values. C++ defines true and false as the values 1 and 0, respectively, but any nonzero value is interpreted as true.

byte—A group of eight bits. Memory in a computer is organized by bytes, so that each byte has a unique address.

cast—An operation that changes the data type of an expression. For example, if you cast the data type of the integer 10 to **double** type, that quantity is changed to floating-point format. (Note that floating-point format involves a different binary representation than integer, even when no fractional portion is involved.) You can perform a cast by using a C++ data cast such as

`static_cast<type>(expression),`

or by using the old C-style cast:

`(type) expression.`

This latter syntax still works on current C++ compilers but is not recommended.

class—A user-defined data type (or a data type defined in a library). In C++, a class can be declared by using the **class**, **struct**, or **union** keyword. In traditional programming, such a type can contain any number of data fields (called *data members* in C++); object-oriented programming adds the ability to declare function members as well. These, in turn, define operations on instances of the type.

code—Another word for "the program." The word *code* implies the programmer's point of view, rather than that of the user, who only sees the end result at runtime. When C++ programmers speak of "the code," they are usually referring to the source code, which is the group of C++ statements that make up the program.

compiler—The language translator that reads your C++ program and produces machine code and (ultimately) an executable file, which can actually be run on the computer.

constant—A value that is not allowed to change.

constructor—A member function called when an object is created. A constructor tells how to initialize the object. A constructor has the same name as the class in which it is declared, and it has no return value. (But a constructor *implicitly* returns an instance of the class.)

control structure—A way to control what happens next in a program. Control structures can make decisions (albeit limited ones), repeat operations, or transfer execution to a new program location. The **if**, **while**, **for**, and **switch** statements are all examples of control structures.

copy constructor—A special kind of constructor in which an object is initialized from another object of the same type. The compiler provides a copy constructor for each class if you don't write one.

data member—A data field of a class. Unless it is declared **static** (a keyword not covered in this book), each object gets its own copy of the data member.

declaration —A statement that provides type information for a variable, class member, or function. A function declaration can be either a *prototype* (which contains type information only) or a *definition* (which tells what the function does). In C++, every variable and function except for **main** must be declared before being used.

default constructor—A special constructor that has no arguments; this constructor tells how to initialize an object when it is declared without arguments. The compiler provides a default constructor, but only if you write no constructors of your own. As a consequence, if you write any constructor, the compiler takes away the automatic default constructor and then objects cannot be created without an argument list. You can prevent being surprised by this behavior by always writing your own default constructor.

definition, function—A series of statements that tells what a function does. When a function is executed, program control is transferred to these statements. See also *function*.

destructor—Not as lethal as it sounds. A destructor is a member function that performs cleanup and termination activities when an object is destroyed. The declaration of a destructor is ~*class_name*(). Not all classes need to have a destructor, but it's necessary in cases where objects of that class own a system resource (such as memory) that needs to be given back when the object goes away.

directive—A general command to the compiler. A directive is different from a statement in that it does not declare a variable or create executable code. For example, the **#include** directive causes the compiler to include the contents of another source file.

encapsulation—The ability to hide or protect contents. One of the advantages of object-oriented programming is that enables you to define units (classes and objects) that are like "black boxes" to their users, in which the internals cannot be interfered with. You do this by declaring members to be private.

exception—An unusual occurrence at runtime—usually an error—that requires immediate handling by the program. An example of such an occurrence is an arithmetic overflow. If the program cannot handle the exception, it is forced to terminate abruptly, by default. C++ exception handling (not a feature of classic C++, but one that is now considered standard in up-to-date compilers) uses the **try**, **catch**, and **throw** keywords to centralize the handling of runtime errors in your program.

expression—One of the fundamental building-blocks of a C++ program. Generally speaking, an expression is anything that has a value. However, **void** expressions do not have values. Expressions can be as simple as a number or a variable or—through the use of operators—you can form smaller expressions into larger ones. When you terminate an expression with a semicolon (;), it becomes a statement. See Appendix C for more discussion of expression syntax.

floating point—A data format that can store fractional portions of a number as well as numbers in a much larger range than the integer (**int**, **char**, **short**, **long**) formats. On a computer, floating-point numbers are stored internally in binary (base 2) and displayed in decimal. Consequently, rounding errors are possible. Many ratios of integers—such as 1/3—cannot be stored precisely in floating-point format, although they can be approximated to a certain precision.

The principal floating-point type in C++ is **double**, which stands for "double precision."

function—A group of statements that carry out a task. There is no limit to the number of things a function can do, but ideally all the actions carried out by a particular function should have a closely related purpose.

Once a function is defined and declared, you can execute it from anywhere within a program. This is termed *calling* a function. You only have to define a function once—or not at all, if the function is defined in a library or another module—but you can repeat its effect any number of times by simply calling it. Consequently, the use of functions is the most fundamental technique for writing reusable code.

GCF (greatest common factor)—The highest integer that divides evenly into two numbers. For example, the greatest common factor of 12 and 18 is 6; the greatest common factor of 300 and 400 is 100.

global variable—A variable shared by more than one function in a module—that is, by functions in the same source file. You declare a global variable in C++ by declaring it outside of any function. (In a multiple-module program, you can even share a global variable among all the functions in the program by using **extern** declarations.) A global variable is visible from the point where it is declared, forward to the end of a source file.

header file—A file that contains a series of declarations and (optionally) directives; it is intended to be included (through use of the **#include** directive) in multiple files. This is a time-saving device; it saves programmers from having to enter the individual declarations directly in each source file in a project. Remember that variables, classes, and functions all have to be declared in C++ before being used; this is why header files are helpful.

IDE (integrated development environment)—A text editor from which you can run the compiler. This allows you to write, compile, and run programs, all within the same application.

implementation—This is a word with many different meanings in different contexts; but in C++ it usually refers to a function definition for a virtual function. Sometimes I also use the word "implemented" to describe how the C++ compiler generates machine code to carry out actions in a program.

indirection—Accessing data indirectly, through a pointer. For example, if pointer `ptr` points to variable `amount`, then the statement `*ptr = 10;` changes the value of `amount` through indirection.

inheritance—The ability to give one class the attributes of another, previously declared class. This is done through subclassing. The new class automatically has all the members declared in the base class. (Exception: a class does not inherit constructors.)

inline function—A function whose statements are inserted into the code of the function that calls it. In a normal function call, program control jumps to a new location and then returns when execution is complete. This does not happen with an inline function.

When you declare a member function and place its definition inside the class declaration, it is automatically made an inline function.

instance/instantiation—The word *instance* is nearly synonymous with *object*. Any individual value or variable is an instance of some type. The number 5 is an instance of **int**, and the number 3.1415927 is an instance of **double**. Every object is an instance of some class. When a class is *instantiated*, it is used to create an object.

integer—A whole number, or rather a number with no fractional part. This includes the numbers 1, 2, 3, and so on, as well as 0 and negative numbers -1, -2, -3, and so on.

interface—This is another word with many different meanings in different contexts. In this book, I've used it to refer to a general set of services that different subclasses can implement in their own ways. In C++ you use an abstract class to define an interface.

literal constant—A numeric or string constant (such as 5 or "Mary had a little lamb"), as opposed to a symbolic name that is made into a constant (through use of the **const** keyword).

local variable—A variable that is private to a particular function or statement block. The benefit of local variables is that (for example) each function can have its own variable x, but changes to x within one function won't interfere with the value of x in another. This feature—a kind of functional right to privacy—is a cornerstone of modern programming languages.

lvalue—A "left value," meaning a value that can appear on the left side of an assignment. Variables are lvalues; constants are not. Other lvalues include array members and fully dereferenced pointers.

member—An item declared inside a *class* (which is a user-defined type). Data members are equivalent to the fields of a record or structure. Member functions define operations built into the class.

member function—A function declared within a class. Member functions (sometimes called "methods" by other languages) are an essential aspect of object-oriented programming. They define operations on objects of the class.

nesting—Placing one control structure inside another.

newline—A signal to the display monitor that says "Start a new line of text."

object—A unit of closely associated data that can have behavior (in the form of *member functions*) as well as data. The concept stems from the old concept of "data record"—for example, all the information on one company employee might make up a single record. The concept of object is similar but more flexible. By writing member functions, you can give objects the ability to support operations; furthermore, because of how *polymorphism* works in C++, the knowledge of how to carry out an operation is built into the object itself, not the code that uses it. The type of an object is its *class,* and for a given class you can declare any number of objects. Simply stated, an object is an intelligent data structure.

object code—A term that has no connection with objects or object-oriented programming whatsoever. The object code is the machine code generated by a compiler. This code is then linked to library code to create an executable file (an .EXE file in the Windows and MS-DOS worlds) that can actually be run.

object-oriented programming—An approach to program design and coding that makes data objects more central, enabling you to define data objects by what they do as much as what they contain. The object-oriented approach starts by declaring classes, which are flexible user-defined types. A class can then be used to declare any number of objects. Three hallmarks of true object orientation are *encapsulation, inheritance,* and *polymorphism.*

OOPS—A user's cry when he realizes he's deleted the contents of his hard disk. Also, an acronym for object-oriented programming systems.

operand—An expression involved in an operation. One or more operands combine to form a larger expression. For example, in the expression x + 5, x and 5 are the two operands.

operator—A symbol that combines one or more expressions to form a larger expression. Some operators are unary, meaning that they apply to only one operand; other operators are binary, meaning that they combine two operands together. In the expression x + *p the plus-sign (+) is a binary operator and the asterisk (*) in this case, is a unary operator.

overloading—The reuse of a name or symbol for different—though often related—meanings. In C++, overloading takes two forms. *Function overloading* lets you use the same name any number of times to define different functions, requiring only that each function have a different argument list; the compiler resolves calls to the function name by examining the types of the arguments. *Operator overloading* lets you reuse operators (such as *, +, or <) by defining how the operators work with objects of your own classes.

pointer—A variable that contains the address of another variable. (A pointer can also be set to NULL, in which case it does not point anywhere.) Occasionally, I use the phrase "pointer to" to mean "the address of." Pointers have many uses in C++, some of which are described in Chapter 6. In general, pointers are valuable because they give you a way of passing a handle to a chunk of data without having to copy all the data itself.

polymorphism—The scariest word in object-oriented programming. What it means, really, is that *the knowledge of how to carry out an action is built into the object itself,* not the code that uses it. Consequently, a general operation (such as cout << *p in Chapter 17) can be carried out in an unlimited number of ways—all without having to alter or recompile the statement cout << *p in the calling program. If the type of object pointed to changes, the effect of the statement changes even if the main module or program isn't altered or recompiled. The fact that the execution of a single statement can take many forms gives rise to the word "polymorphism" (Greek for "many forms").

precedence—The rules that determine which operations to carry out first in a complex expression. For example, in the expression 2 + 3 ^ 4, multiplication (*) is carried out first, because multiplication has higher precedence than addition. See Appendix A for a summary of operator precedence in C++.

prototype—A function declaration that gives type information only. (It is not a definition.)

pure virtual function—A function that has no implementation (that is, no definition) in the class in which it is declared. This creates a general function to be implemented in subclasses.

reference—A variable or argument that serves as a handle to another variable or argument. A reference variable is an alias for another variable. A reference argument is similar but is implemented underneath the covers by the passing of a pointer. If you understand pointers, references are easy to grasp: essentially, they produce pointer behavior without the pointer syntax.

RHIDE—An integrated development editor that can be downloaded along with the free, shareware GNU C++ compiler (included on the CD). See also *IDE*.

source file—A text file containing C++ statements (and, optionally, directives).

statement—A basic unit of syntax in a C++ program. A C++ statement is roughly analogous to a command or a sentence in a natural language such as English. As with sentences, there is no fixed length to a C++ statement. It can be terminated at any time—usually with a semicolon. A function definition consists of a series of statements.

string—A series of text characters, which you can use to represent words and phrases—or even complete sentences. In computer programming, people use strings to handle alphanumeric data.

The C and C++ languages support strings as arrays of **char**—the **char** type being an integer large enough to hold an ASCII code, corresponding to a single text character. A terminating null (ASCII 0) indicates the end of a string. In addition, newer C++ compilers support an easier-to-use **string** class, which saves the programmer from worrying about how much storage capacity to allot for each string.

string literal—A text string enclosed in quotation marks, giving a constant string value. When the C++ compiler sees a string literal, it stores the characters in the data segment, and then in evaluating the code replaces the string literal with the address of the data. Writing a string literal, therefore, produces an address expression of type **char***.

subclass—A class that inherits from another class. The subclass automatically includes all the members of the base class, except for its constructors. Any explicit declarations in the subclass create additional or overridden members.

text string—See *string*.

variable—A named location for storing program data. Each variable corresponds to a unique location in program memory (its *address*) where data is stored. In addition to name and address, each variable also has a specific type (such as **int**, **double**, **char**, or **string**) that determines its data format.

virtual function—A function whose address is not determined until runtime (this is also called *late binding*). This feature gives virtual functions—which otherwise look identical to standard functions—a special flexibility. You can safely override a virtual function in a subclass, knowing that no matter how an object is accessed, the right version of the function will always be called; so, for example, a function call such as `ptr->vfunc()` will call the object's *own* version of vfunc rather than the base-class version. Virtual functions are closely linked to the concept of *polymorophism*.

In ancient Rome, *virtu* meant "manliness"; in modern parlance, *virtual* means "to have the quality of." This example of (otherwise regrettable) chauvinism has one redeeming feature: it suggests that to take one's place in society, one's behavior was paramount; one had to have the right quality. In computer technology, if something is virtual, it emulates the behavior of the real. It can be used just like the real thing.

Index

informIT

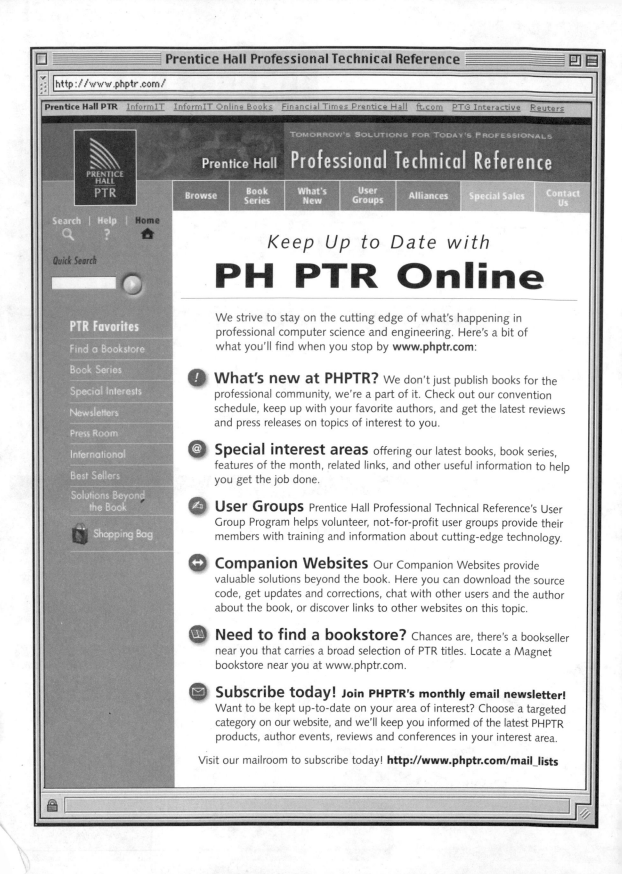

Prentice Hall Professional Technical Reference

http://www.phptr.com/

Prentice Hall PTR   InformIT   InformIT Online Books   Financial Times Prentice Hall   ft.com   PTG Interactive   Reuters

TOMORROW'S SOLUTIONS FOR TODAY'S PROFESSIONALS

Prentice Hall **Professional Technical Reference**

Browse | Book Series | What's New | User Groups | Alliances | Special Sales | Contact Us

Search | Help | Home

Quick Search

PTR Favorites

Find a Bookstore

Book Series

Special Interests

Newsletters

Press Room

International

Best Sellers

Solutions Beyond the Book

Shopping Bag

Keep Up to Date with

PH PTR Online

We strive to stay on the cutting edge of what's happening in professional computer science and engineering. Here's a bit of what you'll find when you stop by **www.phptr.com**:

What's new at PHPTR? We don't just publish books for the professional community, we're a part of it. Check out our convention schedule, keep up with your favorite authors, and get the latest reviews and press releases on topics of interest to you.

Special interest areas offering our latest books, book series, features of the month, related links, and other useful information to help you get the job done.

User Groups Prentice Hall Professional Technical Reference's User Group Program helps volunteer, not-for-profit user groups provide their members with training and information about cutting-edge technology.

Companion Websites Our Companion Websites provide valuable solutions beyond the book. Here you can download the source code, get updates and corrections, chat with other users and the author about the book, or discover links to other websites on this topic.

Need to find a bookstore? Chances are, there's a bookseller near you that carries a broad selection of PTR titles. Locate a Magnet bookstore near you at www.phptr.com.

Subscribe today! **Join PHPTR's monthly email newsletter!** Want to be kept up-to-date on your area of interest? Choose a targeted category on our website, and we'll keep you informed of the latest PHPTR products, author events, reviews and conferences in your interest area.

Visit our mailroom to subscribe today! **http://www.phptr.com/mail_lists**